Untold Tales *of the* Hasidim

The Tauber Institute Series for the Study of European Jewry

Jehuda Reinharz, General Editor
Sylvia Fuks Fried, Associate Editor

The Tauber Institute Series is dedicated to publishing compelling and innovative approaches to the study of modern European Jewish history, thought, culture, and society. The series features scholarly works related to the Enlightenment, modern Judaism and the struggle for emancipation, the rise of nationalism and the spread of antisemitism, the Holocaust and its aftermath, as well as the contemporary Jewish experience. The series is published under the auspices of the Tauber Institute for the Study of European Jewry—established by a gift to Brandeis University from Dr. Laszlo N. Tauber—and is supported, in part, by the Tauber Foundation and the Valya and Robert Shapiro Endowment.

For the complete list of books that are available in this series, please see brandeis.edu/tauber.

David Assaf
Untold Tales of the Hasidim: Crisis and Discontent in the History of Hasidism

Jehuda Reinharz and Yaacov Shavit
Glorious, Accursed Europe: An Essay on Jewish Ambivalence

Eugene M. Avrutin, Valerii Dymshits, Alexander Ivanov, Alexander Lvov, Harriet Murav, and Alla Sokolova, editors
Photographing the Jewish Nation: Pictures from S. An-sky's Ethnographic Expeditions

Michael Dorland
Cadaverland: Inventing a Pathology of Catastrophe for Holocaust Survival

Walter Laqueur
Best of Times, Worst of Times: Memoirs of a Political Education

*Rose-Carol Washton Long, Matthew Baigell, and Milly Heyd, editors
Jewish Dimensions in Modern Visual Culture: Antisemitism, Assimilation, Affirmation

Berel Lang
Philosophical Witnessing: The Holocaust as Presence

David N. Myers
Between Jew and Arab: The Lost Voice of Simon Rawidowicz

Sara Bender
The Jews of Białystock during World War II and the Holocaust

Nili Scharf Gold
Yehuda Amichai: The Making of Israel's National Poet

Hans Jonas
Memoirs

Itamar Rabinovich and Jehuda Reinharz, editors
Israel in the Middle East: Documents and Readings on Society, Politics, and Foreign Relations, Pre-1948 to the Present

Christian Wiese
The Life and Thought of Hans Jonas: Jewish Dimensions

Eugene R. Sheppard
Leo Strauss and the Politics of Exile: The Making of a Political Philosopher

Samuel Moyn
A Holocaust Controversy: The Treblinka Affair in Postwar France

Margalit Shilo
Princess or Prisoner? Jewish Women in Jerusalem, 1840–1914

Haim Be'er
Feathers

*A Sarnat Library Book.

DAVID ASSAF

Untold Tales *of the* Hasidim

Crisis & Discontent *in the* History *of* Hasidism

Translated from the Hebrew by Dena Ordan

BRANDEIS UNIVERSITY PRESS Waltham, Massachusetts

Brandeis University Press

Manufactured in the United States of America
Designed by Katherine B. Kimball
Typeset in Walbaum by Integrated Publishing Solutions

First Brandeis University Press paperback edition 2011
ISBN for the paperback edition: 978-1-61168-194-9

Originally published in Hebrew as *Ne'ehaz basevakh: Pirkei mashber umevukhah betoldot hahasidut/Caught in the Thicket: Chapters of Crisis and Discontent in the History of Hasidism* (Jerusalem: Zalman Shazar Center for Jewish History, 2006).

This project was published with the generous support of the Lucius N. Littauer Foundation.

Library of Congress Cataloging-in-Publication Data
Assaf, David.
[Ne'ehaz ba-sevakh. English]
Untold tales of the Hasidim : crisis and discontent in the history of Hasidism / by David Assaf ; translated from the Hebrew by Dena Ordan. — 1st ed.
p. cm. — (The Tauber institute series for the study of European Jewry)
Includes bibliographical references and index.
ISBN 978-1-58465-861-0 (cloth : alk. paper)
1. Hasidism—History. I. Ordan, Dena. II. Title.
BM198.3.A8813 2010
296.8'33209—dc22 2009053149

And thus you will comprehend what an ordeal child rearing is for these zaddikim; for this is their greatest trial. For while they proclaim the name of God, blessed be He, in the world, and stand in the breach and return individuals to the straight and narrow path, in their homes a foreign growth develops, the very antithesis of the essence of their task to expand the boundaries of and spread holiness . . . And this prevents them from disseminating sanctity, and counters their aspiration to intensify sanctity and reveal the divine aspect in the world, when it is thrown up to them: "Look at your own sons, look at how they behave; how can you demand of others to observe the Torah and the commandments?"

—*Zikaron misheli*, introduction and preface by the admor [Ben-Zion Rabinowitz] of Biala (Jerusalem: Megamah, 1989), 199

Contents

Preface to the English-language Edition

In every respect a historical study, *Untold Tales of the Hasidim* also seeks to tell a compelling tale. True, this book has all the trappings of critical academic writing, including notes and a detailed bibliography, yet it also possesses features of mystery, drama, and tragedy, whose spellbinding powers I hope can be glimpsed among the lines, words, and letters, placing matters in a new and surprising light.

While writing this book, I found myself on more than one occasion overstepping the bounds of the circumscribed field of the historian who deciphers papers and documents, reconstructs events from a variety of sources, and interprets and evaluates facts. Alongside moving experiences—especially while tracing the tragic fate of Moshe, Shneur Zalman of Lyady's youngest son, or reading the heartfelt confession of Rabbi Yitshak Nahum Twersky—I found myself swept into a craft whose affinity to that of the historian I had never before considered: detective work. I saw myself as a sleuth who illumines dark corners with his flashlight, looks for the faded hand- and footprints of forgotten figures, seeks treasures hidden from every other eye and ear, pokes around in smoking ruins and destroyed cabins, and tries to fit tiny mosaic stones into the rough outline and fine tracery of the picture of the past.

As Yaacov Shavit put it: "The detective seeks to prove—after the requisite winnowing—that no fact is fortuitous and that every fact has 'meaning' within a given system. Both detective and historian seek to portray a chain of events over a given time span in a specific location and to bestow an explanation and 'meaning' on these events . . . The detective—like the historian—believes that it is possible to describe and restore the past 'as it really was.'"[1] In setting out to assume the detective's mantle, the historian proceeds without weapons or search warrants, armed only with self-assurance and the optimistic belief that it is possible to reconstruct what others have tried to obscure. Confident in his ability to analyze and reconstruct, and in the overt and covert knowledge he has amassed on the topic of his study, he utters a prayer that he will neither fail nor lead others astray. Although admittedly demanding, the task of the historian-detective is one of the most satisfying ones in the realm of historical study.

The seven chapters of this book treat the hidden and the forgotten—or, perhaps more precisely, what has been concealed or deliberately suppressed. They describe anomalous individuals and dramatic episodes from the nineteenth and early twentieth centuries that were pushed to the sidelines of the glorious history of Hasidism. Ignored by the spokesmen and writers of this large movement, they were consigned to some hidden corner. All because of the discomfort they aroused, and in line with the popular aphorism: "Don't air your dirty laundry in public."

Testimony of the extent to which concealment and silencing made entire chapters vanish from the history of Hasidism comes from early-twentieth-century remarks by Rabbi Yehuda Leib Zlotnik (Avida) regarding the terrible Sabbath desecration attributed to Rabbi Menahem Mendel of Kotsk (he supposedly doused the candles, and some say he made heretical pronouncements at the same time): "Yet something occurred in Kotsk of which nary a soul dares speak. Everyone knows there is some truth to this matter, yet the heart does not divulge it to the mouth. *I wonder, if anyone living today knows what actually occurred,* and when the remaining hasidim from the past generation come to the Kotsk episode, they look heavenward, fearfully stutter 'hmm . . . hmm . . . ,' and fall silent."[2]

But no one can keep the dirty laundry hidden forever. It has a habit of fermenting, bubbling over, and loudly bursting forth; any attempt to clap a lid on the boiling kettle is doomed to failure. Self-appointed watchmen have restrained and tried to suppress the embarrassing truth or "knowledge"—no matter what its nature or interpretation—but to no avail. And when concealment failed and an unpleasant truth burst forth to ostensibly threaten the faithful, a variety of tactics were employed in the Sisyphean struggle over "memory": disregard or denial, erasure and blurring, twisting and rewriting, alternative interpretations, and even the creation of a new fictional story with the polemical power to undermine the dangerous "false truth" and replace it with a different, acceptable, holy truth.

Originally published in Hebrew in 2006 by the Zalman Shazar Center for Jewish History (with the title *Ne'ehaz basevakh: Pirkei mashber umevukhah betoldot hahasidut*), this book aroused immediate interest, and a second printing appeared only a month after the original publication. Articles in popular newspapers, reviews in academic journals, lively debates on Internet forums, and rumors and recommendations by word of mouth all brought enhanced interest, among the ultra-Orthodox camp in general, and the hasidic one, in particular. Given this intense attention, the appearance of an English edition was natural. To my delight, Brandeis University Press decided to publish the English version of this book. Special thanks are due to

Sylvia Fuks Fried for her initiative and support throughout, and to Phyllis Deutsch, editor in chief, University Press of New England. I also thank Jeanne Ferris for her close reading and sharp-eyed copyediting of the book, and Jeffrey K. Weiss for preparing the index.

The English and the Hebrew versions of this book are not identical; various changes have been introduced in order to adapt this version to the needs of the English reader. The chapters are ordered slightly differently, and appendixes containing texts and documents have been omitted, as has one chapter that appeared elsewhere in English.[3] Moreover, long footnotes have been shortened or cut out entirely, particularly those containing detailed bibliographical information in Hebrew or in Yiddish, intended for the reader with expertise in this material. Alongside these deletions and abridgments, I have made corrections and added new data that have come to my attention since the publication of the Hebrew version.

The English version was translated by Dena Ordan, of Jerusalem. Words do not suffice to describe her good taste, knowledge, meticulousness, and devotion to this difficult task. I owe her a debt of gratitude. There is inadequate space to list all the names of the teachers, colleagues, and students who have helped me on this path, supplying bricks and mortar, pointing out mistakes, or bringing new and old sources and studies to my attention. I thank them all. I must also express my appreciation to the Zalman Shazar Center and its director, Zvi Yekutiel, for their full agreement to this book's publication in English. Finally, my profound gratitude to my wife, Sharon, and our four children—Avishag, Netta, Hillel, and Mishael—is not readily translated into words. To you, my beloved ones, I dedicate this book by paraphrasing the words of the famed poet Shlomo ibn Gabirol: You are my rock and my refuge . . . morning and night.

David Assaf
Jerusalem, 2010

Translator's Note

Each translation project in the field of Judaica presents its own set of difficulties and decisions. No system for spelling or transliteration of personal and place names meets the complicated need to remain true to the original, yet to provide a reader-friendly text. In this book, personal names of rabbinic and other figures appear in their Hebrew, and not in their Anglicized or Yiddish forms (thus Moshe, not Moses or Moishe). An attempt has also been made in the text to use more familiar forms that do not indicate a final *heh* or the *shwa na*, for example (Shlomo, not Shelomoh). As for geographical names, this book uses the familiar Jewish (or English) spellings (thus Apta, not Opatów), based mainly on Gary Mokotoff and Sallyann Amdur Sack's *Where Once We Walked: A Guide to the Jewish Communities Destroyed in the Holocaust* (rev. ed., Bergenfield, N.J: Avotaynu, 2002). The transliteration system for Hebrew makes no distinction between *aleph* and *ayin*, between *het* and *heh*, or between *kaf* and *kuf*, on the assumption that the reader who knows Hebrew will recognize which is appropriate. The letter *tsadi* is rendered *ts*, and no hyphens separate the definite article *ha* (or other particles) from the rest of the word. In addition, *shwa na* is not always indicated, nor are letters with a *dagesh* doubled. The transliteration of Yiddish follows the system on the YIVO Institute for Jewish Research website. Words like "zaddik" that have entered the English language appear in their usual English forms. Unless otherwise indicated, all emphases in the quotations are the author's.

Abbreviations

BT	Babylonian Talmud
CAHJP	Central Archives for the History of the Jewish People
IMHM	Institute of Microfilmed Hebrew Manuscripts
NLIS	National Library of Israel
PT	Palestinian Talmud

Introduction

Two entwined themes crisscross and bind the chapters of this book: one is the anomalous, strange, and aberrant individuals who did not keep to their predecessors' straight and narrow path, but chose to carve out their own instead; the other is literary "memory wars," the battles ostensibly fought over persons, events, phenomena, and processes between various, often opposing, traditions. It is also possible to define this study as an attempt to pinpoint the delicate phase at which their preservers and interpreters recast unconventional biographies or closed historical events, reshaping them at will.

Many individuals—prominent and ordinary, scholarly and ignorant, impassioned and vested—stand at the crossroads of the twisted paths of human memory. To date, the always dramatic, sometimes tragic, stories of the individuals (or groups) caught in the thicket of family, community, or tradition are but dimly illumined in the broad study of Hasidism—as is the price they paid for being "other." All of this book's protagonists either fell on the margins of their society or found themselves between worlds, achieving neither tranquility nor fulfillment in the frameworks the hasidic and ultra-Orthodox settings offered (and mainly imposed on) their children. The disquiet their aberrance aroused among their contemporaries also reverberates in the means used to shape collective memory and internal historical writing. A combination of truth and fiction, these means are uncovered here through corroboration by, and contrasts with, many additional sources. The interpretive categories of "polemical" and "apologetic memory" are also employed; they serve to identify reactions—defensive and offensive alike—to alternative constructions of memory. Not only are these various memory traditions (including maskilic ones and those emerging from critical and academic research) acquainted with each other, but they also converse among themselves, both overtly and covertly.

Each of these chapters of crisis and discomfort stands as an independent unit. Readers of this book could justifiably inquire, what links the Seer of Lublin's fall from the window of his house in 1814 with the conversion, six years later, of Moshe, the son of the first Habad rebbe? Or what connects the cruel persecution of the Bratslav Hasidim in the 1860s and Yitshak Nahum Twersky's heart-rending early-twentieth-century confession? My answer is that they share not only the status of aberrant or discomfiting events, or the fate of those rejected or made other, but also the masking of these events. This book aims to reveal the hidden, both to disclose what actually happened and why, and also to demonstrate how the truth was obscured or endowed with an alternative interpretation.

To some extent, this is also the tale of individuals born into prominent hasidic families who failed to find their place: Moshe, the emotionally disturbed son of Shneur Zalman of Lyady, who converted to Christianity and thereby shamed his family and Habad Hasidism; Menahem Nahum Friedman of Itscan, a scion of the Ruzhin dynasty, who devoted his life to hopeless mediation between Hasidism and Western culture; and Yitshak Nahum Twersky of Shpikov, a descendant of the Chernobyl dynasty, whose soul was rent by an existential conflict that time alone cured. The story is sometimes one of a large group, notable for its oddity—such as the Bratslav Hasidim, who took comfort in being the victims of their hasidic brethren's scorn—and sometimes one of marginal individuals, who pushed their way or were forced into the eye of the storm—such as the brilliant scholar Akiva Shalom Chajes of Tulchin, who fought Hasidism his entire life, even after he joined its ranks. All paid a price for their aberrance. Linking them is the fascinating human tale that emerges from the historian's joining of scattered and shattered sources.

Emerging from this book's examination of the aberrant is another feature that connects some of the chapters: a unique, defined social group that can be termed the "scions of hasidic rebbes" (referred to in hasidic circles as *benehem shel kedoshim*—the sons of saints). Dov Sadan first noted this phenomenon in his introduction to the collected poems of Yaakov Friedman, the son of the zaddik Shalom Yosef of Mielnica: "This poetry's birthplace comes from within the reality and symbolism of the hasidic world and from the tension between adherence to, and the struggle with, Hasidism. This phenomenon applies to a worthy group of poets, the grandsons and great-grandsons of hasidic rebbes, who transmuted their ancestors' dominion over souls in matters of faith for their own kingdom, where they rule over the spirits of artistic freedom . . . *But the question of what befell the rebbes' grandchildren who left the fold is a serious one.*"[1]

Sadan returned to this issue in 1976: "I was sitting [at a lecture] in the dining hall of Kibbutz Merhavia looking over the audience, with whose family origins I was acquainted, and they included descendants of Elimelekh of Lyzhansk, and of Levi Yitshak of Berdichev, and of Hayyim of Chernovtsy, and of the Maggid of Zalozits, and of the 'Holy Jew,' and of Shlomo of Radomsk, among others . . . and if I picked them out one by one their numbers would be legion. *And the question is whether these great numbers, their blessing, and their multibranched nature, are accidental.*"[2]

Following in Sadan's footsteps, I tried to determine if it was indeed possible to find shared characteristics among the descendants of rebbes "who left the fold," particularly those who longed for poetry, art, and beauty. Was their similarity fortuitous, or was it the logical outcome of the stresses of their upbringing as the children of hasidic rebbes?

A leading premise of this book is that this was not simply a chance occurrence. Yet its multiple manifestations are not necessarily a product of Hasidism or of their upbringing, but are mainly the fruits—sweet or sour, depending on the observer's perspective—of the contrary trends shaping the world of Eastern European Jewry from the late eighteenth century until the Holocaust. If there is a common, elemental experience shared by all Jews in the modern age it is the tortuous, contradiction-filled encounter between the preservers, guided by glorification of the past and preservation of tradition, and the innovators, whose vision of a future Jewish society leans both on a fresh interpretation of tradition and on the secularizing forces of modernity. Dozens of sources, books, and studies describe this always tense, crisis-laden encounter. This book, however, examines its presence in less likely, and ostensibly more protected, venues: within the hasidic way of life, among its rebbes and their followers. By no means a marginal sect, Hasidism was a powerful, high-status group with massive influence on Jewish life. But even within the supposedly stable world of the zaddikim and their devotees, some were incessantly tossed between tradition and crisis, between old and new, between the conservative forces of religious and familial authority and the enticing, destructive forces of modern life. In touching upon disquieting and discomforting episodes, the chapters of this book attempt to break down these sweeping statements into discrete components.

The opening chapter, "'Lies My Teacher Told Me': Hasidic History as a Battlefield," sets the background for this book. It poses the question of how ideologically oriented groups approach embarrassing episodes, and it demonstrates some of the historiographical strategies employed to confront such affairs in various ultra-Orthodox circles, including hasidic ones.

Chapter 2, "Apostate or Saint? In the Footsteps of Moshe, the Son of Rabbi Shneur Zalman of Lyady," is the longest in the book. Devoted to reconstruction and examination of one of the most disconcerting episodes in hasidic history—the conversion to Christianity in 1820 of Moshe, the beloved son of the founder of Habad Hasidism, Shneur Zalman of Lyady—the bulk of the chapter traces the convoluted paths of memory and the various interpretations of this episode as absorbed by hasidim and maskilim, apostates and historians, each with its own polemical and exegetical cast.

Chapter 3, "One Event, Multiple Interpretations: The Fall of the Seer of

Lublin," treats the different explanations attached to a strange event: the fall of the famed zaddik Yaakov Yitshak Horowitz, known as the Seer of Lublin, from the window of his house, which led to his death nine months later, in 1815. Was this fall the result of the Seer's mystical efforts to hasten the advent of the messiah, as the hasidim claimed? Was it due to inebriation, as the maskilim asserted? Or was it perhaps a failed suicide attempt?

Chapter 4, "'Happy Are the Persecuted': The Opposition to Bratslav Hasidism," surveys the history of the internal struggle against an anomalous group within Hasidism: the Bratslav Hasidim. This struggle, which has accompanied the history of this unique hasidic group from its inception to the present, assumed particularly violent dimensions in the 1860s. The decoding of this strong antipathy showed its source to be the Bratslavers' refusal to accept any leading hasidic authorities other than their own already deceased leaders. This chapter also reveals the modus operandi of Ukrainian zaddikim and the unique patterns of hasidic "takeovers" of Jewish communities.

Chapter 5, "'Excitement of the Soul': The World of Rabbi Akiva Shalom Chajes of Tulchin," is devoted to the enigmatic figure of Akiva Shalom Chajes of Tulchin (1815–68), a fierce mitnaged who, in his youth, apparently composed mocking diatribes against the zaddikim, but upon reaching maturity changed his stripes and became a hasidic rebbe in the small town of Dubova. His multifaceted, contradictory personality has been subjected to prejudicial treatment in various sources, each with its own agenda—from works by the writer Micha Yosef Berdyczewski to family, local, and hasidic memory traditions—which try to crack Akiva's secret and explain his change of heart. This consideration also reveals the nature of some strange controversies that divided various hasidic groups in the southern regions of the Pale of Settlement, first and foremost, the *kadavar* controversy.

Chapter 6, "'How Times Have Changed': The World of Rabbi Menahem Nahum Friedman of Itscan," describes the unique world of Menahem Nahum Friedman of Itscan (1879–1933), and his literary output, entirely devoted to naive, harmonistic mediation between the hasidic world and European philosophy. This thoroughly modern activity amazed the surrounding hasidic society, which found this bizarre phenomenon hard to swallow. The chapter surveys several of his unusual treatises as well as his problematic acceptance in hasidic memory, which ranges from total disregard or a hidden polemic against him to a call to do away with his books.

The final chapter, "'Confession of My Tortured, Afflicted Soul': The World of Rabbi Yitshak Nahum Twersky of Shpikov," focuses on an extraordinary document, a letter penned in 1910 by Yitshak Nahum Twersky of Shpikov (1888–1942), the son of an eminent zaddik. What occasioned this letter was Twersky's imminent departure from his seemingly sheltered Ukrainian court for Galicia, in order to meet (for the first time) and wed his prospective bride: the daughter of the famed Belzer rebbe. In surprisingly rich language, this piercing, intimate, historical and psychological document unfolds Twersky's convoluted emotional paths and dual existence within the hasidic court that he so hated and despised. The chapter explores the familial, social, and historical context of this rare document, and provides a full translation of the confession.

There is yet another important, tragic, and tortured figure whose story merits telling, but who does not take his rightful place in this book devoted to crisis and discontent in the history of Hasidism: Dov Ber (Bernyu) Friedman of Leova (1820/21–76), a son of the famed zaddik Yisrael of Ruzhin. In 1869, disgusted with his followers, Bernyu resigned from his hasidic throne, the first rebbe to do so. Kidnapped and brought forcibly to his brother's Sadigura court, he was rescued by local maskilim. Bernyu remained for a time in nearby Chernovtsy, in the home of a radical maskil, where he desecrated the Sabbath, ate nonkosher food, and published an open letter in the Jewish press voicing his aversion to Hasidism and announcing his affinity for Haskalah. His shocking story aroused much public interest but ended with a whimper. Several weeks later, Bernyu returned to the Sadigura court, where he remained in isolation until his death in 1876. The dramatic twists and turns in the life journey of this zaddik, a son of a zaddik—which resonated in the contemporary press, numerous polemical tracts, and lampoons—opened a Pandora's box that discomfited all the branches of Ruzhin-Sadigura Hasidism and sparked an intensely violent dispute in the hasidic and Orthodox worlds of the 1870s. Bernyu's biography and the history of the Sandz-Sadigura dispute merit separate study of a scope beyond that of this volume. I hope to have the opportunity to tell their stories in the future.

1 "Lies My Teacher Told Me"

Hasidic History as a Battlefield

It is unnecessary to publicize the inadvertent sins of the great, worthy rabbis. Of these sins, only a modicum should be revealed and the majority hidden, especially as these rabbis are now in the "world of truth," and would certainly find this revelation disturbing. —*Beit Rabbi*[1]

In 1995, in a book titled *Lies My Teacher Told Me: Everything Your American History Textbook Got Wrong*, James W. Loewen debunked axioms long held dear in American history textbooks.[2] For me, this book sparked the question of how graduates of hasidic institutions would react if given the opportunity to subject the history of their movement—as marketed by the mechanisms shaping and preserving their society's collective memory—to critical review. Naturally, this question applies to all ideologically oriented educational systems, in every time and place; my spotlight, however, is trained on the hasidic and the ultra-Orthodox systems.

Were hasidim dismayed by the fact that admired rabbis and zaddikim, like Yisrael of Ruzhin, Moshe of Kobrin, or Shmuel of Salant were unable to write?[3] Did they find the claim that the Seer of Lublin's fall from his window was a drunken accident, and not the result of his attempts to hasten the messianic era, embarrassing? And what of Moshe, the son of the founder of Habad Hasidism, who converted to Christianity, or Bernyu of Leova, who joined the ranks of the radical maskilim? And this is but a partial list.[4] In other words, how does hasidic society confront unpleasant facts (assuming that they are not wicked or libelous accusations), and what are the ramifications for a society such as the hasidic one of tackling disconcerting aspects of its history?

How, for example, would an inquisitive Belz or Chernobyl hasid react to the astounding confession found in this book's final chapter, which remained hidden in manuscript form for some ninety years? In it Yitshak Nahum Twersky of Shpikov, a scion of a celebrated hasidic dynasty, openly bares his tortured soul and his dual existence in his much-hated hasidic court: "I constantly have free thoughts, but I am obliged to observe my ancestors' most minute stringencies of observance; I have good taste and love beauty, but I am obliged to wear the clothing of the uncivilized"—referring to the *shtrayml* and *kapota*, still worn by present-day hasidim who might read his words. Twersky continues: "Thus do I live out my life here, a dark gloomy life, without a spark of light, without a shadow of hope."

About to travel to Galicia to wed a young woman he has never met, he imagines the Belzer court as a madhouse ruled by bestial fanatics: "They are frozen, fossilized, standing constantly on the same level as our ancestors in Poland three hundred years ago. And if they have developed . . . they have done so only in the sense that they have heaped more restrictions on their ancestors' restrictions and added stupidity to their stupidity." He goes on with a graphic, harsh description of the narrow, petty, and ugly hasidic world, from which he longs to escape.

Until recently, what was known in Belz and Chernobyl circles regarding the young rebbe of Shpikov was simply the fact of his marriage to the daughter of the renowned Belzer zaddik, Yisakhar Dov Rokeah. Twersky did not serve as a hasidic rebbe and chose to be a communal rabbi instead, but this was by no means unusual. In Belz and Chernobyl collective memory, Twersky and his family—consumed by the Holocaust—retained the image of martyrs and paragons. How would a hasid raised on admiration of the past and the sanctity of the zaddikim respond to the revelation of Twersky's dark, hidden side?

The educational and collective-memory systems of ultra-Orthodox society possess the ability to readily encompass such "embarrassments." Consciously or unconsciously guided by the principle subsumed by the ancient Talmudic saying "whoever says that David sinned is merely erring" (BT *Shabbat* 55b), the ultra-Orthodox consider sins of the outstanding individuals of each generation—and naturally, each period and each circle has its outstanding leader—to be nonexistent, but even if they do exist, they can be reduced, rationalized, or reshaped as meritorious. This glorification of the past receives an antithetical portrayal in a story involving the Besht's contemporary Rabbi Nahman of Kosov. The story goes that upon coming to a certain community, not only did Rabbi Nahman lead the prayers without prior permission, he even diverged from the time-honored Ashkenazic prayer rite. Although irritated by his presumption, "when they heard words sweeter than nectar and honey issuing from his mouth, they took pleasure in it and kept silent." But, when he finished, they furiously demanded, "How did you dare to stand before the ark without permission and to change the order of the prayers from that followed by our fathers and forefathers who were the leaders of their generations?" To which Rabbi Nahman provided the somewhat anarchistic answer: "Who says that they are in paradise?"[5]

But such radical or critical comments are rarely heard at present. An uncontested consensus reigns: our forefathers, the leaders of their generations, are in paradise, and their honor is sacrosanct. Notwithstanding the winds of change blowing in contemporary *haredi* society, and its increasing exposure to international and secular trends, *haredi* society erects barricades against the indiscriminate penetration of sensitive, enticing, or dangerous information into its midst.

Seen from this perspective, in the hands of irresponsible outsiders, history in general—and the history of Hasidism in particular—not only threatens but also constitutes a weapon against tradition. Wielding this weapon are unscrupulous and ignorant scholars, who follow in the footsteps of the detested maskilim, Hasidism's brazen opponents. To these scholars, the faithful ascribe a desire to innovate at any price and an avid search for sensationalism. Witness the following diatribe by the Habad researcher and bibliographer Haim Liberman against modern academic research, as personified by Gershom Scholem and his disciples:

> Hasidism has now acquired the "merit" of being a topic of scholarly inquiry. Articles and entire books devoted to the study of Hasidism have recently been published. But *by all rights this topic should be handled by experts: namely, the hasidim themselves.* As members of the inner circle, born and bred in Hasidism, imbibing it with their mother's milk and living in a hasidic environment, all the paths, methods, and streams of Hasidism are clear to them; they possess expertise in its literature, customs, and oral traditions. Only they have a true sense of Hasidism and for them alone is it proper to undertake its study. It is to be regretted that outsiders and unripe students educated in a foreign environment and possessing extrinsic attitudes toward Hasidism, who derogate the honor of the eminent leaders of Judaism, have chanced upon this field . . . They bring their prejudices to the study of Hasidism, deliberately and incorrectly attributing to it aspects of their own imagination. They introduce distortions, and reach vain conclusions through empty casuistic discussion. Even though they lack the training to study Hasidism, they pretentiously adopt the stance of men of science, and pretend to be governed only by neutral, unbiased academic standards and to show no favoritism.[6]

This is not the place to reconstruct this controversy's reverberations. I simply note a fact that speaks for itself: on the one hand, the scholars Liberman critiqued largely accepted his comments regarding specific points.[7] On the other hand, his generalization regarding empty casuists, ignoramuses, and distorters among academic researchers might also have been favorably received if all the hasidim dealing with historical writing had also come to the field without bias. But the intensive, recent study of what is termed Orthodox historiography provides countless examples—some of which will be discussed here—of ignorance and rancor; of crude or sophisticated cover-ups, both overt and covert; of forgery and prejudicial rewriting; and of denial of unpleasant facts employed by the "experts: namely, the hasidim themselves."[8]

This well-entrenched stance, according to which critical study improperly reveals aspects of Hasidism, continues to guide internal hasidic historiography. Here is another example of a hate-filled diatribe against academic scholarship. In the editors' introduction to a 1991 reprint of a well-known 1805 letter by Rabbi Yehezkel Panet describing the learned circle active in the court of Menahem Mendel of Fristik (afterward at Rimanov), they bemoan the decline of the generations, which has been so severe that only select individuals comprehend this holy document's immense importance. Much to their chagrin, this letter has also sparked interest among scholars of Hasidism. In their dismay, they lump together all researchers, "both *haredi* and secular":

> Recent years especially have seen the rise of so-called researchers of Hasidism, both *haredi* and secular, even including some who have left the fold, heaven forfend, who distort the original image of Hasidism, treating hasidic works as if they were academic books, in which each researcher does as he pleases: takes things out of context, places mistaken emphases, and stresses what he seeks to link to his erroneous notions. And whereas *haredi* researchers do their work privately and are satisfied with the *haredi* press, dressing their remarks in the guise of the history of Hasidism, or as the delineation of a particular rebbe's personality . . . the secular researchers and other afflictions *who study Hasidism in the impure universities* have transformed Hasidism into a political party, the rebbe into a party chief, the rabbis into activists, and the hasidim into rank-and-file supporters (and even this letter has become a historical document, and as a propaganda letter for Hasidism and for the writer's rebbe, it is not to be mentioned).[9]

While the harsh words directed at the "impure universities" are nothing new, the spotlight trained on students of Hasidism from the *haredi* camp requires explanation. Who are these researchers? If up until a generation ago, Habad hasidim were in the forefront of historical activity, a similar awareness of the past has recently developed among additional hasidic groups. Many hasidic courts boast research institutes, publishing houses, and periodicals in which amateur historians publish manuscripts, documents, and other material relating to the hasidic past. This essentially modern activity is often couched in conservative ideological terms: as a struggle to preserve the sanctity of the past and to prevent external distortion of the truth. Note the following typical polemical quotation from a hasidic periodical originating among the Skvira hasidim (of New York), which discusses the importance of the project devoted to the zaddikim of the Chernobyl dynasty: "It has a necessary aim: to preserve its way of life, *so that strangers will not come and defile it* by writing treatises on the history of the zaddikim which discontent Torah scholars, and because of our manifold sins *such treatises are many, written by coarse fools whose uncircumcised hearts do not reach the slightest comprehension of the holy zaddikim's greatness* . . . and regard them as ordinary people."[10]

The history of Hasidism accordingly resembles a battlefield on which two opposing armies are deployed: defenders of "holy" history and "coarse fools" who seek to despoil and defile that history. Is a dialogue, or coexistence, possible between these two worlds? Ostensibly, this is unthinkable. Recent scholarly studies, like their maskilic and heretical predecessors over the past two centuries, are taboo and are not available in *haredi* bookstores. Only individuals drawn to external wisdom read them—in secret, far from prying eyes. But notwithstanding this apparent enmity and distrust, the situation is not nearly so dichotomous. Indeed, any academic involved in the study of Hasidism can point to a few, God-fearing hasidim who are their most faithful readers. Motivated by their love of the secrets of the past, they permit themselves a taste of forbidden honey. More than any other audience, they respond intelligently, correct mistakes, and provide additional sources, new and old, according to their expertise. Thus, the publication of this book in Hebrew sparked dozens of such responses—in writing, by telephone, and in e-mails.

Who are these readers? Hopelessly infected by insatiable historical curiosity, these amateur historians come from all sectors of *haredi* society. Their fields of interest encompass the history of the Torah world, the rabbinate, and Hasidism. Armed with broad knowledge, sometimes arcane and sometimes piquant, they are conversant with all branches of traditional literature, both exoteric and esoteric, as well as with some academic studies. Not only have they developed protective mechanisms to grapple with the critical view of Jewish history, at times they seemingly derive particular pleasure from exposing controversies, disputes, and embarrassing events. Yet these individuals would never consider recording or publishing these comments within their own camps.

This ambiguity toward uncomfortable moments from the past (and even more so toward embarrassing moments in the present) is not restricted to relatively closed sectors of society, but can also be identified among open communities fearful that contending with failure may threaten the rightness of their vision or the integrity of their path. The ability to handle unpleasant episodes in a critical fashion and the willingness to consider change, or even to pay a price for mistakes, mark an optimistic, proud, and confident society. A society in crisis, or one suffering from a lack of confidence or self-esteem, tends to adopt a defensive attitude toward criticism and a hesitant one toward the past, viewing the exposure of its secrets as posing a mortal danger to its stability.

The U.S. Supreme Court Justice Louis D. Brandeis once commented: "Publicity is justly commended as a remedy for social and industrial diseases. Sunlight is said to be the best of disinfectants; electric light the most efficient policeman."[11] He made this statement not as a historian seeking the truth but as a concerned citizen, based on his conviction that the masking of wrongdoing, evil, and corruption harms society, whereas public transparency is not just beneficial but also possesses healing, restorative powers. Yet the magnitude of the emotional response evoked by these questions in different circles does not simply reflect extroversion and innovativeness as opposed to introversion and conservatism, it also highlights great sensitivity toward symbols of the past and the group ethos, whether celestially or terrestrially sanctified. Seen from this perspective, the past is not neutral. We cannot relate to it simply as "what was, was." Rather, it constitutes a dynamic basis for the formation of a shared social identity. A society engaged in a constant struggle to maintain its values and on the defensive against snares, which compulsively defines the borders of identification with its past, will be content with nothing less than a sanctified, pure history.[12]

Encounters with a disconcerting past or with the memory of discomfiting events give the community of rememberers doubts about their path, and the bitter taste of failure. For historians—especially historian-detectives—whose research is not aimed at meeting group spiritual needs and who certainly bear no responsibility for the shaping of collective memory, these events pose a special challenge. Such historians seek to unravel the mystery and to arrive as closely as possible at the truth, both as it was and as it was interpreted. Fueling their attraction to the dramatic and dark sides of history, to hidden or downplayed events, is neither spite nor an overarching morality, but rather the intense allure of the concealed.

It is precisely those discomfiting events and aberrant individuals, which some have sought to erase or to hide from prying eyes, that spark the imagination of the writer, poet, and historian-detective. An understanding of the mechanisms of suppression reveals the complexity of ostensibly straightforward events and contributes to a more refined portrayal of individuals who have been perceived as one-dimensional, holy saints from birth. It also unmasks the sensibilities of those who choose to hide the truth, the clumsy or elegant steps taken to this end, and their strategies for dealing with the sudden revelation of data that elude the silencing mechanisms.

Orthodox Historiography's Strategies of Memory and Repression

> What appears in the above-mentioned book regarding the dispute between our holy rabbi of Lublin . . . and the Holy Jew of Pshishkha . . . are words that should not be heard, let alone uttered, and certainly not printed. A word to the wise is sufficient.
> —Hayyim Elazar Shapira, *Divrei torah tinyanah*[13]

Each chapter of this book considers at length the strategies employed by hasidic traditions of memory to address embarrassing episodes. The attempt to formulate a cohesive interpretive framework for these episodes conjures up the scholarly term "Orthodox historiography," widely used to refer to various means of recording the past commonly found in *haredi* circles.[14] Essentially, Orthodox historiography differs little from other branches of ideologically biased historiography or any other official histories. Does *haredi* historiography possess characteristics that distinguish it from maskilic, communist, and right- or left-wing historiography? In my opinion, the differences inhere not in the historiographies' essences but in their tones or styles. All share a programmatic agenda that seeks to sanctify, and to promote, specific insights, explanations, or values, and all use varied means to restrict the ability of their opponents or rivals to achieve a fair presentation of their views. All view the quest for truth or restoration of the past as it was not as an end in and of itself, divorced from other important values, but as an additional means of opposing antagonists and forwarding the group's agenda. Nonetheless, Orthodox historiography, the focus of this book, does possess unique literary features, some of which will be discussed below.

Present-day *haredi* society, to which Hasidism belongs, functions within a modern democratic environment whose mass media exhibit an ever-growing interest in this society. Accordingly, its members face, on occasion, the danger of public revelation of embarrassing incidents involving the *haredi* elites, or exemplifying the undermining of old-world values, whether these assume the form of financial corruption, theft, fraud, domestic abuse, sexual aberration, or rape. The memory-agents of current *haredi* society are not just, as in the past, the life stories of eminent individuals, or the oral traditions passed from father to son, or the authoritative rebbes, rabbis, and teachers in various educational settings. In the thick of those who shape *haredi* collective memory, we also find *haredi* political figures—who receive wide coverage in the secular press—and *haredi* journalists and other media personalities.

More than any other force, the flourishing *haredi* media of the last generation, both printed and broadcast, have shaped their consumers' agenda. But they are not guided by the masthead logo of the *New York Times*: "All the news that's fit to print." Essentially recruited media, they do not see their role as disseminating information at any price; indeed, at times their function is actually to conceal. Well-attuned to their mission to nurture, preserve, and protect the values of the *haredi* society with which they identify, these media are moreover self-appointed to provide the *haredi* answer to prying eyes. The secular press, paradoxically accused of prejudicial one-sidedness, has in some respects become for the *haredi* media the heir and partner of maskilic literature, on the one hand, and of academic historiography, on the other hand—seen as possessing destructive, and not curative, tendencies.

Investigative reporters' interest in episodes of corruption, financing of yeshivas, police records and courts, forces the *haredi* media—even its independent, politically unaffiliated branches—to take a stand on how to present embarrassing facts. Heightening these dilemmas is *haredi* society's profound dependence on the kosher *haredi* press for news of their circles (alongside oral rumors, still a strong alternative communication route). Barring exceptional cases, the *haredi* media largely utilize a dual memory strategy: they overlook defects and flaws within the holy community, creating the facade of a harmonious society that obeys traditional authorities, notwithstanding its multilayered stratification; and they also aggressively trumpet the hollowness of the surrounding society. The *haredi* media will never report the arrest of the son of a *rosh yeshiva* for election fraud, or the sexual abuse of young men by the head of the *kolel*, or the wife beating of a rebbe's son, but they do highlight secular society's hedonism and moral corruption.

However, the picture is far from simplistic. At times, internecine hatred and dissension in the *haredi* world, despite its largely shared worldview and lifestyle, has the opposite effect. An uncontrollable desire to blacken the opposite side unleashes inhibitions and overrides the desire to silence or hide. Polemical tracts, hate-filled placards, and provocative wall posters (known as *pashkevilim*), both signed and anonymous, are an accepted, long-standing method of disseminating subversive, disconcerting material, at times with the blessing of the authorities backing one side or another. The result is public broadcasting of embarrassing information, which would ordinarily have been silenced or made to disappear. The sophisticated, complex, and conspiratory nature of this information indirectly contributes to the undermining of the ostensible solidity of the accepted descriptions of the past, characterized by simplicity, naiveté, and harmonistic tendencies.

Between "Honor" and "Truth": The Toldot Aharon Inheritance Dispute

A recent example comes from a bitter inheritance dispute between twin branches of one of Jerusalem's most fanatical and insular hasidic sects: the Toldot Aharon group. This controversy not only sparked a nasty wave of violence but was also accompanied by the issuing of publications containing harsh mutual accusations. Each of the rival parties—followers of the two contesting brothers, the sons of the rebbe Avraham Yitshak Hakohen Kohn, who died in 1997—publicly accused the other of having forged the dead rebbe's will. Alongside strong personal vilification, these accusations were backed by photocopies of documents and other supporting evidence grounded in modern scientific methods, such as statements by graphologists and police investigators. As put forth in its introduction, the rationale for the publication of the first treatise, *Nes lehitnoses* (To fly a banner), turns out to be a surprisingly modern historiographical aim: the disclosure of truth for its own sake and, ostensibly, not for practical advantage:

> The purpose of this book is not to change the reality created after our rabbi's death . . . nor is its purpose to make financial claims. Its main goal is simply "so all shall know"; it aims to uncover the ways of a zaddik and the pure truth of our rebbe's will, and to restore our rabbi's honor, may his memory protect us, and to unmask the hypocrites who pretend loyalty to our rabbi . . . and to his will, and impute wrong to others . . . This book and the revelation of the truth of the will and testament will give the forgers no rest . . . But it is obvious that they will stoop to any means, perverted as it may be, to preserve their lies. We are also aware that they have great power and can unbalance people . . . Therefore, we announce in advance our intention not to be dragged into provocation. There will be no further response regarding the matter of the will beyond what is written in this book. To all arguments, rationales, announcements, letters, lampoons, etc. issued by the other side, the reader will find the answers in this book.[15]

This book's editors attempt to grab the stick of historical writing by both its modern and conservative ends. On the one hand, they portray themselves as guided by a search for the pure truth, which they seek to uncover as it is, even if this leads to the embarrassing conclusion that the will was forged;[16] on the other hand, they pretend that, for them, the ramifications of this truth hold no practical interest. Also, by committing themselves in advance not to respond to the expected counterattack, they prepare a strategic path of retreat. And this counterattack was not long in coming: another book appeared in response. Feeling themselves the injured side, its authors place no trust in their opponents' self-righteous stand, and lament: "Indeed, the results . . . are most embarrassing, though they feel that they have achieved their aim thereby: *they have ground the honor of the Torah into the dust; openly trampled the honor of the rabbinic court; mocked Torah scholars as if they were vain, empty members of our people* . . . Whence all the commotion? . . . Why scrabble at this rehashed issue, which is accompanied not only by controversy and dispute but also by burning hatred, and which accomplishes nothing.

But no, they roll pious eyes heavenward and display their kosher hooves, as if their entire aim were to arrive at the truth . . . Are all means of vilification acceptable?!"[17]

This quotation's juxtaposition of "honor" and "truth" is not accidental. Preservation of the "honor of the Torah" or of "Torah scholars" is not just a fundamental value of conservative Orthodoxy, it is also a defensive (or, in this case, offensive) mechanism against the tempting, authoritative voice of history (as a representative of the "truth") and against those who scrabble in it. It is noteworthy that the other faction also refers to the concept of honor; however, it associates the rehabilitation of the dead rabbi's honor with the revelation of historical truth.

Concern for the Torah's honor in no way deterred the authors of the counterattacking booklet from presenting an alternative past, as it was from their perspective. Not surprisingly, the second tract also exhibits a stylistic conflation of polemical *haredi* defensive-aggressive rhetoric with testimony- and document-based historical and philological analysis. Although its authors maintain that they were forced to answer their detractors in the same coin, the outcome is similar: an amalgamation of the conservative-*haredi* and modern-historical approaches. And, almost predictably, the back cover of the book displays a proclamation signed by five prominent rabbis decrying the first book as "a lampoon, vain futility . . . the reading of which is prohibited and *which should be purged from the world.*"

There is, of course, a distinction between current events, more difficult to deny or distort, and those of the recent or distant past. Additional ethical and educational criteria influence the description of the distant past, leading to the shaping and marketing of a harmonious, fabricated past.

Arming for Battle: Lies, Bans, and Censorship

As we saw above, the dissemination and suppression of embarrassing information are intertwined. Tightening this dialectical weave of revelation and concealment is the easy access to means of publication, trustworthy or not, in the form of newspapers, independent publications, or online forums that provide maximum exposure but at the same time allow full preservation of anonymity. These conduits, both old and new, for disseminating and absorbing information and rumors somewhat counterbalance the suppressive trend and mechanisms of official censorship. The entirely new phenomenon of *haredi* Internet forums tolerates free expression on all topics, revelation of well-kept secrets, and spirited discussion between supporters and detractors alike. Even a random sampling of the dynamic, popular forums divulges the surprisingly subversive dimension of this virtual *haredi* communication.[18] Chats on these forums in the wake of the publication of the Hebrew edition of this book focused on the fate of Moshe, son of Shneur Zalman of Lyady, and reveal the difficulty that even open-minded participants experienced in accepting dismaying facts at face value, and the participants' profound need to rationalize and explain.

In late 2000 I published a comprehensive Hebrew study in *Zion* (a quarterly published by the Historical Society of Israel), titled "Convert or Saint? In the Footsteps of Moshe, the Son of Rabbi Shneur Zalman of Lyady." This study, an expanded version of which appears as this book's second chapter, treated Moshe's conversion to Christianity. Despite weak denials by Habad spokesmen, the fact of the conversion itself—whether it was of his own free will or through force and enticement—is incontestable. But the sources attest to yet another detail: Moshe suffered from mental illness. Whether or not he was of sound mind when he converted, this ostensibly supplies an excellent explanation for the conversion: as a private, contained failure, that of an insane individual, it in no way constitutes a blot on the hasidic movement. Nonetheless, Habad writers did not embrace this explanation. Indeed, their position was that if this event actually took place, it was an embarrassing blemish to be removed, hidden, or denied. Denial only intensified their discomfort, as Shneur Zalman of Lyady's failure to raise his son in the hasidic path could be attributed to the Habad movement as a whole.

The alternative-history strategies adopted by Habad historiography in response to the public airing of this episode by nineteenth-century maskilim are covered in greater detail in chapter 2. They include: (a) a strategy of vagueness—namely, no denials, but no prominent reporting of this embarrassing event either; (b) a corrective strategy—namely, the provision of purportedly true evidence that bestows a happy end on the story (in this case, stories of Moshe's wandering and repentance, without identifying his sin); and (c) the tactic of denial—that is, total rejection of the existence of the discomfiting episode and the substitution of a kosher biography for Moshe.

The prime representatives of the strategy of vagueness are Rabbi Hayyim Meir Heilman and his important study of the Habad dynasty, *Beit Rabbi.* Its adoption is readily understandable: no person would willingly tell his audience that his father, son, or rabbi had sinned. But, although Heilman did not see fit to publish everything he knew, he was also not prepared to pen any lies. Because the book's plan required that he mention all of Shneur Zalman of Lyady's descendants, his adoption of the strategy of vagueness was a natural and logical solution. Heilman also used the corrective strategy in the form of popular rumors and tales current among nineteenth-century Habad hasidim, which in this case probably sprouted from below. The outstanding representative of the tactic of denial is the sixth Habad rebbe, Yosef Yitshak Schneersohn (Rayyats). Although almost certainly acquainted both with the historical background and some of the facts of the case, he fabricated an alternative biography that transformed Moshe the convert into a strong opponent of Christianity and its representatives.

An ingenuous hasid nurtured solely on internal Habad literature would certainly find such a terrible step by one of Shneur Zalman of Lyady's holy descendants unthinkable. But, notwithstanding its sensational nature, my initial publication of this episode aroused little interest in the *haredi* street. The reporter who covered the story for the local Jerusalem paper *Kol ha'ir* pressed the Habad spokesman to answer some questions about the Moshe episode—he naturally issued a strong denial—but other than that, no statements from hasidic spokesmen were forthcoming. From the hasidic perspective, this was the appropriate technique: it was certainly preferable to ignore this publication, than to enter the dark alleyways of controversy, an approach that could raise additional embarrassing queries. After all, he who is ignorant cannot ask questions. How many hasidim read *Zion* or *Kol ha'ir*? Better to keep silent and let the story return to hibernation.

But this was certainly not the case for a new, detailed three-volume work examining the personality and philosophy of the Gaon of Vilna, *HaGaon*. Authored by Dov Eliach, who belongs to the world of the Lithuanian yeshivas, its appearance on the *haredi* book market generated a tempest that has yet to die down. Although far from critical or academic, Eliach's book shows conversance with various source documents and even modern research, on which he draws copiously (but without so noting).[19] There is nothing unusual about this book, except for the fact that Eliach crossed the line by devoting the third volume to the Gaon's antihasidic campaign. Not only did Eliach highlight this generally suppressed matter and cast aspersions on great hasidic leaders, he even dared to hint that, although weakened, the eighteenth-century excommunication of Hasidism, signed by the Gaon of Vilna, had never been canceled.[20]

The ensuing storm in the *haredi* street led to the banning of the book and the excommunication of its author. A Jerusalem periodical titled *Olam hahasidut*, whose masthead reads "devoid of gossip and politics," devoted almost an entire issue (no. 88, Shevat 2002) to debate with "that scribbler who entered the public arena." Not content with decrying his bold insolence, the newspaper also imputed to Eliach ignorance and failure to understand the sources. A clear measure of the rage aroused by this book is the illustration on this periodical's front cover, which depicts *HaGaon* being consigned to the flames of a hasidic auto-da-fé.

Given the Vilna Gaon's status as one of the most admired and outstanding rabbinic figures in his and subsequent generations, hasidim certainly find his antihasidic campaign embarrassing. How could such an eminent figure not only fail to perceive the great light of Hasidism but also authorize its violent persecution? Although they attributed this failure not to Hasidism but to

FIG. 1.1. Front cover of the Shevat 2002 issue of *Olam hahasidut*, showing Dov Eliach's *HaGaon* being consigned to the flames

the Gaon and the mitnagedic faction, the hasidim still sought an explanation for his stance and actions. In his study of the Gaon, Immanuel Etkes notes three main Orthodox historiographical trends in the treatment of this issue: an apologetic approach, ascribing a positive outcome to the polemic for the future shaping of Hasidism; a harmonizing approach, viewing this as a spiritual dispute in which the leaders of each faction displayed mutual respect; and intentional forgetfulness, whether in the guise of false modesty—the claim of unworthiness to treat this subject—or of complete disregard. Etkes sums up his discussion: "Most authors who have dealt with this topic from an orthodox Jewish point of view have shared this difficulty in accepting the picture of the past in which the Gaon appeared as a zealous and uncompromising warrior against Hasidism . . . So we see that, in places where the myth of the Vilna Gaon continues to play a vital role and to serve as a focus of identification, critical history is not exactly a welcome guest."[21]

It is therefore not surprising that *haredi* society's main source of information on the Gaon, the treatise of the late *haredi* writer Betsalel Landau, *HaGaon hehasid miVilna*, first published in 1965 (Jerusalem: Usha), entirely omits the Gaon's antihasidic campaign. (It does, however, devote a long chapter to the Gaon's antimaskilic campaign.) Naturally, Eliach suggests that Landau's book originally contained a chapter on the Gaon and Hasidism, but that internal *haredi* pressure led to its deletion.

Why a stormy reception for Eliach's book on the Vilna Gaon, and total silence on my publication of the sad episode of Shneur Zalman's son Moshe? The answer lies not in contextual and stylistic features or each topic's inherent interest, but mainly in the authors' identity and authoritativeness, as well as the availability of their writings. By and large, *haredi* society takes no interest in academic studies, ostensibly stamped with bias and hatred. Not readily available in any case, these studies are not likely to come to the attention of the *haredi* public. But it is a different matter altogether when a *haredi*, "one of us," who writes in the *haredi* style, has rabbinic approbations, and even claims rabbinic backing for his literary output, is involved. The scholarly journal *Zion* is not sold or read in *haredi* Bnei Brak, Jerusalem, or Kfar Habad. It was therefore preferable in the case of Moshe to refrain from comment in hopes that this episode would remain confined to the few curious, learned individuals already in the know. *HaGaon*, on the other hand, written in a combative style by an observant Orthodox Jew and widely distributed among bookstores catering to a *haredi* audience, could neither be ignored nor forgiven.

Is the story of *HaGaon* exceptional? The following two relatively recent examples demonstrate excoriation, and excommunication, of God-fearing *haredi* authors, this time by Lithuanian mitnagedim.

In 2002 Rabbi Nathan Kamenetsky published a detailed, multifaceted treatise, *Making of a Godol: A Study of Episodes in the Lives of Great Torah Personalities* (Jerusalem: Hamesorah)—a two-volume work, some 1,400 pages long, on his father, Rabbi Yaakov Kamenetsky (1891–1986). The father had been head of the Torah ve-Da'at yeshiva in New York and was considered one of the greatest twentieth-century Lithuanian Torah scholars.[22] The book by his son—himself a *haredi* rabbi and teacher in a prestigious Jerusalem yeshiva—aroused great anger and was rapidly banned and taken off the market.[23] Critiques of this book, which touches on other prominent rabbinic figures as well, noted its "severely debasing remarks, derisiveness, degradation and *hotzo'as sheim ra* [defamation] against several figures among *gedolei horabbonim* [leading rabbis]," (for example, their portrayal as possessing such common personality traits as jealousy and competitiveness, overbearingness or impatience, and even a propensity for pranks). Other grounds for rejection included its infusion of "spurious opinions and incorrect *hashkofoh* [outlook]" (such as its criticism of the hushing up of the truth in *haredi* works, or the claim that great Torah scholars took an interest in additional fields of study alongside the Talmud and Halakha, including philosophy, *musar*, or Hasidism). The ban, signed by a long list of important *haredi* rabbis, including some with no knowledge of English, still stands; the author cannot reissue his book.[24]

Another writer recently targeted by *haredi* censorship is Nosson Slifkin, a young *haredi* Jerusalem rabbi who calls himself the Zoo Rabbi. Notwithstanding his youth, several of his books have been banned as heretical (because, for example, of his belief that the world is millions of years old and that his attempt to prove this in no way contravenes Judaism).[25] A manifesto issued by Rabbi Yisrael Eliyahu Weintraub accused the author of twisting rabbinic statements "*so that they would be consistent with the opinions of academics, may they bite the dust*—and that the author defers to them in the maskilic style of former days." Rabbi Mikhl Yehuda Lefkowitz, an elder statesman of the Israeli Lithuanian yeshivas, added "the hope that the disseminator of heresy [Slifkin] will *burn all of his books* and publicly retract all that he has written."[26]

As the topic of the day in the *haredi* street, these banned books sparked a lively, fascinating debate in the *haredi* and modern Orthodox Internet forums, which disseminated the news of the ban. Individual copies of *Making of a Godol* are still sold secretly and even offered at outrageous prices on public auction sites.[27]

Self-Restraint, Deletion, and Retouching

Books in disfavor with certain rabbis (or with activists closely associated with them) can therefore be banned and even burned or otherwise destroyed. But this is uncommon. The prevailing *haredi* modus operandi seeks to ward off embarrassment and ensuing controversy; therefore, their memory-preserving mechanisms largely employ censorship, both external and internal. The long-standing tradition of *haskamot* (approbations) for books of Torah scholarship, and the rabbinic committees and spiritual guides found at almost every *haredi* newspaper, avert the publication of works the *haredim* view as harmful to their interests. But the main method of censorship is self-restraint on the author's part.

Self-censorship, in the Original and in Translation

One figure who reveals the policy of self-censorship is Rabbi Nosson Zvi Kenig (d. 1997). Kenig, who specialized in the history of the Bratslav hasidim and published treatises and letters from manuscripts, refers to this policy in his introduction to a book of nineteenth-century letters by Bratslavers. On his own initiative, he showed this material to "the prominent elders among our group, and consulted with them as to what should be published, what hidden things should be revealed to the public, *and what should not be printed and should remain hidden. And we deleted several letters . . . and did not print them for clandestine reasons.* Sometimes we only omitted part of a letter, marking the ellipsis with 'etc.'"[28] Thus, in a letter from 1865 in which Bratslav hasidim from Teplik, Podolia, complained of their cruel persecution by Yitshak Twersky of Skvira and his followers, Kenig—himself a Bratslav hasid—consistently replaced the Skvira rebbe's name with "etc."[29]

This spontaneous self-censorship was grounded not in fear of revealing Torah secrets, but in the author's piety and sincere desire to preserve the honor of zaddikim. This trend characterizes many sectors of Orthodox writing. The best-known example is the fate of *Der Chassidismus*, written in 1901 by the *haredi* German author Ahron Marcus under the pseudonym Verus (truthful one). Many pages of the Hebrew translation were censored because they were inconsistent with the standards then current among *haredi* leaders; nonetheless, the editions of the translations differ vastly among themselves. Thus, fifteen pages devoted to the embarrassing episode of Bernyu of Leova, "mistakenly" printed in the first Hebrew translation published in 1954, were omitted from the second, 1980, edition. The rationale provided in the preface to the latter was that this certainly reflected the wishes of the author and translator, both by then deceased.[30]

The motto "It is the glory of God to conceal a matter" (Proverbs 25:2) guides the kind-hearted concealers and censors who either act autonomously or under the aegis of their rabbis;[31] at times, however, the hiding of "a matter" results from shifts in editorial opinion. If in the prior example, the most recent editors exercised deeper censorship than their predecessors, in the next example, the latest editor revealed what his predecessors had hidden. A Habad publisher censored the surname of the maskil Aryeh Leib Mandelstam (1819–89) from a friendly, complimentary letter sent by the zaddik Menahem Mendel Schneersohn (known as the Tsemah Tsedek). The publisher did so because he "felt that it dishonored the rebbe to publish his 'praises' of Mandelstam, the maskil." But before long, this letter appeared in a Habad publication with Mandelstam's name in full, "for the book's editor decided that this in no way harmed the rebbe."[32]

Taking the significant differences into account, these phenomena merit comparison and contrast with the techniques of censorship and rewriting used by other indoctrinating societies.[33] If this seems harsh, additional examples follow.

Retouching and Airbrushing

Zekhut yisrael, a four-volume anthology of stories and testimonies regarding various zaddikim compiled by Rabbi Yisrael Berger of Bucharest (1855–1919), is considered an important, kosher source. In one volume, Berger printed the story of the Seer of Lublin's mysterious fall (treated in detail in chapter 3 of this book). Naturally, Berger cited the hasidic version of this event; but he also inserted, in square brackets, the following remarks by one of the Seer's disciples: "The holy rabbi, our teacher Yehuda Leib of Zaklikov, said that *he*

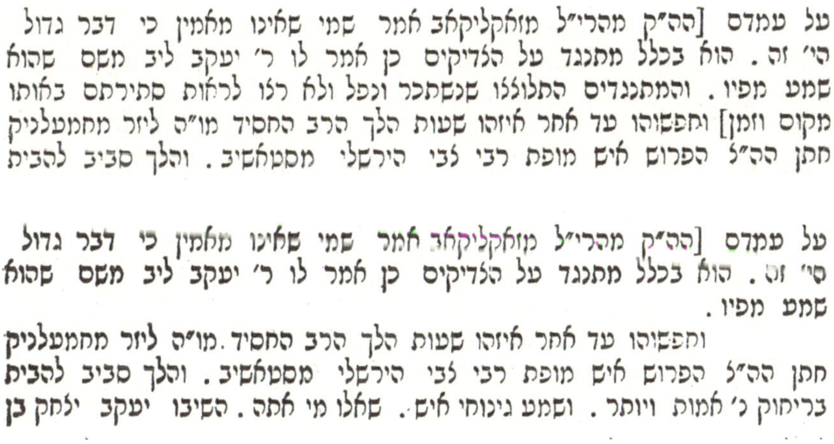

על עמדם [הה"ק מהרי"ל מזאקליקאב אמר שמי שאינו מאמין כי דבר גדול
הי' זה. הוא בכלל מתנגד על הצדיקים כן אמר לו ר' יעקב ליב מפה שהוא
שמע מפיו. והמתנגדים התלוצצו שנשתכר ונפל ולא רצו לראות סתירתם באותו
מקום וזמן] ותפסוהו עד אחר איזהו שעות הלך הרב החסיד מו"ה ליזר מחמעלניק
חתן הה"ל הפרוש איש מופת רבי צבי הירשלי מסטאשיב. והלך סביב להבית

על עמדם [הה"ק מהרי"ל מזאקליקאב אמר שמי שאינו מאמין כי דבר גדול
הי' זה. הוא בכלל מתנגד על הצדיקים כן אמר לו ר' יעקב ליב מפה שהוא
שמע מפיו.
ותפסוהו עד אחר איזהו שעות הלך הרב החסיד. מו"ה ליזר מחמעלניק
חתן הה"ל הפרוש איש מופת רבי צבי הירשלי מסטאשיב. והלך סביב להבית
בריחוק כ' אמות ויותר. ושמע ניגוני איש. שאלו מי אתה. השיבו יעקב יצחק בן

FIG. 1.2. The text of the first edition of *Sefer zekhut yisrael hanikra eser orot* (Piotrkov, 1907), above, and the censored version (Warsaw, 1913), below. Although the retouched lines create the impression of a break between paragraphs, the censor forgot to erase the first square bracket from the original.

who does not believe that this was a great thing is an opponent of the zaddikim. This is what Rabbi Yaakov Leib of that place told him, who heard it from his mouth. *And the mitnagedim joked that he was drunk and fell, and they refused to see that their interpretation contradicts the facts in that time and place*" (*Eser orot*, 91). The italicized sentences provide evidence of another view, one that does not see the fall as "a great thing." Berger, of course, totally rejected this view. Yet someone evidently found this reference to the mitnagedic opinion objectionable, and starting with the next edition, published six years later, these lines were erased from the book.[34] As seen from the illustrations above, no graphic means were used to hide the erasure's blatant traces, and those responsible did not even notice that the initial square bracket remained in place.

This was not the sole change introduced between the first and subsequent editions of the book. In the section devoted to Yisrael, the Maggid of Kozhenits, the first edition contains a story omitted from the later ones. Because of its rarity, I cite it in full:

While I was in Kalushin for the Sabbath, my cousin, the famed zaddik Rabbi Meir Shalom, of blessed memory, told me that when Motele, the son of the Maggid, may his memory protect us, died, the Maggid said upon his return from the funeral: "In the western lands it is the custom that a marriage agreement is sealed by the man slapping his intended bride so hard that she loses a tooth, and this is the *kinyan.*" And these were his very words: "he strikes her until her tooth falls out."[35]

This is, without a doubt, an exceedingly strange tale. According to this story, after his son's funeral, the Maggid of Kozhenits stated that the Jews of the western lands (the Maghreb, especially Morocco) seal a marriage contract by the groom's striking the bride until he knocks out a tooth. But what is significant here is the moral of the tale: for the Maggid, the death of his son was like a divine fist in his face, and this blow constituted a marriage between him and God. But why was this story ripped out? Perhaps because of its oddity, or perhaps due to fear that naive readers might mistakenly think that this practice was real, or perhaps because someone simply denied this story and either decided that it never happened or that it was not consonant with the Maggid's memory. In any event, this story was expunged from all subsequent editions; the page was shortened, and the following section appended to the previous one.

Pasted-over Pages

The six-volume lexicon *Meorei Galicia: Encyclopedia of Galician Rabbis and Scholars*, by Rabbi Meir Wunder, bears witness to an individual's erudition, diligence, and single-minded devotion to a task. However, anyone consulting this important compendium must bear in mind the author's self-imposed restrictions, grounded in his personal religious worldview and sense of his audience's wishes; naturally, he also had to maneuver between conflicting interests and familial and other pressures (including the need to fund such a large project). Consequently, Wunder deliberately avoids any mention of controversial issues or embarrassing incidents. Nor can we expect full, detailed, objective historical descriptions from an author who declares that his book brings Jews closer to Judaism through knowledge of their past, and that it serves as a genealogical source among hasidic courts before finalizing a match for their descendants or hasidim.[36] In line with Wunder's policy, the long entry on Rabbi Hayyim Halberstam of Sandz, for example, devotes only three lines to the dramatic controversy with Sadigura, and the tragic fate of Bernyu of Leova receives a mere two lines in his entry.[37] Similarly, the participation of dozens of rabbis in this controversy is simply alluded to in their entries.[38] In a personal conversation, Rabbi Wunder confirmed the purposeful nature of this avoidance of "the negative" and noted that this principle also dictated his inclusion of the complimentary openings of missives between leading rabbis, but not of the derogatory statements found in the body of the letters.

Naturally, the definition of "negative" is open to interpretation. Despite his stated policy, in one instance Wunder was forced to make postpublication alterations. Volume one of his encyclopedia, which appeared in Jerusalem in 1978, contained a brief entry on Elimelekh Ashkenazi of Horodenka, a Torah scholar and Chortkov hasid who died in 1916. Based on the data at his disposal, Wunder reported Ashkenazi's participation in the founding convention of the Mizrachi movement in Galicia, which was held in Lemberg, and his election as chair. Afterwards, his fellow townspeople testified that he founded a Mizrachi branch in his hometown. In all fairness, Wunder noted "an emphatic denial by Ashkenazi's grandchildren."

After this volume's publication, these grandchildren, who had evidently become ultra-*haredi*, decided that any association with National Religious Zionism dishonored them and stained their grandfather's memory. They coerced Wunder into printing a new page, which he then pasted in the remaining volumes of the encyclopedia in his possession. This updated page censored the "sensitive" lines, rewriting Ashkenazi's biography not on the basis of new data but in accordance with his descendants' wishes.[39]

Omissions between Editions

Reference was made earlier to the Sandz-Sadigura controversy, sparked by what the hasidim viewed as the zaddik Bernyu of Leova's shameful defection to the maskilic camp in Chernovsty in 1869. In its wake, Hayyim Halberstam of Sandz excommunicated all the branches of Sadigura Hasidism and demanded that Bernyu's brothers publicly denounce their sibling's ugly step. He also asked that they abandon their ostentatious customs, viewed by him as heretical and as deviating from Hasidism's original path. Like the Vilna Gaon a century earlier, this leading rabbi of his generation embarked on a merciless, but hopeless, campaign against what he saw as a group that jeopardized the world of traditional Judaism. In this case as well, the violent dispute ended only with the deaths of the protagonists in 1876. And, here too, it turned out after the fact that the leader of the campaign had erred in his assessment of the danger and failed to achieve his aims. This controversy's fascinating story requires more space than is at my disposal here, and I hope to tell it elsewhere. In any event, notwithstanding traces of this ancient hostility, at present these hasidic groups generally live in harmony. As was true for the other crises and incidents mentioned here, few references to Bernyu's fate, the steps taken by the protagonists, or the feud's accompanying conceptual and social polemic appear in hasidic—namely, Sadigura or Sandz—literature.

This is illustrated by *Rabenu hakadosh miTsanz*, a comprehensive, three-volume work published by the late Jerusalem mohel and Sandzer hasid Yosef David Weisberg (the book was ghostwritten by the above-mentioned Meir Wunder). The preface to the first edition (1976) explicitly states the author's intention to ignore the controversy initiated by its protagonist, Hayyim Halberstam of Sandz:

> My object in writing the book was to enhance the glory of Heaven and to acclaim the way of Hasidism, particularly that of our saintly rabbi . . . For that reason I have omitted many things that are not likely to teach a proper, ethical way of life, or actions in the conduct of the rabbi that we do not understand, and *therefore the affair of the well-known controversy that broke out in 1869 has been omitted,* although our rabbi was involved in it with all his might and stormy nature. The imprint of that controversy was apparent in the Jewish world for many decades, *but in our own time, the rabbis have made peace among themselves, and the relations between the grandsons of the two dynasties are cordial, while both are engaged in the struggles for the strengthening of Judaism in our generations.*[40]

It is superfluous to point out that this stance contradicts the self-evident axioms of historical study. To quote the historian Jacob Katz: "In principle, no aspect of a person's life or creativity stands outside the biographer's sphere of interest."[41] Weisberg, of course, did not view himself as a critical biographer, nor was historical reconstruction his aim. Guided by educational, not historiographical, goals, Weisberg had no qualms about using patently anti-historical tools to realize his mission.

Some twenty years later, when copies of the first edition were no longer available, its author initiated the publication of a new edition. This edition (Jerusalem, 1997) differed from its predecessor in only one respect: the preface was reset, omitting the above-cited paragraph. Now, even the author's apologetic and justificatory rationale for self-censorship was seen as problematic and derogatory; therefore it had to go! And why? Lest the curious reader inquire what "well-known controversy" had been omitted and seek information elsewhere, thereby besmirching the honor of the zaddikim.

But this is not the sole example of censorship in the book. The editor's stringency led him to use a method we have met before: retouching. One chapter mentions a Yiddish biography of Hayyim Halberstam by Yehoshua Rocker (Vienna, 1927). This book naturally covered the controversy with Sadigura in detail, from the pro-Sandzer viewpoint. What was permissible for Rocker, who boasted on the title page that he would cover the biography of Rabbi Hayyim Halberstam "up to the terrible controversy between Sandz and Sadigura," was not permissible for the hasid Weisberg. The title page of Rocker's book appeared in Weisberg's work, but as is clearly visible in the illustration opposite, the "hazardous" words were crudely blocked out.

Similar self-censorship was exercised by Moshe Hanokh Greenfield, a Sandzer hasid who produced an edition of some one hundred of Hayyim Halberstam's letters. Because of these letters' importance, not just in illuminating the lives of zaddikim but also as a source of God-fearingness and other salutary qualities, he noted that he had "printed everything I could

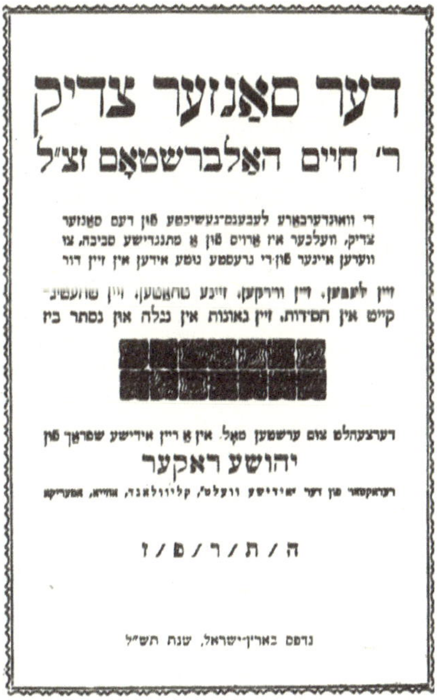

FIG. 1.3 (right). The title page of Yehoshua Rocker's *Der sanzer tsadik* (Vienna, 1927). The original subtitle states that the book treats the biography of Rabbi Hayyim Halberstam "up to the terrible controversy between Sandz and Sadigura."

FIG. 1.4 (left). In the description of Rocker's book and the photograph of its title page found in Yosef David Weisberg's *Rabenu hakadosh miTsanz* (Jerusalem, 1976, 1:370), the lines mentioning the controversy between Sandz and Sadigura were erased and retouched.

find." At the same time, he issued the following caveat regarding "everything": "Naturally all the letters relating to the well-known controversy so forcefully led by the holy rabbi of Sandz have been deleted. It is not for us to attempt to reach those peaks, *and we must not awaken this affair, but should rather let it remain in its place.*"[42]

The Conversion of Antagonists

Finally, I note two novel strategies employed by the various branches of Orthodox historiography to address discomfiting facts. The first follows the belief that a good offense is the best defense. It is thus possible to express partial or even full agreement with the facts and, at the same time, to avoid blame either by supplying a different interpretation of the facts, or by indicting the other party. The second strategy co-opts the antagonist by embracing him and converting him into "one of us." Here we find an interesting distinction between hasidic and nonhasidic writing. A number of examples follow.

Rabbinic Approbations for Ribal's *Te'udah beyisrael*

Elsewhere I have noted a surprising fact about the zaddik Yisrael of Ruzhin, seemingly inconsistent with our expectations of a hasidic leader. Rabbi Yisrael lent financial support to the publication of the works of the maskil Yitshak Ber Levinsohn (Ribal) of Kremenets (1788–1860), termed "the Russian Mendelssohn" by his admirers and "the devil's spawn" by his Orthodox detractors. Although the exact nature of their relationship is unknown, Levinsohn was related to the zaddik, as he states. Yisrael of Ruzhin assisted the publication of two of Levinsohn's works, *Te'udah beyisrael* and *Efes damim*.[43] This fact, which discomfited both hasidim and maskilim (other than Levinsohn, who recounted it) was either ignored or hidden and, therefore, no need to explain it ever arose.[44]

But Yisrael of Ruzhin was not the only prominent rabbinic figure to support the publication of *Te'udah beyisrael*. The first edition of this book (Vilna and Grodno, 1828) contained an approbation signed by Rabbi Avraham Abele ben Avraham Shlomo Poswoler, an eminent scholar who headed the Vilna rabbinic court. How could this inescapable but embarrassing fact be explained?

As an outstandingly skilled representative of contemporary "Lithuanian" historiography, Dov Eliach neither ignores nor blurs this fact in his book *HaGaon*, discussed above. Indeed, he confronts it squarely, offering an explanation that both clears Rabbi Abele's name and, at the same time, places the blame squarely in the maskilic camp. Without solid proof, but based on what he terms "simple logic," Eliach unhesitatingly makes the approbation's publication nothing but a fraud forced on the rabbi by fear of the government:

> How the maskilim and the scholars that followed them struggled to portray the gaon, Rabbi Avraham Abele . . . as a moderate, with some sympathy for maskilic ideas; after all, he gave an approbation to the book *Te'udah beyisrael* . . . And it turns out, that this Ribal had supporters in the corridors of power, which he employed to accomplish his plot . . . Why then should we be surprised to find the signature of the gaon, Rabbi Abele, one of the outstanding halakhic authorities of his day—which Ribal needed in order to get an official stamp of approval—prominently displayed in the front of the book? The fear of the czarist regime was at work here . . . The story of the "approbation" represents another giant step in the maskilic campaign of impudence and forgery. After all, not only do we find here a distorted description of a given situation, but also that they themselves were responsible for manufacturing the "proof," namely, "the approbation," which they then turned around and used to prove their point.[45]

This demonization of the maskilim, which apparently balks neither at distortion nor forgery, serves a dual function: it preserves the honor of an eminent scholar, a student of the Gaon of Vilna, who ostensibly supported maskilic ideas, and exposes maskilic crimes—namely, their use of unacceptable means to promote their doctrines. But not only is there no evidence that Rabbi Abele granted this approbation unwillingly, this was, moreover, not the only maskilic book for which he wrote an approbation. We have three other approbations, all of which were indisputably published during his lifetime, and whose authenticity was never denied.[46]

Approbations by Lithuanian Rabbis for Shlomo Dubno's *Biur*

Eliach more than successfully confronts several embarrassing facts in his book. Another illustrative example of his technique comes from his interpretation of the attitude of Lithuanian rabbis toward the maskilic *Biur* (a commentary on Moses Mendelssohn's project, the German translation of the Bible), and toward Shlomo Dubno, a distinguished scholar and grammarian, in particular.

Dubno was a member of Mendelssohn's close circle; Mendelssohn credited him with the *Biur* project and with composition of the commentary on Genesis. But in 1781, while engaged in writing the commentary on Exodus, a rupture took place between the two, perhaps against the background of a financial dispute, or perhaps due to Dubno's discomfort among Mendelssohn's disciples; the reason remains unknown.[47] Dubno left Berlin for Vilna, where he tried to reissue his commentary, replacing the German translation (which was of course unnecessary in Lithuania) with the traditional Rashi commentary and Targum Onkelos. Although this edition was never printed, Dubno did acquire approbations from important rabbis, including Hayyim of Volozhin and his brother, Rabbi Shlomo Zalman (Zalmele), who showered praise on both Dubno and his commentary. Shmuel Yosef Fuenn, the Vilna maskil and editor of *Hakarmel*, published some of these approbations as early as 1861.[48]

Eliach, who consistently erases any traces of positive interaction between the Vilna Gaon and his disciples and the Haskalah, or between them and external wisdom,[49] refused to place credence in this document. According to Eliach, the maskil Fuenn had a vested interest in rewriting history, in order to demonstrate support for the Haskalah by the Gaon and his disciples. Therefore, even though well aware of its existence, in his biography of Hayyim of Volozhin (*Avi hayeshivot*, Jerusalem: Makhon Moreshet Hayeshivot, 1991) Eliach ignores this approbation and omits it from his list of this figure's other *haskamot*.

Recently, however, an autograph copy of these very *haskamot* by Rabbi Hayyim of Volozhin and his brother came to light among the microfilms in the National Library of Israel. Thus, Fuenn was neither a liar nor a forger. In an article penned with polemic fervor, Yehoshua Mondshine criticized their concealment:

This constitutes yet another example of "a generation that judges its judges." Instead of following the light of their generation's outstanding figures, they attempt "to cast" them in their own "light." *And when they apprehend that he does not walk in their "paved path" they try to "return him to the straight and narrow" and to have him "toe the mark"*. . .That is what they did to the Vilna Gaon, when his words were not sweet to their ears . . . and it is their intent to do the same to the greatest of his students . . . and all this is part of a general trend aimed at "rewriting" the history of Lithuanian Jewry . . . primarily of its capital Vilna, which became a center from which Haskalah spread.[50]

Here Mondshine strongly denounces biased "Lithuanian" writers of Eliach's ilk, who retouch history to harmonize with the contemporary *haredi* outlook. There is no reason, Mondshine argues, to hide eminent Lithuanian rabbis' ascertainable affinity for, and favorable attitude toward, Haskalah and maskilim. Whereas, in his opinion, hasidim examined not only a book's contents but also its writer's sanctity—and if either was found to be "flawed," they refused to study it—adherents of the mitnagedic and of the *musar* movements followed the principle of "accept the truth from whosoever states it," whether maskil or apostate.

Eliach was caught in a trap of his own devising: on the one hand, the maskil Fuenn neither lied nor committed forgery; on the other, Rabbi Hayyim of Volozhin had indeed granted an approbation to a book penned by a confirmed maskil. How then could he save his rabbi's reputation? The answer lies in the second method mentioned above: co-option. Anyone who allies Shlomo Dubno with the hated maskil Mendelssohn is mistaken; actually a pure, God- and sin-fearing individual, Dubno abandoned Mendelssohn upon realizing the inherent dangers of the latter's path. Eliach counterposes Dubno's *Biur* to Mendelssohn's translation: "Dubno's *Biur* is entirely holy, and Mendelssohn's translation is totally secular." As a means of separating Dubno from the maskilic coterie of Berlin, prominent rabbis adopted him; hence, the approbations by Lithuanian rabbis for Dubno's commentary "all testify to the rejection of the Haskalah and of its founding father."[51]

Eliach, now forced to acknowledge the accuracy of the statement by the much-detested Fuenn, could not resist a final attempt to lob his guilt onto his opponent's side of the court. Having deliberately hidden Rabbi Hayyim's approbation because it was incompatible with his doctrine, Eliach now accused Fuenn of concealing a different *haskamah* from the same booklet, that of Rabbi Shmuel, who headed the Vilna rabbinical court, because this apparently "contradicted his worldview, and was inconsistent with his orientation."[52] Eliach went even further in a comment aimed at members of his camp: "What a pity that even observant Jews [such as Mondshine] often display complete faith in maskilic works of this type [like Fuenn's], even when this concerns the honor of the most distinguished Torah scholars, and do not regard them with suspicion . . . This is especially true in the case of Haskalah, which is close to maskilic hearts, about which they produce many lies and half-truths, as noted earlier. This must be distinguished from their use of historical facts, in which they have no vested, personal interest, and which can be considered free of ulterior motives."[53]

These remarks distil the main features of Eliach's historiographical approach: maskilim are always suspect; only in the absence of a personal stake is their testimony reliable, like the neutral testimony of a non-Jew with no vested interest. This, of course, contrasts with Eliach and his coterie, who regard themselves as above suspicion of any personal interest and only have the honor of the distinguished rabbis before their eyes. Paradoxically, this is the very same Eliach who was accused of mocking the leaders of the hasidic movement in his book, of mentioning them "offhandedly and with typical maskilic coolness, and of applying a vulgar interpretation" to their doctrines.[54]

Yitshak Satanow: A Maskil or a God-fearing Jew?

From an outside observer's perspective, the polemic I am about to discuss, which hinges on a single vowel, is exceedingly strange. But for the scholar of Orthodox historiography, this is an intriguing test case: a fairly recent debate preserved in a series of publications, which not only cuts across traditional camps but also reveals their attitudes toward Haskalah and maskilim.

The polemic's inception lies with one Hayyim Krauss, who thought that the traditional vocalization of the word הגשם in the phrase from the daily prayers הרוח ומוריד הגשם (who causes the wind to blow and the rain to fall) should be pronounced with a *segol* (*e*), rather than a *kamats* (*a*). He collected approbations from important rabbis belonging to both the mitnagedic and hasidic camps and published his innovations in a wide-ranging book titled *Kuntres birkhot hahayyim* (The blessings of life). He proposes that the *kamats* was the innovation of none other than a maskilic figure—the writer, publisher, and grammarian Yitshak Satanow (1732–1804):

> The source of the change in the word *hageshem* . . . is the prayer book *Vaye'etar Yitshak* composed by someone named Yitshak Halevi of Satanow. He was a member of the maskilic circle in Berlin and printed his book in that circle's publishing house, in Berlin, in 1785 . . . These maskilim, as is well known, aimed to change tradition, and in his introduction to the above-mentioned prayer book, Satanow uses abusive

language toward the ancients, who certainly do not deserve such remarks. Nonetheless, I cite several lines from this work . . . Indeed, it is known that "that man" of Satanow was not just a grammarian, and not just a maskil, but somewhat more . . . and this is what appears regarding him in G. Kressel's *Cyclopedia of Modern Hebrew Literature.*[55]

Here Krauss cites Kressel's lexicon at length and determines the untrustworthiness of "that man" (a term usually used to refer to Jesus). Krauss goes on to quote Israel Zinberg's denotation of Satanow as "half a believer and half a heretic."[56] Krauss collected concrete and linguistic data to prove his stance, also quoting zaddikim and rabbis who stated that anyone who uses the pronunciation *hagashem* "needs looking into." An early-twentieth-century halakhic authority, Rabbi Shaul Rosenberg of Hungary, argued that even if the grammarians were correct, we have no desire for their "honey": "Those that say *hagashem*, it appears that the reason for this is because the grammarians of earlier generations, most of whom leaned toward heresy, raised this matter. Accordingly, we have no desire either for their correction, or for their honey or their sting, and even if it were good, we would not follow their version in any thing."[57]

Shortly thereafter, a young Bratslav hasid named Sar-Shalom Marzel pounded Krauss into the dust. Armed with an approbation from Rabbi Yosef Shalom Eliashiv, Marzel published a book titled *Kuntres mashiv haru'ah* (Who causes the wind to blow). In it, he supplies proofs to justify "our holy custom, the custom of our fathers and the great rabbis of former generations" to place a *kamats* under the *gimel*, and to say *hagashem.*

My concern here is not with the details of the polemic itself but with Satanow's status as an authoritative source. Marzel takes issue with the claim that Satanow was a maskil. Indeed, according to Marzel, Satanow was a righteous, kosher Jew. Unaware that Kressel and Zinberg were twentieth-century scholars, Marzel innocently thought them to be nineteenth-century maskilim. In the heat of his debate, Marzel takes them to task for libelously attributing "Enlightenment" to Satanow in order to blacken his name among the God-fearing:

Especially when palpable hatred emerges from between the lines of the above-mentioned lexicon . . . and it is the person who testifies to these facts [Kressel], who must be judged. And the reason for what is found in the (external) works condemning the author of *Vaye'etar Yitshak* to death, this is because of his loyalty to God and his Torah, which aroused these demons' anger; they therefore wrote lampoons in order to create dispute and confusion . . . so that his remarks would not be accepted by the public . . . And I *wonder greatly*, how that author had the gall to rely on something written by some writer named G. Kressel (whose identity and reputation we neither know, and perhaps need not know), who barely reaches the ankles of the *wondrous Torah scholar, Rabbi Yitshak of Satanow*, and to thereby grind his honor in the dust.[58]

The "rain" debate lived on in the form of many additional and witty tracts, whose discussions slid to additional matters (such as the nature of the grammarian Wolf Heidenheim).[59] This brief presentation suffices to show how even such a prominent maskil as Yitshak Satanow—publisher, obsessed writer, talented forger of ancient texts and rabbinical approbations, a man of indisputable maskilic leanings—could be co-opted and transformed into a religious authority, duly "converted" and drafted in favor of one or the other side in a controversy.[60]

"I Too Am Not Objective": History as It Should Have Been

The already mentioned strategies of memory and repression are by no means the only ones available; moreover, these and additional strategies rarely function in isolation but are rather mutually supportive and intertwined. I conclude this discussion of *haredi* historical writing with a unique, frank confession of the prejudicial, one-sided nature of historiographical writing in general, which accuses other authors—whether Lithuanian mitnagedim or critical historians—not only of engaging in similar tactics but also of reluctance to admit this. Yehoshua Mondshine, a Habad hasid, bibliographer, and outstanding scholar of the hasidic world, blames researchers—rightfully so, to a large extent—for directing their demand for objectivity only at hasidic sources. These sources are "prime suspects," he complains, immediately rejected, ostensibly because of their partiality and loyalty to their rabbis and their own camps, whereas the maskilim and mitnagedim, who have their own "zaddikim," are generally awarded uncritical acceptance. The writings of the mitnagedim—as Mondshine amply demonstrates—are definitively biased, and when necessary, their authors deliberately forge sources and distort documents. Mondshine's essay concludes with an instructive personal confession: "Like many of my predecessors I too am not objective; unlike them, however, I admit to this fault. Of my readers I make the following request: will *you* please try to be objective!"[61]

The historian Immanuel Etkes responded to this appeal: "In point of fact, the critical scholar is also liable to err. The naive view that it is possible to deal with history with complete objectivity has long since faded away. However, there is a great difference between a scholar committed to discovery of the truth and to striving for it—aware of his or her limitations and of the relative character of historical research—and a scholar bound by religious or ideological commitment who declares that no research can be objective."[62]

Naturally, the *haredi* camp contains talented researchers of the past, endowed with both extensive knowledge and common sense. But when their wanderings in the paths of history bring them to dark alleyways, to critical points where facts may conflict with their worldview, or cause distress and dismay, they find themselves caught in a thicket of contradictions: to what extent should they seek, and reveal, the truth?[63]

Indeed, notwithstanding its obvious nature, we cannot overlook the absence of one strategy in particular: recognition of historical truth as it was, and as reflected in the extant sources. But recognition of the truth carries innate dangers. The truth imposes itself on its discoverers, forcing them into direct confrontation with its outcomes, even if this means full or partial admission of failure. Direct, open statements of the following type—indeed, such and such an episode took place and yes, it is embarrassing and unpleasant, but let us see what can be learned from it—are largely absent from Orthodox historiography.

The mechanisms shaping and preserving historical memory among groups with a religious, ideological, political, or educational agenda (including Hasidism) do not always take an interest in history as it was but rather in a form that can be called history as it should have been. Memory is a prime educational tool, and any unauthorized interpretation can shake the foundations of an ideological world in need of nurture and protection from its enemies.[64] To this end, "special agents" are empowered to supervise and shape historical memory—to highlight or suppress some of its parts, to study it intensely or blur its traces, to censor it ruthlessly or "convert" it—in order to continuously market an unswerving picture of a pure, harmonious past. These mechanisms are not always overt; after all, this is not some dark, organized conspiracy imposed from above. Although at times governed by self-aware sophisticated mechanisms, as demonstrated above by examples from Orthodox historiography, by and large the past is shaped in a spontaneous, naive manner of which even its memory agents are unaware. But whether sophisticated or simplistic, coarse or refined, all of these mechanisms have a shared basis: the recognition that the past and how it is remembered have the power to shape both present and future.

2 Apostate or Saint?

In the Footsteps of Moshe, the Son of Rabbi Shneur Zalman of Lyady

> On more than one occasion we have seen that many of those who converted were the great-grandchildren or grandchildren of the holy rabbis. For they are unfaithful, and use not their intelligence to weigh their deeds. Even their fear of God is a rote commandment copied from their forebears. And when one of them makes a small breach in the fence erected by his forefathers, he then strides through like a ferocious beast or wild ass in the desert. If he experiences a slight mischance, he rages at God and his Messiah and at the religion of his forefathers.
> —Wolf Ehrenkranz, *Hazon lamoed* (Iasi, 1858), 43

Among the mitnagedim, Berl Katzenelson once related to Dov Sadan, there is a saying concerning the hasidic custom of singing "bam-bam." The mitnagedim interpret this as an acrostic that stands for "Bernyu Moshenyu-Beide Meshumadim" (Bernyu and Moshe are both converts),[1] as referring to Dov Ber (Bernyu) Friedman of Leova,[2] Yisrael of Ruzhin's son who in 1869 abandoned his hasidim and went over to the maskilic camp, and to Moshe, Rabbi Shneur Zalman of Lyady's son who converted to Christianity, the main protagonist of this chapter.

For the reader's convenience I provide a table of the Habad rebbes.

Name	Title	Dates
Shneur Zalman of Lyady (Rashaz)	Ha'admor Hazaken; the Alter Rebbe	c. 1745–1812
Dov Ber	Ha'admor Haemtsa'i; the Mitteler Rebbe	1773–1827
Menahem Mendel Schneersohn	Ha'admor Tsemah Tsedek	1789–1866
Shmuel Schneersohn (Moharash)	the fourth admor	1834–82
Shalom Dov Ber (Rashab)	the fifth admor	1860–1920
Yosef Yitshak Schneersohn (Rayyats)	the sixth admor	1880–1950
Menahem Mendel Schneersohn (Ramam)	the seventh admor	1902–94

The margins of nineteenth-century hasidic history contain many incidents and failures—cases of individuals who strayed from the fold—that the hasidim would be content either to forget or to suppress. Although the two figures mentioned above are among the most conspicuous examples of individuals who shamed their prestigious families and their hasidic branches, other individuals also left a stain on Hasidism.[3] Hasidic tradition generally had them repent prior to death, lest they die as heretics or as non-Jews.[4]

"Would That My Parents Had Been Cruel": Straying Children of Zaddikim and Rabbis

The prophet Isaiah stated: "I reared children and brought them up—And they have rebelled against Me!" (1:2). It is an open secret that the intimacy and intensity of family life and child rearing in presence of a famous, admired leader are not easy. On the one hand, many advantages accrue to the leader's children: unmatched conditions for spiritual development, acquisition of the father's traits and imitation of his ways, and enhanced status as the father's natural heirs (which is also seen in the political and artistic arenas). On the other hand, the demanding framework in which they are raised and educated poses many dangers to their development and can lead to emotional immaturity. Moreover, expectations by family and admirers that all the leader's descendants will continue the exact path set down by the leader, without diverging even an iota, leave no room for anomalous individuals uninterested in following the trodden path or in assuming their destined posts. In this sense, the social and emotional pressures with which the children of zaddikim or rabbis grapple differ little from those of the offspring of kings or nobles, or of prominent political, literary, or artistic figures. The response to these pressures takes the form of a variety of relief-bringing mechanisms, ranging from repression to awareness of living a dual, divided existence,[5] and to harsh antagonism manifested in the crossing of all red lines: fleeing from the assigned post, or denying family tradition—or, in extreme cases of bitter despair, turning their backs on their religious and national identity. We will have occasion to meet various figures fitting these models in the chapters of this book.

Needless to say, the behavior of these individuals sears parental hearts and lives with a sense of bereavement and failure, which is especially conspicuous among prestigious families whose brilliant sons became maskilim or heretics. These children were no less affected than their parents, as the memoirs of the maskil Yehuda Leib Levin (Yehalel; 1844–1925), the grandson of the zaddik Moshe of Kobrin, illustrate: "My parents' anguish and their sighs depressed me. Alas, would that my parents had been cruel, would that they had excoriated and humiliated me, or had lifted a hand to punish my rebelliousness, for then I would have already departed and found my path in life. But my merciful, kind parents, who loved me more than themselves, melted and tortured me with their tears and their distress, and though my heart was torn by pity I was unable to still or to calm them."[6]

The story of Lipman Lipkin (1846–75), the son of *musar* movement founder Yisrael Salanter (1810–83), typifies this intergenerational rift. This talented young man was profoundly influenced by Haskalah ideas. At the age of fifteen, he abandoned his famous father's house and went to study in Königsberg and Berlin; he was eventually awarded a doctoral degree from Jena University, in Germany, and the degree of magister from St. Petersburg University. He patented a mechanical device and became a well-known figure in Russian and British scientific circles. As far as we know, Lipkin remained a faithful Jew, but his father, who vainly tried to effect his return to the Torah world, refused to forgive or forget his leaving home. An 1865 report in *Hamagid* announced the arrival of the "maskil Lipkin" in Königsberg after a scientific course of study in Berlin, and informed the readers that he now intended "to complete his studies in all matters of wisdom and knowledge." The reporter went on to provide Lipkin's lineage, explaining that this learned person was none other than the son of the eminent rabbi Yisrael Salanter. His offering of the following opinion—"it also honors his righteous father, the *Gaon*, that he did not prevent his son from acquiring learning in the university, so that Torah and wisdom might be united in his son, to the glory of our people"—prompted a strong, emotional denial by that "righteous father," Yisrael Salanter: "As the truth is a lamp to the feet of the righteous who walk about in the land, I am obligated to make it known before the people that the honor is not mine, as was written [in the report] concerning my son . . . but the opposite is the case. The thing is very much to my dislike, and my heart is saddened concerning the path which my son wishes to pave for himself. Whoever loves his soul and is able to speak to the heart of my son, to change the desire of his spirit not to go against the spirit of my heart and my will, will do a great favor to a downcast one such as I am today."[7]

It is difficult not to recognize this father's vulnerability and pain. Faced with the possibility that his private failure might be applied to his entire educational mission, he issued this personal statement explicitly detaching himself from his son's path, lest suspicion arise that paternal love could in any way alter his beliefs and worldview.

"And to Anger You I Will Convert": Parent-Child Relations and Conversion

The tense, loaded relationships between famous parents and their offspring provide a dramatic backdrop for their stories. Especially well known in Jewish circles in the modern era are the tragedies that affected such prominent figures as Mendele Mokher Sforim (Yaakov Shalom Abramowitz), whose beloved son Meir converted to Christianity; Shimon Dubnow, Ahad ha-Am, and Mordekhai Ben-Hillel Hakohen, whose daughters married into Russian Orthodox families; and Rabbi Eliyahu Klatskin of Lublin, whose son Yaakov, a renowned philosopher and ardent Zionist, abandoned Judaism and married the daughter of a Protestant minister.[8]

Most intriguing is the story of Lucian, the son of Y. L. Peretz, who hated his father, loathed his literary works, and detested anything related to Judaism. His friend, the playwright Peretz Hirschbein, wrote: "In his emotional makeup Lucian was an assimilationist . . . he devoted all his powers to convincing me that Jews were atrophied physically . . . 'Jews must merge with a healthy nation—he would counter—and do you know with whom? With the Latvians! They are the only ones who can save the attenuated Jewish blood.'" Hirschbein went on to note: "This did not occur only in Y. L. Peretz's home. There are many such examples in our world, in which the sons of eminent parents were consumed by jealousy, and did not desire to remain in the shadow of their great parent. Far from their fathers, by virtue of their own personalities, they beat their heads against the wall—seeking to create their own path in life, without the aid of their father's name."[9] Among the ranks of those born to famous parents who rebelled by converting we find not only those on the verge of assimilation (like Theodor Herzl's family members, most of whom converted, committed suicide, or went insane), and not just children of maskilim,[10] or the scions of those who had already abandoned the Torah world, but also the descendants of famous rabbis, from both the mitnagedic and the hasidic camps, who themselves adhered strictly to Jewish law and practice but failed to inculcate them in their children.[11]

Upon learning the bitter truth that their daughter Chava has fallen in love with a non-Jew and converted, Sholem Aleichem's fictional character Tevye the dairyman, a simple Jew, comforts his wife with the observation that they will be neither the first nor the last to undergo this experience. Nonetheless, Tevye cannot help but ask why his beloved daughter has dealt them such a blow: "How then, you ask, could she have gone and done such a thing? Well, to begin with it was just our rotten luck . . . And then too, someone must have put a hex on her. You can laugh all you want at me, but (though I'm not such a yokel as to believe in haunts, spooks, ghosts, and all that hocus-pocus) witchcraft, I tell you, is a fact—because how do you explain all this if it isn't?"[12]

Tevye's explanation appears more like an attempt at self-deception. Blind, bad luck that struck him, which could have as easily struck his neighbor, and the bewitching of his daughter are two sides of the same coin. On the one hand, ordinary individuals lack the ability to cope with witchcraft or to change their luck; on the other hand, this deterministic rationale releases both parents and the surrounding society from self-examination, and from accepting responsibility for failure. More significantly, this explanation obviates the need to understand the actual underlying causes of the crisis and the true motivation for conversion (but does not release Tevye and his wife, as readers of the story know, from sitting *shiva* for their daughter who converted).[13]

A mixture of anguish and pangs of conscience, of compassion and hatred, are the main emotional motifs that characterize the conversion experience in the child-parent context. On more than one occasion, the allegedly "simple" cases—conversion against a romantic background—reveal the blurred boundary, crossed unawares, between intergenerational crisis and religious or national tensions. Typical is an early-twentieth-century Yiddish folk song that tells the sad tale of a Jew from Kobrin whose daughter converted to Christianity. All her parents' pleas fell on deaf ears. Not only had their daughter fallen in love with a non-Jew, she also found the nerve to exact revenge on her people: "Sisters and brothers, dig yourselves graves! And to anger you I will convert, making the sign of the cross."[14]

That Jews in czarist Russia converted is by no means an earthshaking historical revelation. Notwithstanding the imprecise data for the first half of the nineteenth century,[15] the number of converts was not negligible.[16] Among the varied motivations for conversion, four main reasons can be isolated: (1) the material gains and socioeconomic opportunities afforded by integration into Russian society (like access to higher education or residence or work permits);[17] (2) extreme dislike for their coreligionists or families, accompanied by the desire to shame them and to exact revenge;[18] (3) a strong conviction of the veracity and superiority of the Christian path;[19] and (4) "neutral" conversion, especially against the background of interfaith romantic ties.[20] With the enhanced processes of acculturation, secularization, and assimilation in the modern period, the latter motive naturally gained in importance.[21] But whatever their incentives, having instantly severed their ties with Judaism, these converts were not necessarily welcomed by the Christian majority and continued to be haunted by their Jewish pasts.[22]

If the abandonment of tradition and the shift to Haskalah, and certainly secularization and assimilation, were a terrible tragedy for traditional Jewish society, conversion was even more so. In this respect, traditional and maskilic attitudes[23]—and later, the national and Zionist ones[24]—differed little. All viewed apostasy (in Hebrew *shmad*, meaning destruction) as an extreme step of national and religious betrayal that symbolized despair, weakness, and self-hatred, and at the very least an educational failure that not only left the convert but also his parents, his family, and his close environment under a cloud.

Polemic and Apologetic Memory

Shneur Zalman of Lyady's beloved youngest son Moshe also belongs to the ranks of Jewish converts to Christianity. The tragedy of his conversion, which took place in 1820, left a lasting imprint on the Schneersohn family and on Habad Hasidism. A century ago, Alexander Ziskind Rabinowitz (Azar) noted: "One subject remains virtually untouched by writers in our day—the history of the Schneersohn family."[25] Since he penned those words, much progress has been made in the study of Habad Hasidism, its literature, and the history of its leaders, with hasidim, writers, and academics sharing in this task. But the dramatic episode of Moshe remained a hidden secret. That Rabinowitz skirted this episode is not surprising; after all, his article opened by praising this group: "Habad Hasidism can justifiably be proud that only a very few of its members have left the fold."[26] Indeed, even those intimately acquainted with this group and its history were barely aware of Moshe's life story.

The partial and contradictory nature of the data, coupled with the blurring of their traces in hasidic historiography, make it difficult to track the story of Moshe's apostasy, one of the stranger episodes in hasidic history. As opposed to the manifold oral traditions, few written sources have survived. Arriving at a full, trustworthy reconstruction of these events is seemingly beyond our reach.

But even if the full picture eludes us, there is still at our disposal sufficient information to outline this episode's main strata, discuss old and new sources, and—most important—identify its different memory paths, which transform it from a juicy anecdote into an event of profound historiographical significance. These memory paths fall into one of two categories: that of polemical memory, largely based on prejudiced traditions, which aim to expose and condemn; and of apologetic memory, which seeks to blur and exonerate. Attuned to each other's existence, these opposing memory traditions carry on both overt and covert polemical dialogues among themselves. As opposed to interfaith polemic, with its differing exegeses of shared, canonical texts, this memory path focuses rather on different interpretations of a witnessed historical event, whose existence only a few deny.

To date, the study of polemics between the various branches of Eastern European Jewish society in the eighteenth and nineteenth centuries has stressed the spiritual or the ideological realm—namely, the debated interpretations of written sources. But a broader application of the categories of polemical and apologetic memory facilitates consideration of what divided the hasidim from their opponents. The following chapter, which treats the fall of the Seer of Lublin from the window of his house in 1814, examines another embarrassing historical event in hasidic history, discussed for decades in hasidic, mitnagedic, and maskilic sources. Not only did each group "remember" the circumstances leading up to the fall differently, but each memory tradition—which was cognizant of its rivals' existence—sought to defend its stance against that of the opposing tradition. The different memory traditions for the story of Moshe's conversion exemplify this process even more strongly.

Shaping the discussion are the main cluster of sources that have been preserved regarding Moshe's life: (1) recently discovered archival documents; (2) maskilic memory traditions preserved in letters and memoirs; (3) non-Jewish sources, penned mainly by apostates; (4) hasidic memory traditions; and (5) the sparse historiographical treatments of this matter, both in the critical, academic tradition, and the hasidic, Orthodox one.

"He Has Regained His Former Strength": Moshe Prior to His Conversion

Few definite details are known regarding Moshe's biography prior to his conversion, but he was probably born in 1784, and he died before 1853.[27] The youngest of Shneur Zalman of Lyady's (Rashaz) sons, he had two older brothers—Dov Ber (known in Habad as the Mitteler Rebbe), who later assumed his father's post, and Hayyim Avraham (d. 1848), known for his modesty[28]—and three older sisters: Freyde, Devorah Leah (the mother of the third Habad rebbe, Menahem Mendel, known as the Tsemah Tsedek), and Rachel. The oldest, Freyde, was famed for her unusual erudition and for her special relationship with her father, Shneur Zalman; the other two sisters died during their father's lifetime.[29]

According to the archival sources discussed below, the first signs of Moshe's mental illness emerged when he was eight years old. He received medical treatment, and from the scant information available, it appears that his illness alternated between remission and outbreak during his childhood. The documentation also indicates that, in 1801, his father Shneur Zalman made the rounds of Vitebsk, St. Petersburg,[30] and Smolensk in search of a cure for Moshe. In fact, one of the doctors who examined Moshe in 1820 testified that he had treated him nineteen years earlier. The intervals of good health, the admiration of his father's court, and the strange youngster's obvious talents cushioned Moshe from prying eyes, and even enabled him to marry.

On the night of the 15th of Kislev 1797, "the wondrous youth, our teacher Moshe" was elected into the Liozno burial society, an honor all of Shneur Zalman's family members enjoyed.[31] A week later, during the festival of Hanukkah,[32] Moshe married Shifra,[33] the daughter of Zvi Hirsh of Ule, a town in Vitebsk Province, not far from Lyady and Vitebsk. Of Zvi Hirsh nothing is known, but it appears likely that given the status of his other sons-in-law—Leib and Yitshak—Zvi Hirsh was one of Shneur Zalman's veteran hasidim. After all, only a staunch admirer would be willing to overlook Moshe's defect (although he may have believed that Moshe had been cured); for him, the ultimate objective would be to enter into marital ties with the rebbe's family.[34] As was the custom, Moshe moved to his in-laws' home, and the in-laws supported the young couple for several years. At a later date, Moshe apparently received an appointment as a communal rabbi.[35]

Habad sources report his father's special fondness for Moshe; they also note that, because of his excellent memory, Moshe was honored with the task of repeating his father's talks for hasidim who had not been present when they were originally delivered: "During our rebbe's lifetime . . . golden-tongued Moshe would repeat our rebbe's hasidic talks in their entirety exactly as delivered, and would also record them in their entirety (and we saw a large book with all these writings and notations)."[36] Some of these notations, known as *hanahot*, have been preserved in Moshe's own handwriting.[37] Aside from these notations, no other Torah exposition, thought, or letters by Moshe are known to be extant.[38]

In 1812 Shneur Zalman and his family abandoned Lyady and fled east before the Napoleonic invasion,[39] joining the Russian army on its retreat into the interior. A letter by Dov Ber documented the circuitous route of the large, sixty-wagon caravan[40] and the travails of the journey. Shneur Zalman died in a remote village on 27 December 1812 and was buried in the town of Hadyach in Poltava Province.[41] Dov Ber, who had been sent to Kremenchug to rent apartments for the entire family, was not present at his father's deathbed; neither was Hayyim Avraham, who was ill that day.[42] After the funeral, the family traveled to Kremenchug, where news reached them of the plundering and burning of all the houses in Lyady by the French forces; accordingly, they decided to remain in Kremenchug until the summer of 1813.

But Moshe and his family did not take part in this perilous journey and evidently remained in Ule, or nearby.[43] After all, not every Byelorussian Jew abandoned his home and property, nor did everyone who fled enjoy the protection of Russian officers. A letter sent by Moshe's brothers indicates that Shneur Zalman sent a special messenger to Ule to fetch Moshe as well; this messenger apparently failed in his mission. From the vague wording of the letter, we can deduce that Moshe did attempt, albeit unsuccessfully, to flee east (without his family) in order to join his father and brothers. He made it to Shklov, where he was taken prisoner by the French army and accused of spying. Interrogated and sentenced to death, Moshe was released when his captors realized that the supposed spy was emotionally unbalanced.[44]

Traces of Moshe disappear for a time. Just a month after their father's death (early in 1813), we find his brother Dov approaching some hasidim in

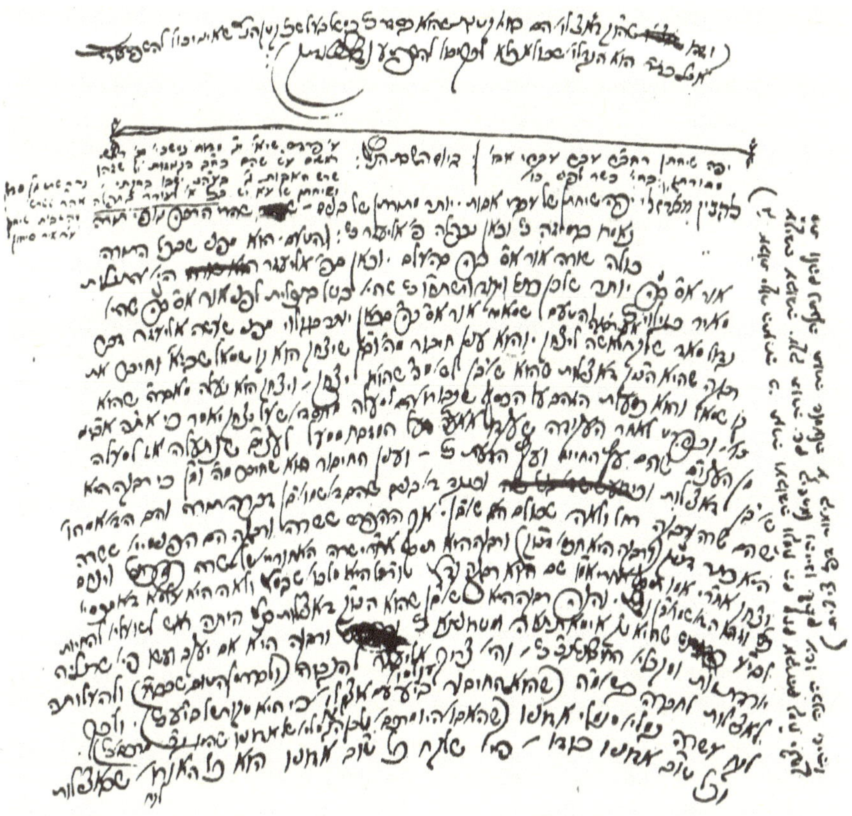

FIG. 2.1. An 1803 talk by Shneur Zalman of Lyady, copied by his son Moshe. The corrections are in the Tsemah Tsedek's handwriting.

Vitebsk with a request for help in locating his brother: "And my main request is that you inform me of the well-being of our beloved brother Moshe, and of his entire household, whether he was saved from the conflagration, and where he now resides. By so doing you will restore us and my mother the rebbetzin . . . And if you could get a letter from him to us—how good and pleasant that would be."[45]

In late 1813 the two brothers, Dov Ber and Hayyim Avraham, returned to Byelorussia and settled in the town of Lubavitch in Mogilev Province. From that time on, Lubavitch became the capital of Habad hasidism.[46] But Dov Ber did not automatically inherit his father's position. Other hasidim contested his claim to be the preferred candidate, first and foremost Shneur Zalman's leading disciple, Aharon Halevi Horowitz of Staroselye (1766–1828).[47] Not only did Dov Ber have to secure his position as successor to the Habad throne, he also had to support his family members, now penniless, and to build a new hasidic court. Over the course of this year, faithful Habad hasidim undertook a widespread fundraising campaign in order to meet these needs.[48]

An archival document relating to Dov Ber's arrest in 1825 indicates that this campaign netted at least 35,000 rubles, a huge sum. The money was turned over for inspection and distribution to Dov Ber, whose "decisions were not to be questioned."[49] Indeed, the rebbe recorded how the money was to be distributed among Shneur Zalman's children, sons-in-law, and grandchildren. Regarding his brother Moshe, he wrote: "To my brother Moshe, his wife and young daughters I make an outright gift—not out of obligation but out of good will, to please our late father—of 3,000 rubles, of which he received 1,000 some time ago, and the remaining 2,000 rubles will of course be sent to him from the overall amount, through his wife Shifra."[50]

Compared to what other family members received, this was a paltry sum. But why should Moshe receive a gift at all? Unlike his brothers, who lost their homes and property during the war, he probably had a house that was still standing. The explanation that this was a goodwill gesture to please their dead father may allude to Moshe's special circumstances, and his need for funds to underwrite medical treatment for his emotional disorder. There is no doubt that the relationship between the brothers was strained. In some letters from this period, to be mentioned below, Dov Ber took a harsh tone with his brother for issuing derogatory statements on Hasidism. The fact that Dov Ber determined that the money was intended for Moshe's wife and daughters, and would be entrusted to his wife, is also indicative of Moshe's mental condition at the time.

Interestingly, in the beginning of the above-mentioned document detailing the dispensation of funds among his relatives, Dov Ber recounts that he vowed to disburse the money "*in order to remove the strictures his father issued against him [Dov Ber] on several occasions during his lifetime, because of the anguish caused to him in hidden circumstances* . . . accordingly, [Dov Ber] decided . . . to take upon himself, while at his father's gravesite, this manner of conduct, *in order to be absolved of, and to do penitence for, all his sins.*"[51] What anguish did he cause his father, and what "hidden circumstances" led Shneur Zalman to chastise his son and made Dov Ber a penitent? If ever discovered, these mysterious circumstances would certainly shed intriguing light on the tense Schneersohn family relations.

In any event, in 1814 Moshe was still considered worthy of joining his two brothers in signing an approbation for the *Tanya* and for the introduction to *Shulhan arukh haRav*, both basic texts composed by their late father.[52] Some subsequent editions of these books omitted the signed approbation and the introduction, sparking speculation that this omission was related either to the "inheritance war," in which Moshe ostensibly participated,[53] or to the stain of Moshe's apostasy.

Sometime before 1817 Moshe experienced another physical crisis that was undoubtedly emotional as well. His recovery was noted in a letter dated Nisan 1817 from his mother, the rebbetzin Shterna, to the hasid Yitshak Doktor Gill of Dubrovno: "And my son, as well, the famed Rabbi Moshe, has, thank God, *regained his former strength*, and his family members are all alive and well. He has settled in Ule. Nothing else is new."[54]

Was this a bad winter cold, or some deeper crisis that had passed? The use of such strong expressions for a minor illness appears unlikely. With the revelation of the archival material, it is now obvious that Moshe's mother was referring to a temporary remission of the harsh mental illness from which he had suffered since childhood. Evidently, his traumatic wartime experiences—his status as a French prisoner of war, and his narrow escape from execution—had an impact on his mental state, making his illness resurface. The documentary evidence clearly indicates that, beginning in 1813, many doctors in various towns attempted to cure Moshe. In search of a cure, he made his way to Staryi Bykhov in Byelorussia, Seree (part of the Duchy of Warsaw until 1815), Vitebsk, Vilna, Tilsit, and Königsberg in Prussia, eventually returning to Ule.[55] Apparently his mother the rebbetzin was noting his safe arrival.

In 1816 Dov Ber sent a letter to three of his close followers, containing harsh words and obscure comments about one of his opponents, referred to as "the snake," because of his poisonous mouth and pen. In this letter, he mentions the difficulties caused by "what is happening with our well-known brother, etc."[56] Dov Ber's remarks are obscure; nevertheless, they imply that he now faces exigencies greater than those of dealing with the embarrassment of his strange brother—namely, the followers of his late father who refuse to accept his authority.[57] The continuation of the letter, which was omitted in the censored version published by Habad and marked by an ellipsis, contains more harsh statements regarding "our well-known brother." From them, we learn that Moshe liked to drink, and that, after imbibing punch, poisonous remarks against Hasidism dripped from his sharp tongue; Hasidism, he claimed, was uninnovative and passé.[58] Nor can we argue that the reference is to someone other than Moshe. This is clear from another document linked to the above-mentioned investigation, dated 1825—a survey by the Russian investigators of the stages of, and documents related to, Dov Ber's interrogation. They wrote: "Kissin [the informer] also presented a letter written by Shneur [Dov Ber] to three of his friends, containing dark, twisted, and regrettable expressions, from which we can understand that he laments the decline of the hasidic camp . . . This letter contains the following section in which Shneur berates his brother and addresses him using these words: 'Know my brother, that the upshot is that these things are naturally opposed: they attempt to humiliate Hasidism at the same time as the practice of fund-raising spreads.'"[59] Without going into the precise meaning of these remarks, we can at least establish that this paragraph has been censored by the letter's editor. The original explicitly stated: "For he [Dov Ber] laments the decline of the hasidic camp and *primarily the indifference of his brother (who later converted).*"[60]

The conversion indeed took place in the summer of 1820. Moshe, the rabbi of Ule, then thirty-six years old, married and with children, converted to Christianity. What motivated this terrible act, and what were its consequences? The many, varied versions of the answers to these questions are treated below.

There is another verifiable fact in Moshe's biography, one not directly related to Moshe himself. In 1843, his family (his wife, children, sons-in-law, and their offspring) emigrated from Russia to Palestine (first to Hebron and later to Jerusalem). Although it would be convenient to see this move as the result of the shame ensuing from Moshe's act,[61] the gap of more than twenty years makes this unlikely.

Leon Yulievich or Piotr Aleksandrovich? The Archival Testimony

When I first published my study of Moshe in 2000, I noted "my regret that, to date, we have no official records of this episode," and my "hope that the rich Russian archives contain documents able to shed light on it."[62] This statement relied on the testimony of Shaul Ginsburg and Shimon Dubnow—two eminent historians of Russian Jewry who had addressed this affair—regarding their disappointing search for documents relating to Moshe in the archives of the Holy Synod in St. Petersburg prior to the October Revolution.[63] I had no inkling of how rapidly the discovery of new documents would take place. Shortly after my article's publication, two files covering the 1820–21 period, which documented Moshe's conversion and its circumstances, were located in the Minsk archives. Whatever Moshe's motives, this rich material leaves no doubt as to the fact of his conversion.

The two files in question are housed in the National Historical Archives of Belarus, in Minsk, and contain official documents and private correspondence in Russian, Polish, and even Latin, all connected to the conversion of "Rabbi Leon Shneyer."[64] Initial examination of this material yielded the findings summarized below.[65]

The earliest document in the file, dated 1 July 1820,[66] contains a statement made by the rabbi of Ule, Moshe Zalmanovich Schneersohn, to Josaphat Siodłowski, the assistant Catholic priest in that town.[67] In this affidavit, Moshe announced his long-standing wish to convert to Catholicism. He further stated that, upon becoming aware of his desire, his fellow Jews kept him under close watch and even beat him, in order to keep him from carrying out his plan. Nevertheless, he never abandoned his desire to accept the true religion of Jesus Christ, as attested in the Holy Scriptures and by all the prophets. Moshe requested the priest's protection, and asked the priest to instruct him in the tenets of Christianity and baptize him. Signed by Moshe in Russian and Hebrew, this affidavit was witnessed by various individuals, among them military officers, civil servants, and nobles, and an additional local priest named Grigorii Eliashevich; all the signatories attested that this was the rabbi's wish, and that he was of sound mind in taking this decision.[68]

Following the penning of this affidavit, Moshe came under the aegis of the Catholic priest. Three days later, on the afternoon of Sunday, 4 [16] July, the week of the fast of Tisha beAv, Moshe was secretly baptized in the home of the priest Siodłowski. He was then moved to a monastery in Beshenkovichi, fifty kilometers southwest of Vitebsk, in order to receive instruction in Christian dogma. Having become convinced that Moshe was emotionally disturbed, the local priest and doctors there recommended that he be returned to his family. Moshe was accordingly sent back to his family in Lubavitch for about six weeks. We cannot know or even imagine what happened during this period—how his brothers, wife, daughters, and followers received him, what they asked him, or how he replied.

But Moshe's case again came into the official eye. At the request of the civilian governor of the Vitebsk Province (to which Ule belonged), the civilian governor of Mogilev Province (to which Lubavitch belonged) extracted Moshe from his family for a battery of medical tests. Convened on 18–20 July [30 July–1 August], the commission, whose members also included a priest and a police representative, examined various documents and interviewed Moshe. Notwithstanding Moshe's lucid answers, which indicated that he was not permanently insane, the commission ruled that he suffered from mental illness. The priest disagreed. Convinced that Moshe was feigning madness because of Jewish pressure, he suggested that Moshe be sent to the Catholic monastery in Polotsk (in Vitebsk Province) to prepare undisturbed for his examination on Catholic dogma. But the priest was overruled, and the decision was reached to return Moshe to his family.

Thus, Moshe once again found himself in his brothers' keeping. Over the following weeks, the Habad hasidim made efforts both to shelter him and to forestall a repetition of his act. In September, the elders of the Jewish community in Vitebsk and Moshe's brothers Dov Ber and Hayyim Avraham dispatched letters of complaint to officials in Mogilev and Vitebsk Provinces. The report found in the extant letter from the brothers (the one from the communal leaders is missing) sheds light on the complex background to this affair, whose details and unfolding were not always entirely clear even to those directly involved.

The main figure in this affair was Pod-Polkovnik (Lt. Col.) Mikhail Alek-

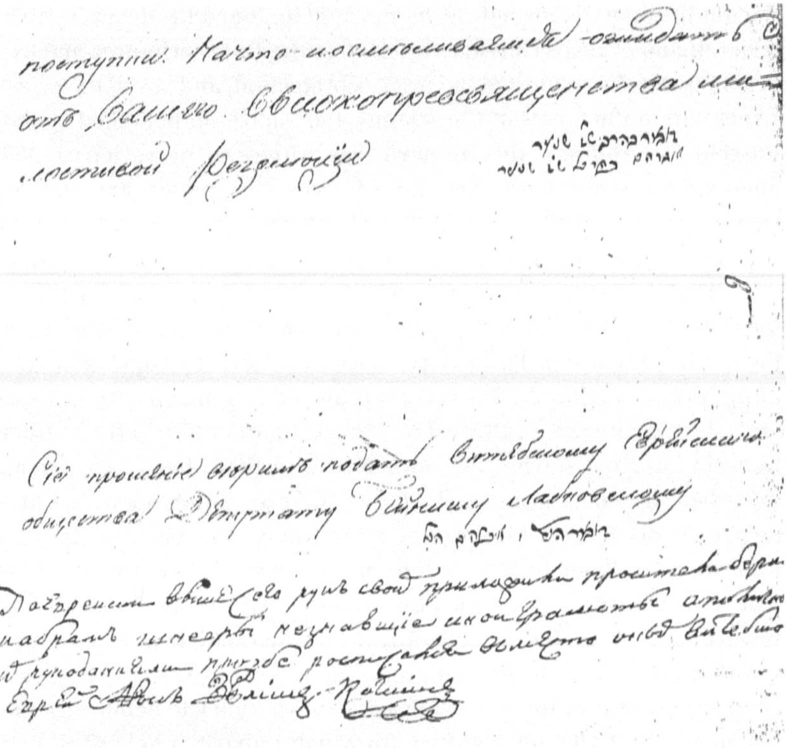

FIG. 2.2. The last page of the letter by Moshe's brothers, Dov Ber and Hayyim Avraham. Their signatures (in Hebrew) appear on lines 3 and 6.

seevich Puzanov, an artillery officer who resided in Ule and was determined to see Moshe convert. In those days, when members of the armed forces were billeted in the homes of local residents—occasionally to the residents' liking (and for handsome pay), but mostly not to their liking[69]—Puzanov apparently lived in a stone house belonging to Moshe's wife's family. Asked by the family to move from the stone house to a less comfortable wooden one in the same courtyard, this officer sought, so Moshe's brothers claimed in their letter, to exact revenge. Taking advantage of Shifra's absence (as she was probably responsible for keeping an eye on her husband), the officer prevailed upon Moshe to come to his home for tea. However, no tea was imbibed; rather, Puzanov served alcoholic punch, getting Moshe drunk. Other documents claim that he also fed Moshe nonkosher food. The officer then had Moshe sign a letter expressing his desire to convert to Catholicism. Next, Puzanov shaved off Moshe's beard and sidelocks and sent him, accompanied by soldiers, to the local priest. The priest did not delay. Even though aware of Moshe's mental illness, he took Moshe under his wing and baptized him several days later.

On 8 [20] September 1820, a letter of complaint signed by Moshe's brothers reached the office of the archbishop of the Roman Catholic Church in Russia, Stanisłav Siestrzeńcewicz Bohusz.[70] A well-known figure in church circles, Bohusz, who lived in St. Petersburg, was involved in Moshe's conversion from the start. Moshe was still in his family's care at the time this letter was written. Its declared aim was to ward off the efforts by the priest Eliashevich and the officer Puzanov to baptize Moshe once again. The brothers also spelled out Moshe's long-standing mental illness (other documents indicate that it first emerged in 1802), and their father's futile attempts to find a cure, noting that Moshe enjoyed short periods of remission and was generally in good health until 1812. A sharp downturn took place during the Napoleonic wars, when Moshe was a French prisoner of war. Held in Shklov on accusations of spying, and condemned to death, Moshe was freed when his captors realized that he was mentally unbalanced. The metropolitan's laconic reply, sent through the Vitebsk dean, indicated his refusal to discuss Moshe's health at that juncture.

October saw another turning point in this affair. While in his family's care, Moshe managed, through unknown means, to send word to the Russian Church in Mogilev of his desire to convert, this time to Russian Orthodoxy. This change of religion was not unusual. Other apostates to Catholicism acted similarly, in the former Polish regions of Lithuania and Byelorussia in particular. In the wake of Moshe's declaration, on 9 [21] October the consistory of the Russian Orthodox church in Mogilev requested the baptismal certificate from its Roman Catholic counterpart.

If the letter from the Russian consistory accurately reflects Moshe's testimony, it reveals not only procedural irregularities in the baptismal ceremony performed in Ule, but also Moshe's confused state of mind. In his letter, Moshe states that he underwent baptism to Catholicism of his own free will, but that he did so in order to escape Jewish persecution in the form of beatings, insults, and threats. His godparents were, he stated, the officer Puzanov and Yustina Aleksandrovna Reutt, daughter of the estate owner (Alexander Petrovich) Reutt. As it was customary to rename the convert after the baptism, Moshe was given the name Piotr Aleksandrovich (evidently, for his godmother's honorable father). From the complaint, and from other documents as well, it appears that several requirements were not met: the baptism went unrecorded in the church's baptismal book, the required number of witnesses was not present, Moshe was baptized only once, and the event was not reported to the police or to the baptizing priest's superiors.

Based on Moshe's request, the Polish deacon Zranicki, from the major district town of Lepel (in Vitebsk Province), was called upon to verify the details of the baptism and to secure the baptismal certificate. Zranicki, who evidently opposed the conversion, exceeded his brief and initiated an independent investigation, sparking Archbishop Bohusz's ire. Zranicki requested

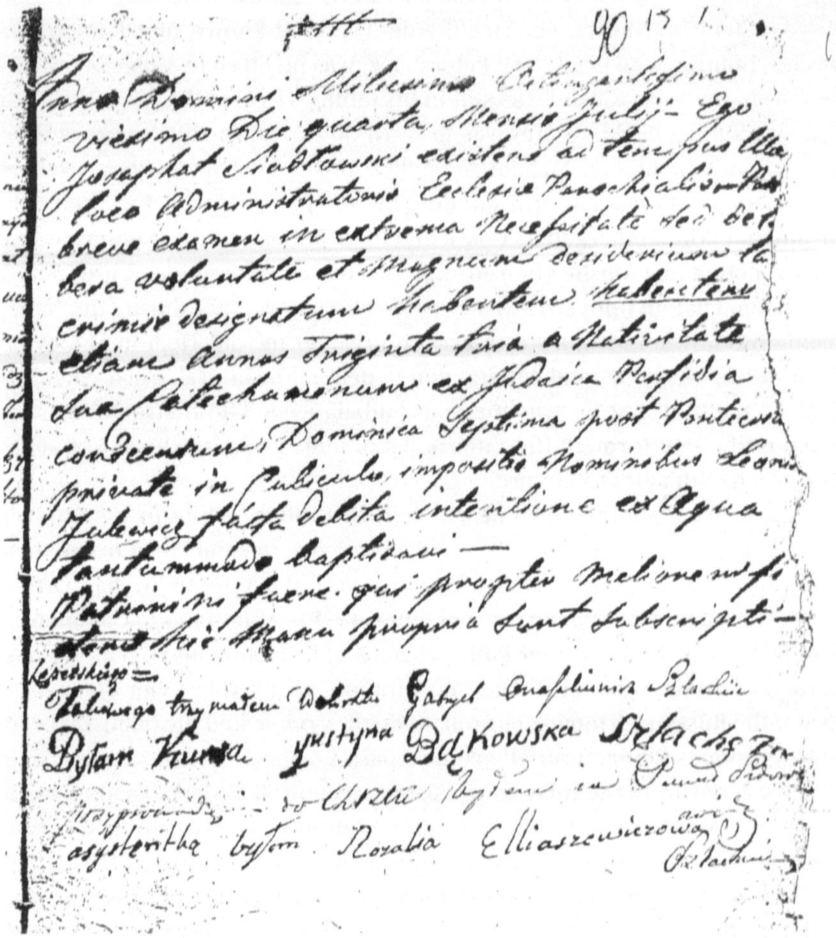

FIG. 2.3. Moshe's baptismal certificate. In it, the Catholic priest Josaphat Siodłowski certifies that the baptism took place on 4 July 1820, the seventh Sunday after Pentecost. The certificate reflects a fixed Latin text, in which only the names of the person baptized and the witnesses change. Lines 11–12 contain Moshe's new name, in Polish: Leoni Jolewicz.

the original baptismal certificate from Father Siodłowski, and took depositions from Puzanov and four other supposed witnesses to the ceremony. It quickly became apparent that these witnesses were not the same as the ones cited by Moshe and Siodłowski. Yes, a woman by the name of Yustina was present, but she was Benkovska, not Reutt. Moreover, from other sources, we know that the Ule town noble was named Ignace Reutt, not Alexander. Above all, Moshe's Christian name was Leon Yulievich; the name Piotr Aleksandrovich never existed. This emerges clearly from the Latin baptismal certificate Siodłowski appended to his letter.[71]

Siodłowski admitted to Zranicki that the baptismal certificate had been penned on a separate sheet signed by Moshe. This he attributed both to an accompanying sense of urgency and to an unnamed superior's opposition. Two of the witnesses stated that the ceremony was held secretly at the priest's home, and not at the church, as was the usual practice. We have no knowledge of the identity of this superior or the nature of his objections; it may even have been Deacon Zranicki himself. In any event, it is likely that the Catholic Church's objections to the conversion were based on doubts regarding either Moshe's sincerity or sanity,[72] or on generous Jewish bribes.

Having completed his investigation on 13 [25] November, Zranicki reported to the Catholic consistory in Mogilev that he was unable to locate the original baptismal certificate, and that following lengthy discussions with Siodłowski, he was convinced that Moshe had not been properly baptized. The hastily penned conversion certificate was probably not authentic, as one of the signatories, Pavel Sidorovich, denied having witnessed the ceremony. At this point, notwithstanding the doubtful nature of the conversion—and mainly because Siodłowski and Puzanov insisted that the ceremony had been correctly performed—the consistory dispatched an official announcement to the governor of Mogilev Province, dated 15 [27] November 1820, declaring the baptism of the rabbi Moshe Shneyer in the Catholic church in Ule valid. His Christian name was Leon Yulievich.

Late November [mid-December] saw the intervention of the minister of the interior, who directed the governor of Mogilev Province to remove Moshe from his family and to transfer him to St. Petersburg. This was at the explicit request of the minister of education and religion, Prince Alexander Nikolaevich Golitsyn,[73] a member of Alexander I's close circle, who had been following these events. The letters preserved in the document files make Golitsyn's dilemma clear. On the one hand, the Jews consistently argued that Moshe was mad, and the St. Petersburg Jewish deputies requested that Golitsyn hand Moshe over to his family for treatment.[74] On the other hand, the Catholic consistory in Mogilev explicitly stated that it found the medical records unconvincing; moreover, it claimed that the baptism ceremony had been implemented correctly, that Moshe was mentally balanced, and that only among his Jewish brethren did he pretend madness due to fear.

Moshe, who was then living in the residence of Bohusz, the Catholic archbishop, now underwent extensive medical examinations. In January 1821, the doctors, whose names appear on the document, determined that he was mentally ill. One even recalled having treated Moshe nineteen years earlier and expressed hope for a cure, even if it was lengthy and costly. Golitsyn refused to assign government funding to Moshe's treatment and asked that his friend Bohusz return Moshe to the Jewish deputies, so that they could

FIG. 2.4. Prince Alexander Nikolaevich Golitsyn

underwrite the costs of his care. The crux of the problem was not simply the expense, but whether or not Moshe's conversion was valid—as the Catholic consistory of Mogilev claimed—or not, perhaps because of the indisputable fact that he was mentally ill.

As noted, Golitsyn recommended acceding to the Jewish deputies' request, but on the condition that no Jews be allowed in Moshe's presence while he was undergoing treatment. Priests, however, would be allowed to discuss the tenets of Christianity with him. Bohusz refused. He wanted to keep Moshe in his home and under his wing. In the course of the treatment, which lasted for months, Moshe received instruction in Christianity from the famed German Catholic mystic and preacher Johannes Gossner, a recent newcomer to St. Petersburg.[75]

In August 1821, Golitsyn again corresponded with Bohusz. From this letter we learn of Czar Alexander's order that Moshe not be returned to his wife. "I said to the czar," Golitsyn wrote, "that if the cure requires additional costs, the funding will come from donations by good Christians and not from government monies, and the czar agreed."

On 29 August [10 September], Moshe's condition took a turn for the worse. Ivan Orlai, the eminent St. Petersburg physician who was treating him, reported that Moshe was experiencing serious seizures and asked permission to transfer him from Bohusz's private residence to the hospital. Five days before Rosh Hashanah, on 10 [22] September 1821, Moshe was admitted to the renowned Obukhovskaya Hospital, which specialized in the treatment of nervous disorders. Orlai noted instructions from the military ruler of St. Petersburg to the head doctor to place Moshe in a private room. This appears

FIG. 2.5. The German Catholic preacher Johannes Gossner

to be the last certifiable information about Moshe's fate. From this point on, he drops out of sight. The absence of any later documents in his file supports the supposition—raised elsewhere, as we shall see—that Moshe died shortly after being admitted to the hospital.

To sum up the archival evidence: There is complete agreement that Moshe suffered serious mental illness, beginning in his childhood (which surprisingly neither prevented him from marrying, nor kept the Jews of Ule from accepting him as their rabbi). Evidently, he enjoyed brief periods of remission until he finally succumbed to the disease, perhaps in the wake of the traumatic events he endured during the Franco-Russian war. There is also concurrence that a Russian officer influenced Moshe to convert. The documents also point to the problematic nature of the baptismal ceremony. Performed in July 1820 in the Catholic church of Ule, it was carried out carelessly, did not follow all the rules of Catholic ritual, and was not properly recorded. Moreover, because it was illegal to convert someone who was not of sound mind, the various branches of the Catholic church were loath to admit Moshe's insanity. Their recognition of Moshe's mental imbalance would invalidate his conversion. In addition, the archival sources indicate that, after converting, Moshe was returned to, and subsequently removed from, his family for varying periods of time, in order to undergo medical examinations. Concurrent with the investigations of his conversion, Moshe announced his desire to join the Russian Orthodox Church. In the end, Moshe was declared a Catholic and was relocated to St. Petersburg, where he received private treatment at the home of Archbishop Bohusz. When his condition worsened, Moshe was hospitalized.

This extensive documentation, which requires further examination, still leaves us with no concrete explanation for Moshe's true motives, apart from insanity (the medical nature of which remains uncertain). Also missing is documentation of Moshe's fate, which, as we shall see below, was a debated matter as well.

"He Had Done So in Sane, Sound Mind": Maskilic Memory Traditions

The matters discussed in the archival documentation outlined above were known only to its correspondents. Nonetheless, the traces of the act itself, which took place over several months, played out before a broad audience, Jewish and non-Jewish alike. Sholem Aleichem's story "The Lottery Ticket" describes the lightning speed with which news of a conversion spread through a small Russian town: "Suddenly, no one knows how or where, something explodes, like a bomb from the sky, like an earthquake. The people awaken, start to run. They run this way and that. 'What is it? Where? What happened?' The story of Yisroel-the-*shammes*' son was like that bomb. It tore the town to pieces and woke up everybody. They were all as upset and excited as if this had to do with their own health or livelihood, as if this was the only thing they had to worry about. Some dropped their work, others left the table with their food untouched and went off to the marketplace to see what was going on."[76] This was undoubtedly the case for the Moshe affair. But the vow of silence taken by the many Jewish witnesses exercised its influence: so great was the shame that the secret did not pass their lips.

A similar mantle of silence and secrecy shrouded comparable contemporary events among other distinguished families. And indeed there were those who compared the disaster that beset Habad to similar disasters striking their counterparts. A matching case was that of Avraham Peretz. This son-in-law of the notable Yehoshua Zeitlin of Shklov—a well-known patron of rabbinic scholars, himself a scholar and the son of a scholar (his father served as a rabbi in Lubratov, Galicia)—converted to Christianity in St. Petersburg. Zeitlin's great-grandson, the writer Shaul Yisrael Ish-Horowitz (1861–1922), recounted the secretive atmosphere in his parental home and the parallels their contemporaries drew between the two episodes: "Regarding this sad event [Avraham Peretz's conversion], the leading mitnagedim and even our family members used to whisper among themselves from time to time. *But not a soul dared to utter a denigratory remark or to reveal the secret*, in line with the principle 'the heart does not divulge to the mouth' . . . And at the same time, a similar event took place in the home of the admor of Lyady. It was then said: God meted out measure for measure—for the sins of factionalism and schism in Israel he took the dearest ones of the opposing camps."[77]

As is usually the case in these circumstances, the earliest extant written sources come from the maskilic camp. The much later hasidic reactions and their counterinterpretations already take into account, and confront, the maskilic memory traditions, both printed and oral.

Yitshak Ber Levinsohn's Letter to Yosef Perl

The earliest source referring to Moshe's conversion is a letter sent on the eve of Rosh Hashanah 1820 by the maskil Yitshak Ber Levinsohn (Ribal), then living in Brody, to his friend Yosef Perl (1773–1839) of Tarnopol:

> I now find myself obliged to report some current events to his honor: 1. Rabbi Zalman Liozner, the head of the Habad faction, was survived by three sons, Reb Ber, Reb Moshe, and Reb Avraham. And it came to pass after their father's death that conflict broke out between Reb Ber and Reb Moshe, each of whom wished to fill his father's place. And Reb Ber sat on the throne of the rabbinate in the town of Lubavitch in the land of Raysen [Byelorussia] . . . but his brother Moshe outstripped him and was appointed rabbi of the town of Ule. The conflict between them began about two years ago [and lasted] until Reb Ber defeated Reb Moshe. Upon seeing that Reb Ber had become greater than he, Reb Moshe approached the priests and converted. And although there had been a schism between the two factions in Habad—for the previous two years Habad had split into two factions—they made peace among themselves, and collected much money and bribed the priests and the town and provincial officials to return Moshe to them, claiming that he was incompetent and insane. And Reb Moshe shrieked like a crane and stated that he had done so in sane, sound mind, and wrote a letter to Prince Golitsyn recounting the entire matter. And the news reached Czar Alexander. The czar sent for Reb Moshe and had him brought to St. Petersburg in order to interview him and to determine whether he spoke the truth, for he was portrayed as incompetent and as having been subjected to undue influence. And this Reb Moshe had already been sent to St. Petersburg and came before the czar. This event took place just a month ago. I heard every word last night from Reb Mordekhai Shapira who came from Berdichev, because the sons of Rabbi Yitshak Levi . . . of Berdichev are related to this Reb Moshe,[78] and there is unceasing talk.[79] I later heard about it from a recent arrival in our region from Odessa, the famous scholar Reb Yosef Landau of Prague, and he told me that he heard it from officials in Kiev. And the hasidim around here go about aimlessly, and are jumping out of their skin, and would harm themselves if they could.[80]

Thus, news of Moshe's conversion reached Galician maskilim with lightning speed. In noting that the event had taken place but a month earlier, Ribal nearly hit upon the actual date of the conversion. However, he places Moshe's arrival in St. Petersburg earlier than does the archival material, which indicates a mid-December 1820 date. This illustrates how rumors can even precede their realization.

The fact that the tragic, human side of Moshe's conversion held no interest for Ribal is difficult to overlook. He appears to take malicious pleasure in the confusion of the hasidim, who allegedly seek to commit suicide ("harm themselves"). Like many of the contemporary maskilim, Ribal disseminated juicy antihasidic information, gossip and half-truths, for use in the maskilic polemic with, and satirization of, Hasidism.

In his letter, Ribal notes two sources of information: Mordekhai Shapira, who learned of the case from Berdichev hasidim, and Yosef Landau, whose informants were Kievan Russian officials.[81] According to these sources, the background to this episode was a family quarrel regarding the succession to Shneur Zalman. When Dov Ber gained the upper hand, Moshe refused to accept the verdict and converted of his own free will, as a means of revenging himself on his family. Well publicized, the conversion even aroused the interest of Alexander I himself; consequently, Moshe was summoned to St. Petersburg.

Notwithstanding the antihasidic nature of this letter, we must note that the document in question belongs to friendly personal correspondence and does not come from a satirical propaganda broadside intended for publication. Even if aimed at serving Perl's satiric needs, the tone of the letter is informative, not satirical, in nature. Ribal and Perl would naturally prize such rumors, as proof of Hasidism's inherent dangers.

Ribal's report raises several points: (1) the conversion took place in 1820; (2) the background to the controversy was a familial succession battle; (3) the matter came to the attention of high officials in the regime (Prince Golitsyn and Alexander I, who ostensibly met with Moshe); and (4) the episode greatly discomfited the hasidim, who tried to restore the erring son to their midst through a variety of means: bribing church and government officials and announcing that Moshe was unbalanced. Some of these points concur with the archival findings; others do not. Thus, the date of conversion is accurate. But did Moshe actually meet Prince Golitsyn and Czar Alexander? Golitsyn's intense involvement clearly emerges from his testimony in the above-cited letters. Even though he mentions the czar's interest in this affair, it is difficult to imagine that Moshe actually met the czar; indeed, to date, no documentary evidence indicates that such a meeting took place. Furthermore, the conversion's ascription to a succession war is unfounded. In making their way from Mogilev in Byelorussia to Berdichev and to Kiev, these rumors conflated Moshe's conversion with the disputed succession to Shneur Zalman. As noted earlier, this dispute, which Habad tradition does not deny, took place not between the brothers but between Dov Ber and Aharon Halevi Horowitz of Staroselye. Evidently unaware of Aharon's name or of this succession dispute, it appears likely that Ribal (or his informants) combined the conversion with what was seen as a possible motive.

But not only is the link between the failed succession attempt and the conversion specious, it is also surprising. After all, Moshe had a far simpler option at his disposal, one often chosen by the sons of zaddikim and other unsuccessful candidates in succession battles: simply to withdraw from the main group and to found a rival court (as Aharon of Staroselye did). Clearly, the radical step of conversion does not require a connection either to disappointed hopes for succession, natural as they may be, or to the desire for revenge.

The material Ribal passed on to Perl undoubtedly pleased him greatly. Despite its potential, because Perl's witty antihasidic satire *Megaleh temirin* (Revealer of secrets) had already appeared a year earlier, he was able to introduce Moshe only as a minor character in his *Bohen tsadik* (Test of the righteous): "Afterwards, I showed him a treatise that I had in my satchel. I once took this treatise from the secretary of a zaddik who was recording his rabbi's doctrines, and he had approbations from the contemporary zaddikim. I told him of my intention to publish this treatise which was left to us by the blessed zaddik, our teacher *Magkar ben hatsadik miZalin.* He did not see or look at the book, but only said: I knew the author's father, the zaddik of blessed memory. I have heard the son's name, whose good reputation is already known."[82] This strange name is the numerical equivalent in Hebrew of "Moshe the son of the zaddik of Liozno." Only those in the know could decipher this delicate allusion to the man "whose good reputation is already known."[83]

Moshe Berlin's History of Hasidism

Another maskilic source on the Moshe affair is a Russian memorandum from 1853 prepared by the maskil Moshe Berlin of Shklov, who held the title of *Uchony Yevrei* (learned Jew) for the Byelorussian region (even though he spent most of his life in St. Petersburg). His *Istoria Hasidisma* (History of Hasidism), which is extant in manuscript, aimed to bring what he saw as the hidden dangers of Hasidism in general, and of Habad in particular, to the attention of Russian officials. Berlin wrote:

> The death of the first zaddik (Shneur Zalman) in the Byelorussian district sparked debate among the hasidim regarding the choice of his successor, as Zalman was survived by three sons. The eldest, Moshe, had a certain reputation as a scholar, but he was wedded to his desires, behaved immodestly, and did not observe Jewish law strictly. The youngest son, Avraham, although a simple, straight individual, was not a scholar; he could therefore not succeed his father. The middle son, Berke, was also no

scholar, and he too was wedded to his desires. But being, on the other hand, a clever, hardworking, and talented preacher, he knew how to draw attention and to attract the love of the communal elders by various means, such as flattery, distributing honors, and the like. In order to keep his older brother Moshe from blocking his aspiration to take his father's place, Berke persecuted and humiliated him as much as he could, driving Moshe to the brink of despair. Consequently, and in order to carve out an independent path to fame, and to embarrass his brother Berke, Moshe converted to Christianity. The hasidim, who found this most disturbing and troubling, tried every means to return him to Judaism but to no avail. And Moshe himself, whose conscience was not clear, went insane and died in St. Petersburg.[84]

Motivated by a stubborn battle with Habad (whose leaders entered the fray and fought him until they succeeded in having him dismissed from his post),[85] Berlin can by no means be regarded as an unbiased witness. Although he collected data on the Habad rebbes, especially targeting the Mitteler Rebbe, for whom he had little regard, and his son-in-law, the Tsemah Tsedek, Berlin's sources are not readily ascertainable. In the absence of known links between him and Ukrainian and Galician maskilim, it appears that Berlin relied mainly on traditions culled from local maskilim, hasidim, and government officials. But Berlin's memorandum contains some mistakes—Moshe was not the oldest but the youngest son (an error that will be repeated in other maskilic sources), and he was not a party to a war of succession—although his remarks regarding Moshe's end merit consideration. According to Berlin, Moshe converted in order to shame his brother. But, as a result of incessant humiliation and pangs of conscience, he went insane and died in St. Petersburg. Berlin provides no date of death, but it had to be prior to 1853, the date of the memorandum. As Berlin's memorandum was internal—meant only for the eyes of government officials—the next step in this discussion is to determine if the details embedded in his comments made their way to other witnesses.

Perets Smolenskin and Pesah Ruderman's Interpretation

The first two printed reactions in Hebrew to the Moshe episode—until that point still in the realm of deniable rumor—appeared in the radical nationalist periodical *Hashahar*, then the main forum for antihasidic discourse. The initial response appeared in 1869, the first year of *Hashahar*'s publication. In a poem titled "Hamishtage'a" (The madman), Perets Smolenskin (1840?–85), the journal's editor, mocked the hasidic way of concealing the crime, whenever one of its holy members deliberately violates moral standards, by claiming that "he has gone mad!"[86]

Mainly devoted to the contemporary episode of the zaddik Bernyu of Leova (the son of Yisrael of Ruzhin), who had just published an open letter in the Jewish press announcing his defection to the maskilic camp, the poem informed readers of what had taken place "more than fifty years earlier" in Lithuania:

That awesome holy one [Shneur Zalman] had two sons:
Moshe the firstborn acquired wisdom.
His second son Dov followed his eyes
and to the wisdom of Judaism failed to lend his ears.

"Dominion will fall to me after my father's death,"
so thought the eldest son to himself during his father's lifetime.
But after his death he saw that his hopes were in vain,
the exalted office was placed on his brother's shoulders.

Bloody murder—cried the firstborn in rage—
He of uncircumcised heart [Dov Ber] dazzled the eyes of the foolish with bribes!
The uncircumcised one was raised up to teach the ways of heaven,
therefore the teacher chose the faith of the uncircumcised!

He thought and he spoke, and implemented his plot
to desecrate his brother's name and that of the congregation he taught.
He chose a new faith and denied his own faith,
but the hasidim exclaimed in unison: "He has gone mad!"

Smolenskin appended two notes based on current rumor; however, they bear no relationship to the truth. Regarding Dov Ber, the Mitteler Rebbe, he wrote: "Rumor has it that he fell ill with syphilis, and died," and regarding Moshe, he commented: "The following tale is transmitted orally in Lithuania, that the firstborn, Moshe, who excelled in Torah wisdom, imagined that he would inherit his father's place after the latter's death, but the other [brother] had a rich father-in-law, who bribed the leading hasidim to choose his son-in-law instead. Upon learning that his opponents had overcome his allies, in his towering rage he shouted in Yiddish: 'If the goy can become a rebbe, then the rebbe will become a goy.' And afterwards he converted. But, in order that the zaddik not be embarrassed by his brother, the hasidim announced that he had gone mad." This is the first recorded appearance of this witticism, henceforth to be applied to Moshe and his acts, namely, if the goy (Dov, supposedly an ignoramus) can be a rebbe, then the rebbe (Moshe, the scholar) will become an actual goy (non-Jew)!

A native of Monastyrshchina in Mogilev Province, Smolenskin had little sympathy for Hasidism, even though he had frequented the Lubavitch court in his youth. His *Hato'eh bedarkhei hahayyim* (The wanderer in the paths of life, originally published 1869–71) contains a colorful, but cruelly critical, description of hasidic life in "Tsavua'el" (hypocrisy-ville), namely Lubavitch. Smolenskin times his hero's arrival for 19 Kislev, the date on which the hasidim celebrate the first Habad rebbe's release from jail, also describing, in passing, the rebbe (the Tsemah Tsedek) and his five sons. Although Smolenskin portrays himself as an expert on hasidic matters, his knowledge was actually slight. Smolenskin undoubtedly spent no more than a few months at the Lubavitch court.[87] The stories he repeats regarding Moshe, to which he may have been exposed during this time, were unfounded and present the antihasidic, rumor-mill version of the apostasy. Thus, Smolenskin was not aware that Shneur Zalman had three sons. Like many other earlier and later maskilim, he thought that Moshe was the firstborn and a scholar, while Moshe's brother Dov Ber was corrupt, and Smolenskin fell into the trap of seeing the "succession war" as the explanation of Moshe's conversion.

Several years later, in 1875, Smolenskin published a series of articles by a young maskil named Pesah Ruderman (1854–86), who represented himself as a former Habad hasid. Reportedly a witness to hasidic tales and rumor, he too recounted something of Moshe's fate:

> Shneur Zalman of Lyady, the Alter Rebbe, was survived by three sons and one daughter, Menahem Mendel's wife.[88] The oldest son Avraham was one of those whom Smolenskin terms (in *Hato'eh bedarkhei hahayyim*) "neither fish nor fowl." Lacking any talent for exoteric or esoteric Torah knowledge, he had no hope or thought of taking his father's place. The youngest, Moshe, the hasidim say, was exceedingly handsome and his father's favorite because he excelled in Talmud and Halakha, was freedom-loving and enjoyed singing and dancing. After the Alter Rebbe's death he sought to assume his post, but his brother, Dov Ber, who had little exoteric, but much esoteric, knowledge, used hypocritical, hidden means to depose his brother, besmirching his name, saying that he defiled himself by eating non-Jewish bread and loving a non-Jewess (the hasidim still whisper about Moshe's affair with the high officer's daughter who became pregnant) . . . And they so embittered his life until he threw off the yoke and converted; eventually, he went mad and died in a Moscow hospital.[89]

Apart from the fictional succession war, which we have already met in his predecessors' works, Ruderman's account rounds out Smolenskin's in several respects: (1) the background to the succession war inhered in the intellectual gap between the clever, talented son, Moshe, and Dov Ber, an ignoramus, hypocrite, and schemer; (2) Dov Ber and his followers instigated rumors that Moshe ate nonkosher food and was in love with, and impregnated, the daughter of a Russian officer; and (3) Moshe's conversion was an act of desperation, as the hasidim had embittered his life. Finally, he went insane and died in a Moscow hospital.

Any attempt to evaluate the reliability of Ruderman's account must consider that it derives from a harshly polemical, antihasidic article. The remarks of this self-defined "former hasid,"[90] who aims to attack Habad Hasidism, must be seen as essentially untrustworthy, especially with regard to his biased portrayal of Dov Ber. Note, moreover, the following inaccuracies: not only was Hayyim Avraham not Shneur Zalman's oldest son, but the contemporary rebbe, Menahem Mendel, was married to Shneur Zalman's granddaughter (the daughter of the Mitteler Rebbe), not his daughter. And if what every hasid knew was not obvious to Ruderman, how can we trust his testimony regarding sensitive material unknown to most hasidim?

Nonetheless, we must note several details, some of which (like Moshe's death from insanity, already mentioned by Moshe Berlin) also appear independently in other sources. Ruderman correctly rejects the "romantic" motivation—a juicy rumor that certainly took wing—as groundless defamation and gossip. Had there been any truth to this rumor, Ruderman and others would have unhesitatingly applied it to the conversion. But, given the current lifestyle of Eastern European Jews, and especially the strict supervision in hasidic courts, even such avowed enemies of Hasidism as Ruderman were aware of the extreme unlikelihood of an affair between a married hasid with children and a Russian officer's daughter.[91]

The Testimony of Avraham Ber Gottlober

The testimony of the maskil Avraham Ber Gottlober (1810–99) sets us on a new track. Gottlober also called himself a former Habad hasid (having joined this group after his marriage), but unlike his predecessors, he was actually well acquainted with this branch of Hasidism, and with its literature and traditions. He first makes casual reference to the episode of Moshe in a footnote to his polemical article "Et la'akor natu'a" (A time to uproot), which sought to defend the Mendelssohnian legacy from Perets Smolenskin's harsh attack:[92] "And an important rabbi from the hasidic sect, Rabbi Shneur Zalman of Lyady, suffered such an episode. His eldest son Moshe, who was already serving in the rabbinate, left Judaism and converted to Christianity. Can we blame all such eminent persons for [the behavior of] their children and disciples?"[93] These remarks display Gottlober's clear intuition of Smolenskin's blunt attempt to place the "sins" of the Berlin haskalah generation—assimilation and alienation—at Mendelssohn's door. Gottlober in no way found Mendelssohn responsible, or to blame, for the sins of his children and followers. Just as Gershom Me'or Hagolah bore no guilt for his son's conversion, or Nahmanides for the conversion of his disciple Abner of Burgos, so too Shneur Zalman bore no responsibility for his son's apostasy. Gottlober's brief remarks contain the now familiar mistake—Moshe, as noted before, was not the firstborn but the youngest son—but this makes no difference in this context.

The same mistaken birth order is repeated in Gottlober's memoirs, first published in 1880 (though written much earlier). Here Gottlober provides a detailed version grounded in memories of his youth and his family life. Although we can assume his familiarity with Ruderman's remarks, he provides a totally different picture, especially of Moshe's end:

Dov Ber's older brother, named Moshe, converted. He settled in the royal capital of St. Petersburg and then went mad and died. Some say, that he first lost his mind and then left his faith. Ultimately, Kabbalah was his downfall, for his mind was too limited to encompass its secrets . . . and he went insane. They claim that he composed kabbalistic secrets and hints on making the sign of the cross.

In my youth, when I studied in the study house in Chernyakhov,[94] and was eating at my father-in-law's table . . . a tormented, elderly, and sick pauper was brought to the study house, pulled in a wagon hitched to a single, starved horse, as the poor at that time were sent from town to town and from village to village. And he agreed to remain in the small room attached to the study house for several days, as was customary in hasidic settlements, and sometimes a few hasidim prayed there privately. This individual fasted all day, every day, and broke his fast in the evening on bread and water alone, nothing more; he slept on the ground with no pillow, and did not utter a word, except for the prayers, which he recited according to the Habad rite, and with that group's customary gestures. My father of blessed memory went to see him, and he stood and honored my father by hinting at his majestic appearance and good looks, for my late father was indeed very handsome and well known. To the few questions my father posed he answered in writing, and his handwriting was extraordinarily beautiful and his language was clear and accurate. But he revealed neither his name nor his origins nor the purpose of his travels. Several days later he was provided with a wagon at his written request and he traveled on. *Afterwards it was said* that this man was Moshe, the son of Rabbi Zalman. My father, who had known Zalman, testified that the man's face resembled that of Zalman, and let those who know for certain be praised![95]

Notwithstanding Gottlober's maskilic bias and lifelong grudge against Hasidism, he retained warm feelings toward Habad and its zaddikim.[96] Aware of Moshe's conversion, Gottlober referred to it openly, but he did not link it to a succession war. Moreover, he made no effort to describe Dov Ber as an ignoramus and Moshe as an intellectual; on the contrary, he described Moshe as possessing limited intellectual ability. It was Kabbalah that drove Moshe insane, to the extent that he even composed a kabbalistic work on the secrets of the cross (a bizarre allegation that we will meet again).

Gottlober's innovation lies in the alternative tradition regarding Moshe's end: he did not remain a convert, but repented and went into "exile" (*galut*), undertaking a life of wandering and distress. He made the rounds of the Jewish communities in the southern part of the Pale of Settlement, in the provinces of Volhynia and Kiev, and not in the northeastern regions of the Pale where he had been active (Ule, Lubavitch, and Mogilev) or central Russia (St. Petersburg and Moscow). As we shall see below, this geographical transfer typifies all the other witnesses that support, and depend on, this version—namely, the hasidic ones. In it, they found a means of rehabilitating Moshe's negative image, thereby creating a counterpoint to the maskilic memory tradition first echoed by Smolenskin and Ruderman.

It would be convenient to argue that Gottlober's testimony forms the basis for the story of Moshe's exile as woven in hasidic sources. But as we shall see below, the story of the exile appears in written Habad sources that predate, and are independent of, the publication of Gottlober's memoirs. Gottlober not only supports but also strengthens the hasidic version. Clearly, if a prejudiced maskil of his ilk, who never missed a chance to blacken Hasidism, testified that Moshe repented, his remarks must ostensibly be trustworthy.

The hasidic sources are discussed later in this chapter. For now, note that this part of Gottlober's testimony is clearly unfounded. Not only does he issue a cautionary remark: "let those who know for certain be praised"; moreover, the poor, sick wanderer who came to the Chernyakhov study house[97] reportedly did not utter a word. Communication proceeded through signs, or in writing. He refused to identify himself, and his identification as Moshe relied mainly on rumors and on testimony after the fact (Gottlober's father recalled the resemblance *after* the rumor had spread regarding the pauper's resemblance to Shneur Zalman).[98]

How are we to understand the link that Gottlober creates between the mysterious wayfarer and Moshe, tenuous as it may be? At present, three unverifiable possibilities exist. First, Moshe did not die of distress and madness but—as Habad sources will also claim—repented and wandered among the towns of Volhynia. Not only is this version the most difficult to verify, it raises other questions to be discussed later in this chapter. Second, as early as the 1820s, young Gottlober, his father, and his fellow townspeople internalized popular rumors regarding Moshe's repentance, and connected them with a strange wayfarer who passed through their town. Although this seems likely, a caveat is in order: no early sources confirm the existence of such rumors close to the time of Moshe's conversion, and the story of Moshe's "exile" first appears in 1876, in the letters of the Habad hasid Zvi Chaikin, to be discussed below. And third, it is also possible that the elderly Gottlober linked an episode he witnessed in his youth with the new hasidic tradition that spread beginning in the mid-1870s, and that this link was a figment of his imagination.

Ephraim Deinard's Version

This discussion of the maskilic traditions concludes with a brief look at the remarks of the renowned and contentious writer, traveler, and publisher Ephraim Deinard (1846–1930). Deinard visited Lubavitch, where he reportedly met the Tsemah Tsedek and his sons.[99] But Deinard's strong aversion for things hasidic, and especially his strong hatred for Habad, whose members he termed "the most evil hasidim and most dangerous to the teachings of Judaism,"[100] clouded his judgment, making it difficult to rely on his comments in the absence of external proof. He wrote: "Rabbi Zalman was survived by two sons. The firstborn, Moshe, was a learned man, who felt himself worthy to inherit his father's place, rather than his younger brother Dov Ber, who was a sly ignoramus. Knowing that he would be unable to establish hegemony in his father's town, where it was known by all that he was not worthy to take his father's place, Dov Ber went afar and settled in the city of Nezhin in Chernigov Province, a town populated by ignorant hasidim . . . and his brother Moshe, who saw that his brother's plot to take his father's place had succeeded, remained alone like a bush in the desert, became angry, and left his people and his religion, and hid from human eyes."[101]

Evidently familiar with his predecessors' remarks, not only does Deinard not add any new evidence, but he introduces mistakes. Like Smolenskin and Gottlober, he incorrectly describes Moshe as the firstborn, not the youngest, son; and like Smolenskin, he knows of only two sons (Gottlober does not mention Hayyim Avraham or how many sons Shneur Zalman had). Another mistake places Dov Ber in Nezhin; actually, this was where Dov Ber was taken ill, died, and was buried on his return from a visit to his father's grave.[102] Deinard derived the supposed intellectual gap between the brothers and Dov Ber's shifty nature from Smolenskin and Ruderman. In short, Deinard's version neither adds to nor detracts from our inquiry. He repeats his version of events regarding Moshe in several of his elegantly produced editions of his works, including his *Alata.*[103] Note Gershom Scholem's remarks on this book's questionable value: "An astounding book! Nearly every sentence contains lies and falsehoods—whatever is stated more confidently, 'facts,' dates, links between events—all are emasculated, incomprehensible, or simply fabricated. It is impossible to critique each and every sentence. What a waste of good paper!"[104]

"He Was in His Right Mind": The Apostates' Testimony

That Jewish sources silenced Moshe's story is entirely comprehensible; but what explains the absence of traces of this episode among interested non-

Jewish parties—the clergy, missionaries, and apostates? Intensive missionizing efforts among the Jews of the Pale of Settlement in the period after the Napoleonic wars, especially from 1817 to 1825, throw this question into greater relief.[105] Russian missionary groups founded Bible societies with the czar's encouragement, and Alexander I gave millenarian Anglican missionaries such as Lewis Way and Alexander McCaul a sympathetic hearing. At their audience with the czar, these missionaries outlined their plans for mass conversion of the Jews; in return, Alexander gave them permission to act in the region of Congress Poland (but not in the Pale of Settlement).[106] Moshe's conversion, with its strong reverberations, could have crowned these efforts. Nonetheless, few surviving Christian printed sources refer to his case.

Joshua George Lazarus's Ebenezer

Surprising testimony about Moshe's case from a Christian perspective comes from an Anglican convert named Joshua George Lazarus (1799–1869). His book *Ebenezer* combines a personal memoir with a description of Eastern European Jewish society and missionary propaganda calling on Christians to abandon their negative attitude toward Jews and to befriend them.[107] A Jewish native of Riga, Lazarus converted in Liverpool in late 1836, along with his second wife and two children. His book opens by declaring that his remarks are directed primarily to his family: to inform his children of their father's roots and of his path to the Christian faith. Friends who read his manuscript encouraged him to reach a wider audience through publication.[108] Its anonymous introduction portrays this book as the continuation of McCaul's well-known *Old Paths*, which claimed to have "shaken, by the blessing of God, the whole fabric of *rabbinism* to its foundation."[109]

Lazarus's book belongs to the nineteenth-century genre of Western Christian writing on traditional Jewish society in Eastern Europe, North Africa, and Palestine. This genre frequently combined travelogues, personal experiences, and memoirs with ethnographical and historical notes to add a supposedly scientific veneer.[110] It also incorporates missionary propaganda, aimed at uncovering the "mistakes" of the spiritual leaders—namely, the rabbis—who lead the Jews astray.

Ebenezer devotes a fascinating chapter to Habad Hasidism. In it, Lazarus recounts how, as an eighteen-year-old newlywed living in the home of ardent mitnagedim, he became curious about hasidic customs. He saved up and traveled secretly to Lubavitch, remaining there for several months. During this time, he was exposed to hasidic practices and even met and conversed with the rebbe (Dov Ber, the Mitteler Rebbe) at length.[111] This largely sympathetic, trustworthy portrayal exhibits detailed knowledge of hasidic customs and contemptuously rejects mitnagedic claims. According to Lazarus, Hasidism and Christian doctrine display close affinity: "The fuel is ready, and a living spark is only needed to kindle the fire."[112] It is therefore worthwhile becoming acquainted with the hasidim and investing in propaganda efforts: "And we may here say with Paul [Romans 10:14–15]—How shall they know if they have not heard? And how shall they hear if it is never preached to them?" By way of strengthening this argument, Lazarus tells of Moshe, who accidentally discovered the "truth" and converted. Lazarus portrays Moshe's tragic end—imprisonment and death in an insane asylum—as a heroic example of martyrdom for Jesus:

> I may here mention an instance of the readiness of the Khasidim to receive the truth as it is in Jesus when made known to them. In the year 1828, I think, a Russian General happened to stay with the brother of the rabbi above-mentioned [Dov Ber], whose name was Rabbi Moshe. This General, who, I now perceive, must have been a good christian, conversed with the rabbi about christianity, and gave him a New Testament, which he diligently read so that in three nights he was by the grace of God convinced of *the Truth*, and wished to make an open confession of his faith. The General fearing that this might occasion a disturbance in the place amongst the Jews, thought it prudent to send him to Petersburg. There the rabbi was baptised, i.e. immersed, according to the custom of the Greek Church [Russian Orthodox Church].[113] Within a week or two after his baptism, he found many things in that church contrary to what he read in the New Testament, and was particularly offended by their image-worship, against which he began to preach in their own church, and was shortly thrown into prison for his zeal. The Jews also considering his conversion to christianity as a blot on their nation, took advantage of this opportunity for taking vengeance upon him, and by giving large bribes to corrupt men in power, they obtained a decision against him of insanity, and cast him into an asylum where he soon died of grief. The Jews to this day maintain that he was mad. They allege in proof of this, the fact of his having preached against the church of which he was apparently a member, being either unable or unwilling to distinguish between the christianity of the New Testament, and that corrupt form of it in the Greek Church, against which alone the rabbi protested. I was formerly of the same opinion, and thought him mad; but since the Lord has been pleased to reveal His Son to me, I am now convinced that he was in his right mind, and suffered for righteousness' sake. We have here an instance in our day, of a martyr of Jesus being persecuted even unto death by Jews and Gentiles.[114]

Lazarus erred regarding the date ("the year 1828, I think") and place of Moshe's conversion. Nor was he aware of Moshe's original conversion to Catholicism. However, his information regarding the involvement of a Russian officer, Moshe's transfer to St. Petersburg, and his death there are accurate. His testimony is biased; after all, his main goal was to prove the po-

FIG. 2.6. Illustration from the title page of Joshua George Lazarus's *Ebenezer* (London, 1841)

tential for conversion among hasidim,[115] and the superiority of Anglicanism over Russian Orthodoxy. Implicit in his remarks is the perhaps unwitting confession that the main motive for Moshe's conversion was mental unbalance. There is not even a hint of the succession war.

Ostensibly, Lazarus's remarks indicate exactly the opposite of the claim of mental illness. Deeply convinced of the truth of Christianity, Moshe took the appropriate step. His end is also depicted as the result of intellectual integrity: his inability to come to terms with the contradiction between the principles of the New Testament and Russian Orthodoxy's pagan practices. Indeed, Lazarus notes time and again how icon worship and incense burning are not just deviations from the original spirit of Christianity, but constitute an emotional barrier between Jews and the message of Christianity, mistakenly equated with the Russian Orthodox Church.

To the outside observer, Lazarus's claim seems untenable: is it remotely possible for a person to reach an independent decision to convert within three days? Yet examination of conversion stories, no matter what religions are involved, illustrates the often abrupt nature of the process. Converts report a sudden enlightenment or revelation—over moments or days—that completely transforms their lives. In other words, conversion is not always a lengthy process accompanied by agonizing doubts, but can take the form of a sudden resolution, with full preparedness to pay its price.[116]

But even if we accept this phenomenon, it remains doubtful that a Torah scholar like Moshe, educated in the Talmudic way of thinking and the ancient harmonizing pilpulistic tradition, would be deterred by a "difficulty" in his new world and would act in such an extreme fashion. Not only does the archival material clearly testify to a long process of conversion as well as severe mental illness, but Lazarus himself also admits that he at first thought Moshe unbalanced. The fact that the Jews paid a generous bribe to hide their shame does not contradict this estimation. Only his own conversion changed Lazarus's perspective. Nonetheless, his confession merits examination, for we would not expect one convert to speak unfavorably of another who had converted before him. The presentation of Moshe's conversion as resulting from a mental breakdown would give rise to suspicions regarding impure motives and lack of stability and would accordingly cast doubts on the verity of other Jews' conversions, including that of Lazarus himself.

"A Civil Servant"?

A year later, in 1842, testimony relating to Moshe by another convert, Bonaventura Mayer, appeared in his German travel book.[117] A Viennese professor of languages, Mayer traveled throughout Eastern Europe from 1825 to 1826, and his description of Jewish society there displays a particularly favorable attitude toward Hasidism. In commenting on Habad, he notes that their relatively small numbers in no way reflect their importance. Whereas other hasidic groups hate them and claim that Habad hasidim pursue the "devil's path" in Kabbalah, Mayer attributes their hatred to Habad learnedness, to their greater expertise in spoken and written Russian as compared to all other hasidim. Regarding Moshe, Mayer wrote: "Despite all this, his [Shneur Zalman's] oldest son converted to Christianity before the death of [Czar] Alexander [in 1825], and he is now a civil servant. On the other hand, the younger son [Dov Ber] inherited his father's place and continues to act in his spirit."[118]

The offhand, innocent concluding remark is outdated, for it confuses the younger and older sons. Moreover, this book's publication took place some sixteen years after Mayer first heard about Moshe (it is unlikely that the two met). Mayer makes no statement as to Moshe's end, but his comments imply that, at least until 1826, six years after his conversion, Moshe was effectively living as a Christian.

Did Moshe convert in order to obtain a post in the Russian bureaucracy? Although this motive applied to many converts who sought a livelihood and advancement, there is no reason to suspect that this was Moshe's impetus.

Perhaps Mayer, a Jew who converted in order to gain a professorial position at the University of Vienna, projected his personal reasons onto others. If Moshe recovered from his illness—and no conclusive evidence exists for either his recovery or the date of his death—it is possible that he was awarded a job in the Russian bureaucracy. This, however, would have been a logical outcome of, and not the reason for, his conversion. After all, once Moshe had cut himself off from Jewish society, he would need to support himself financially. His knowledge of Russian—also mentioned explicitly in Habad sources, as we shall see below—might have facilitated his ability to obtain a civil service job usually reserved for Christians alone.

Surprisingly, Mayer's remarks receive backing from an independent source of value only as a curiosity: a letter sent in May 1888 by the writer Sholem Aleichem to the historian Shimon Dubnow, then just beginning his investigation of Hasidism. Sholem Aleichem recounted that a good friend of his, from Kiev, "a particularly original individual," claimed that "a member of one of the royal branches descended from the Besht converted and served as a civil servant in some government office for a long period of time in St. Petersburg." Sholem Aleichem wondered if this information interested Dubnow.[119] Moshe, of course, was not descended from the Besht, but who can argue with rumors or legends?

There are some chronological inconsistencies between the information provided by Lazarus and that given by Mayer. As noted, Mayer's information comes from his visit to Russia in 1826, whereas Lazarus tentatively attributes Moshe's conversion to 1828. Given that we know the actual date of the conversion, we cannot rely on this dating. Must we totally reject Lazarus's testimony on this basis? If he mistook the date of the conversion, is his report of Moshe's date of death inaccurate as well? The tradition placing Moshe's death in a mental asylum is consistent with the archival report of his admission to the Obukhovskaya Hospital in St. Petersburg, after a severe fit (though we cannot confirm that he died there), and with the independent accounts by Berlin and Ruderman (although they disagree as to place, citing St. Petersburg and Moscow). Nor does it contradict Mayer's testimony (which is backed by Sholem Aleichem's letter). Accordingly, we can tentatively assign Moshe's death to around 1828, though at present we lack further confirmation.

As an aside, I quote the remarks recorded by the book collector Leeser Rosenthal (1794–1868), found in an entry on the *Tanya* in the catalog of his private library: "When the French came to the land of Russia, for fear of the enemy the above-mentioned Rabbi Zalman fled to the town of Vitebsk, where no Jews lived, and died there. And one of his grandsons became a Greek Orthodox Christian and built a chapel on his [Shneur Zalman's] grave."[120] The origins of this strange item, with no foundation in fact—as if a Greek Orthodox chapel would have been erected on the grave of Shneur Zalman of

Lyady!—are difficult to determine. (Furthermore, Shneur Zalman was not buried in Vitebsk, where Jews have always resided; he died near Kursk and was buried in Hadyach.)[121] Yet, this rumor, evidently of non-Jewish origin, spread widely, even reaching Rosenthal in Amsterdam.

In concluding this section, let us return to the question with which it opened: why are there only scant traces of Moshe's conversion in printed Christian sources? After all, having enjoyed little success in their efforts to convert Jews during Alexander I's reign,[122] Moshe's case could have served as an outstanding rallying point for missionary activity. It is also well known that one must exercise caution with regard to the reports of missionaries and apostates. Not only do they enthusiastically testify to Jewish willingness to convert, but they also transform thoughts and hopes into historical reality, without any basis in fact.[123] Why then was Moshe's case so little publicized?

From the above-mentioned archival material, it is certain that this episode was known to a wide circle of government and church officials, both in Mogilev Province and in the capital. However, given Moshe's doubtful sanity and the questionable nature of his baptismal procedure, the consensus apparently was that publication of this event would harm rather than help church interests. If there is any factual basis to Lazarus's testimony, after his conversion, Moshe revealed himself as a fanatic, who not only embarrassed the Jews but also the priests who had helped him convert. Ostensibly, the fact of his madness or fanaticism did not have to be revealed to all; it was possible to simply note the conversion of the son of a prominent hasidic leader. Perhaps the large Jewish bribe to the officials in charge, attested to by Lazarus (and which seems logical), also contributed to this episode's suppression. Another possibility is that Moshe disappeared: he either died soon after being hospitalized, or perhaps, as the hasidic legend treated below claims, escaped and returned to Judaism. In any event, as they were unable to produce the person in question, partisan Christians may have preferred to hold their peace.

In the Historian's Workshop

Shimon Dubnow's Historical Investigations

The late nineteenth century saw the awakening of scholars' interest in Moshe. First and foremost among these scholars was Shimon Dubnow, whose 1890–91 correspondence with Shmaryahu Schneersohn of Warsaw, one of Shneur Zalman's great-great-grandsons, attests to his interest in Moshe.[124] But, notwithstanding the intriguing material Dubnow collected,

Moshe receives no mention in his works, not even in his comprehensive *Toldot hahasidut.* This can be attributed to three factors. First, the cutoff point for Dubnow's book was 1815; as the conversion took place in 1820, there was no need to include it. Second, Shmaryahu Schneersohn repeatedly requested that Dubnow refrain from inquiries about Moshe, due to the preponderance of rumor and legend over fact. Perhaps this convinced Dubnow, even though he did sometimes investigate rumors. And third, Dubnow was well disposed toward intellectually inclined Habad Hasidism and was attracted to Shneur Zalman's charismatic personality.[125] Dubnow may have preferred to keep this episode hidden, rather than spoil the favorable impression of Habad by inserting a sensational, undocumented story. In any event, Shmaryahu Schneersohn's letters preserve an early Habad account of Moshe, which enables the historian to trace the stages of the hasidic memory tradition.

In a 31 May 1890 letter to Dubnow, Schneersohn detailed the biographies of the Habad rebbes at length. In touching upon Shneur Zalman's sons, he was forced, probably unwillingly, to insert the following parenthetical remark: "Regarding his third son Moshe it is best to maintain historical silence, for the details are all obscure and of doubtful facticity."[126] Dubnow nevertheless requested further details on Moshe. Schneersohn begged him not to focus on this figure, whose affairs in no way contributed to Dubnow's proposed history of Hasidism: "Regarding his third son Moshe, I again beg you to remain silent, for everything that happened to him is hidden in fog, and the many contradictory legends make it difficult to arrive at the truth of this matter. And, as your aim is to write the history of Hasidism in general, and of its glorious rabbis, mentioning this episode will bring no benefit, and will only shadow his [Moshe's] reputation. I am confident that you will honor my request."[127] Schneersohn's next letter to Dubnow added further details on Moshe culled from his relatives:

> Regarding Moshe, the son of Shneur Zalman of blessed memory, even if we compiled all the stories we could with difficulty extract a single truthful sentence. But I affirm that I myself heard this in Lubavitch from the admor Rabbi Shmuel, the son of Menahem Mendel of blessed memory. I met with him when I was in Lubavitch about fourteen years ago and he told me the following: "Did you hear the rumor that Reb Moshe died recently in a small town in Volhynia, where he was sheltered in the poorhouse for a number of years? And they did not know his identity until just before his death, because he commanded that the inscription on the gravestone read 'Moshe, son of the admor Shneur Zalman, *ba'al Hatanya* ve-*Hashulhan arukh.*' And this report was confirmed by an official from the local burial society in that town." So he told me. And I did not delve into details or ask him in what town or on what date, or how this report reached him. Therefore I cannot vouch as to whether this story contains a speck of

truth; but among the many legends, we may accept this one too. He who says less will come closer to the truth than he who tells the tale.[128]

This first internal testimony to Moshe's end comes from his close kin. If Schneersohn's memory was reliable, this conversation took place around 1877. Today, we know that the source of the "report" transmitted by Shmuel Schneersohn (the Tsemah Tsedek's youngest son) to his relative Shmaryahu Schneersohn was a hasid named Zvi Chaikin, whose letters will be discussed below. Note that Shmuel—who, as we shall see, took special interest in Moshe—omits to mention where Moshe died. This lacuna was filled at a later date, when Habad tradition linked Moshe to the town of Radomyshl, in Kiev Province. However, Shmaryahu Schneersohn voiced his uncertainty as to the story's accuracy and doubted whether it was possible to arrive at the truth.

As mentioned earlier, Dubnow acceded to Schneersohn's plea and refrained from mentioning Moshe in his studies. But in the margins of Schneersohn's letter, Dubnow penned the following data he had collected for his personal use:

More about Moshe, the son of Shneur Zalman, who, according to the stories, converted, I heard from Rafael Imanuel of St. Petersburg (in winter 1890/1): said Moshe fled from his home to Mogilev, where he observed Greek Orthodox Christianity and stayed in the monastery or in the bishop's home. Then, emissaries sent by the rebbe from Lyady or Lubavitch (1814?) came to redeem him through words or money, and they imagined that he was forced to convert to Christianity. And when they arrived in Mogilev to engage in their intercessory efforts, they were brought to the bishop's home, and he came out to meet them accompanied by the above-mentioned convert Moshe. When the bishop saw the emissaries he crossed himself and made the sign of the cross over Moshe. Then the emissaries said: "Woe to us that we have seen you thus! How did you become caught by heresy?" Moshe answered, "Actually, the bishop made a mistake, because he formed the sign of the cross from the forehead to the navel as is the practice, but this is not according to the Kabbalah, which requires first awakening from below and then from above. Accordingly, the sign of the cross should be made from navel to forehead." The emissaries divined that Moshe had lost his mind. Bitterly disappointed, they returned home.

The story also spread that when Ber seized the reins of power instead of his older brother, Moshe was angered and cried out: "If a goy (Dov Ber was considered to lack scholarly ability) can become rebbe, then the rebbe can become a goy," and he went and converted. And the reason was that Reb Ber the younger [of the two] (whose father, after he achieved fame, married him to the daughter of a wealthy man from Vitebsk) had the support of the wealthy and prominent members; but Reb Moshe, the firstborn, who was married while his father was still poor and unknown and living in poverty in Liozno, only had the support of a minority; therefore Reb Ber seized the rulership. And then Shneur Zalman's disciple Aharon of Staroselye split off from Reb Ber and founded his own sect.[129]

The material collated by Dubnow, which contains the usual confusion of birth order, seemingly adds some new details. The main ones are that the conversion took place in the Russian Church in Mogilev (as we know, this is incorrect; Moshe was baptized in the Catholic Church in Ule), and that the Habad hasidim, knowing nothing of the circumstances of the conversion and thinking it forcible, tried to extract Moshe, but desisted when they realized he was insane. Nor did Dubnow determine when the conversion actually took place (he thought it was around 1814) or establish its underlying motives. One interesting detail is the story of Moshe's kabbalistic expertise in making the sign of the cross, which almost certainly originated with the rumor cited by Gottlober: "They claim that he composed kabbalistic secrets and hints on making the sign of the cross."

It is difficult to ignore the modern interpretive overtones of these late-nineteenth-century accounts of Moshe's story. The pithy witticism about the rebbe who became a goy, first encountered in Perets Smolenskin's poem, certainly cannot be considered reliable historical testimony (after all, who among its reporters could have quoted it precisely as stated?). It must therefore be regarded as an antihasidic joke introduced to the episode after its occurrence,[130] part of a polemical interpretation ascribed to the act of conversion. Nor does the story that "spread" provide historical evidence; it is more in the nature of a folk fable, in tune with the radical socialistic atmosphere of Russia in the early 1890s: Moshe's political protest against the hasidim's preference for a rich ignoramus over an impoverished scholar. But apart from the hasidic tradition that his father favored him, we have no evidence of Moshe's scholarly ability. And certainly, consideration of Dov Ber's writings, letters, and activity, rebuts any claim that he was an ignoramus.[131]

As noted above, Dubnow neither made use of, nor published, these data. Nonetheless, as seen from an April 1910 Yiddish letter from his friend Yehuda Novakovski, this episode continued to pique his interest.[132] In this letter, Novakovski, a native of Chernigov Province and descended from a Habad family, related what his grandfather told his mother, "quietly, sadly, and in a cracked voice." His comment that "despite some slight differences, the story almost replicates what you told me" indicates Dubnow's sustained interest in sources relating to this episode. Novakovski recalled that the story was kept hidden from the children, but that his mother—from whom he heard it—testified that "she remembered the event almost word for word, because its content, and the accompanying secrecy, as well as the deep pain exhibited in speaking of it, left a profound, indelible impression":

Mosheleh, the son of the Alter Rebbe, had a brilliant mind; he was thought the best of the sons. When the Alter Rebbe returned home, *Mosheleh began to act like a fool, and to say incomprehensible things. He said that the old God was dead and that a new God must appear, and similar nonsense.* You can imagine what a storm raged in the house. The Alter Rebbe, of blessed memory, said that this was all the fault of Avraham Hamalakh [the angel]. Moshe finally left the Alter Rebbe's home and no one knew to where he had disappeared. Once the Alter Rebbe joyfully announced to his hasidim: "My Moshe has returned to the straight and narrow." But the hasidim feared to ask for details. Immediately after the rebbe's death a letter arrived from Moshe—from whence it was sent is unknown; he hid this well—which said: "I announce to you that, heaven forfend, no embarrassment will be caused in the world to come to my father of blessed memory because of me." It then became clear that he was living somewhere or other and that he had fully repented. But his traces vanished and what became of Moshe remains unknown to this day.

Both overall and in its details, this story contains no kernel of historical truth, and its writer clearly has no actual knowledge of the history of Hasidism.[133] Interestingly, the conversion receives no mention here. Moshe's tragedy instead focuses on his sudden madness and flight from home, placed in Shneur Zalman's lifetime. Lacking any factual basis, this story represents another innocent attempt by the hasidim in Novakovski's hometown to explain to themselves Moshe's strange behavior.

Dubnow mentioned Moshe again, this time in a letter of 15 November 1912 that Dubnow sent from St. Petersburg to Shmuel Abba Horodezky, his fellow researcher of Hasidism:

Regarding your inquiry about the son of *Hatanya* who converted—his name was Moshe—I can only tell you that I too investigated and found nothing beyond several lines in Avraham Ber Gottlober's memoirs (in *Haboker or*) and fragmentary reports from Schneersohn family members who try to conceal the matter with nonsense. Some recount, for example, that Moshe went mad and abandoned the correct path because his brother Reb Dov Ber was "anointed" rebbe after Shneur Zalman's death, and then shouted, "If the goy has become a rebbe (Dov Ber was no Talmudist and was not fit to tie Moshe's shoelaces) then the rebbe will become a goy." He then went and converted in Mogilev, the provincial capital, and some say he fled to Moscow. In St. Petersburg I have at present found no documentation regarding this matter, and it remains an unsolved mystery to this day.[134]

This letter as well contributes no new information. We have already encountered the rumor concerning Moshe's flight to Moscow in Ruderman's remarks, with which Dubnow was familiar.[135] In any event, it is interesting that, even though he came up empty-handed in St. Petersburg, Dubnow did not abandon his search for archival documentation on Moshe.

Shaul Ginsburg and Zvi Chaikin's "Apocryphal" Letters

The convoluted tale of Moshe acquired yet another twist in January 1931, when the Russian-Jewish historian Shaul Ginsburg published a popular Yiddish article in *Di tsukunft* (The future). In this article on the "legend and the truth regarding the Alter Rebbe's son who converted," Ginsburg surveyed the information known about this affair.[136]

The article opens by noting the difficulties that hamper the reconstruction of the actual events: hasidic literature virtually ignores Moshe, and Habad hasidim are not forthcoming. If coerced, they supply information unwillingly, with a wink or a hint. We, on the other hand, Ginsburg writes, are free to state unequivocally what happened: Moshe converted. Ginsburg could not fix the exact date of the conversion and speculated that it was around 1814, a short time after Moshe's signature last appeared in one of his father's published works;[137] nor could he determine Moshe's motivation for this act. Having failed to garner any intelligence from the hasidic elders, who had certainly heard the story from their fathers and grandfathers, Ginsburg reported that he could only compile the many conjectures. Of these, the main ones ascribed the conversion either to a romantic involvement or to an internal family succession dispute, both of which we have seen in earlier sources.

Finding none of these explanations satisfactory, Ginsburg suggests an entirely different stimulus: events related to the Franco-Russian War. To recall, when the French invaded Byelorussia in 1812, Shneur Zalman and his family fled Lyady. Ginsburg conjectured that Moshe became friendly with a Russian officer or missionary during their wanderings, and that this individual influenced his decision to convert. What transpired afterward remains unclear, though it is certain that Moshe died as a Christian in a Moscow hospital.

But Ginsburg's conjectures are no less speculative than those of his predecessors. First of all, the eight years separating the conversion and that flight make its influence questionable; secondly, as we saw earlier, Moshe did not flee with his father.

However, Ginsburg's main contribution in this article is his Yiddish translation of two previously unknown Hebrew letters composed in 1876–77 by a Habad hasid named Zvi Chaikin[138] and, according to Ginsburg, intended for internal hasidic consumption. In order to downplay and reduce the blow of the conversion, which could not be entirely eliminated, it was necessary to anchor the hagiographic tale of Moshe's repentance in trustworthy "witnesses" to be disseminated among the hasidim—namely, letters and oral rumors. In his assessment of these letters testifying to Moshe's death as a kosher Jew, Ginsburg termed them apocryphal.

Chaikin's first letter, written in early 1876 and addressed to his friend Levi Yitshak,[139] relates a marvelous, moving tale. Two weeks earlier, Chaikin had encountered a rabbi from Ostropol who oversaw fundraising for the land of Israel in Kiev Province. The latter told him that "some thirty years earlier," while he was living in Fastov,[140] a stranger wearing linen clothing and carrying a large staff arrived in town during the summer. This man spoke with no one, and it was not even certain whether he was Jewish. After staying in that town for several weeks—no one knew where he slept—he continued his wanderings. The following winter, shortly before his death in 1827, Mordekhai of Chernobyl visited Fastov. All the townspeople came out to greet him, including that wayfarer, who pushed his way through the crowd in order to reach Rabbi Mordekhai. The zaddik noticed him, "got up, warmly gave him his hand, but spoke not a word with him; they only made signs to each other." The wayfarer subsequently disappeared, and all those present realized that "he was a worthy Jew, but hidden." Naturally, this prompted investigation. It turned out that he slept in the local poorhouse,[141] whose watchman testified: "There were four roofed columns in front of the poorhouse, and when he wanted to sleep, he would command the watchman to tie his hands to each of two columns and each of his legs to another two columns, and that is how he slept."

Several years later, while the narrator was living in Ostropol, he had occasion to return to his father-in-law's house in Fastov. One day that wayfarer entered the house and requested "a small donation for that day's needs." While the narrator was escorting him out of the house, the wayfarer "recited profound Torah [exposition] until he reached the Torah on the fourth leg;[142] he then ceased speaking and left." Several years later the narrator's father-in-law ended up in Radomyshl. There, the members of the burial society informed him that the mysterious itinerant was on his deathbed. He hurried to the poorhouse along with the agents of the burial society, who asked the dying man whether he had any sons who should be informed of his death. He answered, "That's my business; I will inform them myself." When asked what to write on his gravestone, he answered, "I am Moshe, the son of the Rav Hagaon R. Shneur Zalman of Lyady." You must decide, Chaikin concluded his letter, whether or not to show the letter to the admor Shmuel Schneersohn (Moharash).

Shmuel Schneersohn's interest in Moshe's biography emerges clearly from Chaikin's second letter (1877), which he addressed directly to the fourth rebbe. Chaikin first recalls having sent the rebbe information the previous year. He then announces that, in accordance with the rebbe's explicit request, he had traveled to Fastov in order to personally investigate, and collect testimony on, this matter:

> I must inform his honor as to the results of my investigation in the above-mentioned town. The rabbi, Reb Mikhl, the Ostropoler rabbi's father-in-law, who was in Rado-

myshl when the well-known person died, and saw and heard him identify himself before he died, has been dead now for about six years. But his other son-in-law, named Yosef Mikhls, remained in Fastov . . . He is a very important person in that town who also collects money for the Holy Land, and he knew of this matter, as witnessed personally and from his father-in-law's remarks . . . But I did not find him at home, for he was out collecting money as an emissary. However, I spoke of this matter with his son, a valued young scholar, who promised that, as soon as his father returned from his journey, he would inform us by letter whether he affirmed his brother-in-law's statement . . . This young scholar also promised, that, God willing, after Passover his father would be in Radomyshl collecting funds, and he would then investigate the gravesite and ascertain whether or not there is a tombstone there and what the inscription says.

This too that young man did. He approached an elderly man in the town and said to him: "I heard that some time ago there was a man in this town who altered his appearance and dress, and wore despicable clothes and cork shoes on his feet, and spoke with no one, and no one knew who or what he was, until the Maggid, the holy rabbi, Mordekhai of Chernobyl, arrived . . . and that man pushed his way into his presence, and when [the Maggid] saw him he stood up and gave him his hand, and spoke with him in signs, and then he left. All then understood that he was a great man." This is what the young scholar said to the old man and he asked him if this was true, and if he remembered anything of this episode. And the elderly man answered: "It is true and certain, and they said that he was the son of the rabbi of Lyady." That was what he recalled.[143]

As described here, the improbable chain of transmission also lacks internal logic: the original witness (Mikhl of Fastov, the Ostropoler's father-in-law) was dead; his son-in-law (Yosef) was away from home, and only an anonymous elderly local affirmed what appear to be planted recollections of an event. Ginsburg concluded that these letters were exemplars of a widely disseminated hasidic genre. Although the name of the town where the penitent lived and died differed in the story's variants, all shared a similar core: the legend that Moshe repented and was buried as a kosher Jew, which, Ginsburg concluded, left the honor of the dynasty intact.

Certainly, the fact that Zvi Chaikin's identity was unknown heightened Ginsburg's suspicions that these letters were forged. At present, however, we can establish that the hasid Chaikin existed, as did the others mentioned in his letter.[144] Nonetheless, the hagiographic features interwoven into Chaikin's so-called authentic stories—repeated from witness to witness—make it impossible to treat them as valuable testimony from which we can reconstruct aspects of Moshe's past.[145]

Irrespective of their verity, these letters are intriguing for another reason: the date of Chaikin's letter and the story recorded therein are consistent with Shmaryahu Schneersohn's letter to Dubnow, in which he recalled first hearing similar details from Shmuel Schneersohn in 1877. This makes it virtually certain that Chaikin's letters served as Shmuel's source of information.

Chaikin's first letter was penned shortly after the publication of Pesah Ruderman's mocking remarks in 1875, which comprised the second reference to Moshe's conversion in printed Hebrew material. It is at least feasible that the publication of Ruderman's remarks triggered a felt need in the Lubavitch court to formulate an official answer for internal questioners and doubters; it is equally possible that true interest arose in a lost family member's past.[146] Thus full and partial reports circulated—perhaps only among the inner circles—regarding Moshe's repentance and wanderings. By 1880 some of these rumors may also have reached Gottlober, who recorded them.

Moreover, contrary to the setting of Moshe's death in 1878 by the sixth rebbe (Rayyats), Chaikin's letters indicate that, by early 1876, Habad hasidim regarded Moshe as having been long dead. This constitutes yet another example of Rayyats's unreliability as a historical source, not only as an interpreter of history, but also as a preserver of ostensibly straightforward family traditions of births and deaths.[147]

Notwithstanding Ginsburg's firmly expressed opinion about apocryphal letters and a systematic coverup, the existence of letters besides Chaikin's relating to Moshe remains speculative. In this case, however, letters and rumors are interchangeable: in some instances, a letter documents a rumor; in others, a letter forms the basis for a rumor. Indeed, the rumors documented in Chaikin's letters underwent further, sometimes independent, reworking. The next stage in the grounding of the hasidic legend—its integral incorporation into Habad historiography—will be treated below.

The Amplification of Maskilic Legend

Two months after its publication, the Yiddish writer A. Litvin responded to Ginsburg's article.[148] He proposed observing Moshe from a tragic, human perspective: the price Hasidism paid for its revolution in Jewish life. As with every revolution, the harshest price was exacted from the families of the founders and leaders. Not only did Hasidism face external threats (from mitnagedim and maskilim), it also had to deal with divisive internal forces. Entwined with struggles for honor, prestige, and money were conceptual and theological disputes, creating family dramas reminiscent of inheritance disputes in royal courts, dramas that take us behind the scenes of this major socioreligious movement.

Litvin cites additional informants. The writer and psychologist Fischel Schneersohn, also a descendant of Rashaz,[149] recalled that this episode was not discussed in the family circle; he was well aware of it, nonetheless. He also recalled the hasidim telling the tale of a pointed dispute that erupted between Barukh of Mezhibozh, the Besht's grandson, and Shneur Zalman of Lyady against the background of the latter's fundraising attempts in Barukh's territory. In the course of this dispute, Barukh demanded that Rashaz pay him the respect due someone who puts on the Besht's phylacteries; Rashaz responded that Barukh ought to check whether or not the phylacteries had a flaw. When checked, the Hebrew letter *yod* was found to be missing from the headpiece. Enraged, Barukh cursed Shneur Zalman, saying that because of the disqualification of the phylacteries, one of his sons would leave the faith ("You took a *yod* out of my phylacteries, therefore I will take a *yid* [Jew, in Yiddish] from your children").[150] According to Schneersohn, because of this blot, the hasidic elites of Galicia and Volhynia refused to contract marriages with Rashaz's grandchildren; his grandsons therefore sought out superior scholars for their daughters by way of demonstrating that scholarship compensated for this shame.

The information imparted to Litvin by Perets Smolenskin's brother Yehuda Leib Smolenskin is of greater interest.[151] He recounted that Moshe was the most talented of Rashaz's sons, beloved alike by his father and the rank-and-file hasidim. For them, Smolenskin believed, talent, not birthright, determined succession. But Dov Ber, Rashaz's firstborn son, who coveted and won his father's throne, did not accept this principle. And in the course of the dispute Moshe uttered the now familiar witticism: "If a goy can become rebbe, the rebbe can become a goy." After converting, Moshe settled in St. Petersburg. Within a short time he became an archimandrite (or held some other religious title) and served as the leading clergyman at one of the city's major churches. Naturally, Jewish society was in an uproar, and a delegation was dispatched in an attempt to return him to the fold. Moshe refused to admit them and shortly thereafter disappeared entirely from the city. Both the police and the top clergy searched for him in vain. For some time thereafter, Smolenskin related, when a St. Petersburg Russian met a Jew, he would mockingly inquire: "And where is our Moshko? Tell me, where is our Moshko?" A rumor current among maskilim and mitnagedim asserted that Moshe had drowned; others claimed that he had returned to Judaism and secretly made his way to Palestine, where he spent the remainder of his life in prayer and self-mortification.

The new information in Smolenskin's account pertains to Moshe's rapid advance in the hierarchy of the Russian church and his mysterious disappearance. None of this has any firm evidentiary basis; apparently, Smolenskin compiled an eclectic collection of rumors. The two traditions regarding Moshe's end are improbable. The drowning version current among opponents of the hasidism, according to Smolenskin, features the literary, folkloristic motif of "measure for measure": drowning was the appropriate punishment for a convert who was baptized in water.[152] The rumor of his flight to Palestine was probably grounded in the knowledge of his family members' immigration there, and in the Holy Land's status as a refuge for penitents.

Litvin wrote that, separate and apart from the question of its reliability, Smolenskin's account shocked and impressed him. At the time, for fear of injuring Orthodox readers' sensibilities, he dared not publish his data;[153] but once Shaul Ginsburg had gone public, this version of the Moshe affair also deserved a hearing. Litvin thought Chaikin's letters authentic and of historical value; but he agreed with Ginsburg's surmise that Russian officers or clergy who accompanied the family during their flight from Napoleon had influenced Moshe. From his many inquiries in various hasidic courts in Galicia and Lithuania prior to World War I, it became clear to Litvin that this supposition had some basis: from time to time, missionaries in the guise of penitents or religious Jews undergoing a period of exile succeeded in penetrating the hasidic courts and ensnaring innocent hasidim.[154]

The "Flight" of Barukh, Shneur Zalman's Father

We now come to an apparently different episode—only briefly mentioned by Litvin, who did not fully appreciate its significance. It has to do not with Shneur Zalman's son, but rather with his father, Barukh, who late in life made his way from Lithuania to a remote Hungarian town in the Máramaros-Sighet region. Litvin's informant was Rabbi Yekutiel Yehuda Grünwald, a researcher of Hungarian Jewish history.[155] According to Grünwald, Reb Barukh was a confirmed mitnaged who accepted the Vilna Gaon's ruling that Hasidism was a heretical sect; he accordingly demanded that his son abandon Hasidism. Upon his son's rebellious refusal, the father went into exile without informing his family. And, in order to prevent his son from contacting him either during his lifetime or after his death, he refused to reveal his identity during his wanderings. Litvin was unable to recall whether Grünwald related this story as fact or fiction, but he also noted that few verifiable reports had survived, and that this story did not pass the lips of Habad hasidim.

Grünwald published this account in a 1921 article on the history of Hasidism in Hungary:

> A wondrous thing do we find in the history of Hasidism in our land. Rabbi Barukh, the father of the zaddik Shneur Zalman . . . suddenly disappeared from his land . . . fled from his home and left his honored son and came to Hungary, where he worked as a melamed for several years in Munkatsh, and for some years in Solish[156] . . . where he is buried. Everyone finds this astounding. Why did Reb Barukh relinquish his son's status and wealth for a place where he was unknown, and live the grief- and penury-filled life of a melamed? The elders of Solish relate the following tradition: When Reb

Barukh became ill and the burial society saw that his end was near, they asked him where his sons lived, but he refused to reveal this information. Several years later, his son, the zaddik Shneur Zalman of Lyady, came to Solish. He gathered a quorum of ten men, went to his father's grave, removed his shoes and begged his father's forgiveness. Now I think that the explanation is apparent: this elderly man opposed Hasidism, and when he saw that his sons did not heed him, he left them and their wealth and came to Hungary, where Hasidism had spread less widely.[157]

Naturally, Habad historiography places this story in an entirely different light. According to Hayyim Meir Heilman, the author of *Beit Rabbi*, what occasioned Barukh's departure was his inability to tolerate the honor bestowed on him by his son; accordingly, he left Liozno, where Rashaz was then living, and "wandered afar and went into exile from town to town. And everywhere he went, when he came to the synagogue all recognized that this was no ordinary pauper . . . until he came to Hungary, to a town named Solish . . . where he remained for several years until his death . . . and they inquired whether he had sons and where they resided in order that they be informed of his death. And Reb Barukh told them that he had four sons in Russia, all rabbis (and one of our rabbis related that he stated: two must be informed, one requires only a hint, and one does not need to be informed, as he will know on his own)."[158]

We have here two divergent historiographical traditions, each of which suggests a different interpretation for an undisputed historical fact: Barukh's burial in the remote Hungarian town of Solish. Of equal historical value, neither the antihasidic nor the hasidic interpretation allows us to reconstruct events, but only sheds light on trends of polemical and apologetic memory.[159] Whatever the reasons for Barukh's departure and wandering, hasidic traditions reveal surprising similarities between the portrayal of the grandfather's death and the expiatory death of Moshe, who seemingly followed in his footsteps. Both grandfather and grandson cut themselves off from their families in mysterious circumstances, went into exile, lived in total anonymity, and even refused to reveal their identity with their dying breath. Both requested that only their first names be engraved on their tombstones,[160] and both stated that there was no need to inform their families, as whoever needed to would know on his own.

The tale of Rashaz, the admired leader of Byelorussian hasidim—thousands of whose followers bowed to his authority—who failed miserably on his home ground because neither his father nor his son followed his path, is certainly dramatic and tragic. But before the observer gives free rein to psycho-historical and literary insights, we must remember that the attribution of mitnagedism to Barukh is without foundation, and that Moshe left the fold after his father's death, rather than during his lifetime.

In concluding this section devoted to the historian's workshop, it is necessary to note that, by and large, historical scholarship in the past generation has paid scant attention to Moshe, touching on him only in passing.[161] Yisrael Klausner's treatment of the episode exemplifies the discomfort even straightforward historians experienced. In a 1943 monograph on Moshe's grandson Hayyim Zvi Schneersohn, himself a colorful personality, Klausner did not hesitate to explicitly mention the conversion, quoting the testimony of Tuvia Solomon, a Jerusalem elder acquainted with Hayyim Zvi: "With that son of the Rabbi of Lyady there was an episode that grieved the family and the Habad hasidim: he converted . . . and later repented."[162] Thirty years later, when a second edition of this work was published by Mossad Harav Kook, this modest comment was rewritten from an apologetic standpoint: Moshe was not mentioned by name, his conversion made to disappear, and the episode was simply termed "a disaster."[163]

"The Time Has Come for Moshe's Story to Be Revealed": Hasidic Memory Traditions

The Habad traditions on the matter of Moshe's conversion are especially complex. Understandably, the creation of this tangled weave of apologetic and didactic traditions cannot be divorced from the historical or historiographical awareness of leading Habad spokesmen. If other hasidic circles would have entirely hidden such an event, Habad's intense involvement in history, self-documentation, and invention of the past made this episode impossible to ignore. This fostered the creation of a new, more palatable tradition that combined masking of the truth with a polemic targeting maskilic and academic interpretations, and which engaged in an attempt to derive positive lessons from this dismaying affair.

It was its debut in modern historiographical works on Hasidism that forced Habad spokesmen to confront the Moshe episode squarely. Prior to that point, it was possible to maintain a smoke screen; the episode was not recorded, and whispered rumors alone were exchanged among the few individuals in the know. Familiar not just with the oral rumors and Chaikin's letters, but also with the printed Hebrew material by Smolenskin, Ruderman, and Gottlober, the inventors of the Habad memory tradition naturally distilled from the latter what suited their needs. Thus, Gottlober's description of Moshe's going into exile dovetailed with the testimony from Chaikin's letters and with the apologetic need to fashion a happy ending: indeed, there was an episode, but it ended well.

The Habad version of Moshe's fate—whose precursors we have already met in the letters of the hasidim Chaikin and Shmaryahu Schneersohn—had

FIG. 2.7. Rabbi Hayyim Meir Heilman, the author of *Beit Rabbi*

its origins in the court of Shmuel Schneersohn. It was formulated and published in two main versions: in the 1902 edition of *Beit Rabbi* by Hayyim Meir Heilman, the most important biographical work on the Habad rebbes; and in a 1942 letter by Yosef Yitshak Schneersohn (Rayyats), which provided Moshe with an alternative biography.[164]

Beit Rabbi*'s Blurring of the Truth*

Notwithstanding its brevity, Heilman's treatment of this episode conveys his barely concealed discomfort. He outlines Moshe's family tree, noting that Moshe was a signatory (along with his brothers) to the introduction to the first edition of his father's halakhic work *Shulhan arukh haRav*, and of the approbation to the first edition of the *Tanya*, published after Shneur Zalman's death. Heilman goes on to say:

> What happened to him afterward is well known. And it caused our rabbis and our flock great grief, and he was saved after great effort with the help of God, and since then his whereabouts remain unknown. And they sent the members of his household to the Holy Land . . . Indeed, in recent years it has become known that he stayed in the towns of Poland, and went in exile from place to place, or was in the forests, etc., and would come to town to beg for donations for his basic needs, meager bread and scant water, whether for weekdays or the Sabbath, and if they wished to give him more he refused to take it on any account. And he slept in the study house with a stone for a pillow and bound his legs with rope. No one knew who he was or what he was doing,

only a few individuals knew that he was our rebbe's son and they said that he strongly resembled our rebbe in his looks.[165] He was actually in the vicinity of the towns of Kiev and Zhitomir, and was spotted on several occasions in Cherkas at the home of the holy rabbi Yaakov Yisrael,[166] and in Chernobyl at the home of the holy rabbi Aharon.[167]

Toward the end of his life he was taken ill in a town near Zhitomir. Upon realizing that he was at death's door, they called in the burial society. Before he died they inquired as to his name and that of his father so that they could be inscribed on the tombstone. He replied, "Write Moshe on the gravestone, and that you do not know his father's name; write thusly." Next they inquired where his family resided so that they might be informed, and he answered: "They will know on their own." Then he died. And his honored resting place is there . . . And when I was in Berdichev I saw the elderly men who knew and saw him and they recounted all this regarding him, adding many appalling details.[168]

This account leaves the reader with the distinct impression that Heilman knew more than he was willing to impart. Although he did not deny the fact of the conversion, he refrained from naming it, in line with his dichotomous worldview with its "love of the truth above all," on the one hand, tempered by his sense that it was not necessary to tell the entire truth, on the other. With regard to disconcerting matters, he wrote: "It is unnecessary to publicize the inadvertent sins of the great, worthy rabbis. Of these sins, only a modicum should be revealed and the majority hidden."[169] At the same time, Heilman went to great lengths to provide firmer, and ostensibly more reliable, grounding for the story of Moshe's exile by citing the testimony of the elderly men who were acquainted with him. Recall that this story, first written and published by Gottlober, was consistent with Chaikin's letters and with the rumors current in Moharash's court. Heilman skirted the obvious questions: what terrible sin made Moshe go into exile, from what was he saved, and what occasioned great grief? No individual would mortify himself or seek penitence for a minor sin. As molded by Heilman, the story of Moshe's death—for which he provides no date—is the hagiographic story of the death of a hidden saint. As noted earlier, the shaping of this story reflects the decisive influence of the description of the death of Rashaz's father Barukh, who also died in exile and similarly refused to divulge his name and lineage on his deathbed.[170]

Perhaps his lack of knowledge as to the conversion's exact date made Heilman link the immigration of Moshe's family to Palestine with the grief he had caused, creating the impression that this was forced on them. But, as we have seen, the two events are unconnected; his family left Russia around 1843, twenty-three years after Moshe's conversion.

FIG. 2.8. Rabbi Yosef Yitshak Schneersohn (Rayyats), the sixth Habad rebbe

Yosef Yitshak Schneersohn's Trail of Denial

In subsequent Habad historiography, Heilman's account underwent apologetic expansion in a tradition invented by the sixth Habad rebbe, Yosef Yitshak Schneersohn, who has been characterized as someone who "subordinated the writing and documentation of history to the needs of the making of history."[171] An independent Habad tradition corroborates this rebbe's particular interest in the story of Moshe and in the revelation of a "new truth" regarding his matter: "On the occasion of the founding of the Hatamim association, the admor Rayyats said to the rabbi of Fastov, *'the time has come for Moshe's story to be revealed.'* And he showed him eleven hasidic volumes composed by Moshe containing lofty matters. And he added that no one else knows of them."[172] Rayyats alludes here to the existence of apocryphal writings by Moshe known to him alone. These writings, which encompass not only Torah exposition and Hasidism but also "lofty matters," prove Moshe's Torah erudition.[173] Like other suddenly discovered early writings, they are grasped as an authoritative source with the ability to overturn subversive interpretations. But the rebbe does not specify what makes this the "time" to reveal the truth. The Hatamim association mentioned in this tradition was founded in 1934;[174] but three years before Rayyats's comments, Shaul Ginsburg had published his article on Moshe's conversion and the hasid Chaikin's letters. It seems likely that this article had come to Rayyats's attention and catalyzed his attempt to recast Moshe's reputation.[175]

The first documented evidence of Rayyats's treatment of Moshe's story comes from a letter posted to one of Chaikin's descendants in Shevat 1922. Rayyats wrote:

When Czar Alexander I was in Babinovichi[176] . . . the Mitteler Rebbe came there for an audience with the czar. His brother, the holy rabbi Reb Moshe, accompanied him. And the bishop of Vyazma (who was expert in the holy tongue and whose knowledge of Judaism outstripped that of the bishop of Smolensk)[177] envied him. Aided by the governors of Vitebsk and Mogilev Provinces, [the bishop] engaged in a religious debate with the holy rabbi, Reb Moshe. The debate concerned principles of faith. They were silenced, and the holy rabbi, Reb Moshe, prevailed. But after this victory the bishop dealt with him shrewdly, and the governors arranged another debate (to which Moshe was forced to agree) in Vyazma. Here they spread libelous tales of their victory . . . and he was placed under arrest—his pleas were all to no avail—until one of the prisoners in his room died suddenly. And amid the confusion and panic, the holy rabbi Reb Moshe left the prison, and went to Orsha.[178] There they informed him that the authorities had been seeking him, so he went on to Volhynia Province.[179]

As we shall see, this version contains the kernel of the expanded, detailed story later developed by Rayyats. Entirely directed at creating a counter-history for Moshe, it engages in a polemic with the other version.

The next stage in the expansion of the legend came on 9 Heshvan 1942, in the form of a letter sent to a member of the Montreal Schneersohn family. This letter contains Rayyats's answer to a question regarding "the head of our family . . . Rabbi Moshe":

I learned much from what I heard from my honored grandmother . . . Rivka . . . who heard it from . . . her father-in-law . . . the Tsemah Tsedek . . . regarding the fit of jealousy he had—namely, the holy rabbi, Rabbi Moshe—when the governor of Mogilev Province presented him and his honorable exalted brother . . . to Czar Alexander I when the latter visited the city of Babinovichi, which is near Lubavitch. He [Moshe] felt that they had not been suitably honored, for he presented them after the nobles. Moshe berated the governor in the presence of the chief bishop of Smolensk, for he [Moshe] spoke several languages.[180] And the bishop insulted Moshe as well as the Law of Moshe, and Moshe made a biting reply. And this sparked a religious debate that was held during the month of Heshvan in 1815. Held in the monastery in the town of Jarcevo,[181] Smolensk Province, in the presence of the leading clergy of the provinces of Smolensk, Tula, and Nezhin,[182] this debate lasted for about a month. After he defeated the priests, they decided to transfer him to one of the districts in Kiev Province or to Vladimir in inner Russia.[183] And following the synod's[184] order to transfer him to Vladimir, on the fourth day, while closely guarded by two priests and by armed soldiers, while they were lodged in the village of Andreyevka, near Moscow, a deep sleep fell on all, and the holy rabbi, Rabbi Moshe, escaped. And God, blessed be He, gave him strength, and he ran for nearly a day without noticing the cold or the deep snow on the way—later he himself wondered how he ran and on what paths—until arriving in the town of Oryol.[185] There he made himself known to Rabbi Moshe Leib Jacobson, from Pogar,[186] who hid him in his home for several days. From thence he made his way to Volhynia. *The date on which the holy rabbi, Rabbi Moshe, was rescued was Wednesday night, 19 Kislev 1815*. His family traveled to the Holy Land . . . and he went into exile from 1815 until Sivan 1878. He was born in the town of Liozno in 1784 and died in 1878 in Radomyshl, in Kiev Province, where he is buried.[187]

Before addressing the main points of this letter, note that the sixth Habad rebbe names Moshe "the holy rabbi." This must be equated with an unequivocal denial of the act of conversion; otherwise, how could the rebbe bestow such an honorific on Moshe? He had the option of refraining from its use; alternatively, he could have called him "Reb Moshe," as Heilman does in *Beit Rabbi*. This denial of the conversion—both here and elsewhere—strikingly reflects Rayyats's deliberate dissociation of Moshe's exile from any hint of a need for repentance. In the absence of sin, repentance is unnecessary; therefore, the purpose of Moshe's exile was not religious mortification but to hide from the authorities.[188] Moreover, the story is framed in opposition to the maskilic interpretation, which attributed the conversion to the disdain of Moshe, the scholar, for his brother Dov, the ignoramus. Here the opposite is the case: it was the governor's disparaging behavior toward his brother Dov Ber that sparked Moshe's zeal and ultimately led to the dramatic events portrayed here.

The forced, polemical nature of this story is grounded in Rayyats's inability (or lack of desire) to detach it from its original context: the arena of Christian-Jewish conflict. But instead of the embarrassing, inexplicable conversion, Moshe now stands at the center of a different conflict: a medieval-style religious debate, in which Moshe and Judaism emerge with the upper hand.

The questionable reliability of Rayyats's sources is the least of this story's many weaknesses. Even if we accept this train of transmission from his grandmother, who heard them from her father-in-law, what we have here is a century-old collection of rumors. More problematic is the absence of any evidence of a month-long interfaith debate held in some monastery. No Jewish-Christian interfaith debates ever took place in czarist Russia; we can speculate that this story adopts the literary framework of famous religious polemics (like the one held in Barcelona in 1263, in which Nahmanides defeated the priests but was forced to flee to the Holy Land). Rayyats's dramatic tale is therefore molded in typical hagiographic fashion: the hero possesses the emulation-worthy attributes of ingenuity, devotion, and courage.

One of this story's outstanding hagiographic markers is the claim that

Moshe's release occurred on the 19th of Kislev, the same date on which his father had been released from jail in 1798, from that time on an annual day of celebration in Habad.[189] Additional allusions to Rashaz can be identified in the plot to exile Moshe to Vladimir and in his bold escape to Oryol; these were the towns through which Shneur Zalman and his family passed while fleeing Napoleon's forces.[190] This transforms Moshe's flight into a remake of his father's. The whitewashing of Moshe in this tradition incorporates not only his extraordinary courage but also a typological resemblance between him and his eminent father.

Above all, the story's greatest weakness lies in its failure to clear Moshe of the stain of conversion. Undoubtedly aware of the conversion, Rayyats did not know exactly when it occurred, and his mistaken ascription of the conversion to around 1814 apparently derives from Shaul Ginsburg's article. In any event, if the supposed debate was held in 1815 and immediately followed by exile, Moshe clearly could not have converted a year earlier. Moshe's disappearance is adequately explained as ensuing from the debate and his escape from imprisonment. Evidently, Rayyats was unaware of Ribal's letter to Yosef Perl, which attributed the conversion to 1820. This dating, now supported by the archival evidence, would have contradicted and spoiled Rayyats's story, for if this debate ever took place, it could have had nothing to do with Moshe's conversion five years later. Moreover, it appears that Rayyats was also unfamiliar with the letter penned by Moshe's mother, which has Moshe recovering from illness in 1817 and returning to his home in Ule,[191] the same year Moshe was purportedly in hiding from the czarist regime in the villages of Volhynia. Clearly, Rayyats's version of events never took place.[192]

Rayyats put forth this version of Moshe's involvement in a religious debate in other writings, some of which predate the above-cited letter. A treatise titled "The Minsk Debate," apparently written as early as 1931, mentions a similar tradition, which places the "religious debate" in 1817: "In the summer of 1817, when the Russian czar Alexander I traveled from St. Petersburg to Kiev via Vitebsk and Babinovichi . . . the holy Mitteler Rebbe was also invited to be among those at the welcoming ceremony . . . But the Mitteler Rebbe did not speak Russian; accordingly, his brother Rabbi Moshe, who knew many languages, took charge and negotiated with the government authorities, which later caused the religious debate that forced Moshe to disappear, and his family moved to the Holy Land."[193]

Moshe's story underwent reworking in Rayyats's pseudohistorical work *Divrei hayamim hahem* (History of those days). Published posthumously in 1964, it was based on the rebbe's notes. Although undated, it appears likely that these notations postdate Rayyats's arrival in the United States in 1940. In them, he continued to shape the fictional story of Moshe in greater detail.

What distinguishes this version is its revelation of Rayyats's initial, hesitant steps in framing Moshe's biography as someone on the cutting edge of the Christian-Jewish polemic. Using the same literary motifs from which the above-noted story of the debate was concocted, Rayyats now moves the scene back two decades, to Rashaz's second arrest in 1800. Here, too, Rayyats was unable to entirely avoid hinting at Moshe's embarrassing future. But although well aware of this future, he attempts to conceal it from his audience.

According to this version, Moshe accompanied Shneur Zalman on his journey to St. Petersburg in the role of translator.[194] And indeed, "Rabbi Moshe found favor in the eyes of the princes because of his handsome looks, his temperate manners, and his well-ordered speech which showed his overtaking of all in mastery of a pure style of expression in the language of the land. Even more surprising to them was his ability to speak elegant French." Two educated priests were among Rashaz's interrogators, and their questions focused on highlighting the contrast between Judaism and Christianity. Although Rashaz did everything in his power to avoid this polemic, of Moshe it was said:

> He was by nature argumentative, especially regarding religious matters in which he had become interested some three years earlier. He acquired . . . some books in Hebrew and in French . . . and *he acquired expertise in their arguments for their faith*, in their scriptural proofs, and in countering their arguments . . . The priests became aware of Rabbi Moshe's wondrous knowledge of the principles of their faith, and that he was well versed in negating their strongest arguments. And they spoke his praises to one of the senior clergy . . . Rabbi Moshe visited this senior clergyman on several occasions—without the knowledge of our rebbe [Rashaz]—and Rabbi Moshe bested him in debate. Rabbi Moshe's explanations . . . found favor in [Rashaz's] eyes for their logic and common sense, but his style of speech based on his sense of self-worth, *which accentuated his arrogance*, did not find favor in his [father's] eyes . . . *and he berated him for that.*[195]

In this fictional story, Moshe becomes friendly with, and finds favor in the eyes of, the St. Petersburg nobility. He spends hours in their private libraries "reading books that interested him, including *books of faith and heresy in various religions, which held special fascination for him.*" Once Moshe visited the home of "Count Arkadii Zubarov,"[196] where he became involved in an interfaith debate. Moshe spoke heatedly, "and spelled out the deceitfulness and cruelty of the Jesuits as compared to the evil of the Christian priests," but his remarks left "an unpleasant impression" on his audience. The count next arranged for a debate to be held between Moshe and the count's personal priest. Moshe rose to the challenge; his acute speech "made a strong impression on those gathered there, so that even those great in wisdom and in Christian doctrines and faith were at a loss to answer; but they bore a grudge against Rabbi Moshe."[197]

Dissatisfied, Count Zubarov arranged for another debate, this time involving some forty participants. Notwithstanding Moshe's impressively lucid explanations for the development of the Jewish faith and for the mistaken Christian interpretation of scriptural verses as referring to their messiah, his audience was determined to see his defeat. A wealthy hasid named Mordekhai of Lepel,[198] who witnessed this debate, warned Moshe of the potentially explosive outcome of his actions. On finding that his warning had no impact on Moshe, Mordekhai was then forced to approach Rashaz. The Alter Rebbe's response was to recount an event from his past, aimed at expanding the historical backdrop and at presaging for him—and for the readers of Rayyats's book, who knew how to understand one thing from another—what would transpire with regard to Moshe.

As transmitted by Rayyats, Shneur Zalman's fictional memoirs ostensibly contain a unique historical datum: ten of the Maggid of Mezhirech's disciples banded together to wage war against the mitnagedim and decided on the radical step of excommunicating the Vilna Gaon. Only Rashaz's intervention prevented this drastic action: "After the decree of excommunication declared in Vilna in 1783,[199] ten of the elders of the holy group, the disciples of our teacher the Maggid, gathered and decided to place an actual ban on the Vilna Gaon according to tradition . . . Two of the holy circle approached me to join in and I refused. My son Moshe, then about three years of age, was standing nearby, and one of the two angrily said, 'The desecration of the divine name that you fear, will come from him [Moshe].' I replied, 'God will not heed, and deliverance comes from God.'" And for those for whom these hints did not suffice, the writer provided a note: "Such a ban uproots the excommunicate from his heavenly soul, heaven forfend! . . . And when the light of the soul in the body is cut off from the soul's root and being, *then the person excommunicated must inevitably convert, heaven forfend.* And to such desecration of the divine name, our holy admor could by no means agree. And this angered the Polish zaddikim."[200]

Only someone aware of the actual outcome could ascribe expertise in Christian doctrines to Moshe, whose fate involved eventual misuse of this knowledge. Rayyats was certainly cognizant of, and attempted to refute, the rumors that Gottlober published concerning Moshe: the "claim that he composed kabbalistic secrets and hints on making the sign of the cross." Rayyats's tales therefore serve a dual purpose. For those lacking knowledge of Moshe's true fate, they are hagiographic stories that glorify an outstanding personality, a descendant of the most prominent Habad family, who publicly sanctifies the divine name. For the minority in the know, who were aware of the bitter truth, this is a morality tale with a hidden polemical message: do not endanger yourself by seeking things beyond your ken. Moshe—the beloved and talented, but arrogant, son—garnered knowledge of Christian writings and was himself entrapped. It was therefore preferable to maintain distance from dangerous spheres and not to depend on your powers of faith, for that way may lie unthinkable desecration of the divine name. Naturally, this was not uttered aloud, but anyone familiar with the Moshe affair could read between the lines.

In addition to its didactic message, this story reflects historiographical distress regarding Moshe's motives for apostasy. Rayyats provides two, contradictory explanations—both covert and identifiable only by those who already know the truth. The first blames Moshe for the conversion, making it a delayed reaction to the poison of heresy he imbibed while acquiring expertise in Christianity, heretical works, and general knowledge. The second imputes the blame not to Moshe but to an angry curse uttered by the Maggid's disciples, because Rashaz had foiled their attempt to excommunicate the Vilna Gaon.

This second explanation makes Moshe the sacrificial victim on the altar of his father's refusal to participate in the ban, which could have brought terrible desecration of the divine name: possible apostasy by the outstanding rabbi, the Vilna Gaon. The fact that this event purportedly took place when Moshe was three years old largely relieves Moshe of responsibility for his action, making it a predetermined, and inevitable, act. This not only clears Moshe's reputation, it also serves as a polemical response to the anti-Habad witticism linked to Barukh of Mezhibozh's curse that one of Shneur Zalman's sons would abandon his people.[201] Not just a personal spat between Shneur Zalman and an arrogant zaddik, hurt by the fact that his vaunted phylacteries turned out to be defective, this was rather an earthshaking matter involving a ban on the Vilna Gaon, which could potentially wreak disaster on all Jews. In rising above petty vengeance, Rashaz prevented disaster, but his son paid the price. Indeed, other Habad sources take up and expand the story of the ban on the Vilna Gaon, linking it directly to Moshe's fate.[202]

But the varying, even contradictory, pseudohistorical explanations provided by Rayyats for the Moshe episode trouble only the outsider observer. As a rebbe conversing with his hasidim, or writing personal letters in answer to queries or notes consigned to a drawer, he is bound neither to historical reconstruction nor accuracy. Regarding the zaddik Yisrael of Ruzhin, his son recounted that it was his father's practice to recite his teachings and stories in different variations, as "the zaddikim tell their tales to fit the needs of the moment."[203] Rayyats was no exception. His writings are not a trustworthy source for study of the past, but rather recruited, leisure-time literature that, by providing a fictional picture of the past, meets the changing needs of the present.

Local and Familial Memory Traditions

In addition to the two, already mentioned, basic Habad sources—*Beit Rabbi* and the writings of Rayyats—other traditions blossomed, aimed at fleshing out the Moshe episode and adapting it to didactic hasidic needs. The complex subtlety of this process of amplification and dissemination through oral and written rumor makes it difficult to reconstruct. Lacking chronological order, these traditions combine—whether in sophisticated or clumsy fashion—actual facts and testimony with various literary, folkloristic, or hagiographic motifs.

The letters of the hasid Zvi Chaikin constitute the earliest literary exemplars of this phenomenon, but there were additional manifestations of Moshe's story. All share the grounding of a good end for Moshe, and most have the same setting: Ukrainian towns. This reflects a characteristic feature of hagiography: the creation of local traditions linking the hero's birth, youth, life, or death to a particular town. In Moshe's case, many traditions lead to the town of Radomyshl in Kiev Province, some 45 kilometers northeast of Zhitomir.

The "Graybeard" of Radomyshl's Tale

Rayyats's 1942 letter contains a lengthy addition by the editors, taken from what they term "notes by our rabbi from summer 1908 regarding the above matter."[204] Essentially, these notes are nothing more than another compilation of traditions augmenting earlier ones on Moshe's exile. As mentioned above, the exile tradition contradicts the alternative biography marketed by Rayyats—which denies the sin of conversion entirely—for if there was no sin, what sparked a need for punishment, and what occasioned Moshe's need for redemption through mortification? In any event, neither Rayyats nor the editors of his letters paid attention to this inconsistency.

The bulk of the rebbe's notes comprise stories he heard in the summer of 1907 or 1908 from Nahum of Radomyshl, a Habad hasid known as "the graybeard" (*hayashish*).[205] He told a tale of a strange ascetic—nicknamed *der heykhe zeyde* (the tall grandfather)—who lived in the attic of the Chernobyl study house in Radomyshl. Summer and winter found him sitting on the beams that supported the roof, and "he would tie himself to the beams . . . so that he would not fall . . . He would tie his left foot to the beam on which he sat during the day while he slept."

The "graybeard" described the ascetic as follows: "He was very tall and big-boned. But he was nothing but skin and bones; his face was ruddy and yellow; his beard long with some white and some blond hairs." He would mortify himself, eating and drinking small quantities and, "while eating, would tie his left leg to the table leg." He used the charity money given him "to buy wood and chickens for poor women who had just given birth." Toting a heavy sack filled with books and treatises over his shoulder, he wandered between three towns: Ovruch, Chernobyl, and Mozyr.[206] "Not a soul knew who he was . . . but our compatriots . . . knew that he was the son of our master, our great rabbi Reb Moshe, of blessed memory, the youngest son of our eminent rabbi."

The "graybeard" further related that the wayfarer would don two pairs of phylacteries at the same time, as was the Sephardic custom. He never changed his clothes or cut his hair, and the elders of that place recounted that "he was there for about thirty years, and arrived in those very clothes." He was never called up to the Torah except for the Day of Atonement 1854, which turned out to be the year of his death. After his death in Iyyar 1855, he was buried in Radomyshl, near the grave of the zaddik Zeev Wolf of Zhitomir, "and a large tree grew on his grave." The elders also said that close to his death, the members of the burial society inquired: "Does his honor have family that should be informed? And he answered that he had family and that they would know by themselves. They then asked what to write on the headstone. He replied: 'Here lies Moshe,' nothing more."[207]

Although there is no indication of the "graybeard's" age, based on his lineage it appears that in summer 1908 he was almost a hundred years old.[208] Even if his mind and memory remained unclouded, his testimony is not absolutely reliable. From his descriptions emerges a picture of an ascetic, of the type known as "the silent one," found in numerous eighteenth- and nineteenth-century Jewish towns.[209] Unaffiliated with any faction in the community, this ascetic maintained total anonymity and entered into no local economic, communal, or social ties. Even if Habad hasidim were convinced that the mysterious wayfarer in this case—if he ever existed—was Moshe, the proofs are tenuous. Nonetheless, it is not the features that this early tradition shares with previous Habad memory traditions, such as the binding of the ascetic's arms and legs, that make it of interest; rather, its discrepancies with Rayyats's later version are striking. These include a different date of death for Moshe—1855, not 1878—and a different date for the beginning of his exile. According to the Radomyshl elders cited by the "graybeard," Moshe lived in their midst for about thirty years, beginning around 1824 and not 1817, as in Rayyats's later version. Chronologically, this memory tradition is more consistent with the facts known from other sources: we know that Moshe's conversion took place in 1820, and if he repented and went into exile, this probably occurred soon thereafter. The supposed date of death is also more logical, for according to Rayyats, Moshe died at the ripe old age of ninety-six.

But this identification of the "silent" wayfarer as Moshe seems doubtful.

The wayfarer himself never indicated in any way that this was the case and, with the exception of the geographical area and the local Habad hasidim's conviction that he was the "son of their master," there is no proof that he was Moshe. And as explained above, the story of his death, especially his inexplicable refusal to inform his family of his impending demise, is hagiographical in nature. Moreover, the tradition identifying Moshe's burial place in Radomyshl—next to that of Zeev Wolf, a disciple of the Maggid of Mezhirech and the author of the hasidic work *Or hameir*—is problematic because Zeev Wolf was buried in his hometown, Zhitomir.[210]

Thus, the tale of the "graybeard" follows, and freely reworks, the traditions documented in Chaikin's letters. Perhaps this graybeard was one of the elderly men who purportedly knew and saw him, and upon whom Heilman relied for his description of Moshe in *Beit Rabbi.* As noted, Heilman places Moshe's exile in the same geographical region, and casts the story of Moshe's death and conversation with the burial society in a similar mold.

A Madman or One of the Thirty-six Hidden Saints?

Like the tradition of the "graybeard," additional written hasidic sources on Moshe have their origins in oral familial traditions passed down from generation to generation.[211] The following example comes from the Habad *Sefer hatse'etsa'im* (Book of descendants):

> It is told that the holy rabbi Rabbi Moshe, may he rest in peace, once came to Bialystok during the years of his exile. Before he arrived Rabbi Avraham Abele Kosovsky of Bialystok intuited his coming and announced that an important guest was on his way to the town and must be greeted. Suddenly an old Jew carrying a sack on his shoulder appeared. To everyone's great surprise, Rabbi Avraham Abele went over to him; they whispered in each other's ear and parted. Only after they parted did Rabbi Avraham tell them that this was the holy rabbi, Rabbi Moshe, the son of our Alter Rebbe, may he rest in paradise.
>
> It is also related: individuals who met him in the towns where he spent the years of exile, testified that he ate only dry bread and fish stock even on the Sabbath. When asked how long he intended to continue this practice, he replied: "to the end."[212]

Regarding the first tradition, which transplants Moshe from the southern part of the Pale of Settlement to Bialystok, in northeastern Poland, the author notes that he heard it from his father, who heard it from Rabbi Kosovsky's descendants.[213] With regard to the second tradition, he states that he cannot remember its precise source.[214] Clearly, these are variations on the theme of exile first found in Chaikin's letters and Gottlober's memoirs, and elaborated in other internal hasidic traditions like the ones attributed to the "graybeard" of Radomyshl and "the elderly men" that Heilman encountered in Berdichev. Both their lengthy transmission and the shaky foundation of the identification make it difficult to place trust in these rumor-based traditions.

Another tradition of this type is cited by Yeshayahu Halevi Horowitz. The chain of tradition proceeded from Horowitz, a Habad hasid, rabbi, and author who was born in Safed, back to his friend Aharon Shub of Tiberias. The latter related in turn that he had heard the following story in his youth from a hasidic Safed elder named Yaakov Kamenitser:

> He recounted that he was among the young scholars studying in the Kamenets study house. Once a pauper came who spent all day and all night in the study house . . . and also fasted frequently, occasionally partaking of what generous women brought to the poor. This pauper always kept his prayer shawl over his head and his face hidden. When the young scholars experienced difficulty with some Torah matter they would ask him to clarify [it], but he spoke with no one and only hinted that they should bring him paper and ink . . . Once . . . the above-mentioned Reb Yaakov bent under his prayer shawl in order to see his face and was seized with fear and trembling, and had to keep himself from falling, for his face was like the noonday sun . . . Afterwards someone arrived from a different town. When told of this wondrous thing, he replied that this person had also stayed in their town for a time and that it had become known to them that he was Moshe, the son of Admor Hazaken.[215]

The Kamenets in question is Kamenets Podolsk, in Podolia. Obviously, this story has no basis in fact. It is but another reflection of the Moshe narrative that places him in exile in the towns of the Ukraine, living an ascetic life, studying the Torah day and night in the study house, and answering the questions put to him in writing, but generally remaining silent. He keeps his face hidden and does not reveal his identity, which becomes known "afterwards."

Another version, of uncertain origin and background, comes from an anonymous hasid, who claims to have met an individual named "Mikhael Leib." Upon identifying his interlocutor as a Ḥabad hasid, this Mikhael Leib relayed the following information about Moshe:

> While visiting my father-in-law in Fastov, I heard that there was an old man there, the son of Admor Hazaken, and that when he begged, he would take no more than a kopeck . . . He dressed in white linen and even wore linen shoes, which stayed clean . . . Generally, he spent the day walking in the forest and would come to the poorhouse in the evening; he would then tie one leg to one beam and the other to a second beam, and sleep in that fashion . . . *Some said that he was mad; others that he was one of the thirty-six hidden saints.* Once the zaddik Mordekhai of Chernobyl came to Fastov and was lying sick in bed, and everyone came to be greeted by him. When

the zaddik saw that individual he greeted him, said "Aha," and they spoke to each other with signs. Then that person left. From that point on it was more emphatically stated that he was a hidden saint. Subsequently, it was persistently said that he was the son of Admor Hazaken.

Once when I was at my father-in-law's house that person came to beg for alms . . . As I accompanied him out he expounded a teaching on the four legs of the divine chariot, but stopped in the middle, saying "enough." I heard afterwards that he went to Radomyshl . . . and that he died there. That is the tale one Mordekhai Leib told me.

Sometime later, when I was in the presence of the admor Moharash . . . I told him of this, and he asked me to investigate this matter when I visited those places. On one occasion when I was in Kiev, I traveled by postal coach to Radomyshl. I entered the study house and inquired whether anyone remembered an elderly man named Moshe. And they said to me, "You must be asking about the son of Admor Hazaken." And I asked, "How do you know?" . . . They said: "Everyone knows that he was the son of Admor Hazaken." And they showed me an old man, and a beadle who was not particularly elderly, who had known him. And they told me as above that he used to wear white clothing . . . and that he did not attend the Torah reading lest they call him up to the Torah, which would force him to reveal his father's name. When asked for his family name he remained silent, and at times he protested, saying: "What good would it do for you to know?" He slept between the beams of the study house attic as related above. His hair was white from age and he had clearly been blond in his youth. He had long fingers. Before his death they asked him from whence he came, so that they could inform his family. He said that it was unnecessary; they would know by themselves. And he died shortly thereafter. They showed me his grave, which was inscribed with praises, but only his name, Reb Moshe, and not that of his father, appears there.

This is what I heard in Radomyshl and when I recounted it to the admor Moharash, he said the following: "That is the truth," for he knew his physical appearance. And he [the admor] also had in his possession a treatise by Rabbi Moshe of blessed memory containing a passage on the above-mentioned four legs of the divine chariot.[216]

We cannot determine when this tradition was recorded, or whether it derived from a letter or was just transmitted orally. Nonetheless, it obviously freely reworks the testimony of the Ostropol rabbi first cited in Chaikin's letters, in conjunction with the traditions of the "graybeard" and *Beit Rabbi*, and additional, purportedly "documentary expansions": the physical description of Moshe (verified by Moharash); the visit to Moshe's grave in Radomyshl and its laudatory inscriptions; and the parallel between the exposition of the legs of the divine chariot heard by the storyteller and the collected treatises on Hasidism by Moshe in Moharash's possession. This then is another example from the string of local traditions, whose origins in the town of Chernigov we met in Gottlober's memoirs. These traditions tie Moshe to towns in the southwestern provinces of Russia—Volhynia, Kiev, and Podolia—

especially Fastov and Radomyshl. The alternative characterizations of the wayfarer as either a madman or as one of the thirty-six hidden saints also typify the hagiography of hidden saints who, following the revelation of their identity, become local saints.

"He First Lost His Mind and Then Left His Faith"

Our winding, bewildering journey in the wake of the contradictory traditions regarding the lost son Moshe has reached its end. The many sources examined here lead to the inescapable conclusion that Shneur Zalman of Lyady's youngest son, Moshe, decided to convert to Christianity and implemented this decision through baptism in 1820. Despite official Christian doubts regarding the baptism's validity, and efforts by his family to return him to the fold, Moshe stood by his decision. He moved to St. Petersburg, where he was hospitalized at the urging of Prince Golitsyn in order to receive treatment for his long-standing mental illness, an illness that apparently took a turn for the worse under the pressures following his conversion. We lose track of Moshe from that point on, but it is likely that he died shortly thereafter. The writings of Yosef Yitshak Schneersohn (Rayyats), the sole version that denies the very fact of conversion by inventing an alternative biography, do not suffice to controvert this fact, now backed by archival documentation. Other Habad sources hide or ignore the disconcerting truth, or recount only what they believe is its respectable ending, but dare not to deny the conversion entirely.

In traditional Jewish society, the incentive for conversion cannot be reduced solely to an attempt to improve the convert's standard of living, or to embarrass his family and society. Conversion is a dramatic statement of the apostate's wish for a complete break with his past—with his religion, culture, coreligionists, and family—and of his readiness to pay the concomitant socioeconomic and emotional price. Most converts recognize the pros and cons of their chosen step, and the expected personal and familial consequences: on the one hand, total separation from their previous society, accompanied by being targeted as objects of mockery and scorn (this disdain also extends to their family members, who, even though they did not convert, are now doomed to suspicion); on the other hand, an often false welcome in their new social setting, where the convert is viewed as a foreign implant, or even as an unstable, dangerous, and traitorous element, capable of harming his new allies. As no material gain can compensate for such a price, this makes simplistic explanations inadequate.

Certainly, the question of what motivated Moshe's conversion arose as soon as news of the event first spread. Moshe was already an adult, a married man with children; moreover, he was the scion of one of the most eminent families in traditional Jewish society in general, and in hasidic society in particular. As Moshe himself left no explanation for his action, this opened the door to folkloristic and learned explanations, all speculative.

Indeed, by and large, the explanations offered for Moshe's conversion do not meet critical standards. They fall into a number of categories, the first of which can be classified as the *familial motive.* First mentioned by Ribal, and uncritically adopted by maskilim and scholars, it attributes the conversion to the succession war. But this incentive has its source in the confusion of traditions: there was a succession war, but it was between Dov Ber and Aharon of Staroselye. In any event, Moshe converted long after this struggle (in which it appears unlikely that he took part) was decided; any link between his putative disappointment in the struggle and his conversion is not self-explanatory, and no proof exists for this contention. We also find the easily raised but difficult to eradicate *romantic motive*: falling in love with a non-Jew. Not just far-fetched, this lacks documentary support. Pesah Ruderman, who mentioned the spread of such evil rumors, rejected them out of hand. (The dissemination of rumors that Dov Ber died of syphilis is not coincidental.) Then there was the *religious motive*: deep internal conviction in the rightness of Christianity. Seemingly difficult to accept, this motivation is not incredible. The church documents attest that Moshe voiced this motivation while of sound mind (remember that conversion carried out under other circumstances was illegal). The convert Lazarus notes this rationale; in this instance, however, he appears to be projecting his life story onto Moshe. Another motive is the *utilitarian one*: acquisition of a high-status job in the Russian bureaucracy. Intimated by Bonaventura Mayer, this claim has no logical backing, and it similarly appears to be the projection of Mayer's reason for conversion: to receive a position open to Christians alone. Finally, there is the *social motive*—intellectual fraternization with a Russian officer during the 1812 flight from the Napoleonic forces—as suggested by Ginsburg. Militating against this motive is the fact that the conversion took place long afterward, and also that Moshe did not join the rest of his family in their 1812 flight.

Our rejection of all of the above motives leaves Moshe's emotional pathology as the only plausible explanation for his conversion. This impetus appears overtly and covertly in all the nonhasidic sources. That Moshe suffered from mental illness receives incontrovertible support from the archival testimony. Such a dramatic, far-reaching act as conversion certainly involves total emotional disintegration and implosion of all cushioning defense mechanisms and guilt feelings, the background for which we do not and may never know. Partial backing for this explanation comes from the above-cited letter by Moshe's mother, which mentions his evidently temporary recovery from his illness.

The fact of mental illness does not of course rule out the influence of additional factors, some of which, perhaps incongruous or unrealistic in the eyes of healthy individuals, may be seen differently by an unbalanced person. Thus, Moshe's internal motivation for this unusual step may have been buttressed by additional ideological or social considerations after the fact. And this perhaps fueled the rumors preserved by Lazarus, Gottlober, and Dubnow regarding Moshe's criticism of icon worship, his composition of a kabbalistic treatise on the "secrets" of the cross, and his condemnation of a priest who did not cross himself according to kabbalistic doctrine.

The zaddik Avraham Yehoshua Heschel of Apta (d. 1825) courageously noted the prevalence of madness and depression among nineteenth-century hasidim. He attributed these phenomena to an ungovernable impulse to break the existing religious order, to spiritual immaturity, and to emotional imbalance, which ultimately led to emotional and psychological disability. His harsh words are eminently applicable to the case of Moshe: "A person who wishes to ascend to God, level by level, at each level it is necessary that he first receive a call from Heaven, and then he will be given that level . . . For we have seen with our own eyes *many of the hasidim who have gone mad, heaven forfend, or fallen into melancholy*, and where does this come from? . . . For those persons indeed wish to ascend to God, but they did not see the ladder, for they do not serve the Lord gradually but seize something that does not belong to them without any call or permission from Heaven . . . A person should beware of this."[217]

Moshe's postconversion history remains shrouded in mystery: we cannot even establish when and where he died. One chain of tradition has him remain a Christian. In it, he either earns his living as a Russian bureaucrat (Mayer, Sholem Aleichem) or receives an appointment as a priest in St. Petersburg (Yehuda Leib Smolenskin). In any event, he reportedly dies brokenhearted in that city (Moshe Berlin), in a Moscow hospital (Ruderman, Ginsburg), or in an insane asylum (Lazarus). Alongside this tradition is a firm hasidic one, first recorded in the letters of the hasid Zvi Chaikin and in Gottlober's memoirs, in which Moshe repents, goes into exile in the towns of the southern Pale of Settlement, and dies incognito, in Radomyshl. Characterized by wishful thinking, this memory tradition does not deny the fact of the conversion, but it suggests a happy end. First formulated in the 1860s in the court of Moharash, until its publication in *Beit Rabbi*, this version was disseminated by noncanonical means: rumors, "testimony," and private letters.

Concurrent with the publication of new findings by nonhasidic researchers—Ginsburg, Litvin, and Simha Katz—a shift took place in Habad historiography. Rayyats then offered an alternative biography, in which the sin of conversion was erased, and which also engaged in covert polemic with the various insights suggested by other treatments of this episode.

Until the discovery of new archival material in Russia—it seems likely that such material exists[218]—it is doubtful whether we can fully determine the circumstances of Moshe's death. Did he die shortly after converting (which appears probable and has evidentiary support); did he recover from his illness and live as a Christian (either as a bureaucrat or a church official); or did he flee St. Petersburg, repent, and wander among the towns of the Pale of Settlement? The latter fates are extremely improbable. Surely, if Moshe had lived as a Christian, some documentary evidence would have survived. As for the option of flight and repentance, it would be difficult for such a famous individual to remain hidden for so long. Many informers made their living by turning over wanted individuals; moreover, the modern context in which Russian Jewish society operated from the 1860s on precluded a totally anonymous existence. In addition, as conversion from Christianity to Judaism was illegal, the sole means available to a convert seeking to return to Judaism would be to leave Russia—and if that happened, again, some record of it should be extant.

Moreover, if Moshe had indeed returned to Judaism, then Habad historiography would not have turned against him and obscured his memory. Although the Mishnah teaches us: "If there was a penitent, one may not say to him, 'Remember what you used to do!'" (*Baba Metsia* 4:10), the principle of "in the place where penitents stand even the wholly righteous cannot stand" (BT *Berakhot* 34b) would have made Moshe's story an outstanding exemplar of faith. Instead, Habad historiography subconsciously adopted a dual, somewhat contradictory memory strategy: on the one hand, it denied the fact of the conversion and the grief caused to his family by constructing an alternative, heroic biography involving an interfaith debate and flight from prison (Rayyats); on the other hand, it evaded explicit mention of the conversion, but presented repentance and exile as a means of exoneration of sin (*Beit Rabbi* and many oral traditions).

"It Never Happened"? The Ongoing Struggle over Memory Traditions

The story of Moshe's repentance, which played a role in the hasidic-maskilic memory wars, was perpetuated in the struggle between Hasidism and supposedly hostile academic research, to a large extent correctly viewed as maskilic in nature. A 1989 letter published in a Habad organ gave expression to this struggle: "I hereby bring to the readers' attention interesting details arising from two letters describing the last years and death of Reb Moshe, may his memory protect us, living evidence regarding this zaddik, that portray his righteousness and solitary existence . . . The details of the latter's life are obscure . . . *and various 'researchers' have pinned nonsense on this basis*."[219] The convert, the son of saints, has accordingly reverted to the role of zaddik and ascetic for which he was destined from time immemorial. Those who attribute some defect to him speak worthless "nonsense."[220]

Shortly after the publication of this study's initial version (*Zion* 65 [2000]), Menahem Brod, the Habad spokesman, was approached for his reaction. He responded: "It is not the case that some among us are in possession of an internal tradition, that a few individuals know and hide the truth. Just the opposite is true. His [Moshe's] history is known from written and oral sources, *and the conversion is a libel*."[221]

Two years later, in 2002, Moshe's story reemerged with the publication of *The Christian Son of Habad Rebbe: A Rabbinical Scandal* (in Hebrew), by Boaz Eppelbaum. Openly based on my study, this shallow, sensational, and poorly written work presents the story of Moshe in an imaginary and exceedingly strange fashion. Although purportedly a "historical novel," the author clearly lacks any knowledge of either Hasidism specifically or Eastern European Jewry in general. Neither historical nor a novel, apart from being a bibliographical curiosity, this book has no bearing on this discussion. In the wake of its publication, the Israeli journalist Yair Sheleg interviewed Menahem Brod, who again strongly denied the story of Moshe's conversion: *"It never happened; this is simply a fantasy*. Eppelbaum's book does not merit comment, but Assaf's article as well is built on unfounded assumptions. What we know is that Reb Moshe became involved in interfaith arguments with Christians, and that after he ostensibly lost one, he was asked to convert. He refused, and was therefore forced to hide and live incognito."[222]

The appearance of the Hebrew edition of this book (*Ne'ehaz basevakh*, 2006) sparked an intense, fascinating discussion on the *haredi* Internet forum "Atsor, kan hoshvim" (Halt, we're thinking here). This was notable for the interest it aroused, as more than 62,000 people entered the forum.[223] Most of the discussion focused on the chapter about Moshe. The participants included many Habad hasidim, who tried, out of true pain, to protect their heritage and rescue it from an ostensibly new threat, in the form of historical research. One noteworthy participant was Rabbi Shalom Dov Levin, a scholar and well-regarded researcher of Hasidism who currently manages the Habad library in New York. Under the pen name Halavan, he directly confronted me in the online discussion; I, however, posted my response under my real name.

What was intriguing were the updated historiographical positions taken by Habad in this debate. After a failed attempt by several participants to argue that the archival evidence was forged, either by maskilim or by Russian civil servants, and that the conversion never took place, Levin took the lead. He affirmed the new documents' verity, agreed that Moshe suffered from mental illness, but entered a strong claim that there was never any conversion. In his opinion, the Russian officer Puzanov enticed Moshe, forcibly tricking him into signing some document. Moshe, who was mentally ill, had no idea what he was signing and certainly never intended to convert; all he desired was to return home to his family. The sin was thereby transferred from poor, innocent Moshe and laid at the door of the historian David Assaf. The latter was accused of love of sensationalism and hatred of hasidim, especially Habad, which made him hide the truth and engage in malicious, deliberate distortion.[224]

All this demonstrates that even a thousand documents or protocols cannot breach the protective wall guarding the hasid's simple faith in the purity of the Habad dynasty. The history of Moshe, his madness, and his conversion remains silenced to the present day and, prior to the publication of my Hebrew book, were known only to a few within Habad circles. The name Moshe is rare among members of the Schneersohn family and is therefore also rare among Lubavitch hasidim in general; descriptions of his adventures are missing from the current, flourishing Habad publications. Nor has anyone taken the trouble to locate or uncover his gravesite or the accompanying documentation. From time to time, however, Moshe's name emerges to trouble the adherents of Habad Hasidism; it then returns to oblivion.

3 One Event, Multiple Interpretations

The Fall of the Seer of Lublin

> What grips me now and has always gripped me concerning the events assembled in this chronicle, since first long years ago I heard of them and read of them, are the dates—the dates of the actions and the deaths of sundry men. The few generations, which separate me from that time, have told and retold these events. Thence came into being the flesh and blood of this chronicle. What I have added may be called its garment. But the dates are the mighty skeleton beneath. —Martin Buber, *For the Sake of Heaven*, 311

"A Flame Hovering over His Head": The Seer of Lublin in His Hasidim's Eyes

At the end of the eighteenth century and the beginning of the nineteenth, one of the most adulated figures among hasidic leaders and their flock, both in Poland and beyond, was the zaddik Rabbi Yaakov Yitshak Horowitz, better known as the Seer of Lublin (1745?–1815).[1] As his appella-

---

This chapter is an extended version of an article titled "One Event, Two Interpretations: The Fall of the Seer of Lublin in Hasidic Memory and Maskilic Satire," which appeared in *Polin: Studies in Polish Jewry*, Volume 15: *Jewish Religious Life, 1500–1900*, edited by Antony Polonsky and published for the Institute for Polish-Jewish Studies and the American Association for Polish-Jewish Studies by the Littman Library of Jewish Civilization (Oxford, 2002).

tion implies, his renown rested largely in his unique spirituality, here described by the zaddik and mystic Rabbi Yitshak Yehuda Yehiel of Komarno (1806–74), who visited the court in Lublin in 1815, the last year of the Seer's life: "I was privileged to visit Lublin with my late father when I was a boy of nine, and I saw his [the Seer's] face illumined like torches. And when he opened the door to recite *Kegavna*[2] I saw a flame hovering over his head. I was there for the Passover holiday and I witnessed several matters of the holy spirit and of the highest spirituality and his intensely wonderful prayer, a leaping flame."[3]

Some of the Seer's followers even went so far as to draw a sweeping analogy between Jerusalem and the Seer's Lublin court, envisaged as a miniature Jerusalem, the Holy Temple of the diaspora. For such a description, we turn to the words of one disciple, the zaddik Uri of Strelisk (1757–1826): "When one comes to Lublin he should imagine to himself that Lublin is Eretz Israel, that the courtyard of the study house is Jerusalem, that the study house is the Temple Mount, that his apartment is the Porch, that the gallery is the Sanctuary, that his room is the Holy of Holies, and that the shekhinah speaks from his throat. Then he will understand what our rabbi is."[4]

Even in cases where his disciples parted company with the Seer—as happened with Rabbi Yaakov Yitshak, the "Holy Jew" of Pshishkha (1766–1813), and his followers—this did not detract from their esteem for the Seer as their teacher. Indeed, as most of the zaddikim in the following generation were either his direct or indirect disciples, it is by no means an overstatement to call the Seer the father of Hasidism in Poland.[5]

On Simhat Torah (October) 1814, the Seer fell out of the window of his house, suffering critical injuries that eventually led to his death nine months later, on the fast of Tisha beAv (August) 1815. Although these bare facts are not disputed, their interpretation by hasidim, maskilim, and writers differs substantially. Of these varying interpretations, the maskilic version was the earliest. Written in the style of a journalistic exposé, this satiric account followed upon the heels of the fall itself, making its initial appearance even before the Seer's death. The hasidic counterversion, however—with its clearly apologetic and polemical overtones, evidently intended to furnish an alternative to the maskilic version by endowing the fall with mysterious mystical nuances—is late, dating to the early twentieth century.

The following discussion is based on a satirical antihasidic treatise preserved in manuscript form in the library of Yosef Perl in Tarnopol. Titled *Sefer nekiyut uferishut* (Book of cleanliness and abstinence), it describes the Seer's fall.[6] This chapter does not aim to uncover the reality behind the Seer's fall, but rather to trace the transmission of these opposing traditions, showing how their divergent treatments of the fall illustrate patterns of imagery, polemical and apologetic memory, and dispute.

"This Was No Simple Matter": The Fall of the Seer in Hasidic Memory Tradition

In later hasidic sources, the series of events that led to the Seer's death are referred to by the semantically charged term the "great fall." This term has several layers of meaning, both overt and covert. Signifying more than just a tragic accident, it suggests a spiritual fall. Indeed, some hasidic sources link the Seer's fall to his emotional breakdown following his failed attempts to hasten redemption, and the shattering of the messianic hopes he had vested in the Napoleonic campaign in Russia.[7] In brief, in hasidic legend the Seer's fall has a threefold aspect: a physical fall; a personal-spiritual fall; and a military-political fall—Napoleon's failed attempt to invade Russia in 1812, and the dissolution of the duchy of Warsaw in early 1813.[8]

Written long after the event in question, as noted, the two main hasidic sources for the "true" interpretation of the Seer's fall are from the early twentieth century. Apparently written independently of each other, the first is a brief description by the hasidic writer Ahron Marcus (1843–1916) in *Der Chassidismus*, published in 1901;[9] the second is an undated letter sent by Rabbi Yosef Lowenstein of Serotsk (1840–1924)[10] to Rabbi Zvi Yehezkel Michelsohn of Plonsk (1863–1943?). The latter transmitted this letter to his son-in-law Yisrael Berger of Bucharest, the author of the four-volume hasidic anthology *Zekhut yisrael*. Berger published this letter in the volume titled *Eser orot*, first printed in 1907. This section undertakes a detailed analysis of this depiction:

> After the year 5574 [1814], in which was seen how the hand of divine providence brought the fall of the Emperor Napoleon until he was taken captive,[11] many predicted that God's great name would be magnified and sanctified. As for the Rabbi of Lublin, he lived in the constant expectation of divine salvation, that redemption would swiftly come through the messianic king, Amen . . . And he found a propitious time, the night of Simhat Torah, on which all Israel are acquitted after the days of judgment. On Shemini Atseret they drank mead in his house and piled all the empty glasses on the windowsill. He said to his followers: "If we have a good Simhat Torah, then we will have a good Tisha beAv." After the *hakafot* he commanded his followers to remain in the large hall and to guard him watchfully in his special room. And they became as deaf and heard not. Then the rabbi commanded his wife Rebbetzin Beyle to watch over him—"Unless the Lord watches over the city, the watchman keeps vigil in vain" [Psalms 127:1]: the Maggid of Kozhenits died on the eve of Sukkot [1814]; a stone was thrown at the window of the house of the Rabbi of *Ma'or vashemesh*, which broke the window pane.[12] He [the author of *Ma'or vashemesh*] said, "Who knows what is happening there, in Lublin?"
>
> The rabbi sobbed loudly and the rebbetzin suddenly imagined that she heard a

loudly sobbing child knocking at the door, and she forgot his command and went to open the door. When she returned, the rabbi was not in the house. She only saw him snatched from the house through the window. His followers understood that this was no simple matter: it was impossible for anyone to throw himself from this window, for the window was above shoulder height. Moreover, in all the time that he had sat in this room, some fifteen years, he had never approached the window to look at the marketplace. And all the glasses were still standing on the windowsill. [The holy rabbi, our teacher Yehuda Leib of Zaklikov,[13] said *that he who does not believe that this was a great thing is an opponent of the zaddikim.* This is what Rabbi Yaakov Leib of that place told him,[14] who heard it from his mouth. *And the mitnagedim joked that he was drunk and fell, and they refused to see that their interpretation contradicts the facts in that time and place.*][15]

They searched for him until several hours later the hasid Rabbi Leizer of Chmelnik, the son-in-law of the holy rabbi, the marvelous ascetic Rabbi Zvi Hirshele of Stashev, made a circuit of the house, a distance of some fifty cubits or more. And he heard someone moaning. He asked, "Who are you?" and received the answer, "Yaakov Yitshak, son of Meitl." And he emitted a noise. His most prominent disciples gathered and drew lots for who would carry home his feet, his body, and his head.[16] And the holy rabbi, Reb Shmuel of Kuriv,[17] was allotted his head. He saw the rebbe whispering and leaned over to hear, and he was reciting *Tikun Leah*,[18] and the clock read eleven o'clock, which was the time for the *hatsot* [midnight] prayer for him. The holy rabbi Reb Shmuel said, "See our rabbi's sanctity, that even at such a time he worships God."

The rabbi was very ill and his opponents imagined that he would expire that very day. The mitnagedim rejoiced at this and drank wine. When this came to the rabbi's attention, he said, "When I leave this world they will not even be able to drink water." And so it came to pass, for the Seer of Lublin, light of the world, died on the following Tisha beAv.

And the rabbi said that they took him to heaven to receive judgment for trying to force the end of days and sentenced him to be cast down to earth. And the Maggid of Kozhenits spread the corner of his robe to lower him to earth gently, and if not for him not a bone in his body would have remained whole, heaven forbid. It was thus that the rabbi [the Seer] found out that the Maggid had died, and if he had known he would not have initiated his attempt at all.[19]

Although Rabbi Lowenstein of Serotsk's account closely resembles Ahron Marcus's earlier one, it also exhibits some differences. Many details are missing from Marcus's account, such as the lottery held among the hasidim for who would support which parts of the Seer's body. However, Marcus gives information not found in the rabbi of Serotsk's account, such as a description of the first-floor window above the study house,[20] and the involvement of the famous penitent, the physician Dr. Bernhard (Hayyim David of Piotrkov),[21] who was rushed to Lublin to treat the Seer. According to Marcus, when the doctor inquired of the Seer where he had pain, he replied, "My left thigh." And when asked how he fell, the Seer answered: "All the satanic forces of evil set on me. After such a Simhat Torah—such a Tisha beAv." In Marcus's account, the Seer went on to relate that the late Maggid of Kozhenits and his own mother came to his aid and cushioned his fall. Moreover, not only does Marcus's account mute the polemical barb directed at the Seer's opponents ("When I leave this world they will not even be able to drink water"), it lacks the messianic atmosphere so prominently featured in Lowenstein's account ("And the rabbi said that they took him to heaven to receive judgment for trying to force the end of days").[22] Marcus's source for the details of the fall was the rabbi of Sosnovits, who claimed to have heard them from Dr. Bernhard's eyewitness account.[23]

In any event, as presented in hasidic accounts, the fall is a miraculous event distinguished by several irrational features: the great height of the window, so high that even someone as tall as the Seer could barely thrust his head through it; the wineglasses, which remained undisturbed on the windowsill; and the fact that the Seer reportedly never even went near, or looked out of, the window. In the absence of a rational explanation, only the miraculous one remains, supported by the semantic overlap between the Seer's fall and Napoleon's fall, and by the folk etymology equating Napoleon with *nefilah* (fall), based on the Seer's intertwining of his fate with that of the French general.[24] In the hasidic account, guided by his presentiment of impending events and their consequences (even though he remained unaware of the death of the Maggid of Kozhenits a week earlier, on Erev Sukkot), the Seer pointedly requests that his wife and the members of his intimate circle guard him carefully. However, in the spirit of a story whose tragic ending is foreseen, they fail to fulfill this duty. Despite his miraculous survival, the Seer interpreted his fall as a divine punishment for his premature attempts to bring the Messiah, evidently himself believing he deserved a death sentence. It was only the intervention of the deceased Maggid of Kozhenits that cushioned his fall and delayed his death for nine months.[25]

The bracketed statement cited above—attributed to the Seer's disciple Rabbi Yehuda Leib of Zaklikov—that "he who does not believe that this was a great thing is an opponent of the zaddikim," requires further emphasis. Its apologetic and polemical tone can be attributed only to its being a reaction to an alternate interpretation that stripped the fall of its supernatural aspects, as substantiated by the continuation of the account, which explicitly mentions the mitnagedim and their attitude to the fall: "And the mitnagedim joked that he was drunk and fell, and they refused to see that their interpretation contradicts the facts in that time and place." It should be noted, however, that although this brief passage appeared in the first, 1907, edition of *Eser orot*, it was expunged from all later editions of this work, starting with its second edition in 1913—evidently because it could ostensibly be understood as legitimating the alternate version.[26]

As we shall see below, a significantly different explanation was indeed in circulation. If the hasidim interpreted the fall as the physical manifestation of a spiritual fall from a state of mystical elevation, the maskilic satire attributed the Seer's fall to his emotional and physical imbalance, and to his inebriated state. It is not surprising that wine plays an important role in the hasidic source as well. The hasidic source depicts the hasidim merrily indulging in drink on Simhat Torah, as was the custom, placing the empty bottles on the windowsill, where they miraculously remained untouched. Moreover, and here the polemical slant emerges with clarity, the hasidic legend depicts as drunkards not the hasidim, but rather the Seer's opponents. By rejoicing too soon at his impending death, the latter receive a parodic "punishment": the Seer's death on a fast day made it impossible for them to celebrate his death in drunken revelry.[27]

To sum up, the hasidic source represents a dual stance: on the one hand, it presents an internal, positive explanation linking the fall to higher spiritual and messianic matters; on the other hand, it puts forth an external, polemically oriented explanation that satirizes the mitnagedim while simultaneously offering a counterhistory. But who were these opponents who rejoiced in the Seer's expected demise, and why did they use this satiric barb?

"Foolish and Ignorant": The Seer of Lublin in His Opponents' Eyes

Hasidic legend did not overlook the chilly reception afforded the Seer when he moved from Lantzut to Czechov, a Lublin suburb, after 1798: "In those days the city of Lublin was filled with scribes and great God-fearing scholars, but they were all mitnagedim who did not follow the ways of Hasidism, and they viewed anyone following that path as alien, not comprehending that the hasid also worships God, blessed be he, with all his heart . . . and when they heard in Lublin that such a breach had been made near their city, that one person who followed the paths of Hasidism had settled nearby and had begun to attract others . . . then they were greatly incensed and began to despise and to persecute him."[28]

Given what we know of the Seer's charisma and mystical personality, it was in effect well-nigh impossible for his mitnagedic and maskilic critics to ignore the inroads he made among their followers. Their struggle against the Seer focused primarily on undermining his authority and credibility.[29] Ironically, the local mitnagedic rabbi Azriel Halevi Horwitz (known as "the iron head"), who made strong attempts to defame the Seer during his lifetime,[30] unwittingly allowed the Seer to be buried in a choice cemetery plot, near the grave of Rabbi Shalom Shakhna, a leading sixteenth-century Polish Torah scholar.[31]

An additional critic was the militant mitnagedic preacher David of Makov, who used biblical allusions and imagery to mock and ridicule the Seer in his *Zmir aritsim* (Wicked shears). He compared the Seer to Nimrod and Balaam, and his hasidim to the trees that anointed the thorn bush as their king in Jotham's parable (Judges 9:7–21):

> The hasid, Reb Itsik of Lantzut, began to be a man of power, a mighty hunter on earth.[32] Around him gathered flocks upon flocks of hasidim,[33] all gloom and disarray. Excessively involved in feasting, he moved the hour for the afternoon prayer. On the High Holidays all the hasidim come, wavering and wandering, to take shelter in his shade, that he may set his nest on high, and not for nothing did the starling follow [the raven], but because it is of its own kind. Greedy for gifts, familiar with ghosts and spirits . . . he who raises his voice clamorously in prayer is called a *gaon* . . . And he who claps his hands together they call a hasid and rabbi.[34]

He continued:

> Regarding the hasid, Reb Itsik of Lantzut, who never was, nor will be, a Torah scholar, I will open my mouth and say: Oh grape branch, wayward and defiant, see, he teaches?[35] A barren tree among the trees of the forest, foolish and ignorant. Why he is encased in gold and silver, torn apart and ripped, but there is no breath inside it, for he has made ready his heart like an oven while he lies in wait.[36] He sleeps all night and oppression ceases,[37] in the morning he flares up like a burning fire . . . And they came to Baal-peor, as to the chief magician Balaam ben Beor. It shall be night for you so that you have no vision, without meal or sustenance . . . the seers shall be shamed and the diviners confounded.[38]

Another famous mitnaged who mocked the Seer's supposed prophetic powers was the Maggid Yisrael Loebl of Slutsk. In his *Sefer vikuah* (Book of debate), Loebl related that, when he visited their courts, both the Maggid of Kozhenits and the Seer at Lantzut had failed to divine the true nature of a person who presented himself as a simple hasid: "The rabbi of the holy community of Kozhenits and Reb Yitshak of Lantzut are my proof, for they did not divine my true nature when I stayed with them last winter and presented myself as a hasid belonging to their sect. They believed what I said, and prayed for fulfillment of my wishes and desires. And what was my desire? To oppose the heretics that emerge from their ranks."[39]

Both the Seer's renown and the news of his embarrassing fall naturally winged their way to mitnagedim and maskilim in Poland and Galicia. As noted above, an anonymous sardonic account of the fall, apparently based on eyewitness and hearsay testimony, titled *Sefer nekiyut uferishut*, appeared during 1815, prior to the Seer's death in August of that year. Although it remained in manuscript and was never published in full, this satire's contents evidently circulated widely. It was this initial version that effectively determined the attributes of the maskilic interpretation of the Seer's fall.

Ma'asei harav or *Sefer nekiyut uferishut*: The Satire's Transmission and Its Author's Identity

In 1904, Ephraim Deinard published a new edition of the rare, polemical, antihasidic work *Zmir aritsim*.[40] To this work, he appended a short introduction written by the copyist—Mendel Landesberg of Kremenets (1786–1866)—in which this maskil, a friend and contemporary of the maskilim Yosef Perl and Yitshak Ber Levinsohn (Ribal), related how he prepared four antihasidic treatises for publication.[41] This compilation included, in addition to a corrupt copy of *Zmir aritsim* (which Landesberg mistakenly called *Zemer aritsim*),[42] a brief anonymous satire, which he titled *Ma'asei harav* (The rabbi's deeds). Landesberg wrote:

> In the introduction I mentioned a short treatise *Zemer* [*Zmir*] *aritsim hasheni*, which was written by the disciples of the Gaon and published in Warsaw at the same time as *Sefer havikuah*. And *Zmir aritsim* contains much criticism of the deeds of the rabbi, Reb Itsik of Lantzut. I thought that it would be good to copy this treatise into this volume—it includes what happened to the aforementioned rabbi who experienced an impure event, which his hasidic sect viewed as signs of purity—so that the kind reader will understand to what extent the hasidim depart from the truth. This treatise, titled *Ma'asei harav*, was written in 5575 [1814–15], the year that this event concerning the zaddik took place. And I have removed it today from my satchel in order to provide you with a copy of it from beginning to end; and this treatise will be a witness to, and support, *Emek refa'im*.[43]

The "impure event" referred to by Landesberg was obviously the Seer's fall from the window of his house. Landesberg's determination of 1815 as the date of composition is substantiated by examination of the text, which further narrows it down to after the 24th of Nissan 1815,[44] and before the Seer's death on Tisha beAv of that year, of which the text's narrator seems unaware. Two significant points emerge from this dating to mid-1815. First, examination of the introduction—written, it would seem, by Yosef Perl—reveals that the text in question was an initial satiric response to *Shivhei haBesht* (In praise of the Ba'al Shem Tov), first published in late 1814. This work eventually became the polemical focus of Perl's multifaceted creativity, as exemplified in his *Megaleh temirin* and his German *Über das Wesen der Sekte Chassidim* (On the nature of the hasidic sect) in particular. Second, by its very presence in Perl's literary estate, this satire, which preceded the composition of *Megaleh temirin*, necessitates an exploration of possible mutual influence between the two works.[45]

Landesberg did not state who composed this work; however, his remarks make it clear that he simply copied it. As noted, his antihasidic compilation found its way to Deinard, who published its treatises in several pamphlets over the course of the same year.[46]

The satire in question, has, however, received scant attention from scholars, with the exception of Simha Katz and Avraham Rubinstein,[47] who called attention to the different version of the manuscript found in Perl's literary archive.[48] Although torn in places, the manuscript is longer and more complete than the brief version published by Deinard. The flowing, almost uncorrected, handwriting is apparently not an autograph but the work of a professional scribe. Not only does study of this archival copy shed light on the work itself and on its author, but it also enables us to examine how maskilim perceived Hasidism in general, and the Seer of Lublin in particular.

Notwithstanding its fluid handwriting, this copy is evidently a draft, and not the final version of this work. The last two pages contain many parenthetical additions that perhaps reflect some of the alternatives at the copyist's disposal. Many are vulgar in nature (repeated references to urine, excrement, and genitalia); perhaps the copyist was debating whether or not to include these coarse expressions in the final version of the satire. In the published version, these phrases appear as an organic part of the text, with no formal, distinguishing markers.

The text in question was first examined by Simha Katz, the investigator of Perl's archive, who rescued many manuscripts in the 1930s, bringing them from Tarnopol to Jerusalem.[49] Katz penned the following in the margin of the first page of the manuscript: "***Sefer nekiyut uferishut*** (the author of the listing ascribes the treatise to Mendel Landesberg of Kremenets!). But, based on its mention of the book ***Shivhei Alekse*** composed by S.B.H. [Shimshon Bloch Halevi] (as per his letter to Perl from 1817),[50] it appears that it was written by S.B.H. This treatise appears in a short version at the beginning of *Zmir aritsim {ha-rishon}* published by Deinard; there it is called *Maasei harav*. This proves that {Landesberg was} just the copyist and not the author (see ibid., p. {1})."[51] Indeed, in Philip Koffler's list of Hebrew and Yiddish manuscripts in the Yosef Perl archive, we find the following: "*Sefer nekiyut uferishut* about the famous rabbi, of whom it is said that he is a man of God, a hasid, known by the name Reb Itsikl Lanctor [sic]. At present he sits firmly on the throne of Hasidism in the big city of Lublin. It was published at the Charny Ostra press at Sudlikov, in the year . . ."[52]

Comparison of the citation copied by Koffler from the manuscript of *Nekiyut uferishut* that he saw in the Perl archive with the manuscript copied by Landesberg and published by Deinard as *Ma'asei harav* shows that both are versions of the same work. Part of the citation recorded by Koffler appears with the same wording in Landesberg's copy, in the section titled "To the reader,"[53] which is missing from the manuscript preserved in the Perl archive. It appears that the text from the Perl archive lacks its first page, which was still extant in the copy seen by Koffler. This page, which evidently contained a "To the reader" section similar to the one preserved in Landesberg's copy, explicitly noted the title of the work: *Sefer nekiyut uferishut.*

Shimson Halevi Bloch and Shivhei Alekse

As noted, it was Simha Katz who correctly determined that Mendel Landesberg was just the copyist, and that the Galician maskil Shimshon Halevi Bloch (1784–1845) was the author of the satire. A close friend of Shlomo Yehuda Rapoport, and both a disciple and a friend of Nahman Krochmal, Bloch is known primarily for his three-volume popular geographical and historical textbook, *Shvilei olam* (Paths of the world).[54]

The proof of Bloch's authorship of *Sefer nekiyut uferishut* lies in its link to a lost satire titled *Shivhei Alekse* (In praise of Aleksey), a parodic echo of *Shivhei haBesht.* Its protagonist is the Besht's non-Jewish servant, who was his coachman and valet.

In *Nekiyut uferishut,* the narrator recounts to the Seer's followers the wonders and miracles worked by rabbis in the Ukraine, remarking, among other things, that his rabbi (probably Mordekhai of Kremenets) has a gentile servant. This servant is "the grandson or great-grandson of the illustrious gentile *Alekse dem rabines*, the Besht's steward." This transparently parodic remark suggests that, alongside hasidic admiration for their rebbes' lineage and dynasties, they nurture a holy dynasty of gentile coachmen and stewards. The manuscript version, but not Deinard's, of *Nekiyut uferishut* contains the following statement by the anonymous annotator regarding that gentile coachman: "All his powerful and mighty acts *are [recorded in the book?]* Shivhei Alekse, *which, God willing, I shall soon publish.*"

In an 1817 letter sent to Perl, Bloch (then living in Lemberg) declared his intention of writing a satire by that name: "On the importance of the task in which I am engaged will testify a sound witness, my dear friend, the sage Krochmal, not I . . . But since the task is great, and cannot be completed in a short time, the above-mentioned dear friend advised me to complete *Shivhei Alekse* that I had already begun, and to publish it so that the [hasidim] will be frustrated and put to shame, and will be a laughingstock in the eyes of all readers and in their own eyes as well."[55] Apparently what motivated Bloch to create a book of praises centering on the Besht's gentile coachman was the publication of *Shivhei haBesht* in 1814/15 (at Kopust and Berdichev); two years later, however, this treatise was not yet ready. Bloch's letter indicates that he had revealed his plan to Krochmal, one of the leading maskilim in Galicia, who encouraged him to continue this project.

This matter of Aleksey requires further elaboration. Surprisingly, this noted figure of hasidic folklore receives no mention in early hasidic sources. Although *Shivhei haBesht* contains numerous references to the Besht's "Canaanite [Christian] servant" who accompanies him on his travels (and even tried to kill him on one occasion),[56] as far as I can tell he remains anonymous.[57] It was the maskil Yosef Perl who first mentioned this coachman by name. In his *Über das Wesen der Sekte Chassidim*, completed in 1816, Perl pokes fun at "seinem christlichen Kutscher Alexi," to whom the Besht assigned various tasks.[58] The discovery of the reference to Aleksey in the annotations to *Sefer nekiyut uferishut*, written in 1815, make this the earliest source in which this gentile servant is explicitly identified by name.

It is only later, beginning in the 1860s, that we find Aleksey appearing by name in hasidic sources.[59] From that point on, he is elevated to various levels of sanctity, and his personality and doings undergo imaginative expansions that are subsequently adopted by hasidic and by nonhasidic writers and scholars.[60]

The literary significance of this state of affairs extends beyond the use of the name Aleksey and leaves us with one of two possibilities: either the name Aleksey was originally a sardonic maskilic invention, a mocking Ukrainian name for a prototypical gentile that was attached to the Besht's coachman, and later found its way into hasidic literature, where it was quite naturally and naively absorbed; or it was an authentic hasidic tradition, regarding an actual coachman named Aleksey. Initially transmitted orally, this tradition was first documented in writing by maskilim, and it reappeared in hasidic works only fifty years later. In any event, this represents another surprising example of the covert dialogue and cross-fertilization between maskilic and hasidic sources.

Perl's Part in Shaping Nekiyut uferishut

As noted, the manuscript preserved in Perl's archive in Tarnopol is apparently a copy; in any event, it is not an autograph by either Bloch or Perl. Nonetheless, the manuscript illustrates Perl's likely involvement in the final shaping of this work.

First of all, the two opening pages of the satire reflect Perl's spirit: typical of Perl are the marking of the projected audience as hasidic communities everywhere, and the connections drawn between the satire and *Shivhei*

FIG. 3.1. Yosef Perl

haBesht, Nahman of Bratslav's *Sipurei ma'asiyot* (Tales), and Nathan of Nemirov's *Likutei tefilot* (Selected prayers). Also, the purported copperplate of the Seer's fall, to be appended to the book, is directly linked to Perl's satiric method, as exemplified in his *Megaleh temirin*.[61] Moreover, these brief introductory pages contain many idioms typical of Perl's other antihasidic writings. Second, the notes to the manuscript state their author's intention of publishing *Shivhei Alekse* in the near future. But the person who wrote the notes and the author of *Shivhei Alekse* were not necessarily the same; perhaps the annotator—probably Perl—simply intended to publish this work.

Examination of *Sefer nekiyut uferishut* elicits that its original author—evidently Shimshon Bloch—sent it to Perl for consideration, and perhaps for editing as well. Typically, as for other works, Perl seems to have replaced the original introduction with one of his own devising,[62] with the addition of sardonic explanatory comments.[63] The different and later authorship of the notes is definitively established by their author's awareness of the Seer's death—of which the author of the satiric text displays no knowledge—and his comment, "I even walked on his grave." Thus, the notes were written after Tisha beAv 1815, and by a different author. The extant copy of the manuscript containing the entire satire was copied by a professional scribe, most likely a member of Perl's circle who was employed to copy sources and original works.[64]

Sefer nekiyut uferishut: Structure and Content

The narrator of this satire, a maskilic merchant from Białystok, arrives in Lublin on business just after Passover 1815. Upon hearing from two local hasidim that the Seer (referred to as *haroeh*, and not *hahozeh*)[65] has been shut up in his house for some time and refuses to see anyone, the merchant sets out to uncover the truth. He introduces himself as a Jew from the strongly hasidic area of Volhynia who purportedly seeks a blessing from the rabbi, as his wife has failed to conceive for the past five years. First plying the hasidim with drink, he then questions them, obtaining by this means the details of the Seer's fall from his window on Simhat Torah. The narrator's true identity is revealed after he berates the hasidim for their stupidity, for their naive belief in a zaddik who is nothing but a deceiving drunkard. The hasidim, for their part, are unable to accept the fact that what for them epitomized the zaddik's purity and gift of prophecy was nothing more than a sham perpetrated by a pitiful drunk. They accuse the merchant of coming to "make the Seer stink," to which the merchant's ironic response is: "Why do you scream at me? *He* sank and fell and lay outstretched in human excrement, and *I* make him stink?" The printed version of the satire contains a different ending, in which the merchant is joined by a mitnaged, originally from Vilna, who now lives in the Germanized Lithuanian town of Jorborg. These two ideal antihasidic prototypes, the maskil and the mitnaged, join forces in unmasking the zaddik.

Several classic themes of the maskilic critique of Hasidism are well represented in this satiric work. Of these, a major motif is intoxication and love of wine among zaddikim and their flocks.[66] Not only does this unrestrained drinking cause the Seer's embarrassing fall, it also ultimately induces the hasidim to let the secret slip. In addition, implanted in the text we find coarse hints comparing hasidism and Christianity, alongside criticism of the Seer's supposed prophetic powers and continuous access to divine inspiration. Also embedded in the text is an inverse parodic comparison of the Seer of Lublin to the biblical Samuel, similarly known as the Seer, whose rise to eminence came against the background of the corruption of Eli's sons, on the one hand, and of Eli's multiple blindness, on the other hand. The literate reader was certainly aware that Eli met his death in a fall from his chair (1 Samuel 4:18).

The Dionysian and erotic sides of the hasidic experience, exemplified by intoxication and erotic stimulation along with the excessive emphasis on bodily excretion—feces, vomit, and other body fluids—are strikingly enunciated in this maskilic version. As depicted here, the crude, unesthetic, and licentious hasidic ethos is in stark contrast to their professed ideal of purity and abstinence. Even the satire's title alludes to its crass nature via the parodic inversion of the terms "cleanliness" and "abstinence"—key terms in Hebrew ethical literature, synonyms for physical purity and sexual abstinence—to refer to the excrement in which the Seer landed while drunk. The satire's ironic treatment of the life of hasidic purity—patterned on "cleanliness leads to abstinence, abstinence leads to purity, purity leads to hasidism"[67]—highlights hasidic utilization of the study house's outer walls as a public urinal and outhouse, lined "with mire and mud and human excrement." The Seer, who wanted to either urinate or vomit, finds himself in this pile of excrement, and cleanliness in this context appears in its secondary, borrowed meaning of excretion. This unusual crassness—necessary for the book's polemical aim of portraying Hasidism as contaminated by vulgar animality—is perhaps the reason why this satire remained in manuscript.[68]

In addition to its crudity (and in some instances feeding it), the satire's first-person narrative is replete with sophisticated biblical associations and allusions. Although fully appreciable only in the Hebrew original, an excerpt from its account of the Seer's fall follows:

It came to pass when I begged them to tell me the story of the Seer . . . that after they had become drunk, one acceded to me. The ass opened his mouth, and said: "On the twenty-third day of the seventh month, which is the holiday of Shemini Atseret, a day of drinking and rejoicing, when all had come to the Seer's residence, to rejoice with him on Simhat Torah . . . and the Seer drank and became drunk and his gorge rose and he vomited until the people were unable to sit with him—and the Seer could no longer control himself—and he commanded the lad who attended him, saying: 'Place me in my bedroom, for the spirit of prophecy has begun to move in me, and let no man enter. For God will speak with me there.' For he lived in a stone house and his bedroom was a small chamber with recessed and latticed windows all around and the one open window in his chamber was opposite the dung gate, where people go to do their business, which is lined with mire and mud and human excrement . . .

He fell on his bed . . . until the urine rose to his head. He then mounted his bed to the windowsill, and holding his genitals, let his waters hit the ground. He had not yet finished urinating, his flesh was still in his hands, and he reeled and moved like a drunk, and fell full length on his face from the window onto the piles of human waste. He lay there without utterance or words, making only a soft murmuring sound, and no one knew his burial place.

Toward evening, when the hasidim departed, two men who served him came there to relieve themselves. They lifted their eyes and they saw the rabbi lying prostrate like a prophet and that the window was open. They looked at each other in astonishment and were hesitant to approach him, for they said, "he is in the grip of the spirit of prophecy; let us hear what God says to him." They waited a long time but he did not move at all . . . they approached him and turned him over and saw that his "circumcision" stood erect, for it was in his hand. And they shouted: "It has been given as a prodigious marvel to the house of Israel."[69]

As we would expect, the satire ends with a denunciation of hasidic stupidity and hasidic failure to comprehend that the Seer was nothing more than a charlatan.

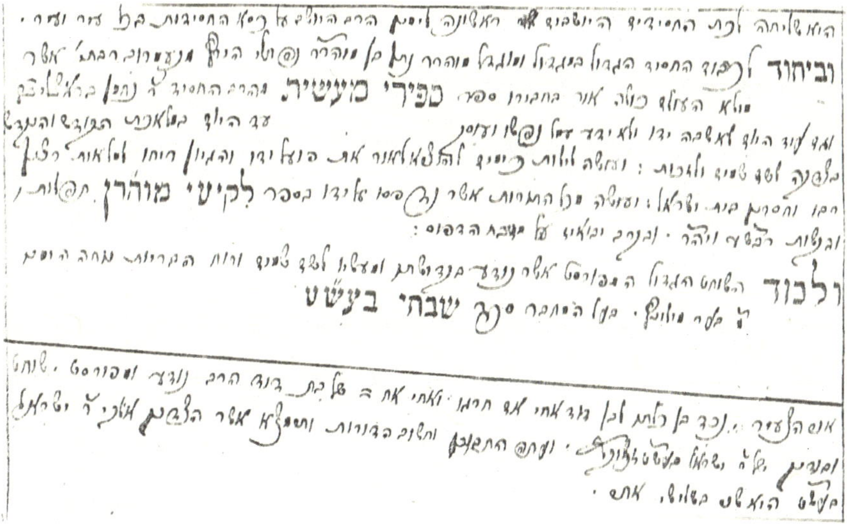

FIG. 3.2. The opening page of *Sefer nekiyut uferishut*

"From Drunkenness and Heavy-headedness I Fell": Tracing the Maskilic Version of the Fall

Although *Sefer nekiyut uferishut* remained in manuscript, and even its short version was not published until 1904, it appears likely that its contents were commonly known, and that the maskilic interpretation of the circumstances of the Seer's fall circulated widely. At least another four nineteenth-century literary witnesses to this tradition are extant: one from the 1840s, written by the satirist Isaak Erter (1791–1851); a second from the 1860s, penned by the journalist Alexander Zederbaum (1816–1893); a third from the 1870s, written by the famed rabbinic scholar Solomon (Shneur Zalman) Schechter (1847–1915); and a fourth from the 1890s, written by the historian Shimon Dubnow (1860–1941).

Isaak Erter's Gilgul Nefesh

Isaak Erter's biting satire *Gilgul nefesh* (Transmigration of a soul) was first published in 1845. As its title indicates, this satire describes the strange transmigrations of a wandering soul, which, in one of its avatars, inhabits the body of a hasidic leader. This rabbi—also the narrator-confessor—is none other than the Seer of Lublin, and Erter reconstructs the circumstances of the fall on Simhat Torah via his confession:

> And I lived like a king among his assembled troops on Sabbaths and holidays, and during the seventh month, on the Day of Remembrance—the New Year—and at the

conclusion of the harvest festival [Sukkot], on the eighth day of solemn assembly, Simhat Torah. And it came to pass that, on that occasion at night, I made a circuit of the *bimah*, uproariously celebrating according to regulation, skipping like a ram and shaking back and forth in God's house as is the regulation. And I drank wine, becoming inebriated according to regulation.[70] And while I was singing, "Abraham rejoices on Simhat Torah," I called out: "Make way! Widen the highway! For all these holy ones have descended to me, together they will come to my prayer house to rejoice with me on Simhat Torah . . . Lehayim, Father Abraham! I will raise the cup of deliverance and drink to the health of my guests. Lehayim, Father Abraham!" And I drank a glass for each and every holy one until I toasted each and every one listed in the book. And when I left off drinking a vision was revealed to me. In this vision I saw my house of prayer spinning, turning over in front of my eyes. I was frightened by this vision, lest I fall down drunk amongst the assembled congregation. I hurriedly called out: "Come exalted holy guests, come to my upper chamber! There we will stay a while together, take sweet secret counsel together on hidden matters." I went to my room, shutting the doors of the upper chamber and locking them.

Then my hasidim said one to the other: "There is none like our master! There is none like our rabbi! He is most holy, he is greatly exalted. For our holy patriarchs have left their seats in divine paradise to come to his synagogue to rejoice with him on Simhat Torah. And he spoke to them in our presence as a man speaks to his fellow man. And he was leaping and whirling with them, calling their names, and he drank to them and we witnessed it. Now they meet in his attic room, consulting together concerning our redemption and salvation, taking counsel to free us from our yoke and to bring a redeemer to Zion, our righteous Messiah. And our rabbi confronted the angel of each nation and a king, and brought him down into the dust. And in overcoming heavenly angels . . ."

While they spoke of these matters, their spirits taking heavenly flight, a young boy came shouting to his father, saying: "Father, I went to relieve myself between the buildings and I found our rabbi lying there dead." All my hasidim trembled and they all raced posthaste out of the doors and windows of the house, and found my body, my holy corpse, cast between the buildings in a place of vomit and filth, under the window of my upper chamber. And all raised an anguished cry, wailing and lamenting. All said, "Because of our sins the zaddik died. Because of our many iniquities he has perished and is gone! Because of our sins Samael overcame him while they wrestled, and picked him up and cast him out the window."

But I was engaged in no battle with Satan or an evil angel, I had a contest with a burning seraph, the burning liquor in my gut. After closing the doors of my chamber behind me, in hopes of ridding myself of the effects of the wine and in an effort to restore myself to my usual state I tried to vomit the wine out the window of my chamber in between the buildings, and from drunkenness and heavy-headedness I fell through the lattice, breaking my neck.[71]

Like his predecessor Ribal—in his 1823 antihasidic satire *Emek refa'im* (Valley of ghosts)—Erter portrays a fictional zaddik who deliberately misleads his foolish followers. They adhere to the absurd belief that their rabbi is closeted with the patriarchs and the angels in a joint attempt to bring the Messiah, and interpret his fall as the result of a struggle with satanic forces. But as the zaddik well knew but did not reveal, he did not struggle with a heavenly seraph, but with earthly wine.[72] In developing this zaddik's literary persona, Erter relied not only on satirical allusions to biblical personages who either shut themselves up in their rooms or died in a fall,[73] but also on realistic elements culled from anecdotes related about various zaddikim.[74] Erter's description of the fall, and the scatological motifs relating to the drunken zaddik rolling in the mire,[75] indicate the influence of the much earlier *Sefer nekiyut uferishut.*

Two other points must be highlighted. First of all, Erter's version of the fall reflects an awareness of the messianic component in the myth of the Seer. He quotes the fear-stricken hasidim, who are convinced that their rabbi is consorting with angels in an attempt to hasten the end of days: "Now they meet in his attic room, consulting together concerning our redemption and salvation, taking counsel to free us from our yoke and to bring a redeemer to Zion, our righteous Messiah." In *Nekiyut uferishut*, however, this messianic aspect is absent; there the hasidim simply interpret the Seer's actions as an attempt to effect a personal ascent of the soul. In any event, Erter's employment of the messianic myth allows us to date its origins more precisely—as certainly no later than that generation. It is also noteworthy that, in Erter's version, the zaddik (i.e., the Seer) dies immediately as a result of the fall, making Simhat Torah the day of his death, a shift that can be seen as the maskilic answer to the orally transmitted hasidic saying—recorded only in late versions—that the Seer's opponents would not even be able to drink water on the day of his death (which was Tisha beAv, a fast day). As Erter's fictional zaddik died on Simhat Torah, his opponents were therefore able to celebrate his death in drink.[76]

Alexander Zederbaum's Keter kehunah

We next find another echo of the maskilic version of the Seer's fall in the 1860s, in Alexander Zederbaum's *Keter kehunah* (Crown of priesthood). In this work, Zederbaum (known by his pseudonym, Erez), editor of the daily newspaper *Hamelits*, painted a broad, but hostile picture of the history of Hasidism. A native of Zamoshch, Zederbaum moved to Lublin following his marriage, remaining there for five years—from 1835 to 1840. Consequently, his remarks on the Seer and his fall may well preserve local traditions, and they form another link in the chain of critical reports on the Seer's fall:

On the night of Simhat Torah 5575 [1814], the Seer closeted himself in his room on the second story of his home. The one window overlooking the wide Jewish street was open;[77] it was very near to the ground. When the spirit of ecstasy settled upon him, he ran to and fro in the room. Moving in haste to look skyward, he lost his balance and fell full-length on the ground. The perpetual uncleanliness of that street saved him from sudden death, for had he fallen on the paving stones he would have smashed his skull and broken his neck, but to his delight there was a mound of refuse there on which he landed. In a flash, the hasidim who were rejoicing on a full glass of wine made a commotion, hurriedly bringing expert physicians to restore him for he had fainted. The fall and the fright set his bones atremble, so that he tossed and turned in pain for nine months, until he died and was gathered unto his fathers on Tisha beAv 5575 [1815]. The hasidim said that the zaddik had put his head out the window in order to grab hovering angels by their robes as a means of hastening the end of days, but Satan succeeded in confusing him and pushing him until he fell through the lattice.[78] Miraculously, they recount, there was a row of empty glass bottles on that windowsill but when he fell he neither broke nor overturned a single bottle.[79]

Zederbaum's version differs entirely from the earlier ones. A comparison shows that Zederbaum provides a more moderate, balanced, and rational presentation of the hasidic version of the events leading to the fall. The Seer is portrayed here not as a drunkard who lost his balance when trying to urinate or vomit, but rather as an excitable eccentric in an ecstatic state, who fell while trying to grab angels by their robes in an attempt to hasten the end of days. Zederbaum's version also downplays the miraculous aspects of the fall by noting that the window was not much above street level, and that a pile of refuse cushioned the Seer's fall. To this rational explanation, he juxtaposes the hasidic version of the Seer's heroic struggle with Satan, who pushed him, and the miracle of the undisturbed wine bottles.

Solomon Schechter's Sihot hanei tsantera dedahava

Shortly thereafter, in 1877, another brief version of the fall appeared in the margins of a short, antihasidic satire, *Sihot hanei tsantera dedahava* (Conversations of two fine fellows), written by Solomon Schechter, a scion of a Habad family, who later achieved fame as the scholar of the Cairo Geniza. Writing under the pseudonym Yahats ben Rahtsa, Schechter published bogus hasidic letters styled after *Megaleh temirin*, in which he mocked the zaddikim of Sadigura against the background of the temporary defection in 1869 of Yisrael of Ruzhin's son, Dov (Bernyu) of Leova, to the maskilic camp in

Chernovtsy. Bernyu subsequently recanted and returned to his brother's court in Sadigura, where he remained in isolation until his death in 1876.

In Schechter's satire, two veteran hasidim and one young hasid are trying to decipher Bernyu's seclusion. They believe that he never went over to the maskilic camp; what happened was that what other zaddikim did covertly, he did overtly. In depicting Bernyu's early seclusion and depression to his hasidim, the narrator recollects the Seer's fall:

> Although we were aware that his [Dov of Leova's] intentions were good, that he wanted to bring the Messiah, why did he have to be so stubborn? The time was certainly not yet ripe. Why did he have to tempt Samael, who had already removed several zaddikim from the world in this fashion, like the holy zaddik of Lublin, who wanted to bring the Messiah. What did Samael do? He tempted the aforementioned zaddik to imbibe large quantities of wine on Simhat Torah. When the zaddik went to his bedroom, he took him and thrust him out the window, killing him—a veritable act of murder. *This gave the heretics an opportunity to say that he was drunk.* And who knows what else might befall our rabbi?[80]

Here Schechter applied the original polemical tradition of the Seer's fall to a new purpose: a satiric blasting of the tragi-pathetic figure of Dov of Leova, a figure portrayed and manipulated by the various contesting factions—hasidim, rabbis, and maskilim—for their own ends.

Shimon Dubnow's Toldot hahasidut

The final transmigration of the maskilic version of the Seer's fall belongs to the early scientific historiography of hasidism. In 1892, the historian Shimon Dubnow, then involved in his Russian studies of the history of Hasidism, issued his well-known call—*Nahpesah venahkorah* (Let us search and examine) inviting the Jewish public to send him material for a history of the Jews in Poland and Russia.[81] One of Dubnow's many correspondents was Yaakov Shapiro, an antihasidic scholar and amateur historian from Międzyrzec Podlaski, who, for remuneration, provided Dubnow with important documents and data on Hasidism in Poland, and even wrote a now-lost treatise on the history of this branch of Hasidism.[82] In one of his letters to Dubnow, he wrote: "Regarding your surprise at the story of the death of the Rabbi of Lublin found in *Keter kehunah*, I have already clarified to you that this is an ancient rumor. I have now seen it among Erter's seventeen transmigrations, the one when the soul entered a rabbi. You can find it there in *Sefer hatsofeh*, my friend, all the details concerning the Rabbi of Lublin's death. And Erter's version preceded the one in *Hamelits* by about forty years."[83]

From Shapiro's remark, "this is an ancient rumor," we can infer that the maskilic tradition that Dubnow found so surprising had circulated among Polish mitnagedim for a long time. In any event, we have seen that its sources were not dependent either on Zederbaum's *Keter kehunah* (*Hamelits*, in Shapiro's letter) or on Erter's *Gilgul nefesh.* In his own book, Dubnow took care to adopt neither the maskilic nor the hasidic version of events. He presents both, though it is not difficult to guess which he thought had greater credence: "The hasidim believe that some element of the 'demonic forces' grabbed him and threw him out of the window, whereas the mitnagedim have a rational explanation: the zaddik drank too much wine during the holiday and became drunk. Upon putting his head out the window he fell out."[84]

The Seer's Fall: A Suicide Attempt?

The Seer of Lublin's tragic fall, and his death some nine months later, marked a turning point in Polish hasidic history. With the death of this foremost of the four "first generation" leaders of Hasidism in Poland,[85] hasidic leadership passed into the hands of the Seer's disciples, who split into many rival dynasties. At their vortex was the court of Pshishkha-Kotsk, and its many opponents.

The Seer's enigmatic personality and the messianic myth linked to him during his lifetime, on the one hand, and the mysterious fashion in which he met his death, on the other hand, fired the imagination of his contemporaries and of following generations. The maskilic exposé of the embarrassing circumstances surrounding his fall found expression in a series of satires and maskilic works, beginning with *Sefer nekiyut uferishut*—written in 1815, while the Seer lay dying—continuing in Erter's *Gilgul nefesh*, published in 1845, and concluding with Zederbaum's publication of *Keter kehunah* in 1867, and Schechter's publication of *Sihot hanei tsantera dedahova* ten years later. It also appears likely that the continued circulation of similar oral rumors and gossip formed the background for the subsequent early-twentieth-century creation of hasidic legend, with its apologetic and polemical explanation of the "true" circumstances surrounding the Seer's fall.

Surprisingly, the maskilic interpretation, which failed to strike roots, did not survive in historical memory, whereas the romantic hasidic myth, with its messianic tinge—notwithstanding its internal doubters[86]—gained in strength. The autobiographical remarks of the hasidic author Yehiel Granatstein are instructive:

> The author, a native of Lublin, recalled: When he was young, still attending *heder*, and at a slightly more advanced age, he would from time to time go—like many other lads

attracted to stories of zaddikim heard and absorbed at home or from hasidic elders in the *shtiblakh*—to the rabbi's study house . . . There, in the open courtyard that provided access to Szeroka Street, he would look at the small window, the window of the dramatically exciting "Fall" . . . From there he would continue on to the aforementioned street and find the spot that informants knew to tell of, the veritable spot where they found the Rabbi of Lublin lying, mumbling, sighing.[87]

Intriguing evidence of the conversion of the site of the fall to a holy place comes from a book testifying to the customs of the admor Hayyim Elazar Shapira of Munkatsh (d. 1937): "When he was in Lublin he entered the holy precinct, that room of the rabbi of Lublin, and recited some psalms there, and saw that window that overlooked the market, which was opened enough to let in air, because it was not fully opened during the fall, just partly. And the window is very small, for naturally a person does not enter through a window, and that is from where the rabbi of Lublin fell."[88]

Another reflection of the conflicting versions of the Seer's fate comes from the conversations of Yitshak Gruenbaum's parents, as reported in his memoirs. (Gruenbaum [1879–1970] was a leading Zionist figure in Poland.) His mother, the Seer's granddaughter, represented the mystical hasidic version, whereas his father, from a mitnagedic background, represented the rational maskilic one. Gruenbaum recounted:

Regarding the Seer of Lublin I heard a story of his death on Simhat Torah day. There were two versions to this story: my mother's and my father's. According to my mother's tale, the Seer foresaw that the Messiah was to descend from heaven on Simhat Torah and that he must go forth and greet him. The rabbi decided to lift himself up and ascend at what he calculated was the moment that the Messiah was beginning his descent to earth. He opened the window, stood on its sill, and went. He failed to rise, fell and broke his neck, and died.

In my father's version this was a simple matter. The rebbe, who drank copiously in honor of Simhat Torah, fell from the window and was killed. Once, when I visited Lublin, friends from a hasidic family showed me the window.[89]

The hasidic version was also incorporated into the works of writers who reshaped it to their needs,[90] and it was even adopted, albeit with some reservations, by historians and students of hasidism.[91] In his seminal monograph *Hasidism in Poland*, Aaron Ze'ev Aescoly stressed the messianic aspect of the Seer's teachings, even unquestioningly accepting the hasidic interpretation of the fall.[92] Martin Buber took matters one step further in his novel *For the Sake of Heaven*, in which he endowed the Seer with that same messianic stamp, even devoting an entire chapter to the circumstances surrounding the fall, again only according to the hasidic interpretation.[93]

FIG. 3.3. The Seer's tombstone in the Lublin cemetery

Obviously it is neither within our power to recreate the Seer's fall, nor to determine which of the conflicting versions is correct. It is possible to cautiously suggest another terrible, even more embarrassing option, only hinted at in the sources: that the Seer's fall was not accidental, but a deliberate suicide attempt. His explicitly reported request that his wife and disciples guard him very carefully may support this possibility. Moreover, according to the hasidic tale, the Seer admitted that he deserved to die because of his attempt to force the coming of the Messiah, and attributed his rescue from death to the intervention of the Maggid of Kozhenits, who had died a week earlier.

Although this is not a psychological study, it is difficult to escape a foray into this realm. Perhaps at that time the Seer suffered deep depression accompanied by suicidal thoughts. Based as it is on vague hints and polemical interpretation, this explanation may seem unfounded, but Zvi Mark recently drew attention to an almost explicit proof, found in a kosher hasidic source: the hagiographic work *Nifle'ot harabbi*, which is entirely devoted to glorification of the Seer of Lublin. This source reports a much earlier suicide attempt while the Seer was still a student of Elimelekh of Lyzhansk:

> When our holy master from Lublin . . . was in Lyzhansk, he would walk up the hill in Lyzhansk with the holy rabbi, R. Zelke . . . of Grodzisk . . . and these righteous ones would seclude themselves there in the profundity of their thoughts. Once the holy rabbi . . . from Lublin . . . was alone with his thoughts concerning humility and excessive abnegation in repentance to the extent that, in his great holiness, *he could find no counsel for his soul other than giving his life. He resolved to do so, and he was approaching the edge of the mountain, to cast himself from it*, but the holy rabbi, R. Zelke . . . sensed his holy thoughts. He placed his hand in the belt of the holy rabbi . . . and did not allow him to do so. He enheartened him with holy counsels and words, as is the manner of the *ṣaddiqim.*

Thus the Seer's suicide attempt was thwarted by his friend Zelke. The story goes on to relate that, for years, the Seer resented his friend for having saved his life. Once, when Reb Zelke came to visit the Seer in Lublin "our holy master was overcome with joy, and said as follows: 'Reb Zelke, I love you greatly, for in the first *gilgul*, you were my son . . . But when I remember what happened in Lyzhansk, I cannot love you wholly.'"[94]

It is highly unlikely that the actual circumstances of the Seer's fall will ever come to light, nor is it important that they do so. Yet close examination of the different versions of the fall highlights the satirical-polemical stamp in each and reveals the convoluted paths of memory building, which are not always guided by the truth as it was. We may compare the hasidic and maskilic traditions to two rivals who seemingly ignore each other. But not only do we possess clear evidence that they are aware of each other and maintain an indirect dialogue, we see how that reflected dialogue has shaped their imagery and their historical patterns.[95]

4 "Happy Are the Persecuted"

The Opposition to Bratslav Hasidism

> There were moments when our flock thought that our rabbi's way was about to end, heaven forfend, such as in the time of the great controversy in Rabbi Nathan's day; as well as in the day of Rabbi Nahman of Tulchin; and similarly when the Communists came to power and said that anyone caught as a Bratslav hasid would be killed; and after the Second World War, when most of our flock in Russia and in Poland was wiped out. Nonetheless, the words of our rabbi, who explicitly promised: "My fire will burn until the coming of the Messiah" still stand and are renewed over and over with greater strength each time, inexplicably.
> —*Siah sarfei kodesh*, 5:184

Three Waves of Persecution

Bratslav Hasidism—its personalities, thought, and ways—is recognized both by hasidim in other sects and scholars of Hasidism as an exceptional phenomenon and a distinct socioreligious branch of the hasidic world. From the sect's earliest days, the strong colors in which its founder, Rabbi Nahman of Bratslav, was painted attracted the interest of observers of this figure and his path. Unable to remain neutral, some observers moved toward amity and wonder; others tended toward suspicion and contempt. The controversy surrounding Rabbi Nahman and the hatred for those who followed his path—who were unable to unite and crown a successor to their dead rebbe, and were therefore contemptuously dubbed the "Dead Hasidim"—have been unceasing. Shadowing Bratslav history to the present is the stamp of enmity on the part of certain zaddikim and their followers, particularly in the regions where Bratslav emerged (the provinces of Kiev, Volhynia, and Podolia). The manifold twists and turns of the sect's history, its unique individual and group portrait, and its varied literary legacy lent Bratslav an impact in mainstream hasidic history far beyond its actual weight in numbers, property, and distribution.[1]

Scholarly study of Hasidism identifies two main waves of persecution of Bratslav hasidim. The initial wave of persecution—led by Rabbi Aryeh Leib of Shpole, known as the Shpoler Zayde (the grandfather from Shpole)—began during Rabbi Nahman's lifetime. Much has been written regarding this controversy, its motivation, scope, and outcome.[2] A generation after the deaths of Rabbi Nahman (late 1810) and of the Shpoler Zayde (late 1811), the controversy was renewed, this time much more forcefully, by the zaddik Rabbi Moshe Zvi Giterman of Savran. His angry blasts targeted the Bratslav hasidim of his day, especially their leader, Rabbi Nathan Sternhartz of Nemirov, Nahman's amanuensis and interpreter.

This controversy, which peaked in 1835–38, was one of the harshest in hasidic history. As the historian Raphael Mahler puts it: "The persecution of the Bratslav hasidim by the Savran hasidim was crueler even than the mitnagedic persecution of hasidim in the previous century."[3] Nonetheless, few data have survived on this controversy and its underlying causes. Not even its motivation, real or imagined, is clear.[4] Was it a direct continuation of the earlier controversy surrounding Rabbi Nahman, in which case one sheds light on the other, or was it prompted by new, entirely different circumstances? Despite the fact that nearly all the testimony to what Bratslav sources term the "great controversy" is cited by Bratslav authors—and therefore tend to exaggerate the harm done them—the truth is readily ascertainable: Bratslav Hasidism was grievously wounded. We hear of beatings and torture, of damage to property and livelihood, murder threats, denunciations, slander, and involvement of the authorities, which eventually led to Nathan of Nemirov's arrest and expulsion from the town of Bratslav. Reportedly, so harsh were these events that "only five individuals from Bratslav withstood the test and continued to worship God as before. But most of the members of the circle in Bratslav could not return to their former level of worship even after God, blessed be he, assisted our teacher Rabbi Nathan, and granted him safety from all the enemies surrounding him."[5] This controversy abated after the death of its two main protagonists: the Savraner rebbe (early 1838) and Nathan of Nemirov (late 1844).[6]

Following Nathan of Nemirov's death, the persecuted, diminished Bratslav hasidim faced a severe leadership crisis. In the absence of a worthy successor to Nathan, combining his unending devotion to Rabbi Nahman's heritage and his outstanding spiritual and practical talent, Nathan's organizational initiatives came to an end. Evidently, the up-and-coming figure in

Bratslav was Nathan's disciple, Nahman of Tulchin (1814–84), who had been groomed as his successor.[7] But, just as Nathan's path to leadership was rocky and faced internal opposition,[8] so too was Nahman of Tulchin's status disputed; evidently, a number of candidates saw themselves as worthy of being leaders.[9] The internal rivalry in Bratslav following Nathan of Nemirov's death must be viewed not just on the interpersonal level—tension between rival leaders—but also against the background of the overall processes of atomization and factionalization affecting Hasidism from the latter half of the nineteenth century. Certainly, intramural leadership struggles impaired Bratslav cohesion; paradoxically, however, external controversy and persecution counterbalanced this inner fragmentation. The degradation and shameful curses the Bratslavers endured, particularly when they gathered at Rabbi Nahman's grave in Uman (in Kiev Province) on Rosh Hashanah eve, were converted into a source of strength that contributed to Bratslav intimacy and an obstinate ability to stand united.[10]

But the anti-Bratslav campaign, which ostensibly died down after the death of the Savraner rebbe, again erupted in the 1860s. The following pages examine the various manifestations of this third wave of anti-Bratslav persecution, in the forefront of which were several Twersky zaddikim belonging to the Chernobyl dynasty. This dynasty ruled highhandedly over most of the hasidic communities in the southwestern provinces of the Russian Pale of Settlement, and had no qualms about taking harsh measures against those who balked at following its orders.[11] The discussion focuses on two events: first, the incitement against, and recurring attacks on, the Bratslavers during their annual gathering at Rabbi Nahman's grave in Uman; and second, the story of a Bratslav ritual slaughterer who was dismissed from his job because he reneged on a promise to the local zaddik not to study *Likutei Moharan.* Based on these and other incidents, I attempt to determine the scope and motives for this conflict, both hidden and overt, as well as the maskilic and hasidic attitudes toward Bratslav during the period under consideration. An ancillary issue in hasidic history from the middle to the end of the nineteenth century is that of "takeovers" by zaddikim of the leadership of new Jewish communities in the Ukraine. Although only indirectly connected to the attitude toward Bratslav Hasidism, the takeovers' centrality to the study of the formation of hasidic towns—towns with a largely hasidic Jewish population—places them at the heart of the discussion here.

"A Fearful, Soul-shaking, Bone-shattering, Dispiriting Scene": The Maskilic Testimony

Maskilic interest in the persecution of the Bratslav hasidim had its inception in a series of articles appearing in *Hamelits* in 1864 with the title "Hasidei

Braslav ve'ir Uman." An anonymous author from Chyhryn, identifying himself only as Alef-Tav,[12] sent Alexander Zederbaum, the *Hamelits* editor, an eyewitness report on events in Uman during Rosh Hashanah 1863. However, this article's acerbity, coupled with Zederbaum's reluctance to anger the hasidim, delayed its publication.[13] After five months had gone by, the author sent a threatening letter to Zederbaum stating that if Zederbaum did not publish his article, he would have it translated into Russian and published with a note stating that he had "sent it to *Hamelits* and that it favored those who walk in darkness and hide their sins." Having concluded that it was preferable to publish the article, Zederbaum introduced the article with a note that he would gladly print the words of anyone who could refute Alef-Tav's remarks.[14]

Alef-Tav's series opened with a firsthand account of what he termed "a fearful, soul-shaking, bone-shattering, dispiriting scene." He began his description by noting that the Bratslavers who came to Uman annually for the High Holidays were true and innocent hasidim who did not diverge from the regulations of the *Shulhan arukh:*

> But suddenly, a band of boys, delinquents, surrounded them on all sides; they too belonged to the Jewish nation. And they flung dirt at them and threw stones, shouting "Bratslaver dogs![15] *Nahmantshikim!*" When those unfortunates saw that they had fallen among scorpions and were confronted by evil intention, they hurried to take refuge in their study house, grasping its corners in order to hide from the steady stream of stones and deadly missiles being shot in raging wrath and overflowing fury. But unto the altar this enemy burst forth with outstretched arm and awesome power, shattering the windows of the house and smashing its utensils without mercy. While you silently wonder for what and because of what all this is happening, a large stone flies with lightning speed and lodges in the forehead of a Bratslav hasid, who falls down in a faint. This angers you and makes your wrath burn, and then another stone is cast at the Torah ark, smashing its doors into fragments!
>
> All this you witness, and your eyes dim, your heart is in an uproar, and your knees stumble, and your mouth involuntarily utters the words: "My God! What is this? Where do I stand? What is the name of this land upon which I stand? And in what year do I witness such a thing?"
>
> Know this: you are in Russia, in the town of Uman, in the year 5623, 1863 in the general calendar.[16]

Next the author briefly outlined the background to this cruel persecution, from the Shpoler Zayde's controversy with Nahman of Bratslav, to the Savraner's controversy with Nathan of Nemirov, recreating from memory the text of the Savraner's excommunication of the Bratslav hasidim.[17] Even though the protagonists of the initial controversies were no longer among the living, persecution of the Bratslavers had not ceased. Not only did the Savraner's adherents remain mindful of their rabbi's command, they were joined by the followers of other zaddikim who wished to fan the flames of controversy. Here the writer clearly alludes to the zaddikim of the house of Chernobyl: "We have heard on more than one occasion hateful, loathsome remarks issuing from the mouths of the rabbi of T. . . and of the rabbi of Sk. . . and their aim was to *obliterate the Bratslavers from Ukrainian soil.*"[18] As we shall see below, the writer was referring to the brothers David of Talne and Yitshak of Skvira.

With respect to their attitude toward the Bratslav hasidim, the writer goes on to say, the residents of Uman are divided into three main groups: (a) the maskilim who protest "the scandalous beating and harsh persecution of fellow Jews just because they hold different opinions, and demand in the name of our holy Torah and of Haskalah love for every person no matter what;"[19] (b) "the fools, the worthless and reckless fellows, and mischievous lads" who actually beat the Bratslav hasidim and throw stones and dirt; and (c) "the remaining residents of the town," namely the hasidim who "absolutely hate the Bratslavers in their hearts, speak harshly of them and impute to them things that never were." The latter, who take intense interest in tales about zaddikim, attribute to dead and living zaddikim the purported command "to destroy the Bratslavers, to make them an object of derision, for they [the zaddikim] promised the assailants and persecutors the world to come and paradise." Upon hearing such promises, the fools rush to wreak their wrath upon the Bratslavers, to the inciters' joy, who watch the altercation and recite the blessing "on having lived and been sustained and therefore able to reach this season, for even ignoramuses and simple people—I copy their exact words—know the divine word and are zealous for his name and his memory that the wicked desecrate. And they praise God not only with their lips but with their hands and fists."[20]

For the writer, the abuse of the Bratslav hasidim recalled Roman gladiatorial combat.[21] Notwithstanding his declaration that he did not belong to the hasidic community—and even if his main aim was to publicly mock the hasidism and their internecine wars, to portray them as petty, small-minded creatures—Alef-Tav's covert sympathies appear to be with the Bratslavers.

From the inception of its antihasidic campaign, maskilic propaganda consistently sought to uncover internal controversies in the hasidic world. This was for two reasons: first, to present Hasidism as a divided, disintegrating social entity at war within, which could unite only defensively against Haskalah and modernity; and second, to present Hasidism as intellectually withered, a movement that, because of faulty values, persecuted not only external, but also internal, opponents. For the maskilim, anti-Bratslav incitement was not just an embodiment of internecine divisions among the hasidim, but also a manifestation of jealousy and evil, and intolerance for other viewpoints. As a member of a minority group in constant friction with traditional society, it was ostensibly easy for this maskilic writer to identify with others persecuted for their desire to express their faith, a right the maskilim sought for themselves. But the outcome of this potential identification could not be cooperation. For all their oddity, the Bratslavers were an integral part of traditional hasidic society, one that preferred enmity and disgrace at the hands of their hasidic brethren to cooperation with the hated maskilim, as evidenced by Bratslav's harsh antimaskilic literature, almost unmatched for its sting.[22]

Following the publication of this three-part article, Zederbaum sought to mask the "political" reasons underlying its initial concealment. He rationalized the delay as grounded in his responsibility to authenticate what he published: "We have investigated and inquired carefully for the past five months and to our regret it is true, and we could not break the principle we have set for ourselves, to impartially report the desecration of the divine name and the degradation of the honor of Israel. It is our hope that the words of the author, written with love and sensitivity, will bear fruit, and it will gladden our heart to hear that the anger between the different sects has ceased, and that the Bratslaver dwells [in peace] with the other hasidim, and that they are treated in good faith."[23]

Zederbaum addressed the persecution of the Bratslav hasidim in his *Keter kehunah.* There he interpreted it as a logical outcome of the divisiveness and enmity that characterize hasidic society:

> See how, in our day, not even a century after the founding of the Bratslav sect, hatred has already grown against them to the extent that they are stoned and thought worse than idolaters; also against those who believe in living zaddikim in our day they [the hasidim] raise a hand, in every place where one sect is more powerful than its sister, to wipe out and destroy them: their ritual slaughterers are outlawed, even though they share the laws found in *Yoreh de'ah;* a prayer leader from their midst does not enable the congregation to fulfill its prayer obligation, even though like them he prays *nusah Sefarad* unchanged; they will not heed a rabbi who follows a different zaddik . . . even if the four parts of the *Shulhan arukh* are open before him and he forms his opinion on their basis. And even though they have not yet decreed that there shall be no intermarriage between them, in actuality, no hasid who is loyal to a particular zaddik would even consider marrying his son or daughter to the son or daughter of a hasid who believes in a different zaddik . . . They have separate synagogues and consider it a sin to pray, even if by chance, in the study house of a zaddik that they do not follow. Nor will they take melamedim for their sons from among the ranks of those they see as harming the Shekhinah because they sanctify a different holy person.[24]

Another maskil impressed by Alef-Tav of Chyhryn's article was Avraham Ber Gottlober, who relates the persecution of the Bratslavers during those years in his memoirs. He too was able to identify the persecutors—the Chernobyl zaddikim:

> To this day, the followers of Rabbi Nahman, who remain faithful to his ways, are more hotly pursued than other hasidic sects. In particular, the hasidim of the town of Uman persecute the Bratslav hasidim when they gather on Rosh Hashanah to pray at the grave of their rabbi who is buried there . . . Every year when they gather there, other hasidim come and call for blows and strike and wound them and these are the names that they call them: "Bratslaver dogs," "*Nahmantshikim.*" As was written in the newspaper *Hamelits* . . . The first to persecute them was the "Grandfather" from Shpole; followed by the rabbi Moshe of Savran . . . *and in our day other rebbes, the sons of the zaddik of Chernobyl,* who are scattered throughout the land, *have arisen against them.*[25]

Gottlober also voiced his wish that the anonymous author from Chyhryn fulfill his promise to publish "the history of Reb Nahman and his hasidim and the reason for the controversy." Was his contemporary Gottlober, with his close interest in the history of Hasidism, unaware of the true reason for the pent-up hatred, controversy, and persecution of the Bratslavers? This was certainly not the case. Gottlober's wish must be seen not as expressing his ignorance, but rather as voicing his desire that the matter of the persecution come to greater public attention through the agency of someone with detailed knowledge of it.

The interest displayed by maskilim such as Gottlober, Zederbaum, Alef-Tav, and many others was ambivalent in nature.[26] On the one hand, they were influenced by Yosef Perl's satiric oeuvre that mocked Rabbi Nahman and his writings;[27] on the other hand, they felt natural empathy for the distress of the persecuted. Even if they could not identify with them or with their beliefs, they still viewed the Bratslavers as a limb of the nation whose unity and reform they desired; accordingly, they sought to find what they viewed as positive characteristics in the Bratslavers—even if their discoveries were of doubtful accuracy.[28]

"Per the Hooligans' Code": The Talne Hasidim's Anti-Bratslav Campaign

As noted above, the zaddikim of the Chernobyl dynasty were in the forefront of the anti-Bratslav campaign of the 1860s, primarily David Twersky of Talne (1808–82), one of nineteenth-century Hasidism's outstanding, most intriguing figures.[29] The fact that Talne hasidim assumed a leading role in the persecution of Bratslav hasidim emerges from the memoirs of the Yiddish writer Mordekhai Spektor (1858–1925), a native of Uman and a scion of a family affiliated with Talne Hasidism. During his childhood, he witnessed, and participated in, the yearly spectacle of abuse. It was only natural that the town youths, including Spektor, saw in these anti-Bratslav incidents an unfailing opportunity for mischief and took part in administering blows.

Spektor, himself the victim of a thrashing at the hand of Bratslavers exacting revenge for Talne harassment, found it difficult to understand both the extreme hatred for the Bratslavers and why Jews beat each other. He recalled that the few Bratslav hasidim who lived in Uman were not harassed during the year, but with the approach of the month of Elul, when the Bratslavers streamed to Nahman's grave, the atmosphere changed: the town filled with hatred. The townspeople refused to have any dealings with the Bratslavers and were unwilling to rent rooms to them, except secretly and for huge sums. The hasidic factions in Uman (Talne, Skvira, Chernobyl, Sadigura, and others), at war among themselves all year long, united briefly against the Bratslavers. Assisting them in their harassment were punks, ignoramuses, and strong men (butchers, wagoners, and the like), who had been persuaded that their actions possessed religious value. Some took advantage of the inflamed religious atmosphere against the Bratslavers to beat up heretics, maskilim, and curious bystanders, as well as women in modern dress (at the time, crinolines were in fashion). Spektor also related that the incessant badgering forced the Bratslav hasidim to hire Russian soldiers for protection, at great expense, while they prayed at the gravesite and in their *kloiz*.[30]

Another who also recounted the harassment of Bratslavers in Uman was the maskil and teacher Elimelekh Wexler (1843–1919). Orphaned at the age of eleven, he was raised in his uncle's home in Uman. This uncle was a Talne hasid, and young Elimelekh, like Mordekhai Spektor, joined the festival of violence and hatred:

> The Bratslavers had built themselves a separate prayer house in Uman. All year long this house stood empty and abandoned, no resident of Uman would enter, because it was abhorrent to them. In my day, Reb Nathan [of Nemirov] was no longer alive, just an old man, named Naftali—not Reb Naftali—was confined in this house of God. He was isolated there almost like a leper; if he ventured outside children would jeer and call out after him: "Bratslaver dog!" and throw dirt at him. Only on Rosh Hashanah was this house filled with festival pilgrims from other towns—nor did they escape humiliating taunts. Crowds of Uman residents used to surround the prayer house, *myself included*, and we threw stones and broke windows per the hooligans' code, with all its stipulations, *for so our teachers and parents instructed us* . . . When Reb Naftali died and they carried his bier past the *kloiz* where I and my young companions studied, we did not follow his bier as was the custom, just the opposite: we remained standing where we were at the windows and our mouths were full of malicious laugh-

ter at his affliction. *So great were the hatred and loathing that had been instilled in our hearts.*[31]

Although Wexler attributed this phenomenon to the instructions of the Savraner zaddik (d. 1838), it is more likely that in the 1850s and 1860s, the wheels of violence were propelled by the orders of the Talner rebbe, whose followers comprised the majority of the Uman hasidim.

Internal Bratslav tradition also tells of clashes between David of Talne's followers and Bratslav hasidim during this period: "Reb Avraham Bernyu, the grandson of our rabbi [Nahman of Bratslav], arranged for his daughter to marry a Talne hasid. On the Sabbath before the wedding, when the groom was called up to the Torah, he [Avraham Bernyu] traveled there and the rebbe, Rabbi David of Talne . . . treated him fondly and seated him in a place of honor by his side. In the course of their conversation, Rabbi Avraham Bernyu asked him: 'They say that your group takes issue with my grandfather.' Rabbi David protestingly replied: 'Heaven forfend! But when they travel to Uman for Rosh Hashanah, they, meaning our flock, bait me and my people until this sparks fights among the hasidim.'"[32]

Thus, there was no disagreement between the sides regarding the fact of Bratslav-Talne conflict in Uman. What was open to interpretation was who bore responsibility for the incitement, provocation, and violence: the Bratslav hasidim, who taunted all the other hasidim and mocked their zaddikim (as David of Talne claimed, with real or feigned innocence) or the Talne hasidim, who harassed a unique minority group just because its ways and style differed from those of all other groups (as the Bratslavers claimed, with real or feigned innocence).

The Rzhishchev Affair and the Edict Forbidding Zaddikim to Travel

Although Alef-Tav of Chyhryn noted his intention of publishing a separate treatise giving details on the controversy from beginning to end, he did not fulfill this promise; a year later, however, he did submit to *Hamelits* another report on Bratslav Hasidism. In this new article, he noted that, for the first time in forty years, on Rosh Hashanah 1864, the Bratslav hasidim were not persecuted in Uman: they were not cursed, thrashed, or humiliated; in fact, they were simply left alone.

He attributed this surprising change to a zaddik—whose name he does not reveal—who had a month earlier gone to the town of Rzhishchev on a fundraising campaign.[33] This town, however, was under another zaddik's control. Naturally, the local hasidim reviled and humiliated the intruder, raining stones on him "until he was but a pace from death." Bruised and humiliated, the zaddik fled for his life from the traitorous town and named the rabbi Y. Y. of Rzhishchev "perfectly wicked, and said that it was forbidden to look upon his visage." As for his hasidim, "they are certainly *mamzerim* . . . and the meat slaughtered by their ritual slaughterers is not kosher, and the prayers of their cantors are an abomination." As was then the practice, the zaddik's followers were almost prepared to inform the authorities that the rabbi of Rzhishchev was dealing in counterfeit bills—"just as they had always done to the Bratslavers." And "all agree," Alef-Tav summed up, "that the quiet that reigned this year between the long-standing contestants [the Bratslavers and their opponents] was rooted in the above-mentioned episode." Some relate that the zaddik who was disgraced explicitly said that "he thought it an honor and a great favor to be stoned and that the Bratslavers were not deserving of such an honor. He therefore ordered that they not be harmed." The author concluded with the hope that this quiet would continue the next year as well, and "that he would see the Bratslaver live a peaceful, secure life with all the hasidim and their rebbes. The Bratslaver will not hate the T. . . and the T. . . will not hate the Bratslaver."[34]

But can we accept Alef-Tav's description at face value? Or is this simply a fiction, or at the very least, an exaggeration? It turns out, however, that the episode at Rzhishchev was widely publicized among the Jews of Kiev Province. The following remarks come from the memoirs of the writer Zvi Kasdai (1865–1937), a native of Dubova in Kiev Province: "Reb Duvidl [of Talne] . . . came to a certain town near Dubova. That town 'belonged' to the zaddik of Rzhishchev. One of the Rzhishchev fanatics lifted a stone and lobbed it into Reb Duvidl's coach. However, Reb Duvidl managed to catch the stone in his hand and, overcome by emotion, said to his hasidim: 'I see this stone as the true devotion of a Jewish soul . . . I envy it' . . . And upon his return home—so they said then—he commanded that this stone be placed among the many precious belongings with which his room was filled, as is well known."[35] The version preserved by Kasdai (who was a newborn in 1865 when these events took place!)[36] represents a later, romantic refinement permeated by the moral lessons attributed to this episode over time. Alef-Tav's account, on the other hand, contemporaneous with these events, retains the atmosphere of interfactional hatred and enmity. The shower of stones with which the residents of Rzhishchev greeted the zaddik, leaving him nearly at death's door, was in Kasdai's account reduced to a single stone, saved by the zaddik as a decorative souvenir.

From the hints embedded in Alef-Tav's account, we can identify the other players. Rabbi Y. Y. is Yaakov Yosef Mendel ben Moshe of Rzhishchev;[37] the zaddik of T. . . is David of Talne; and the T. . . who hate the Bratslavers are the Talne hasidim as a whole. In a note appended to his article, Alef-Tav wrote: "I cannot conceal from the reader the spread of a rumor in our districts that the rabbi's brothers, the famed zaddikim of T. . . [Rabbi Avraham of Trisk?], of Sk. . . [Rabbi Yitshak of Skvira], of Rach. . . [Rabbi Yohanan of Rachmistrivke] . . . and of Ch. . . [Rabbi Yaakov Yisrael of Cherkas? Rabbi Aharon of Chernobyl?], for hidden reasons, appointed the rabbi of T. . . [David of Talne] . . . to travel to Rzhishchev even though they knew he would be entering a scorpion's nest." Given our knowledge of the murky relationships between some of the Chernobyl brothers, this rumor regarding a fraternal conspiracy against Reb David is not surprising.[38] However, given the polemically hostile context of its publication, we can lend it little credence. It must be judged like any rumor that its reporter has deliberately obfuscated (the reference to "hidden reasons").

The events at Rzhishchev also receive mention in a police report dispatched to the governor of Kiev Province on 30 September 1864.[39] Undoubtedly nurtured by information provided by informers from the antihasidic camp, this report had far-reaching consequences for the Ukrainian zaddikim. Forced to intervene in this quarrel, the provincial authorities forbade Rabbi David of Talne (seen as the most deleterious influence) and the other zaddikim to leave their towns and travel among the Jewish communities without official permission. Hasidic sources refer to this edict forbidding travel as "the edict concerning the zaddikim."[40]

In the above-mentioned police report, there is a detailed description of David of Talne's journey a month earlier among the towns and villages of Kiev Province that he had not previously visited, and the method that he and his followers employed in their "takeovers" of these communities. Notwithstanding its antihasidic bias, this description preserves an important record of the typical ways in which entire Jewish communities became the followers of this charismatic zaddik.

Reb David's journey started in July 1864. On 9 August, he reached the town of Boguslav, 100 kilometers southeast of Kiev. He had called upon his many followers in the towns of the region to accompany him to the new communities. To poor hasidim, the zaddik's close followers distributed funds to hire wagons to transport them there; all this was aimed at generating the noisy tumult and festive atmosphere necessary to create a strong impression. The many guests were housed in inns and in the homes of local hasidim. Reb David remained there for eight days and managed to raise about two thousand rubles. The same process unfolded at the next destination, reached on Thursday night: the town of Kagarlyk, some 70 km southeast of Kiev, "where the zaddik arrived with pomp and accompanied by an admiring crowd." Kagarlyk was a "new" place, as yet unvisited by the zaddik; thus, his goal was to "take the reins of ownership of the town into his hands." On Saturday night, one of the zaddik's close followers suggested to the communal leaders that they choose Reb David as their "maggid" and sign an agreement to that effect (the nature of this contract of *maggidut* will be clarified below). Copious amounts of vodka, distributed by the rebbe's followers, flowed during the signing ceremony. Indeed, many signed; those who refused quickly discovered their mistake. That very same evening saw the organization of a melee: the rebbe's supporters broke into the homes of his opponents, smashing their windows and thrashing them soundly. A military band that happened to be in the vicinity was invited to play while the hasidim marched through the streets, passing from house to house, shouting the old messianic slogan: "David, the king of Israel, lives on." One of the zaddik's close followers, who preceded the boisterous mob seated on a horse, exclaimed: "Kagarlyk is ours!" The local rabbi, who had refused to sign the agreement, was expelled from the town. The following day, accompanied by masses of his followers, the zaddik sanctified a new site for the community's graveyard. Once again, vodka flowed and the calls "David, king of Israel" and "Kagarlyk is ours" were heard.

A week later, Reb David and his entourage of some forty hasidim left Kagarlyk for Rzhishchev. Once again, veteran hasidim from the surrounding area were summoned to assist in the "conquest" of the new community, to persuade its Jewish inhabitants to choose Reb David as their maggid, and to expel the local rabbi (named Yosef Mendel in the Russian source).[41]

Upon encountering Talne hasidim on their way from Boguslav to Rzhishchev, three Jews from the village of Rossava inquired as to the purpose of their trip. When the Jews from Rossava revealed their intention of bringing the Talne plot to expel the local rabbi to the attention of the authorities, the Talne hasidim jumped them and worked them over, severely injuring one. They accused these three Jews of being "informers," deserving a death sentence according to Jewish law. Meanwhile, Reb David was received with great honor in Rzhishchev and resided in the home of a local merchant named Leib Ostrovsky. On Friday, the suggestion that the town's Jews sign a contract appointing David as their maggid and that they expel the local rabbi sparked an uproar, in the course of which those who opposed this idea were thrashed and their windows smashed. During the Sabbath prayers several ruffians, followers of Reb David, burst into the synagogue and threatened to rob it if everyone did not swear fealty to Reb David. They also issued death threats against those who had refused to sign, and their family members. One such individual found himself tied up in Ostrovsky's house, where he was struck; he was released only after he agreed to sign. According to the Russian police report, Reb David netted more than 1,500 rubles during his eight-day stay in Rzhishchev. He went next to Rossava, where the same script played out: unbridled violence, uninhibited feasting and imbibing of alcoholic beverages, forcible signing by the town's Jews of the contract appointing Reb David their maggid, expulsion of the local rabbi and his arrest by the

Russian authorities, and the appointment of one of the Talne rebbe's faithful followers in his stead.[42]

There is a huge gap between the picture presented by the Russian police officer's account regarding the zaddik David of Talne's visit to Rzhishchev and the picture given by Alef-Tav of Chyhryn. Not only is there no mention of the zaddik's being stoned or of his embarrassing flight from the town, but in the Russian police report, his visit is crowned with success and the mass fracas is portrayed as having been instigated by David's followers. He apparently remained in town for over a week and filled his coffers with a large sum of money.

A supplementary source on this episode comes from an article published in the Vilna journal *Hacarmel*. In seeking to identify and describe the differences between the Jews of Lithuania and those of Volhynia, its anonymous author touched on the internecine hatred among the hasidic groups:

> And who can describe the hatred that burns in the heart of an adherent of one zaddik for another who cleaves to a different zaddik! The greater his faith in the rebbe he has chosen to elevate to the skies, so too the greater his hatred for the other rebbe to contemptuously avenge himself on him, to humiliate and to raze him to the ground, to the very dust; this therefore is the basis of his antipathy toward his fellow whose heart tends toward a rebbe that he finds despicable. On many occasions the adherents of different rebbes engage in terrible wars, and their mouths call for blows and they thrash each other faithfully! This took place not long ago in Uman and in Tarashcha in Kiev Province,[43] and in other towns as well. About two weeks ago,[44] two camps of hasidim engaged in battle in a small town not far from Kiev named Rzhishchev. And this was the cause of the uproar: it is the custom in this region, when the residents of a town choose a field to serve as their cemetery, or annex a plot to an existing cemetery when this becomes overcrowded, that they then summon the zaddik to whom they have formed an attachment and request that he honor them by coming to perform the consecration. It happened that many of the Rzhishchev residents summoned a zaddik from another town; many others turned to their local rabbi. And a great conflagration broke out between them and they rained blows on each other with unceasing strokes. *And if we desire to expose the zaddikim and reveal their secrets, let us lend an ear to the words of two adherents of two rival zaddikim, for each reveals the secrets of his fellow's zaddik*, bringing his schemes and secret machinations to the light of day![45]

According to this report, the disagreement was sparked by David of Talne's attempt to encroach on the zaddik of Rzhishchev's territory by consecrating a new cemetery.[46] This well-known practice by zaddikim of hallowing new burial ground, to the accompaniment of impressive ceremony, prayer, and supplication,[47] even appears in the above-mentioned Russian police report regarding Kagarlyk. This consecratory act carried not only religious and magical connotations but also, and perhaps primarily, public and societal importance. By turning to a particular zaddik to perform this consecration, the community expressed its members' undivided loyalty toward him; for his part, through this act the zaddik established proprietary rights over the community and its members.

Somewhat later, in 1867, we find Alexander Zederbaum referring to the episode at Rzhishchev. His account contains an electrifying addition that illustrates how far matters had deteriorated:

> It came to pass that when Reb David of Talne set out on his journeys and traveled by way of Rzhishchev, which is the seat of the honorable zaddik Reb [Yaakov Yosef ben] Moshe, that many greeted him with currency. Angered that a stranger had encroached on his territory, the followers of the local zaddik cast stones at the holy guest. And war waxed strong between the two factions, and property was forfeited and great acts of violence engaged in until the local police intervened. And the matter came to the attention of the governor of Kiev and he was incensed at Reb David. Imbued with blazing wrath, the Talne hasidim sought to avenge themselves on the zaddik from Rzhishchev. *And they acted treacherously, sending a letter bearing the forged signature of the zaddik of Rzhishchev to the head Russian priest in Kiev stating that he wished to convert*, and that he would in addition attempt to bring four thousand of his hasidim under the wing of Greek Orthodoxy . . . Nor did the other side remain aloof; it spread calumny to government officials that "David, king of Israel, lives on" is inscribed on David of Talne's chair in gold letters (and rumor has it that this is true) . . . It was said that the governor wanted to exile the holy one to the Caucasus region permanently, without the possibility of travel. And that any who went with him, or traveled to him afterward, there would be but one law for him—to remain there . . . thus, imagine the great joy of the hasidim when the governor changed his mind and confined him to his own town.[48]

The hasidim, Zederbaum went on to say, saw this pardon as miraculous: "And to make the wonder greater, they relate that the governor of Talne . . . heard the verdict issued against the zaddik who resided under his aegis while he was in Paris and hurried back (via a shortcut) to Kiev and recommended to the governor that he withdraw his decree."

Naturally, finding the hasidic explanation wanting, the maskilim provided "a more rational explanation for these events," as Zederbaum notes: "It is well known that the towns in which zaddikim reside flourish because the tax on vodka rises yearly (after all, do hasidim drink sparingly?) and local business is good, and the lords of the town also profit . . . thus he defended the zaddik and explained his troubles away, and the governor acceded to him and lightened his sentence."[49] In any event, the ultimate outcome of the altercation sparked by David of Talne and his hasidim was that the governor "issued a stronger edict forbidding all the known zaddikim to exit the borders of their towns. And the land rested from the journeys of the zaddikim."[50]

Another, parodic echo of these events appears in the chapter "Ketsad merakdin" (How does one dance) in *Masekhet hasidim* (Tractate hasidim), by the maskil Zvi Herman Shapira (1840–98). Then about twenty-five, Shapira penned a sharp antihasidic satire in the form of a Talmudic tractate. It details the means by which "our holy rabbi" (obviously David of Talne) and his followers "conquered" towns:

Mishnah: How does one greet the rabbi [namely, the zaddik]? Upon hearing that the rabbi has come to a certain town, all the hasidim gather in that place. If but a single mitnaged or a heretic resides there, they break the windows of his house and chase him out, breaking up the house and discarding the dust and stones outside the town . . . But if many opponents or heretics live there they proceed as follows: they carry torches from the town from which the rabbi comes to the town for which he is bound. When he is at a distance of four miles, all the hasidim come out to greet him. Every opponent or heretic that they encounter is immediately injured. When they see the rabbi coming they shout loudly: "Long live the king of Israel" three times. And it happened that they called out "Long live the king of Israel" before our holy rabbi, and when this came to the attention of the king of Syria [Russia], he took strict action and placed our rabbi in jail, and the hasidim wasted all their money effecting his release[51] . . . When the rabbi reaches them, they uncouple the horses from his chariot and pull it on their shoulders, and the rabbi expounds Torah on the vision of the chariot-throne until he arrives at that town. Upon entering the town, they again exclaim, "Long live the king of Israel" three times. For each exclamation three glasses of vodka are drunk before and three after, and each glass is accompanied by a curse against an opponent before and a heretic afterward . . . Two who win the lottery carry him on their shoulders to the house especially set aside for him. When they enter the rabbi begins to preach and all the people eat and drink and rejoice and dance and clap hands until they become inebriated . . . and all the hasidim sleep in the street surrounding his house. After awakening, they repeat the previous day's order, and so on the next day, for up to seven days. At the conclusion of the seven days of feasting the rabbi stands and blesses the people that their sexual life will be pure and that there will be no mitnagedim among their progeny. And all the people accompany him for a distance of ten miles . . . and for each and every blessing the people donate redemption money before and after. And he then takes leave of them. When he is at a distance but still just within the range of their vision, they recite the priestly blessing loudly so that he can hear and reply Amen. And all the people sleep in the street and rise early on the next day and return to their homes . . . And with the increase in the number of informers they no longer call out ["Long live the king of Israel"] because of the danger . . . And now, because of our sins, the authorities have decreed that the rabbi cannot leave the boundaries of his town, not even a single step. And why? Because he came to towns where the majority were opponents or heretics and he challenged the wicked.[52]

From this description, elements of which appear in other contemporary hasidic and maskilic sources,[53] it is possible to sketch the takeover of a new town. First of all, the events are intensive and limited to a short period (a week). Their purpose is not simply to force the residents of the town to crown the rebbe and accept his authority as town maggid, but also to unite, and shape the spiritual world of, the local hasidim through cohesion-creating social experiences. These experiences include: mass travel by hasidim after the zaddik's entourage—their entry to the target town empowers the local hasidim and prepares them for the zaddik's visit; a large, colorful reception for the zaddik; the fanning of emotions and violence against local opposition elements ("mitnagedim," or nonhasidic householders and learned individuals, and "heretics," or maskilim) that culminate in property damage, threats, beatings, and even exile; the "coronation" ritual (the exclamation "Long live the king of Israel!") and the "possession" ritual (the consecration of a new cemetery); the celebrations lasting day and night, during which the zaddik is housed in a special dwelling, expounds Torah in public, and gives the crowd lavish meals and limitless alcohol at his own expense; the singing, dancing, and words of Torah on the one hand and of incitement on the other; the joint sleeping arrangements for the hasidim in the street in front of the zaddik's residence; and finally, the signing of the agreement that the zaddik be appointed town maggid and the parting ceremonies for the zaddik, who embarks on his journey to the next town.

But what was the nature of the *maggidut* contract signed by the local community with reference to the zaddik? Here "maggid" does not refer to the traditional preacher hired by the community to deliver a sermon on Sabbaths and holidays; these figures had almost entirely disappeared from nineteenth-century hasidic society. Replacing the moralistic admonitory message delivered by the maggid in the synagogue were the "Torah" and the "hasidic teachings" uttered by the zaddik at the Sabbath table in his court. In the few hasidic places where the title "maggid" was preserved, this now took on a new connotation: a formal, signed agreement that a particular community "belonged" to a specific zaddik and none other. By dint of this contract, the zaddik and his agents enjoyed an economic monopoly in the community and its environs, as well as the sole right to appoint clergy and communal officials. The zaddik set the tone for the community and had the authority to cancel appointments not to his liking. Witness the zaddik Yitshak of Skvira's remarks in a letter to the residents of Teplik, to be discussed in the next section: "You have already given me in writing, a document willingly *signed by all, that you will not do anything without my permission* and, regarding religious matters especially, none shall raise his hand without my knowledge and permission."[54]

Such formal contracts (called *magidus-briv*) were common only among the zaddikim active in the southwestern provinces of the Russian empire (present-day Ukraine), mainly the zaddikim of Chernobyl, Ruzhin, Savran, Linitz-Sokolivka, and their branches.[55] Mordekhai Glubman, a hasid of Shpikov—one of the branches of Chernobyl Hasidism—aptly described the nature of this contract in his memoirs: "This was actual rule. The granting of *maggidut* to the rebbe of a particular town, group, or community meant turning over all public, spiritual, cultural, and economic life to the rule of the rebbe and his hasidim."[56] Zederbaum also described the manner in which the Ukrainian zaddikim "divided" the various communities among themselves in the same fashion and explained the socioeconomic ramifications of that division:

> They divided up the land among themselves as an inheritance . . . when they or their delegates went on their journeys. On these occasions, the local residents joined their ranks, tempted by the counsel of a few enthusiasts, and they crowned them [the zaddikim] as leaders and granted them contracts of rabbinate or *maggidut*, to serve them as protection and refuge . . . Without them, no one is to lift up hand or foot, and in all communal matters, their instruction is awaited, and they send them rabbis, judges, slaughterers, cantors, teachers, beadles, and even bathhouse attendants. As payment, the communities send them an annual head-tax per family, called *ma'amadot*,[57] in addition to gifts for every case, whether good or bad, in addition to the payment they submit when they visit them in their sanctuaries or when the zaddik comes once a year (or more often) to travel from town to town in his realm (a right which, due to their sins, has been abolished these days).[58]

No other direct testimony about the relationship between the events at Rzhishchev and the anti-Bratslav struggle was found; however, a late, obscure Bratslav tradition regarding Reb Sender, the charismatic leader of the Bratslav hasidim in Torgovitsa (forty-five kilometers east of Uman) during the 1860s, apparently alludes to this matter. This group's unusual ways,[59] and Sender's exceptional personality—he was a rich haberdasher who was swept into Bratslav Hasidism and donated all his money to charity[60]—evidently aroused the antipathy of the "mitnagedim," namely, the hasidim who opposed the Bratslavers:

> When the renown of Rabbi Sender of Torgovitsa and his followers spread . . . some of his opponents wanted to give him a sound beating. And they agreed among them-

selves that when their rebbe came to Torgovitsa for the Sabbath, because it was in the *realm of his maggidut*, and Rabbi Sender would certainly also come to greet him as was the custom, they would then catch him and thrash him soundly in punishment for his deeds. And it came to pass that when their rebbe traveled . . . that they wanted to enter some small town where another eminent rebbe dwelt with his hasidim. The local hasidim warned the above-mentioned hasidim not to enter their town, as there were a number of disagreements between them, and their rebbe had commanded that they not allow him to enter the town. But the above-mentioned eminent one insisted on entering the town nonetheless. This immediately sparked a quarrel until they rained blows on each other, *and the eminent one was forced to flee from the town with his followers*. While they were fleeing, the eminent one denigrated the local hasidim, saying to his followers: "*They are not Bratslavers*," meaning that these hasidim were not silent, unlike the Bratslav hasidim who remain silent and act with restraint.[61]

Neither this tradition's moralizing tone, nor the omission of the names of the "eminent ones" and of the place where these events took place, suffices to blur the resemblance to the events discussed above, which took place at the same time and in the same region. It appears likely that the "rebbe of the 'mitnagedim'" was none other than David of Talne, and that the town from which he fled was Rzhishchev. Thus, the Bratslav version has affinities with those of Zvi Kasdai and Alef-Tav of Chyhryn, according to which (and as opposed to the police report) it was David of Talne who lost the battle, and similarly linking his changed attitude toward the Bratslav hasidim to his humiliation.[62]

Thus, the Rzhishchev affair has many sides. Perhaps the vigorous steps taken by the Russian authorities to restrict travels by zaddikim frightened the Talne hasidim and indirectly contributed to the moderation of the anti-Bratslav incitement and violence at Uman for a time.[63]

"The Bratslav Hasidim Eat *Treyf*": The Teplik Scandal

An unlooked-for source further enriches our knowledge of the anti-Bratslav campaign. A manuscript copy of responsa sent to Rabbi Shlomo Kluger of Brody (1785–1869) during the final years of his life contains a number of documents relating the story of a scandal that took place in 1865 in Teplik (thirty-eight kilometers southwest of Uman), in Podolia Province.[64] At the heart of this matter lay a bitter controversy between the Bratslav hasidim in Teplik and the followers of the zaddik Yitshak of Skvira (1812–85), Mordekhai of Chernobyl's son and David of Talne's brother.[65] Given the skimpy nature of the sources on the history of Bratslav Hasidism in Russia in the latter half of the nineteenth century, this correspondence is of special interest.

This affair was highlighted in the contemporary Jewish press in the form of a didactic letter—also published in *Hamelits*[66]—by a maskil named Asher Leml Feingold of Krasne,[67] who was on business in Teplik when these events took place, and in a Yiddish article titled "After Controversy Must Come Peace," published in the newspaper *Kol mevaser*. The anonymous author of that article signed it "not a Bratslaver hasid." But, notwithstanding his sympathy for the "miserable, persecuted" Bratslavers, he places some of the blame for the Teplik affair at their door.[68]

Once again we encounter several versions of an undisputed event, from the perspectives of the aggressors, victims, and outside observers. A study of the versions reveals the human aspects of a sad episode: how their hasidic brethren persecuted the Bratslav hasidim, refusing to come to terms with either their oddity or their unique ways.

According to the Bratslavers, the following was the crux of the matter: Skvirer hasidim living in Nemirov, who had become embroiled in a quarrel with the local ritual slaughterer, Reb Dov, a Bratslaver, libelously informed the zaddik Yitshak of Skvira that the shohet had defamed him. The zaddik—who had the right to make all communal appointments in Nemirov—responded by dispatching a different slaughterer in order to deprive the impertinent shohet of his livelihood. The intervention of several "decent householders," who protested the injustice done to Reb Dov, ended with the latter's traveling to the zaddik's court. There he was forced to sign an agreement that he would not study any of Nahman of Bratslav's books, especially not *Likutei Moharan*. If caught in this "transgression," not only would his shehitah (kosher slaughtering) be invalidated, but he would also lose his hold on the position of town slaughterer.

Not long afterward, the slaughterer regretted his decision. He again traveled to Skvira and informed the zaddik that he was reneging on his agreement, noting that because of his affiliation with Bratslav, his enemies would in any event find fault with him. But, given his prior agreement that such a change of heart would invalidate his slaughtering, making his meat considered unkosher, he asked that the matter be brought before a rabbinical court. Even to tender such a request to an eminent zaddik was audacious; nonetheless, the zaddik was forced to acquiesce. The judges, "decent, eminent individuals who were not from that town"—a clear allusion to the zaddik's potential influence on the Nemirov judges—ruled in the ritual slaughterer's favor.

There was now an eight-year hiatus in the attempt to remove the slaughterer from his post and deprive him of his livelihood, during which time he continued to suffer harassment and minor annoyances. Concurrently, the state of ritual slaughter in Teplik declined sharply. This town, home to a large group of Bratslav hasidim (*kibuts*) from the days of Rabbi Nahman,[69] was also under the Skvirer zaddik's "rule." The two Skvirer-appointed slaughterers did not do a good job, and the townspeople requested permission to hire a new, expert shohet who would be satisfactory to all. The Bratslavers put forward Reb Dov's name, and the idea was accepted by "almost the entire town, all of the Bratslavers, and many of the worthy householders who follow a pure path." But the householders sought the Skvirer rebbe's permission. They sent him a signed request, asking for his approval of the new appointment; they also requested that the zaddik appoint a new shohet in Nemirov to replace Reb Dov, who would move to Teplik.

Here, the Bratslavers contended, the zaddik engaged in treachery. He did not answer the letter, but nevertheless hastily dispatched a new shohet to Nemirov, seemingly agreeing tacitly to the proposed switch. At least, that was how the Bratslavers understood matters. They encouraged Reb Dov to sell his rights to shehitah in Nemirov to the new shohet, only to discover—once Dov had done so—that the zaddik had informed the residents of Teplik that, as the holder of the *maggidut* contract for the town, he was not prepared to ratify Dov's appointment. Dov therefore lost out on both counts; in addition, an appeal by some householders from Teplik who made a special journey to Skvira was to no avail. The zaddik remained adamant.

In Bratslav eyes, this was not simply a struggle against Reb Dov specifically, but against Bratslaver Hasidism and its legacy in general. They could not and did not wish to come to terms with the injustice done them, not just because of the real need for an excellent shohet in Teplik—and no one denied Dov's expertise—but also because they felt responsible for the turn of events and were concerned about Dov's fate, as he now found himself without a livelihood. Accordingly, they refused to accept the Skvirer rebbe's authority and turned to a nonhasidic authority, Rabbi Shlomo Kluger of Brody, for adjudication. That Kluger was esteemed by the hasidim is not surprising. Because he was not affiliated with the hasidic movement, zaddikim and hasidim found in him an objective observer who could arbitrate internal hasidic quarrels, particularly those that at least outwardly touched on purely halakhic matters.[70]

At this stage, the Teplik dayyan, Aharon ben Avraham Yehuda, now became involved in this controversy, but for the non-Bratslav camp. He too penned letters to Shlomo Kluger, claiming to present the majority viewpoint of the townspeople regarding "the scandal in our town." As his first letter, dated 5 Av 1865, predated that of the Bratslavers by about ten days, it appears that each party knew of the other's intention to approach Rabbi Kluger, and that this may have been done by mutual consent. According to the dayyan's account, the Teplik townspeople had freely chosen to accept the Skvirer rebbe's authority and "to fulfill whatever he commanded." With the outbreak of controversy regarding the appointment of a new shohet, it was unanimously agreed to accept the zaddik's ruling on this matter. Both sides therefore traveled to Skvira, and both had accepted the zaddik's decision. The Bratslavers, whom Rabbi Aharon does not mention by name but calls "a tiny minority in the town" or "the subversive party," decided not to heed the zaddik and insisted on choosing a shohet themselves, even though that shohet "had signed a letter in the presence of the Skvirer rebbe making his shehitah forbidden." Aharon the dayyan therefore requested a verdict from Rabbi Kluger as to whether or not that ritual slaughterer's shehitah was to be considered invalid. Two brief letters sent by the Skvirer rebbe to the townspeople of Teplik, which were appended to this first letter, add little to our knowledge of this affair. In them, the zaddik affirmed that he was responsible for all appointments of communal officials in Teplik, and that he was not prepared to ratify the new shohet's appointment at the moment. He asked the townspeople to wait until "he exercised his will, which was that of God," and ruled that "if some shohet comes to the town of Teplik without my knowledge, his shehitah is forbidden."

The Bratslavers also refrained from mentioning their opponent Aharon by name, calling him "a certain dayyan who appealed to the above-mentioned rabbi [of Skvira] and a very great opponent of ours." They portray him as a quarrelsome person, who does everything in his power to incite disputes among the townspeople. To that end, they claimed, even though he harbors mitnagedic leanings, he pretends to be a supporter of the Skvirer rebbe. Naturally, the Bratslav hasidim did not recognize the validity of Aharon's arguments; it is, however, possible to infer their recognition of their position's relative weakness and their willingness to reach a partial compromise. The queries addressed to Rabbi Kluger make it clear that they were prepared to have Reb Dov slaughter meat for the Bratslavers alone and not for the entire community; they even reluctantly agreed that his salary would come not from the communal coffers but from Bratslaver pockets, so long as his shehitah was not outlawed.

Regarding the local dayyan, our sole information comes from his letters and Asher Feingold's letter, which describes him as the true ruler of Teplik. According to Feingold, motivated by his bitter hatred for Bratslav, this former Bershad hasid,[71] a malicious, vengeful man, acted in unison with other hasidic courts to prejudice the Skvirer rebbe against the Bratslavers. Also exceedingly affluent, he lent money at interest and even "owned something like a bank." Most of the townspeople depended on him and his generosity and were, in any event, forced to obey his commands with respect to the persecution of the Bratslavers. In the best polemical tradition of physiognomic stereotypes, he was portrayed as "a short man, as broad as he is tall, with darting eyes, a thick short nose, and a black, almost greenish, complexion."

Feingold's letter provides his account of what he witnessed in the Teplik synagogue on Yom Kippur eve, 1865—namely, the proclamation of a ban against the Bratslaver hasidim issued in the name of Aharon the dayyan: "For the Bratslav hasidim eat *treyf*, therefore all the townspeople are warned not to fraternize with them, not to lend them dishes or borrow any from them, not to live in close proximity to them, and not to rent them apartments. Anyone who has rented them an apartment must evict them immediately; and if he is a melamed, then no youths should be sent to study with him; and if he is poor he shall not receive a stipend or private donations." When Feingold inquired as to the meaning of such a harsh ban, issued on Yom Kippur eve no less, one of the congregants, "whose visage revealed that he was no hasid," replied: "Do you not know? Have you not heard that there is a sect named 'Bratslaver Hasidim' who do not believe in any of the zaddikim of our generation nor do they trust in their salvation, but only glorify the name of Rabbi Nahman of Bratslav . . . and all the zaddikim and hasidim hate them bitterly; although when I see them here they seem to be honest, charitable, and virtuous, *except that they do not believe in the holy ones of this generation* . . . and even if the Bratslavers outnumber each and every sect individually, and even if the hasidim deeply hate each other, they unite to persecute and annihilate the Bratslaver."[72]

It was explained to Feingold that the immediate grounds for the ban was the affair of the shohet Reb Dov, "who disobeyed [the Skvirer rebbe] and studied *Likutei Moharan.*" The dayyan made a public announcement that it was forbidden to eat Dov's meat, and some hotheads even wanted "to break his arm so that he would be unable to slaughter animals." The Bratslavers, who had agreed to pay Reb Dov's salary "from their pockets and not from the communal coffers," approached the Skvirer rebbe on their own initiative and asked him to pronounce Dov's shehitah valid. The zaddik's response was that he had never outlawed it; rather, he had simply objected to Dov's appointment as the Teplik shohet. Precipitating the dayyan's announcement was the shohet's disobedience: he had begun to slaughter between Rosh Hashanah and Yom Kippur, contrary to the zaddik's ruling.

Feingold attested that he verified this account in conversations with others, and even stimulated a hasid, one of the opponents of Bratslav, to talk. The latter said, "with blood boiling and with a loud cry": "How can we stand by complacently when the Bratslavers' wish is fulfilled? We will not back down, no matter what. How much trouble we went to until we were able to humiliate them; shall we now allow them to lift their heads?!"[73] It is perhaps not fortuitous that the Teplik scandal peaked during the High Holiday period, a time during which Bratslav self-confidence was swelled by their communal visit to their rebbe's grave in Uman, on the one hand, and which saw heightened anti-Bratslav incitement by their opponents, on the other.

"They Are Not Beholden to Any of the Leaders of Our Time": The Clash over Obedience

Did the events in Teplik revolve around the obligation to obey the leaders of the generation or the contents of *Likutei Moharan*, or was this simply a local controversy involving economic control of shehitah, disguised as an ideological dispute related to the legacy of persecution of the Bratslav hasidim? Apparently, all of these factors coalesced in this affair.

For the traditional Jewish community, the appointment of ritual slaughterers has always constituted a sensitive sphere: without kosher slaughtering under the supervision of a prominent rabbinic authority, Jewish communal life is inconceivable. Not only did kosher slaughtering generate significant revenues, it bestowed moral and religious responsibilities on those engaging in the activity. For the founders of Hasidism, shehitah was not simply a professional skill; rather, it combined spiritual or mystical rationales with economic interests related to collection of the meat tax. The special hasidic method of slaughtering with highly polished knives became a hallmark of Hasidism and was an unceasing bone of contention between hasidim and mitnagedim.[74] With the rapid spread of Hasidism in the nineteenth century, the "knife controversy" abated,[75] but hasidic slaughterers served as definitive propagandists for Hasidism, their very appointment representing the authority of one zaddik or another over a particular community.[76] Moreover, after the abolition of the *kahal* in Russia in 1844, the meat tax assumed ever-increasing weight in the communal budget. Many parties, some with conflicting interests, divided the income derived from kosher slaughtering: slaughterers, butchers (who sold the meat), tax farmers, communal leaders, and the zaddik (who did not necessarily reside in that community).[77]

The nineteenth century saw many communal disputes regarding the appointment of ritual slaughterers. The most common ploy was to cast aspersions on the existing shehitah's reliability and quality; harsh disputes broke out among neighboring hasidic groups against this background. Threats were bandied, the shehitah was invalidated, and various scare tactics were employed to bring "wayward" shohatim into line.[78] The Teplik affair involving the Bratslavers belongs to this milieu.

As early as the second wave of persecution, during Nathan of Nemirov's day, the matter of ritual slaughterers came to the fore. The reconstructed text of the ban signed by Moshe Zvi of Savran explicitly states: "A melamed from the Bratslav congregation should not teach your children Torah, because this learning will become heresy in his gut. *The shehitah of a Bratslaver shohet is invalid*, nor should a prayer leader be chosen from this evil congregation, for his prayer is an abomination. In general, try to deprive them of the staff of life in any form."[79] Clearly, however, the crux of the struggle was not Bratslav shehitah per se; the outlawing of their slaughterers, melamedim, or cantors merely served as the means to effect the socioeconomic disintegration of Bratslav Hasidism in the post-Nahman era.

Obviously, during the third wave of persecution, the struggle against Bratslav shehitah did not constitute a separate issue, but rather was part and parcel of the various manifestations of opposition to this group. In any event, we confront here a renewed, paradoxical version of the socioreligious struggle over shehitah from Hasidism's early days. Once again we find tension between a minority, separatist-hasidic group, for whom the local shehitah does not meet its standards and is seen as inadequately supervised, and the conservative establishment of the zaddikim, which cooperates with communal forces (the dayyan and the householders) in order to prevent the exercise of independent shehitah, and to retain by this means its authority as the sole appointer of communal officials.

For their part, the Bratslavers were convinced that the shehitah controversy was simply a pretext for perpetuating the initial anti-Nahman and anti-Nathan campaigns: "For the gratuitous dispute regarding him . . . and those who study his books has still not died down."[80] But what was the nature of this gratuitous dispute—above and beyond issues of power and honor—that so directed the ire of zaddikim and hasidim against Bratslav?

It appears that what lay at the heart of the dispute was the obligation to obey the leaders of the generation. From the point of view of Aharon the dayyan and the Skvirer zaddik, the Bratslav hasidim had loudly and openly defied a signed agreement to obey the zaddik, recognized by most of the community as the supreme authority for appointing or removing religious functionaries in the town. Moreover, this breach of discipline could potentially bring about the creation of a separate system of shehitah. This would not just damage the existing system financially (a reason not explicitly mentioned), but it would make the Bratslavers transgress the biblical injunction: *Lo titgodedu* (Deuteronomy 14:1), interpreted in the Talmud as a strict prohibition against the creation of separate factions (*agudot*).[81] The reference to this prohibition, which aimed to preserve the unity of communal customs, is used here cynically and for tactical reasons alone. Anyone familiar with the social reality of Russian Jewry in the latter half of the nineteenth century is aware of the deep rifts in all of its factions, including the hasidic camp. The common axis unifying the members of traditional society was unconditional obedience to the authority of the "leader of the generation." The hasidic leadership found the Bratslavers' refusal to bow to this authority untenable.

Nowhere in his two letters to Shlomo Kluger does Aharon the dayyan identify his antagonists. He simply defines them as "not beholden to any of the leaders [*rosh hador*] of our time" or as "the subversive party that is not beholden to any current leader." In the terminology then current, *rosh hador* (leader of our time) stands for a living zaddik, or an accepted, learned rabbinical authority (like Kluger himself). This characterization of Bratslav Hasidism reflects the author's view of the main flaw he and others found in Bratslav: that they acted on their own authority and did not obey a recognized zaddik or rabbi. For them, the only acceptable authority was that of their dead rebbe, Rabbi Nahman, alongside that delegated to his interpreters and disciples. Indeed, by its very existence, and its success in maintaining a religious, hasidic lifestyle even without the presence of a living zaddik, Bratslav defied a basic principle of Hasidism: its religious dependence on a zaddik who mediates between God and the world, and guides his followers' daily lives.

The offhand mention of the obligation to obey the leader of the generation does not reflect its actual status as a cornerstone of the defensive Orthodox worldview shared by all the members of traditional Eastern European society, hasidic and nonhasidic alike. Despite Bratslav's definitive status as a branch of the new Orthodox society, its open defiance of the obligation to obey the leader of the generation—which was grasped as arrogant insurgency and as an internal attempt to systematically undermine the authority of the living leaders of Orthodoxy[82]—could not be overlooked. This Bratslav brazenness—which was, according to oral tradition, often accompanied by denigration of other zaddikim—angered other hasidim.[83]

Ostensibly, the Bratslavers themselves admitted their guilt on this count. In describing their congregation in Teplik to Shlomo Kluger, they testified that "for many reasons, which they do not seek to explain, they do not turn to any of the eminent ones of the day [*mefursamei hazeman*]." The different terminology used by each side gives precise expression to each one's stance. Aharon the dayyan accuses the Bratslavers of not being "beholden to any of the leaders [*rosh hador*] of our time," namely to a halakhic authority or a zaddik. However, inhering in the Bratslav appeal and willingness to accept Kluger's arbitration is explicit recognition of the authority of one of the leaders of the day who was not a member of their camp. It was not by chance that the Bratslavers specifically chose the term *mefursamei hazeman*, which refers only to zaddikim.[84]

"God Seeks the Persecuted": The Reflection of the Persecutions in Bratslav Historiography

What does the third wave of anti-Bratslav persecution mean in the history of Hasidism in general, and of Bratslav Hasidism in particular? First of all, it is noteworthy that despite the long-standing anti-Bratslav campaign, not a single surviving hasidic source—neither a polemical tract nor a ban (with the exception of the Savraner's letter, of doubtful authenticity)—explicitly identifies the opponent as Bratslav Hasidism. Nor does any hasidic source contain a systematic or theoretical critique of Bratslav leaders, customs, or teachings. For the first two waves of controversy, our information comes primarily from the biased reports of the Bratslavers themselves. What distinguishes the episode at Teplik is its preservation of their opponents' original version, thereby enabling us to compare each side's stance.

Notwithstanding the partial nature of the sources, and the fact that neither of the parties reveals the entire truth, the Teplik affair can be characterized as a local manifestation of a general anti-Bratslav climate in certain hasidic courts. As portrayed, it presents a typical picture of Ukrainian Hasidism in the 1860s, where the inhabitants of towns with a hasidic majority voluntarily turned over the appointment of communal functionaries to an eminent zaddik residing at a distance. But chipping away at this harmonious portrait were the forces of atomization: the zaddik was no longer a sole, all-powerful ruler, and opposition forces were constantly eroding his authority from within. The mere existence of a separatist hasidic sect such as Bratslav, whose agenda and socioreligious interests differed from those of the majority, had the potential to foster discord. Moreover, by its very refusal to recognize the authority of the zaddik accepted by the majority of the townspeople, Bratslav undermined the zaddik's status and economic privileges.

In addition, Bratslav Hasidism consistently maintained its in-group configuration as an intimate, consolidated enclave fueled by its sense of an ongoing threat of persecution, a group that was sadly forced to turn to non-hasidic authorities in hopes that the anti-Bratslav atmosphere would not cloud their judgment. Note, however, that this episode reflects not just the opposition of the Skvirer zaddik and his followers, but of communal bodies as well: the local dayyan and what the Bratslavers called the *kahal*. Even though at that point the *kahal* had been formally abolished in Russia for a time, elements of the communal leadership continued to be called by that name and were viewed—internally, at least—as a functioning body that actively took the Skvirer side. From the Bratslavers' letter, it appears that they saw Aharon the dayyan as a hypocrite only pretending to be a hasid. Motivated by his hatred for the Bratslavers, he was prepared to cooperate with the Skvirer rebbe. On the other hand, "the householders" sided with the Bratslavers; but their numbers and influence in the Teplik community are not easily determined.

It was not by chance that the Skvirer hasidim homed in on *Likutei moharan;* after all, this book had come to symbolize Bratslav Hasidism and was the wellspring of all subsequent Bratslav literature. Rabbi Nahman, who invested much time and effort in its preparation and publication (its first part appeared during his lifetime; the second, posthumously), viewed it as his magnum opus and awarded it mystical value,[85] calling upon his followers to study it constantly. He ascribed many virtues to this work: "It was heard from his holy mouth, that he said that his holy book *Likutei Moharan* which came into the world was the beginning of redemption. And he said, since it is out in the world I greatly desire that it be studied. For it must be studied intensely, until it is known fluently by heart."[86] As is well known, *Likutei Moharan* had an unfavorable, even mocking, reception. But other voices emerged alongside this criticism, and others, not just the few persecuted Bratslav hasidim, studied the book. Some zaddikim, mostly in Poland, expressed their satisfaction with the work and even supplied approbations for its publication (though it appears that they were then unaware that Rabbi Nahman's views were a matter of dispute among the Ukrainian zaddikim).[87]

Naturally, the Bratslavers admired and sanctified this book; they were even prepared to risk their livelihoods and status in defense of their right to study it freely. This did not escape the notice of their opponents, who insulted the Bratslavers by attacking Nahman's literary works. In the 1830s, during the second wave of persecution, we find Nathan of Nemirov bemoaning the ripping and defacement of Nahman's books, primarily by violent youths at adult instigation: "For lads come out and curse and humiliate me in various ways, and once they broke a window in my house . . . and on the last Sabbath . . . there was a great commotion here, for youthful wastrels entered our study house and broke the door and humiliated our flock. And it has happened on several occasions that they have entered our study house, ripping and debasing our holy books in the presence of our flock . . . and one lad ran for his father. And his father came with another man and they thrashed and injured members of our flock."[88]

Nathan went on to describe the forms this humiliation assumed: "For they come and rip the holy books written by our admor . . . and trample them with their feet, and throw them on the garbage heap and filthy places. Has the like been seen or heard? And they think not to look inside the book, to gain understanding of it, to see if it truly merits such debasement."[89] Even during the third wave of persecution, in Nahman of Tulchin's day, we find explicit mention of this practice: "During Rabbi Pinhas of Kublich's day, there was a ritual slaughterer in the town of Kublich, *who greatly debased our rabbi's books. He would rip them and use them to wipe his excretions* and the like. And he persecuted and oppressed our people to annihilation."[90]

Of course, burning or debasing holy books was not a hasidic invention. This ancient tactic of domination possesses two characteristic features of ideological struggles—both within and between religious groups—that cascade into violence: one is the simplistic notion that might makes right; the other, the magical belief that erasure of knowledge makes its creators fade away, and that defacement of pages and words humiliates and degrades those who honor them. It should not surprise us then, given the atmosphere of religious tension—which for Bratslav focused on the High Holiday gathering at Uman—that their opponents perceived their books, holy objects, and symbolic system as a definitive representation of the heretical and provocative foundations of Bratslav thought and behavior. Here we find the hasidim, who had themselves experienced the bitter taste of "book wars" in the past,[91] adopting this tactic not just for their war on mitnagedim, maskilim, and heretics, but also against their fellow hasidim, the Bratslavers.

The outcome of the Teplik affair remains unclear. As far as we know, Shlomo Kluger did not respond to either of the parties to this affair. This was perhaps not only due to his principled opposition to intervention in shehitah disputes,[92] but also to physical weakness. He had almost entirely ceased answering queries at that time.[93]

Of particular interest is the late Bratslav tradition that seeks to reduce the Teplik affair's scope and importance. It unhesitatingly assigns some of the guilt in this matter to the shohet Reb Dov, especially noting his cantankerous nature. According to this ambivalent source, the Skvirer hasidim refused to budge from their position and even designated a spot for disposal of the utensils purportedly defiled by Dov's meat. Dov turned for advice to Nahman of Chyhryn (1825–94), an outstanding interpreter of Rabbi Nahman's works, and one of the few Bratslav hasidim who served as a communal rabbi and head of the local rabbinical court. Nahman of Chyhryn replied: "They should never have accepted your agreement on this matter, nor should you have agreed to it either; both sides have committed injustice." Dov left Nemirov for Bratslav, and from there he moved to Teplik, "and wherever he went controversy was aroused regarding his matter." Finally, Nahman of Tulchin turned to him: "You drew near to us in order to spark controversy against us! Lay down your slaughterer's knife."[94] Dov left off being a ritual slaughterer and immigrated from Teplik to Palestine with his son, eventually settling among the Bratslav hasidim in Safed.[95]

Did all eight Chernobyl brothers participate in the anti-Bratslav struggle? We have already noted the active roles assumed by David of Talne and Yitshak of Skvira. As far as we can tell, the oldest brother, Aharon of Chernobyl (1787–1871) did not participate in the anti-Bratslav campaign, as evidenced by his willingness to have his daughter marry Nahman of Bratslav's grandson,[96] and by his absence from the accounts of this matter. Concerning another brother, Yaakov Yisrael of Cherkas (1794–1876), there is an intriguing source involving Nahman of Chyhryn. According to this hagiographic tradition, Nahman was appointed head of the Chyhryn rabbinical court around 1853. This community, located on the banks of the Dnieper, was contracted through *maggidut* to the zaddik of Cherkas, and Nahman's appointment was made without his approval. The zaddik subsequently interviewed Nahman, recognized his ability, and ratified his appointment.[97] Regarding Yohanan of Rachmistrivke (1816–95), Bratslav sources report that "he took our flock's side, and for several years the Bratslavers prayed in the large Rachmistrivke study house in Uman on Rosh Hashanah, and they always maintained close, friendly relations with our flock."[98]

No information linking the other brothers to the anti-Bratslav campaign has survived: Moshe of Korostyshev (1789–1866) apparently had no court; Nahum of Makarov (1804–51) died before the events of the 1860s; and we have no data regarding Avraham of Trisk (1806–89). In any event, it seems doubtful that this was a familial or dynastic struggle by Chernobyl against Bratslav. At most, what we have here are sporadic outbreaks of controversy connected to specific individuals and circumstances.

The third wave of persecution left only vague, obscure remnants, and no strong marks in Bratslav literature. This requires explanation. After all, since its early days, Bratslav had a wide-ranging tradition of writing and self-documentation, especially with regard to persecution and controversy, for "God seeks the persecuted [Ecclesiastes 3:15] even when the persecutor is a zaddik,"[99] and "happy are the persecuted."[100] This is especially surprising in comparison to the widespread writings about the second wave of persecution, channeled by Nathan of Nemirov into a source of encouragement and emotional strength.

Actually, it is possible to make a generalization here, one not directly connected to the events of the controversy described above. After the death of the great writer Nathan of Nemirov, Bratslav literary creativity nearly dried up. From that point on, the written Bratslav legacy was confined mainly to anthologies, reworkings, and commentaries on Rabbi Nahman's teachings (and even the latter were largely based on Rabbi Nathan's multifaceted interpretive oeuvre), and to imitation of Nathan's epistolary genre. Rabbi Nathan's many letters of spiritual awakening and strengthening sent to his family and disciples achieved canonical status among the hasidim. Copied and reprinted multiple times, they became study material that assisted in the clarification of the values of Bratslav Hasidism, arousing their readers' enthusiasm and enhancing their belief. Nathan ben Yehuda's letters, compiled in *Netiv tsadik*, are a typical example of how this genre was adopted by the Bratslavers; there are other examples, too.[101] Moreover, Bratslav history was recorded only in a fragmentary, opaque fashion: actually, there is almost no extant material for the period between Nathan of Nemirov's literary oeuvre and the late-nineteenth-century writings of Avraham Hazan of Tulchin (most of which were published in the twentieth century). This reflects not just the trend of concealment and self-censorship characteristic of Bratslav Hasidism's dialectic writings,[102] but also its spiritual and material attrition, and its lack of leadership and security in the wake of Nathan of Nemirov's death.[103]

Echoes of this sense of weakness, and attempts at encouragement and fortification appear in various statements by Bratslav hasidim—for example, in Nahman of Chyhryn's *Parpera'ot lehokhmah*, published in Lemberg in 1876, which notes that he himself had been the victim of humiliation. Bratslav tradition recounts that once when he went to prostrate himself on Rabbi Nahman's grave in Uman, "some worthless fellows from the opposing camp threw excrement at him, hitting the rabbi's back."[104] The praise that Nahman of Chyhryn heaped on the Bratslaver hasidim who, despite the increased strength of their "opponents," devotedly and determinedly participated in the great gathering at Rabbi Nahman's grave in Uman is of interest:

> Nonetheless, we gather now especially, at a time when we do not merit our rabbi's physical presence, to hear moralistic preaching from his holy mouth and to taste the sweetness of his pleasant sayings during the time of the enclave, as it was when he was still alive. Nonetheless, we gather around him and rely on his holy merit. Each one cries from the bottom of his heart in purity and great simplicity to merit a return to God, to approach him truly. *And the opponents, upon seeing all this, inquire in wonder, gnashing their teeth*, regarding this yearly gathering which requires much preparation and tiring work: "What do you see? What do you hear?" etc. And we are unable to provide any convincing answer. For this is a deeply individual matter, each one experiences and feels its greatness . . . making this simple, pure worship that requires all the wisdoms, and to worship God in simplicity, *and to do things that in the eyes of others appear mad.* And all is for the love and worship of God.[105]

Similar sentiments appear in a letter of encouragement written by the venerable Bratslav hasid Nathan ben Yehuda to the persecuted Bratslavers in Safed: "All these incidents that we experience serve only to remind us that we are Bratslav hasidim, so that we do not forget for even a day that this name is no empty thing."[106]

The Persecutions Continue

The persecution of the Bratslav hasidim in Uman and elsewhere (in Palestine, for example)[107] continued into the early twentieth century. Here are chosen examples from each decade. In 1868 Avraham Konstantinovski of Tirashpol in Kherson Province related that anyone coming to Uman on Rosh Hashanah "will see the stones slung at those coming to prostate themselves on the holy grave of Rabbi Nahman of Bratslav (which I myself witnessed), and they broke windows on the holiday and struck the Torah ark as well."[108]

In the 1870s we find Michael Rodkinson writing as follows: "And all the persecution that the Bratslav hasidim experience *now as well* (when they travel to Uman to prostrate themselves on their rebbe's grave) at the hands of other hasidim, this is because of the Grandfather [from Shpole] on whom the hasidim rely and therefore do what they do. Only he that knows the secrets of the heart knows who is right! If only there could be peace among the people of Israel!"[109] From the early 1880s, we have the testimony of Nathan ben Yehuda regarding the abasement he suffered at Uman.[110] In 1884 Yitshak Sobol reported in *Hamelits* that the Bratslav *kloiz* is abandoned all year long, but during the High Holidays, when the Bratslavers gather there, they suffer at the hands of "the rabble that does not believe in Rabbi Nahman and delivers a fierce beating, using fists or stones."[111] In the 1890s Ephraim Deinard wrote a similar report.[112] Concurrently, a "sort of ban" was announced against the Bratslavers in Nemirov. They were forced to leave the synagogue premises and to pray separately.[113]

In the early twentieth century, the prolific hasidic writer Yehuda Yudl Rosenberg cautioned his readers against these persecutions: "It is known that because of the controversy between those two zaddikim there are people who debase the honor of the holy zaddik Moharan Braslaver . . . and heap scorn on those who travel to his grave in Uman. Were they wise they would think upon this, that regarding a zaddik silence is more befitting than scornful speech."[114] The writer Micha Yosef Berdyczewski, a native of Mezhibozh, well versed in the hasidic world, provided the following description: "The members of this sect are denigrated more than their brethren. The cautious do not intermarry with them and stalk them. The people of Israel are a jealous nation! So much as stray from the trodden path of custom and prayer rites and you are an idol worshiper."[115] In 1913, Avraham Rechtman, a member of An-ski's ethnographic delegation, provided the following description of the Bratslav hasidim in Berdichev: "They voluntarily isolate themselves from the rest of the town's Jews. Nor are they allowed to participate in public matters, or to be members of any society, no marriages are contracted with them, and no dealings are undertaken with them."[116] This inculcation of hatred was not always effective, however. In his brief memoirs, Zalman Kotliar (1874–1953) of Monastrich (Kiev Province)—who was raised in a Skvirer milieu and absorbed their hatred of the Bratslavers—related how this sparked his curiosity, leading him to travel to Uman for Rosh Hashanah 1896.[117]

Under Soviet rule, persecution of the Bratslavers by other hasidim ceased during the period between the world wars. However, the pogroms that accompanied the civil war in the Ukraine (1917–20) did not bypass the Jews of Uman;[118] moreover, the detachment of the Soviet Union from Poland shortly thereafter also cut Bratslaver hasidim off from the thread that tied scattered

FIG. 4.1. The structure over the grave of Nahman of Bratslav in Uman

Bratslavers to the heart of this Hasidism: Rabbi Nahman's gravesite in Uman. Unable to reach Uman, the Polish Bratslavers (centered in Warsaw, Lodz, and Lublin) made Lublin their alternative gathering place for Rosh Hashanah.[119] As for the few remaining hasidim in Uman and the surrounding area—as well as those who risked their lives to cross the border to the gravesite—they now suffered from the antireligious atmosphere and the heavy hand of the Soviet regime, and from the strong hatred of anticlerical Jewish communists.[120]

In early 1931, when the historian Shimon Dubnow was residing "in the German diaspora, on the outskirts of stormy Berlin," and basking in the completed preparation of his *Toldot hahasidut*, a rumor came to his attention regarding the destruction of the Besht's gravesite in Mezhibozh and of Rabbi Nahman's in Uman. Dubnow chose to conclude his preface with the following moving prophecy: "The regime was awakened to this by the Jewish 'deniers of God,' among whose ranks there are perhaps the great-grandsons of those zaddikim. It suffices to record this event in order to comprehend the revolution that took place in the birthplace of Hasidism two hundred years after the revelation of the Besht. 'An inverted world' created in blood and fire and grounded in tyranny will not last. But what will follow?"[121]

This rumor turned out to be false. The grave had not been destroyed; it was apparently only defaced under the Nazi conquest, when the Jews of Uman were led to the slaughter.[122] A handful of Bratslav hasidim who survived in the town and nearby continued to zealously guard the flame of their rebbe's legacy after the Holocaust, and struggled to maintain their spiritual and physical existence as a religious group under a hostile atheist regime.

"Legacy of a Mistake": An Epilogue?

This chapter has explored the varied expressions of hasidic anti-Bratslav enmity, during the 1860s in particular. Although individuals or groups on the margins of hasidic society (youths, an impassioned mob) carried out its more violent manifestations, zaddikim, rabbis, and communal leaders fanned the flames of controversy. A new ingredient was now added to the tradition of persecution and hatred that had crystallized during the earlier controversies in the days of Nahman of Bratslav and Nathan of Nemirov: the struggle against any who questioned the new Orthodox convention requiring obedience to the eminent leaders of the generation. During the third wave of persecution, economic interests joined with the profound psychological forces that nurture hatred of the stranger and the strange.

The fact that the Bratslav population centers were located in the towns of Kiev, Volhynia, and Podolia Provinces restricted the anti-Bratslav struggle to these regions, mostly to Uman and its environs. The intense atmosphere of religious and social tension fostered by the hasidic milieu—which embraced the southern part of the Pale of Settlement—and the strong influence of eminent zaddikim on daily life, spawned unceasing controversy among the different hasidic groups on almost every conceivable matter. But, as opposed to other hasidic groups, not only did Bratslav willingly accept its legacy of suffering inherited from earlier persecutions, it also continued to adhere to its special ways and refused to accept the obligation to obey the leaders of the generation.

The harsh persecution of Bratslav from within and without Hasidism neither weakened its adherents' faith nor made them despair. From the Bratslaver viewpoint, their persistence even in the face of crisis, humiliation, and the gloomy present was not just a personal and group religious test, but also the realization of Rabbi Nahman's messianic vision.

In the early twenty-first century, some two hundred years after the founding of Bratslav Hasidism, the outside observer of this sect and its history can only hope that its tortured members have reached calm shores. Over the past generation, Bratslav, with its conflicting sects and trends, has made handsome material and spiritual gains. It now ostensibly enjoys growth, and legitimization and recognition in the main. Thousands of copies of its publications are distributed, Rabbi Nahman's tales and doctrines have been translated into numerous languages, and the slogan of one of its more controversial wings—"Na-nah-nahman meUman"—has become a well-known graffito in Israeli society.[123] With the collapse of the Soviet Union, the gates to Rabbi Nahman's gravesite in Uman are again open, and on the High Holidays, tens of thousands of hasidim fill the town, many of whom are not even Bratslavers. It appears, then, that the strong antipathy to Bratslav Hasidism has dissipated and belongs to the distant past.

Yet even today, echoes of the bitter, long-standing hatred toward them can still be heard. A polemical proclamation by the Bratslav hasidim, probably dating from the 1970s, describes the continuing controversy between them and their long-time opponents, the Skvirer hasidim, this time in the United States. And once again, the catalyst for controversy was a Bratslaver's stubborn insistence on studying Rabbi Nahman's books, even though living in a Skvirer neighborhood: "Who will not feel terror at what his eyes see and his ears hear regarding a sect calling itself the Skvirer Hasidim who, whenever they can, take these holy books and tear and burn and debase them in unbelievably degrading ways. And they have ridiculously laughable customs, that cannot be recorded . . . And these individuals have never read or studied these holy books, *and their ugly, shocking behavior is grounded in the legacy of a mistake and on informing by scandalmongers.*" The authors of the proclamation go on to tell of a Jerusalem Bratslav yeshiva student who married the daughter of a Skvirer hasid and was forced to live among the Skvirer hasidim, in the "neighborhood that they built in America."[124] Well liked by his neighbors because of his fine qualities, this young man continued to study Rabbi Nahman's books in secret. "And when it became known to this hasidic sect that he was studying those sacred books . . . the tide turned against him. And just as they had respected him earlier they now began to persecute him greatly and created much trouble for him, and totally abased him, stopping at nothing." They embittered his wife's life, incited her against her husband, and using "ugly temptations" forced her to leave him and to flee to her father's house: "all this because of a single sin: the intense study of the books of the holy admor of Bratslav."[125]

5 "Excitement of the Soul"

The World of Rabbi Akiva Shalom Chajes of Tulchin

> And because he has not yet merited being written about in our literature, I decided to erect a memorial to him . . . for he deserves a place among our recent prodigies.
> —Micha Yosef Berdyczewski, "Tsiyun lenefesh," 72

From Foe to Friend

The end of Rabbi Akiva Shalom Chajes's life (1815–68)[1] could not have been predicted from its beginnings. An acknowledged, incisive Torah scholar and a fervent mitnaged for a significant portion of his life, Chajes served during its final chapter as a hasidic rabbi in the small Ukrainian town of Dubova;[2] an outspoken opponent of zaddikim and hasidim in his youth in the Russian town of Tulchin, Chajes became, in the autumn of his days, an enthusiastic follower of the zaddik David of Talne, whose leadership and hasidic ways we encountered in the previous chapter.

Of their rabbi's stormy past, only legends and fragmentary rumors disseminated by word of mouth (which greatly enhanced their impact) came to the attention of the Dubova residents—including one who would later become one of the greatest Hebrew writers of the revival age, Micha Yosef Berdyczewski. The rumors attributed to Chajes wisdom, knowledge of philosophy and Haskalah, and a history of harsh criticism of Hasidism during his youth—even the composition of antihasidic lampoons. The legends also related that, due to fierce struggles with followers of the Savraner rebbe, Chajes found himself shunned by his fellow Jews of Tulchin. Rumors also told of his flight from Tulchin to forced exile in Austria, of his stay with the famed rabbi Shlomo Kluger of Brody, his throwing off of religious observance, and even of his public desecration of the Sabbath. But ultimately, Akiva Chajes came full circle: he had a complete change of heart and was warmly accepted by Talne Hasidism. The former militant mitnaged received his rabbinic post in Dubova through the openhanded generosity of the admor David of Talne, and in Dubova, Chajes devoted his energies to fighting his new rabbi's battles.

Beneath the legends' hyperbole and concealment lie glimpses of a forgotten, unusual, and tragic figure, whose life took twisting, turning paths. Its various way stations—mitnagedism, rabbinism, Haskalah, and Hasidism—reflect some of the fundamental experiences of traditional nineteenth-century Eastern European Jewish society.

Histories and lexicons have not preserved Akiva Chajes's name and memory. Our knowledge of this figure comes from his writings, which often obscure more than they reveal; his exchanges of responsa with the outstanding rabbis of his day; familial memoirs and rumors that circulated among his contemporaries and their offspring; and a number of hasidic legends that shaped his life story for their didactic purposes. This chapter is devoted to gathering the meager data available on Chajes and to comparing the sources to verify their information. It begins by surveying the definite facts ascertainable from Chajes's surviving literary legacy, and then discusses Chajes's portrayal in family and local memoir literature, on the one hand, and in hasidic memory, on the other hand. Finally, the chapter attempts to determine what trends and rationales shaped his shifting image.

Chajes's Literary Legacy

Born in Tulchin, Podolia, around 1815, Akiva Shalom Chajes was a scion of an ancient, prestigious family, whose main seat was the Galician town of Brody and whose sons served for generations as rabbis, elders, and communal leaders there. One of his forebears was the kabbalistic rabbi Yitshak Chajes (c. 1640–1726), who headed the rabbinical court of Skole and authored *Zera Yitshak*;[3] Akiva took pride in this familial heritage and often quoted his ancestor. That Akiva was an incisive scholar with expertise in all aspects of Torah learning emerges clearly from all the pertinent sources.

Apart from the fragmentary material preserved in the contemporary responsa literature, we know of three or four books written by Chajes. One, which has not survived and which may indeed never have been written, was a polemical antihasidic work composed in his youth, titled *Yesod datenu* (The foundation of our religion). Published either in Frankfurt am Oder or in Lemberg, according to some book catalogs,[4] this book has not yet surfaced in any library, nor is it quoted or alluded to anywhere other than the catalogs.[5] If it was ever written, all traces of this work have been lost.

Two other works—*Nishmat hayah* (A living soul) and *Hitragshut hanefesh* (Excitement of the soul)—were published during Chajes's lifetime; another, a commentary on the prayer book titled *Ikvei shalom*, appeared posthumously. According to Berdyczewski, Chajes left "thousands of manuscripts relating to all branches of Talmudic literature."[6] But even if this is plainly hyperbolic, the following statement by Chajes's son-in-law, Binyamin Horowitz, is evidence of Chajes's rich literary estate: "He left novellae on seven tractates called *Nahalat shivah*, and responsa, and a work on *Siftei kohen* and *Turei zahav* on the *Shulhan arukh, Yoreh de'ah.* And with the help of God . . . I will try to publish them."[7] Evidently, then, most of Akiva Chajes's manuscripts have been lost.

The first work by the man who called himself "the lowly, despised Akiva Shalom Chajes of the holy congregation of Tulchin" was published in Vilna in 1845. Titled *Nishmat hayah*,[8] this work is a commentary on the Yom Kippur confession (*vidui; al het*) and the *Avinu malkenu* (our father, our king) litany; despite their importance to the High Holiday penitential period, Chajes realized that most people did not understand these texts and that, consequently, the sincere penitent did not know exactly how to engage in the process of repentance. Chajes concluded his introduction as follows: "I hoped through this commentary to find favor in God's eyes, that he fulfill my request in his great mercy: 'One thing I ask of the Lord, only that do I seek,' that I will not leave the world without true repentance." Despite the temptation to link these remarks to Chajes's personal repentance from sin, to be treated below, and to his acceptance in hasidic ranks, it is doubtful that they are related. Published when Chajes was about thirty and still living in Tulchin, the transformation in his life apparently took place at a later date.[9]

Chajes's second work, *Hitragshut hanefesh*, a short anthology of kabbalistic commentaries, was published anonymously in Lemberg in 1864. On the title page, the editor, the publisher and controversial author Michael Levi Frumkin (Rodkinson), noted that these excerpts were "prepared for individuals seeking to purify themselves, when deep in introspection and alone with their maker." The author, Frumkin noted, was "very pious, one of the eminent ones of the generation, of blessed memory, who bequeathed us a blessing and, because of his humility, asked that his name be omitted from his holy book." Chajes's authorship of this work emerges not just from its identification in Berdyczewski's two articles but also from its inclusion, thirty years later, in Chajes's commentary on the prayer book *Ikvei shalom.* Written in the Aramaic style specific to the *Zohar*, *Hitragshut hanefesh* in no way hints at its author's name or personality. In his brief introduction to this work—also in imitation of Zoharic Aramaic—Frumkin relates that he received the manuscript from the author, but that the initiative to publish was his. How this manuscript came into Frumkin's hands and why he published it without attribution to Chajes is not ascertainable, nor is it clear why he described the author as deceased four years prior to his actual death.[10] In a memorial to Chajes, Berdyczewski remarked on an incongruity associated with *Hitragshut hanefesh*—namely, that the book's anachronistic style made it popular among the hasidim in particular, who had no idea that its author was an individual whom they had harshly persecuted: "[the hasidim] used to recite chapters from this book during the month of Elul, and would weep at its penetrating profound remarks that pierce the reciter's heart."[11]

In 1898, thirty years after Chajes's death, Binyamin Horowitz of Tulchin, his son-in-law, printed *Siddur ikvei shalom*, a prayer book with Chajes's commentary *Nehora me'alya* (Heavenly light).[12] Actually, this is not a systematic, running commentary—it appears unlikely that Chajes intended to prepare a comprehensive commentary on the siddur—but rather notes to selected parts of the prayer book that Horowitz found in Chajes's literary estate. Horowitz sought both to bring his father-in-law's profound thought to public attention and, at the same time, to improve his economic situation, as he states explicitly in the preface.[13]

Chajes's stature as a Torah scholar, concerned only with halakhic matters, also emerges from exchanges of responsa preserved in the works of eminent rabbis of the day. Among the rabbinic figures with whom he corresponded were Shlomo Kluger of Brody; Yosef Shaul Nathanson of Lemberg; Dov Berush Ashkenazi, who served as rabbi in Slonim and Lublin; Aharon Moshe Taubes of Iasi, Rumania; Meir Eisenstadt, a disciple of the Hatam Sofer from Ungvar, Hungary; and Avraham Teomim of Zborov (and eventually, Buchach). Many of these individuals praised Chajes's knowledge and incisiveness.[14]

"Out of My House, Impure One!" Rabbi Akiva Chajes in Light of Memoir Literature

Neither Chajes's own works, nor his exchanges with various halakhic authorities with whom he probably had no personal acquaintance, hint at his anomalous status in the communities among whom he lived. The main sources for reconstructing this stage of his life come from memoirs written by family members, contemporaries, and fellow townsmen. Each, however, remembered different things or recalled shared matters somewhat differently.

Micha Yosef Berdyczewski

In 1888 the young writer (then twenty-three) Micha Yosef Berdyczewski (1865–1921) published two short pieces devoted to Chajes. Berdyczewski's interest in Chajes stemmed from the fact that his father, Moshe Aharon Berdyczewski, had succeeded Chajes as town rabbi of Dubova. The Berdyczewski family arrived in Dubova in 1873,[15] five years after Chajes's death, when Micha Yosef was about eight years old. Obviously, he never met Chajes but relied on data, rumors, local traditions, and stories heard in his parental home.

"This brilliant rabbi had outstandingly sharp, profound, mental acuity, like one of the ancient ones," Berdyczewski wrote. "He had expertise in all of Talmudic literature: the Babylonian and Palestinian Talmuds and the Midrash." In addition to his knowledge of rabbinics, "he was exceedingly well-versed and expert in philosophical studies, in astronomy and geometry." In Berdyczewski's eyes, Chajes was an extraordinary genius who had the misfortune to be born in the wrong place at the wrong time: "Had he been born in Lithuania, he would have become one of its outstanding prodigies, and would have become one of the spokesmen of the generation . . . but to his misfortune he was born in the Ukraine, the bailiwick of Hasidism." Despite having been born in the heartland of Ukrainian Hasidism—Tulchin was the hometown of the Besht's grandson, the zaddik Barukh of Tulchin (who later moved to Mezhibozh), and to a cluster of Bratslav hasidim—Chajes's "common sense did not allow him to believe in Hasidism." Not satisfied with reservations concerning Hasidism alone, he aired his criticism publicly ("and viewed it as an obligation to open the eyes of others"); thus the hasidim persecuted him and "wished to stab him."[16]

Chajes was ostracized for fifteen years, and not a soul in Tulchin conversed with him. During that time his bread and butter came "from his wife's employment as a storekeeper; he was also slightly involved in bookselling."[17] But Chajes spent most of his time in study: "He studied the Talmud with great devotion, learning up to sixteen hours a day while standing. And when he became sleepy he would stick the lit candle on his hand; when the candle burned down and singed his hand he would awake."[18] What we have here is Berdyczewski's projection onto his admired fellow townsman of the classic model of the Eastern European prodigy he encountered in Lithuania during his years of study at the Volozhin yeshiva.[19]

Berdyczewski also recounted that sharp-tongued Chajes had a mordant wit: "In addition to his eminence in Torah, philosophy, and kabbalah, he had a talent for epigrams, jest, and for trenchant satires."[20] An example of his macabre humor has been preserved in an episode encapsulating his anti-hasidic campaign. According to Berdyczewski, Chajes's antagonist was "the holy rabbi Shlomo of Savran."[21] Forced by their clash to flee to Brody in the Austrian empire, where he came under the aegis of Rabbi Shlomo Kluger, Chajes wrote the following to his enemy from exile: "Two scholars who are at odds in matters of Halakha, one goes to exile etc. [and the other dies]—I have fulfilled my part."[22]

Rabbi Shlomo Kluger, Berdyczewski went on to relate, honored Chajes for his Torah scholarship and was wont to say of him: "None has defeated me, except for Rabbi Akiva." Nowhere in his two pieces does Berdyczewski even allude to a heretical chapter of Chajes's life, to be discussed below. Instead, he contents himself with the following laconic remark: "Late in life he repented and drew near to Hasidism and became a close follower of the zaddik Reb David of Talne and went to live in Dubova, where he died."[23]

Binyamin Halevi Horowitz

Any attempt to delineate the figure of Akiva Chajes must also touch on the brief biographical introduction to *Siddur ikvei shalom* written by his son-in-law, Binyamin Horowitz, also its publisher. Horowitz, himself a Talne hasid, succinctly recorded Chajes's biography from a retrospective hasidic outlook, rewriting and concealing the early, "problematic" part of Chajes's life while highlighting its final hasidic chapter. It goes without saying that Chajes's mitnagedic past is absent from the unusually large number of approbations (fifty in all!) collected by his enthusiastic son-in-law and published in the beginning of the book.[24]

Horowitz supplies almost no new information. He relies on Berdyczewski's remarks and quotes them,[25] but censors those aspects not consonant with the updated image of his father-in-law—in particular, his brush with the hasidim that forced him into exile from Tulchin to another land. In addition, Horowitz underscores the episodes epitomizing Chajes's positive attitude toward Hasidism. Thus he recounts that he heard from Chajes himself of a visit—made at Shlomo Kluger's recommendation—to the well-known zaddik Meir of Premishlan (d. 1850): "And he told me . . . that once he visited the holy rabbi Meir of Premishlan (because Rabbi Shlomo Kluger stated that of him one must say that he possesses the holy spirit). And he [Rabbi Meir] greeted him through an aperture in his door, for he allowed no one to enter his place of learning. And recognizing that Chajes was not argumentative, that he acted with modesty, and was an outstanding scholar, the above-mentioned rabbi did not allow him to depart without opening his door to him and telling him what he perceived and engaging him in an exchange of words of Torah learning."[26]

Shlomo Kluger indeed greatly admired Meir of Premishlan, and the two were longtime friends; Kluger even composed a eulogy on Meir's death.[27] If this meeting between Chajes and Meir of Premishlan really took place, it had to have occurred between 1838 and 1840, a period when Meir of Premishlan confined himself to his room, practiced self-denial, and received almost no callers. This reclusion was interpreted as his means of empathizing with the suffering of the zaddik Yisrael of Ruzhin, then wasting away in a Kiev jail.[28]

Zvi Kasdai

Additional details about Akiva Chajes's colorful personality are given by Zvi Kasdai (1865–1937), a native of Dubova and a childhood friend of Berdyczewski. Kasdai's memoirs, published in 1926, are grounded in local and familial traditions.[29] Like Berdyczewski, with whose articles he was surely acquainted, Kasdai describes Chajes's expertise in Talmudic and rabbinic literature and his knowledge of religious philosophy ("a rare phenomenon in the Ukraine which is awash in Hasidism and which excels—to a large extent—in ignorance"). And, like Berdyczewski, Kasdai testifies to a clash between Chajes and the Savraner hasidim. The precise nature of this controversy remains obscure; Kasdai remarks that Chajes, "being truly learned in Torah, dared to question the erudition of the Savraner zaddik, the sole zaddik in the Ukraine to whom his hasidim have awarded the crown of the Torah." The hasidim persecuted Chajes on that account, and he was forced to flee to Brody, from where he wrote his letter about two scholars at odds. Kasdai adds: "Indeed, the Savraner died that same year."

Ostensibly, knowing the date of the Savraner zaddik's death would help determine the date of the controversy and Chajes's flight; however, matters are not that straightforward. Remember that Berdyczewski identifies this figure as Shlomo of Savran; Kasdai leaves him unnamed and simply describes him as someone his followers saw as an outstanding scholar. But the sole Savraner zaddik worthy of this title was Shlomo's father, the dynasty founder Moshe Zvi Giterman of Savran. A disciple of Barukh of Mezhibozh and Levi Yitshak of Berdichev, this zaddik presided over a wealthy hasidic court in Savran[30] and was regarded—even by his opponents—as a clever, learned leader.[31] Eventually, he earned a reputation for truculence, especially because of his cruel, uncompromising battle against Bratslav Hasidism and its leader, Nathan of Nemirov.[32] Late in life he moved to the nearby town of Chechelnik,[33] where he died in 1838.

Rabbi Shlomo (his full name was Shimon Shlomo) of Savran—evidently Moshe Zvi's only son, who succeeded him as zaddik[34]—was not known for his Torah scholarship, left no writings, and served as zaddik for only ten years, until his death in 1848. After his death, his legacy was split between his two younger sons, Moshe of Chechelnik and David of Savran; we shall have occasion to return to them later.

If Chajes's quarrel was with the dynasty founder Moshe Zvi Giterman, then Chajes fled Tulchin in 1837; if it was with Shlomo, the flight dates to 1847. Earlier, I mentioned Binyamin Horowitz's remarks regarding Chajes's trip to Meir of Premishlan at Shlomo Kluger's recommendation. As noted, this trip could only have taken place between 1838 and 1840; on this basis, the quarrel would have been with Moshe Zvi Giterman, as Kasdai hints. However, other reliable sources indicate that Chajes left Tulchin around 1847 (though not necessarily for Brody); thus Berdyczewski preserves the more accurate tradition, making Chajes's adversary Shimon Shlomo of Savran, and not his father.[35]

Let us return to Kasdai's tale, which has Akiva Chajes fleeing Tulchin—for fear of the wrath of the Savraner hasidim—to the Brody marketplace: "And it came to pass that one of the followers of the Savraner met Akiva in the Brody marketplace and instantly grabbed an ax and chased him with intent to kill. But Akiva escaped to Rabbi Shlomo Kluger's home, and the latter took him in with both hands because of his great Torah learning and protected him against his bitter enemies. And Akiva, so the hasidim went on to relate—left the fold: he read books of heretical wisdom and joined the destroyers—the Berliners."[36]

At first Rabbi Kluger refused to believe the defamatory rumors concerning his disciple, but then an event took place that disclosed his protégé's true nature:

> Once Rabbi Shlomo encountered difficulty in answering a halakhic query sent from Berdichev[37] and was unable to arrive at a decision. After lunch Rabbi Shlomo went into his room and fell asleep. Akiva followed him into that room and wrote an incisive, masterful responsum to the question. He signed it: "I Akiva Chajes." When Rabbi Shlomo awoke and saw Akiva's reply he was seized with violent trembling and shouted as loudly as he could: "Only the Holy One blessed be He can sign 'I', 'I and no other.'"[38] Thus, you are "an other," a heretic, an evil person who teaches Halakha in the presence of his master. Out of my house, impure one! . . .
>
> Akiva immediately left Rabbi Shlomo's house and went—to the harlots . . . he shortened his coat, shaved his beard, openly desecrated the Sabbath, and day by day sank lower and lower into the forty-nine gates of impurity. Until by chance he came to Duvid'l of Talne. "And our rebbe"—thus the Talne hasidim ended their tale—"with his unrivaled watchful eye, immediately perceived that he had a great soul and began to draw him closer until he returned him to the straight and narrow."[39]

The hyperbolic and fictional aspects (attempted murder in the marketplace!) incorporated in this story make it impossible to accept as the plain truth. Kasdai, himself a scion of a family affiliated with Talne Hasidism, claims that he heard these stories from the hasidim themselves. However, the questionable trustworthiness of his remarks—to be discussed below—which remain the sole source for this episode, do not enable us to be sure that it occurred.[40] In the absence of additional, unbiased testimony supporting Chajes's throwing off the yoke of observance, desecrating the Sabbath, and sinking into the forty-nine gates of impurity—indeed, other witnesses undermine its validity—Kasdai's remarks must be viewed as "Hasidiography," an Orthodox hasidic morality tale with a religious, didactic aim. From the Orthodox standpoint, the notion that joining the ranks of the maskilim inevitably led to the depths of sinfulness and heresy was almost axiomatic; moreover, the ultimate fate of those who read heretical literature was preordained. The story of Chajes's lapse is an inverted reflection of the level of fear and defensiveness kindled by the threat of secularization and the powerful temptation of Haskalah. Religious dissoluteness and sexual licentiousness are seen as linked (the first place Chajes went after leaving Kluger was to a whorehouse!). His additional "heretical" actions are all symbolic—the change in dress and external appearance (which symbolizes the desire to assimilate, and the shame of being identified with the traditional collective) and the public desecration of the Sabbath (which marks abandonment of God's commandments)—of the crossing of the lines and a complete break with traditional society. Standing between the heretic and the yawning abyss of sin is the zaddik, who by dint of his prophetic powers identifies the sinner's "great soul" and saves him from destruction.

Before continuing our story, a reexamination of the relationship between Chajes and Shlomo Kluger is in order. Berdyczewski's and Kasdai's remarks imply that Chajes took refuge with Kluger for a time, and that Kluger admired Chajes's learning and saw him as a disciple and friend. And Binyamin Horowitz testifies to hearing firsthand of Chajes's visit to Meir of Premishlan in the wake of Kluger's high praise for the zaddik. Indeed, there are some extant casuistic responsa by Kluger to the "incisive scholar" Akiva Chajes of Tulchin; some signed "his friend."[41] But none of these responsa alludes to a close rabbi-disciple relationship (Kluger never calls Chajes "my student," as he does others); it is possible that they were not even personally acquainted.[42]

Apart from Berdyczewski's and Kasdai's remarks, there is no other evidence that Chajes lived in Brody, and certainly not for any length of time.[43] What is clear is that he lived in Tulchin until 1845 at least (as evidenced by his introduction to *Nishmat hayah*), whereas 1847 found him in northern Bessarabia, in Orhayuv,[44] from whence he continued to correspond on Torah matters with contemporary rabbis. For Passover 1848, we learn of a stay in Lemberg; but a responsum sent that year by Rabbi Nathansohn still addresses him as Akiva Shalom of Tulchin. This was also the case in early 1849, when Rabbi Avraham Teomim posted a responsum to Tulchin.[45] Perhaps Chajes visited nearby Brody in the course of 1848. Nonetheless, his main place of exile was Orhayuv, not Brody. A longer stay by Chajes in a center of Torah learning and of Haskalah, such as Brody, would certainly have left its mark in memoir and maskilic literature.

Mordekhai Glubman

Further data on Akiva Chajes have been preserved in the memoirs of his sister's grandson, Mordekhai Glubman (1872–1943). A native of the Ukrainian town of Shpikov, Glubman had close ties to the local zaddikim.[46] Glubman not only summarizes the known data about Chajes, but also cites original, unique family traditions. His description relates to Chajes's mitnagedic aspect alone; it contains no hints of his departure from Tulchin, or of his residing in Brody, or of any maskilic-heretical period in his life. According to Glubman, Chajes's change of heart involved a shift from mitnagedism to hasidism, not from heresy to hasidism.

"Uncle Akiva" was brother to Glubman's grandmother Menuha. There were, in addition, two other brothers: Shlomo and Pinhas. All three brothers were scholars, "but Akiva was not simply learned in the ordinary sense, but a 'prodigy' in the broadest sense of the word . . . a philosopher and kabbalist. He possessed profound knowledge of the study of the Hebrew language; he was 'a man of many talents.'"[47] Glubman learned much about Chajes from his father and other relatives and friends who had known him. Thus, Noah Zvi, an elderly man from Shpikov who was born in Tulchin and was acquainted with Chajes, told Glubman: "Akiva was one of the prodigies of his day; in our orphaned generation he would be considered exceptional." Regarding his steadfast devotion to study—which we met in Berdyczewski's description—Glubman learned from Liber, one of his relatives, that at night Chajes would remain alone in the study house, studying all night long with one foot on the floor and the other on a bench. Once some other students entered late at night and "found Uncle Akiva standing and studying as was his wont, so deep in concentration that he did not even notice them. They took a piece of chalk and drew a circle around the foot that was touching the floor. When they returned in the morning they found that his foot had not budged from within the circle."[48] From his father, Glubman heard that during his nights in the study house, Chajes would write his novellae on sheets of paper, only to burn them in the candle flame in the morning.[49]

In addition, his father told Glubman that Chajes earned his living as a melamed to the sons-in-law of wealthy householders and as a moneylender. By this means, he was able to save up a goodly sum of money and "was considered a prosperous individual; he lent money in accordance with halakhic restrictions. And when women pawned their silver candelabra and gold jewelry and gems he would run after them to return them for the Sabbath, or for weddings and other family affairs."[50]

"I heard from hasidim and my father verified it," said Glubman, that Chajes was a fervent mitnaged in his youth. This was unusual, as all the Jews in Tulchin were hasidim, mostly Talne hasidim not known for their tolerance: "The hasidim regarded him as 'someone beyond the pale'; after all, how could a Jew exist without 'belief in the sages' and without 'affiliation to a zaddik'; that made him a virtual 'Litvak.' And in those days, in that environment, 'a Litvak' was seen as outside the bounds of Judaism. He was harshly persecuted and libeled; he was identified with the 'Dessauers,' the disciples of Moses Mendelssohn of Dessau."[51]

From the account of another family member, Moshe Waxman of Tulchin, it appears that Chajes was aware of his negative image. Thus, Chajes advised Waxman to conceal their relationship, so that Waxman would not acquire a reputation as a heretic, which would depress his worth in the marriage market.[52]

Rabbi Akiva Chajes's Change of Heart

What made Akiva Chajes turn his back on his past, late in life, and join the ranks of the faithful hasidim? Apparently, Berdyczewski did not know the real reason. He provided the simplistic explanation that Chajes's powers failed him: "At the end of his life, when he found it difficult to continue the battle, he bent his head and turned to Hasidism."[53] A Bratslav tradition, to be treated below, ascribes his change of heart to economic woes: "For lack of a livelihood, he drew near to Reb Duvid'l Talner." These explanations frame Chajes's step as resulting from poverty and despair rather than true conviction in the verity of the hasidic path. Naturally, Talne tradition tells an entirely different story: according to its lights, Chajes the sinner reformed after receiving a personal missive from Reb David. Although its contents remained unknown, the missive's influence was dramatic. Chajes's conversion was thereby given a mysterious, miraculous explanation, and his acceptance of Hasidism was seen not as a step fueled by desperation, but as a voluntary process of surrender and acceptance.

From "Litvak" to Hasid: Mordekhai Glubman's Version

Mordekhai Glubman presents an entirely different explanation, albeit one closer to the Talne tradition. In line with what he culled from "the stories of the hasidim and from his father," the Jews of Tulchin were in need of a rabbi. Akiva Chajes, who saw himself as a worthy candidate, knew that, as a mitnaged, his chances of receiving this post were nil. He therefore sought to disqualify the other candidates. Once the zaddik David of Talne came to Tulchin (the town "belonged" to him by virtue of a *maggidut* contract),[54] and the householders complained to him that "the heretical mitnaged Akiva trips up the rabbis with questions and casuistry like the 'Litvaks' do," leaving the rabbinical throne in Tulchin shamefully orphaned. At the "third Sabbath repast," the zaddik suddenly inquired of the throng surrounding his table if Chajes was there. Akiva Chajes was indeed present, and the rebbe invited him to sit by his side. Akiva attended closely to the rebbe's teachings and requested a personal audience when the zaddik had finished speaking. Their conversation lasted some four hours, and from that time on Chajes was a fervent hasid, to the extent that they used to say that he sat under the admor's table when he spoke words of "Torah." The Talne rebbe reciprocated with honor and love and appointed Chajes as the rabbi of Dubova.[55]

"It was only the merit of the Talne rebbe," Glubman concluded his memoirs, "that kept him from becoming known as the 'Tulchiner *epikoyres* [heretic].' I recall that, as a lad, the elderly hasidim who remembered and knew my uncle would praise his learning, his genius, his diligence; however, they always concluded their praises with 'but.' This 'but,' to the best of my understanding, compared him to one 'who gazed [at forbidden knowledge] and was smitten.' And they concluded: the Talne rebbe found the remedy for his soul."[56]

Thus, Glubman attributes Chajes's conversion from fervent mitnaged to fervent hasid to personal contact and persuasiveness, against the background of the appointment of a new rabbi in Tulchin. Nowhere does Glubman refer to Chajes's flight from Tulchin or residence in Brody. If Chajes never moved to Brody, then he was not under the aegis of Rabbi Shlomo Kluger and did not descend to heresy, from which David of Talne ostensibly had to rescue him via miraculous means.

Glubman does not specify Chajes's opponents, but from his remarks we can infer that they were the Talne hasidim, who comprised the majority of the hasidim in Tulchin. In contrast, the memoirs of Berdyczewski and Kasdai stress the Savraner presence there. For them, it was against the Savraner rebbe that Chajes directed his criticism, and it was the Savraners who were his main enemies. As we shall see below, this identification of Chajes's enemies as Savraner hasidim may shed light on Chajes's late affiliation with the Talne hasidim in particular.

The Talne Hasidim's Version

The Talne tradition mentioned in the opening of this section was preserved in David Leib Mekler's *Fun rebns hoyf* (From the rebbe's court). Mekler

(1891–1976), a prolific journalist and writer, saw himself not as a historian but rather as someone seeking to recover slivers of folklore and images of the past. Indeed, his introduction stresses that he did not collect this material for historical purposes; rather, it should be regarded as a source of folklore and cultural history. In this two-volume work, Mekler interwove historical facts, rumors, and tales that he recorded in New York from his informants: hasidim and admorim, synagogue officials, and acquaintances.[57] Thus, his description of the nineteenth-century Chernobyl and Talne hasidic courts reflects the perceptions reported by Eastern European hasidim in the United States in the late 1920s and their longing for their former, beloved world.

Mekler, who was familiar with Kasdai's memoirs and even mentions them explicitly,[58] appears to have accepted Kasdai's testimony in its entirety, adding to it with literary embellishments of his own devising. We can assume that, had this story entirely contradicted Talne tradition, Mekler would not have published it without reservations. Its inclusion and the addition of details are indicative of Kasdai's memoirs' status as a legitimate, even if not completely trustworthy, representative of authentic Talne tradition.[59]

Mekler told the following tale: Chajes was known among the hasidim as a righteous man and a brilliant scholar, and his reputation spread far. Concurrently, the Savraner rebbe also attained a reputation as a Torah scholar; Chajes, however, had little regard for either the Savraner's learning or his other qualities. It is not clear whether Chajes spoke out against him publicly or whether he simply refused to travel to his court and acknowledge his eminence. In either case, the Savraner hasidim in Tulchin declared war on Chajes, sorely persecuting him until he was forced to flee to Brody, from whence he sent his above-mentioned witty letter about "two scholars at odds." The Savraner rebbe did die in the course of that year, and his hasidim attributed this to Akiva Chajes's curse.

Mekler described Chajes's reception by Rabbi Shlomo Kluger; his signing of the difficult responsum ("I Akiva Chajes"); his expulsion from the rabbi's house (perhaps because of envy, Mekler speculated); and his falling in with the Brody maskilim and abandoning the "straight and narrow." Chajes's wallowing in the forty-nine gates of impurity—Mekler went on to embroider the plot, drawing either on his imagination or on the hasidic tales he collected—made a strong impression on traditional Jews, both saddening and angering them. They wished to take revenge on Chajes, but did not know how. After all, the "Deytshukes" protected him. The hasidim feared that Chajes would become a model for imitation, whereas the maskilim hoped that this would be the case. Indeed, Mekler noted, it was said that because of him, many hasidim left the path. The heretic Akiva Chajes cast a shadow of fear on the hasidic world and all—especially the Savraner hasidim—cursed him, spit at the mention of his name, and prayed for his death. Only the Talne rebbe treated Chajes's deeds with equanimity. In fact, he took an interest in Chajes and his doings, displaying a strange fondness for him. To his hasidim, he said, "Reb Akiva has a great soul that must be saved." Although the hasidim found this difficult to believe, they realized that hidden matters were at stake.

David of Talne therefore wrote a personal letter to Chajes, which he dispatched to Brody via special messenger. None knew its contents, but its results were apparent to all. Upon reading the letter, Chajes immediately packed his bags and traveled to Talne, where Reb David received him as if he were one of his hasidim and never referred to his sins. Akiva became a true penitent, grew his beard and sidelocks, put on hasidic dress again, and was a God-fearing man. David of Talne made inquiries concerning a position for Chajes and awarded him a rabbinic post in Dubova. In return, Chajes demonstrated absolute loyalty to his new rebbe.[60]

Mekler's tale—which, as noted, was heavily grounded in Kasdai's memoirs—abounds with hyperbole and mistaken assumptions. Certainly Chajes was no hasid in his youth. Nor can the rabbinate in Dubova be viewed as much of a prize: after all, this was a tiny, impoverished town, and the rabbi's salary almost certainly a pittance. Also much inflated is the description of the hasidim's fear of Chajes's satanic influence, and the maskilim's abounding admiration for him: there is not a single mention of Chajes's name in contemporary maskilic literature. Nor is Chajes's stay in Brody certain. At the same time, the force driving Mekler's reworking of the material is obvious: the harsher Chajes's sins, the greater the zaddik who wondrously succeeded in rescuing such a sworn heretic from the depths of iniquity.

The updated version of the Talne tradition, published in 1994 in *Netsah shebanetsah*, is of interest. A hasidic biography of David of Talne by one of his descendants, this book aims to glorify him. Drawn directly from Mekler, this enigmatic version mentions neither Chajes nor his town by name:

> A more famous penitent was a brilliant, well-known rabbi. This rabbi became embroiled in a quarrel in his hometown with the local rabbi, because of which the local rabbi's followers began to persecute him. Consequently, he left town and moved to the town of Brody. His heart being filled with bitterness due to these persecutions, he found his way to the band of Brody maskilim and, to everyone's distress, drew closer and closer to them until it seemed that he was straying from the path and had been trapped in their net. All the members of his prominent family who tried to return him to the fold failed. This sad story came to the ears of our rabbi [David of Talne]. All who spoke of him strongly disparaged his desecration of God's name, for before he abandoned the path he had been famed as a prodigy and Torah scholar. Our rabbi said that there was hope for his future and that he wanted to attempt to post a letter to him in

Brody. What our rabbi wrote remains unknown, but after receiving the letter he set out and traveled to Talne to our rabbi. There he sat at our rabbi's table and our rabbi brought him closer and closer until he repented totally within a short time, and our rabbi even went to the trouble of making him town rabbi of Dubova. From that point on the rabbi in question had strong bonds of love for our rabbi and would travel to him as a true hasid.[61]

Even in the absence of Chajes's name, this story obviously relates to him. Here what motivates his departure from his hometown is not his harsh criticism of Hasidism—a fact that emerges from all the memoirs surveyed above—but rather an unspecified quarrel (over what?) between Chajes and the "local rabbi." This rewritten version contains several motifs of interest: Chajes did not descend all the way to heresy but hovered at its edge ("it seemed that he was straying from the path"); and his change of heart—his total penitence—was not the culmination of a long process, but the result of a sudden decision prompted by the zaddik's letter.

The Bratslav Version

More explicit remarks appear in a Bratslav tradition. As is often the case, in line with this group's esoteric traditions, its relatively late transmission does not necessarily indicate lack of reliability:

In Tulchin there was one Akiva Melamed, who was expert in Talmud and rabbinic literature and worthy of being a rabbi. He had expertise in kabbalistic and hasidic literature, but was also knowledgeable in philosophy, scholarly literature, and heretical works to the extent that he even wrote a book mocking the contemporary zaddikim.[62] But he looked like a pious Jew with a beard and long sidelocks. And among his townspeople he was thought to be a learned, pious man.

Once when he was in Bratslav he visited our teacher Rabbi Nathan in order to mock everything he would see and hear in his presence. And, first of all, he asked Rabbi Nathan to say words of Torah. And then Rabbi Nathan recited in the name of our deceased rabbi [Nahman of Bratslav] the short passage from *Likutei Moharan* [1:188] concerning how the zaddik tests a person who comes to find his lost memories to see if he is a pretender . . . When Akiva heard this, and understood how far-reaching Rabbi Nathan's words were, after departing not only did he leave off his mockery, rather, on several occasions, he related this event to various people and praised Rabbi Nathan.

This was Akiva Melamed under whom one of our eminent members studied: Reb Zvi [son of Reb] Pesah of Tulchin, the in-law of Rabbi Nahman Tulchiner at whose hands the above-mentioned Reb Zvi came close to our flock. Once, when he was still a student of his, he said to his rabbi Akiva: "With you who do not believe in the Besht

I do not agree, and I believe in the Besht. But I wonder— to which hasidic sect should I draw near? Thus I inquire, what is your opinion?" He [Akiva] answered: "If you must draw near a hasidic sect, the finest is the Bratslav sect." From that point on the aforementioned Reb Zvi drew near to our flock . . . Said Akiva, for lack of a livelihood, drew near to Reb Duvid'l Talner and asked him to find him a rabbinical post. And he gave him the town of Dubova, near Uman.[63]

"Akiva Melamed" of Tulchin, this tradition's protagonist, is undoubtedly Akiva Chajes; now we also learn that Chajes instructed Zvi ben Pesah, a fellow townsman who became a Bratslav hasid. Once again we encounter a typical hasidic morality tale: an eminent mitnaged who seeks to mock Hasidism and its teachers is captivated by the charms of the rival movement and transformed from foe to friend. According to this account, although Chajes assumed the usual disguise affected by maskilim and heretics—namely, a beard and sidelocks—this did not help him in his encounter with the hasidic rebbe who unmasked him.[64] But in this case the hasidic rebbe is not David of Talne—as in Glubman's memoirs—but Nathan of Nemirov, the leader of Bratslav Hasidism in the generation following Rabbi Nahman's death.

From the Bratslav standpoint, this story's ending is ironic. Although Akiva Chajes spoke favorably of Bratslav Hasidism, ultimately he achieved economic security through the generosity of David of Talne. Between these two neighboring hasidic sects—Talne and Bratslav—there was long-standing enmity. In the previous chapter, we saw how the wealthy, proud Talne court harshly persecuted the inconsiderable, impoverished Bratslav hasidim. The Bratslavers cast their eyes toward Uman, the burial place of their admired rebbe Nahman. This town was close not only to Talne, where the Talne zaddik resided, but also to Dubova, Chajes's last residence. As a means of softening Chajes's move from favoring Bratslav, the "finest sect," to affiliation with their hated rivals, Bratslav memory tradition chose to attribute it not to deep internal conviction in Talne hasidic ways, but to Chajes's economic difficulties.

Moreover, an apocryphal version of the Bratslav story in manuscript contains two lines erased by the proofreader, which were therefore not published: "And Akiva boasted before some of his confidants that he composed the treatise *Magen David* [Shield of David] and that when he drew near to that aforementioned rabbi [David of Talne] he told him that he had written a work on the Torah, and the admor granted him [the rabbinate] provided that he published it under his name [and so it was done?]."[65] According to the censored ending, the zaddik agreed to grant Chajes a rabbinical post in Dubova on condition that Chajes publish his homilies on the Torah under the zaddik's name. Furthermore, it claims that this was actually the case, and that this accordingly reveals *Magen David*'s true nature. Indeed, this polemical tradition, which denies David of Talne's authorship of a work attributed to him, is not unique. It appears independently: the antihasidic writer Ephraim Deinard also claimed that *Magen David* was written by someone other than David of Talne, the teacher Hirsh Lifschitz (the brother of the Orthodox author Yaakov Lifschitz of Kovno) who was then living in Uman.[66]

The Bratslav tradition's transparent explanation of Chajes's affiliation with Talne Hasidism as rooted in a crooked deal between him and the zaddik makes it impossible to rely on this tradition. Even its independent backing in Deinard's version is of little assistance, for Deinard, who sought to belittle the Talne rebbe, cannot be considered a trustworthy witness for anything related to Hasidism. Nonetheless, these two traditions do indicate a widespread disbelief in David of Talne's intellectual ability, and the voicing of doubts as to whether he composed on his own the books attributed to him.[67]

Rabbi Akiva Chajes's Appointment as Rabbi of Dubova and the *Kadavar* Controversy

The final chapter of Chajes's life—during which he served in the Dubova rabbinate—is linked to one of the stormier, stranger controversies in the Ukrainian hasidic world: the *kadavar* controversy. Around what did this controversy revolve?

When he first set out in his role as hasidic leader, David of Talne instituted an innovation in the recitation of the Sabbath and holiday prayer known as *Kedushat keter*. Instead of saying "*Kakatuv* al yad nevi'ekha" (per the Ashkenazic rite used by the mitnagedim and also by Habad hasidim), he asked that his followers say "*kadavar ha'amur* al yad nevi'ekha" (following the Sefarad and ha-Ari rites).[68] In addition, he insisted that his followers pause after reciting the words *lekha yeshaleshu*, and that they then recite the word *kadavar* out loud and in unison. His opponents (the zaddikim of Linitz and of Savran, as we shall see below) refrained from doing this; they asked their hasidim to pause after the phrase *vekara zeh el zeh veamar*, and only then to recite the response *kadosh, kadosh, kadosh* out loud.[69]

This seemingly slight innovation—after all, with the exception of Habad, every hasidic group said *kadavar*, and all, including the Talne hasidim, paused before responding *kadosh, kadosh, kadosh*—this matter swiftly became the acid test of loyalty to a particular zaddik. The Talne hasidim believed that their zaddik's pronouncement came after he experienced a spiritual ascent during which he heard the angelic recitation of the *Kedushah* before God, in which they said *kadavar* and not *kakatuv*.[70] Other hasidim did not find this mystical claim convincing, and the *kadavar* directive—in particular, the pause after *lekha yeshaleshu*—aroused grudges and uproar throughout the provinces of Kiev, Volhynia, and Podolia. *Kadavarnikes* was the appellation bestowed on Talne hasidim; their opponents were *kakatuvnikes* or *kadoshnikes.* Bans were pronounced on the noncompliant, betrothals canceled, partnerships dissolved, and families torn apart. The situation even descended to mutual denunciations and violence: "The terrible discord between those who say *kadavar* and those who say *kadosh* will not be quickly forgotten among the Jews . . . for much blood was shed in its course and some Jewish homes destroyed to the foundation. Because of it several families were impoverished and condemned to oblivion; some tender young wives from *kadavar* families were divorced by their husbands, who belonged to the *kadosh* faction; and there are still some denunciations in the courts of the provincial and the royal capitals!"[71]

As noted above, at the time, the small town of Dubova was under David of Talne's "rule." This rule—embodied in a *maggidut* contract—had manifold socioeconomic repercussions. One was the appointment of the zaddik's followers to key positions in the town's religious infrastructure, and the imposition of Talne customs as a sign of acceding to his authority. Zvi Kasdai, for instance, relates that Chajes exhibited absolute loyalty to David of Talne in this regard as well:

> Engraved in my heart, more than anything else, is the memory of the flogging that the rabbi of our town [Akiva Chajes] received at the hands of the non-Jew, the *pristav* [the gentile chief of police], because of the *kadavar* faith. Our rabbi, a follower of Reb Duvid'l, was naturally zealous for *kadavar*, and outlawed the shehitah of the ritual slaughterer who was a follower of Reb Gedalya Aharon,[72] an adamant opponent of *kadavar.* And the *pristav*, also an opponent of *kadavar*, asked the rabbi to nullify the ban he had placed on the slaughterer's shehitah. And when the rabbi did not accede to his request this inflamed his anger and he raised his whip against the rabbi. And the poor rabbi accepted his verdict and from that time forth all the Talne hasidim knew that a holy rabbi walked in their midst; even to us, the young children, the man was a pure saint, a wondrous legend.[73]

Kasdai repeats this testimony in the continuation: "It is indeed true that Rabbi Duvid'l placed him on the seat of the rabbinate in our town; it is also true that Reb Akiva was entirely devoted to Reb Duvid'l and actually martyred himself for the *kadavar* faith. *With my own eyes* I saw him being flogged in the old study house at the depraved hands of the drunken *pristav*, with the opponents of *kadavar* mocking him and enjoying his shame, and he accepted the verdict and was flogged for his rabbi's honor and for the sanctity of his teachings."[74]

In Talne tradition as well, the *kadavar* controversy appears as a cardinal event in Chajes's life. Mekler, heavily influenced by Kasdai as noted earlier, frames this "especially tragicomic episode" as a reflection of Talne weakness. As a fervent supporter of *kadavar*, Chajes was persecuted on that account by his rivals and enemies in Dubova—namely, the Sokolivka hasidim with whom the local shohet was affiliated.[75] Naturally, his opponents did not sit idly by, after Chajes responded by outlawing the "heretic's" shehitah. Although a harsh controversy broke out in the town, none dared to question the rabbi's decision. The sole individual to do so was local police chief. This non-Jew had no especial interest in how the *Kedushah* was recited, but he did know how to accept bribes. In this instance, having been bought by the Sokolivka hasidim, he persecuted the Talne hasidim and, upon hearing of Chajes's outlawing of the shohet, decided to force him to rescind his decision. Mekler's dramatic, colorful description paints at length the *pristav*'s arrival at the study house and his flogging of Chajes in the presence of throngs of pro- and anti-*kadavarnikes*. Despite the lashes, Chajes refused to back down; this increased his honor in the eyes of David of Talne, who saw him as a saint and martyr.[76]

But did Kasdai actually remember or witness this event as he declared? Chajes died in 1868, when Kasdai was a child of three or four,[77] making it doubtful that he actually witnessed these events; perhaps he just preserved a family tradition (his father was a Talne hasid and one of the *kadavarnikes*). Nonetheless, the event described is apparently based in reality: controversies between neighboring hasidic sects over areas of influence were commonplace, and the outlawing of shehitah was a legitimate tactic in these struggles. Moreover, the Talne hasidim were famed for their combativeness. The outlawing of the slaughtering of the Dubova shohet, who was affiliated with Sokolivka, was part of a general Talne campaign against small, regional hasidic sects whose followers refused to bow to the Talne rebbe's authority.

Tension between the Talne and the Sokolivka hasidim peaked in 1867–69, around the time of Chajes's death. Kasdai recounted its terrible consequences:

> Reb Gedalya Aharon of Sokolivka was Reb Duvid'l's most fanatical opponent, for he [David] encroached on his territory when he moved from Vasilkov to Talne.[78] Because of their *kadavar*, one of Gedalya-Aharon's hasidim set fire to the Talne *kloiz*. The *kloiz* burned down; several Torah scrolls were also burned with it . . . Regarding Reb Yitshak-Yoelikl, Reb Gedalya-Aharon's oldest son, the Talne hasidim made libelous denunciations because of which he was sentenced to hard labor in Siberia but, with the assistance of influential people who stood by his side in St. Petersburg, his sentence was commuted and he was sent to Kherson Province instead of to Siberia, and he chose the town of Kantakuzova, on the Podolia border, as his residence in order to dispossess the zaddikim of the Chernobyl dynasty, who also adhered to *kadavar*.[79]

These serious outcomes of such a trivial controversy—seemingly derived from an imaginary world of hyperbole—cast doubts on Kasdai's trustworthiness. But, in fact, a denunciation did lead to the exile of the zaddikim of the Linitz-Sokolivka dynasty, and they underwent a lengthy period of humiliation and suffering.[80] Hasidic historiography, including that of the Linitz hasidim, tends to obscure the internal background of these events and points an accusatory finger only at the maskilim and the Russian authorities; but vague hints indicate that hasidim, termed the "falsely sanctimonious," were at the center of this ugly tale.[81]

Thus, the Sokolivka hasidim paid dearly for their opposition to *kadavar*; it turns out, however, that they were not the only ones to question this custom. The Savraners also refused to bow to David of Talne's authority and rejected the recitation of *kadavar*.[82] Their objection is unaccountable as, after the death of the zaddik Shimon Shlomo Giterman of Savran, his daughter and two of his sons married members of the Chernobyl dynasty.[83] The latter, raised in the Chernobyl court, remained there until they became independent zaddikim in their own right.[84] But these marital ties did not prevent—and perhaps even encouraged—constant tension and mutual clashes between the various courts.[85] Particularly notable was the opposition of David of Savran (the son of Chajes's former enemy) to the *kadavar* custom instituted by David of Talne (Chajes's patron in those days).[86]

From this vantage point, it may also be possible to interpret Chajes's attachment to Talne Hasidism and his heroic adherence to the custom of reciting *kadavar* not just as identification with David of Talne's leadership and Talne Hasidism's special way of worship, but also as consistent with his ancient war on the Savraner hasidim and the Savraner dynasty.

In the Thicket of Memory

It is difficult to cut a swath through the thicket of various traditions and legends regarding Akiva Shalom Chajes. All the witnesses point to a figure of outstanding intellect—a proud, confident Torah scholar who opposed Hasidism, even though active in social settings in which opposition to Hasidism, let alone militant opposition, was anomalous.

The reasons for Chajes's opposition to Savran Hasidism remain obscure. Perhaps they stemmed from a lack of regard for Hasidism in general, or perhaps they were linked to Chajes's personal disapproval of Shimon Shlomo, Moshe Zvi of Savran's son. In any event, around 1847—the year of this zaddik's death—Chajes left Tulchin. He apparently lived in Orhayuv, Bessarabia, for a short time and then returned to Tulchin.

The story of Chajes's expulsion from Shlomo Kluger's home and his leaving the fold is not well founded. Chajes's exile in Brody is first mentioned by Berdyczewski, whose remarks, however, contain no hints of Chajes's "secularization." This motif appears in Kasdai—some seventy years after the events in question—and after that in the late Talne tradition cited by Mekler. Not only is there no other supporting evidence, it is difficult to imagine that such a dramatic episode—the secularization of an outstanding Torah scholar—would have gone unremarked in the many maskilic sources and the extensive memoir literature on Brody. Although it is possible that Chajes spent some time in Brody and was even friendly with Kluger, Kluger's responsa contain no clues to a personal relationship between them.

Brody, the capital of Galician Haskalah, came to represent the paradigm of a maskilic, heretical town.[87] An important branch of the Chajes family resided in Brody,[88] and even David of Talne lived there for a year and a half.[89] What could have been more natural than to add Akiva Chajes to the roll of its residents? It appears then that folktale-forming mechanisms were responsible for the Talne tale of Chajes's secularization, for this story meshed well with his militant biography. As absorbed by Kasdai (reportedly from the stories related by the Talne hasidim in his hometown of Dubova), this tradition attempted to explain the sudden about-face in Chajes's life, on the one hand, and on the other hand, to aggrandize the supernatural powers of the zaddik David of Talne, who successfully rescued a famous sinner from the pit. Kasdai himself admitted that Akiva Chajes was "crowned with various legends, of which it is impossible to know how much is the truth and how much simple hyperbole";[90] accordingly, his testimony cannot be considered reliable.[91]

The fact of Chajes's appointment as rabbi of Dubova by David of Talne is undisputed. But the reasons for his change of heart—from a mitnaged to a hasid—have yet to be fully examined: was this a perfunctory, despairing step prompted by his inability to earn a living, or a deliberate, wholehearted action? By never explaining the reason for this shift, Chajes opened the door to speculation, and it remains doubtful whether the true explanation will ever come to light. Ironically, Akiva Shalom Chajes struggled against hasidim and Hasidism for nearly his entire life: as a young mitnaged in Tulchin against the Savraner hasidim and their leader Shimon Shlomo Giterman, and in his old age, in Dubova, as a Talne hasid against the Sokolivka hasidim, who refused to bow to the authority of his zaddik and to accept *kadavar*.

6 "How Times Have Changed"

The World of Rabbi Menahem Nahum Friedman of Itscan

Hasidism and Philosophy

The following tale is told of the Hebrew linguist Moshe Aharon Wiesen (1878–1953), who as a youth in Galicia served one of the zaddikim of the day. Summoned by the zaddik, he was informed that he must leave the court—heretical books had been found in his possession. Upon querying the zaddik, Wiesen discovered that the book in question was Avraham Shalom Friedberg's *Zikhronot leveit David*.[1] He asked, "Rabbi, how do you know that this book is heretical? Have you read it?" To which the zaddik replied: "Although not heretical in content, it is utterly, innately heretical, for I assert that any *me'etl is a heretic.* Namely, any author who does not write the self-effacing phrases *mimeni hatsa'ir* [by the youthful one] or *me'iti hakatan* [by the insignificant one] on the title page, but rather uses the word *me'et* [by], certainly cannot be considered one of the God-fearing."[2]

This anecdote's bite lies in its use of the word *me'etl,* which for Yiddish speakers carries the ring of the diminutive for *met* (a dead person). And the wicked, as is well known, are "called dead in their lifetimes." This witticism mirrors the spirit of the age, in which many of the faithful were engaged in a fruitless battle against anything so much as exhibiting traces of the new. In the eyes of the fanatical preservers—devoted hasidim, in particular—not only was anything new biblically prohibited, but even the old could be seen as new: innovators were harshly denounced and punished.[3] But within those very same circles, in that very time and place, we encounter other, surprisingly novel phenomena.

This chapter invites the reader to make the acquaintance of a remarkable individual, Menahem Nahum Friedman of Itscan (1879–1933). This zaddik—

himself the son of a zaddik—rabbi, and halakhist not only dared to write *me'et* ("by") in the books he published, he also departed from custom by using square Hebrew print (not Rashi script), and Arabic numerals (not Roman ones or Hebrew letters) for pagination.[4] Moreover, his books are notable for their distinctive content, style, and sources. Indeed, his writings and philosophical essays on the human psyche, on dreams and their interpretation, and on aesthetics and beauty demonstrate profound knowledge of the best of world thought and literature. They boldly rely on and quote sources whose assimilation into traditional Jewish literature was inconceivable in the hasidic milieu, then or later.

Whether Friedman made his acquaintance with these sources in the original or through secondary citations, he meanders through world literature at will: from Plato, Aristophanes, and Epicurus to Spinoza, Kant, Schopenhauer, Hegel, and Leibniz, ending with Goethe, Schiller, Nietzsche, and Sienkiewicz. Friedman had a working knowledge of some foreign languages (especially German and Latin, and perhaps French), read philosophical and scholarly books and journals, and perused newspapers. He recounts trips made to Italy (he even visited the Vatican), the North Sea, Switzerland, Germany, and France, and describes—perhaps for the first time in rabbinical Jewish literature—landscapes and nature.[5] He penned personal observations on works of art,[6] and on classical musical compositions.[7] His clear, fluent Hebrew possesses none of the features of quotation-saturated, casuistic rabbinic writing, nor of the convoluted, error-ridden writing characteristic of hasidic homily. Anyone browsing through his works will find it surprising that a hasidic rabbi from Romania authored them—not just because of their startling cultural breadth, but also because of Friedman's facile, systematic mode of intellectual thought and the marginality of Hasidism, kabbalah, and mysticism in his world, just from the viewpoint of citation.[8] Moreover, in Friedman we find an ultra-Orthodox leader who fearlessly crossed the line; openly identified with Herzlian Zionism; took a strong critical stance against Agudat Yisrael, of which his father-in-law, Yisrael of Chortkov, was a leader; and published a bold halakhic decision taking a lenient position on autopsies.[9]

The rabbi from Itscan is one of those figures, who, while treading the edge of the highway, attempt to widen it and turn it in fresh directions. Among Eastern European hasidic Orthodoxy, the boldness of his thinking is unmatched—not in terms of his level of learning or penetration, or his gift for written expression—but for its intellectual courage, broad range of interests, receptivity to the spiritual assets of European culture, and ability to expand the boundaries of religious thought.

The following pages describe the literary oeuvre of an extraordinary figure, who blossomed in the hasidic milieu and was forgotten, deliberately so in the last generation. This delineation of our protagonist's world and environment also counterbalances and refines the prevailing view that the world of Eastern European Hasidism in the late nineteenth and early twentieth centuries was fanatical and closed. In the course of the discussion, I raise and try to answer the following question: how did the surrounding hasidic society react to and digest such a complex, unusual phenomenon as Friedman, and to what extent did it accept or reject his innovativeness?

Biography

Nahumnyu, as he was called, came into the world on 25 November 1879.[10] This great-grandson of the famed zaddik Yisrael of Ruzhin (1796–1850)—the founder of the most important hasidic dynasty in Galicia and Romania, whose scions headed wealthy, powerful, and influential hasidic courts—was born in Shtefanesht, in northern Moldova (Romania), on the banks of the Prut near the Bessarabian border. This town's claim to fame rested in the presence of a branch of the Ruzhin dynasty, which, from 1852, had made Shtefanesht the seat of its court. Our protagonist was named after the court's founder, the zaddik Menahem Nahum Friedman (c. 1825–68), Yisrael of Ruzhin's son; he was succeeded by his only son, Rabbi Avraham Matityahu (1847–1933).[11] Following in the path of the dynasty founder Rabbi Yisrael, both father and son gained a reputation for rarely expounding Torah in public. Of the father it was said, "that he acted with simplicity and spoke simple words"; the son was renowned for never having spoken words of Torah publicly during his sixty-five-year tenure as rebbe.[12] Nonetheless, both were forceful, admired leaders with obedient followers.

In a society in which lineage played a central role in determining social status, the younger Menahem Nahum boasted illustrious forebears in both his maternal and paternal lines. On the side of his mother, Batsheva, he was a great-grandson of Yisrael of Ruzhin (she was the daughter of the Shtefanesht dynasty's founder); on the side of his father, Rabbi Avraham Yehoshua Heschel Friedman, he was a grandson of Rabbi Yitshak of Buhush (1834–96), the leading zaddik in Romania in the latter half of the nineteenth century, himself a grandson of Yisrael of Ruzhin.[13]

Menahem Nahum's mother died in 1887, at the young age of twenty-eight, when he was eight.[14] Ten years later, he entered into matrimony with Miriam, the daughter of Rabbi Yisrael Friedman of Chortkov (1854–1933).[15] In line with the prevailing practice among the hasidic elites, this was a match made within the larger family unit: as the granddaughter of the founder of the Chortkov dynasty, Rabbi David Moshe (1827–1903), Miriam was also Yisrael of Ruzhin's great-granddaughter. In short, Menahem Nahum's lineage

FIG. 6.1. Rabbi Menahem Nahum Friedman of Itscan

placed him at the apex of the hasidic elite; great things were expected of him. And it was evidently this same prestigious lineage that protected him from condemnation for his atypical path.

After his marriage, Menahem Nahum spent several years at the Galician Chortkov court, supported by his father-in-law, who was not yet a practicing zaddik. But, despite his eminent lineage, Menahem Nahum's identifiably maskilic leanings prevented the young groom from obtaining the goodwill of the Chortkov hasidim.[16] In 1907, before his thirtieth birthday, he left Chortkov for Itscan in Austrian Bukovina,[17] where he served not as a hasidic rebbe but as a rabbi.[18] As this small community included few hasidim, Menahem Nahum was able to indulge his outstanding intellectual curiosity and to spend his time studying and acquiring Torah and general knowledge. Especially drawn to philosophy, he began to study medieval Jewish rationalistic literature—which never comprised part of the hasidic bookshelf and which was identified with the maskilic camp from the late eighteenth century on—and current German philosophy. Like other enlightened Torah scholars in previous generations, Menahem Nahum was exhilarated by his exposure to world literature and new realms of thought, aesthetics, and art. Unlike them, however, he tried to digest these riches and to incorporate them into a moderate, harmonistic Orthodox approach. He saw as his mission mediation between Judaism and the world of philosophy and enlightenment, which he believed were complementary, not contradictory. His entire literary output, six books and many essays, was devoted to this goal.

In 1914, with the outbreak of World War I, Menahem Nahum fled to Vienna.[19] In this, he followed the many Galician admorim—including his father-in-law, Yisrael of Chortkov, and his relatives Yisrael of Husyatin (1857–1948), Yitshak of Boyan (1849–1917), and Avraham Yaakov of Sadigura (1884–1961)—who, along with their families, now made the Austrian capital the seat of their hasidic courts.[20] There he encountered the zaddik Hayyim Meir Shapira of Drohobych (1863–1924)—a descendant of the Maggid Yisrael of Kozhenits and of Rabbi Yisrael of Ruzhin—who was a fervent Zionist. Evidently, it was through this friendship that Menahem Nahum drew closer to the national Zionist idea, and both men were active in the Histadrut Yishuv Eretz Yisrael.[21] During that period, Menahem Nahum published several blunt, polemical essays opposing Agudat Yisrael,[22] even though his father-in-law was one of its leading figures.[23] In Vienna, he was also exposed to the latest philosophical and psychoanalytical trends.

Menahem Nahum returned to Itscan in 1919, after the war's end. Several years later, most likely in 1923, he moved to Shtefanesht, his birthplace and the center of his hasidic dynasty. There, his childless uncle, the zaddik Avraham Matityahu Friedman, who was extremely fond of Menahem Nahum, groomed him as his successor; thus Menahem Nahum served as "young rebbe" and as the rebbe's semi-official substitute.[24] Hasidim who came to see his uncle also approached him with their request notes (*kvitlakh*) and to ask for blessings and advice.[25] Concurrently, Menahem Nahum continued his Zionist activity and served as the chairman of the Shtefanesht branch of the Jewish National Fund. Influenced by the fact that the fund's offices were situated in the rebbe's courtyard, some members of the hasidic community came to openly identify with Zionism. Further evidence for Menahem Nahum's support of Zionism comes from his purchase of land on Mount Carmel, evidently intended for his future residence.[26]

During the 1920s, Menahem Nahum developed cancer,[27] which perhaps explains his frequent trips to Western Europe over the course of that decade.[28] In 1933, when he was fifty-four years old, his condition worsened. He traveled to a sanatorium near Vienna, died there, and was buried on 21 Sivan 1933.[29] As he died exactly one month before his elderly uncle, he never became an admor.[30] With Avraham Matityahu Friedman's death on 21 Tammuz 1933, the Shtefanesht dynasty came to an end; it no longer exists as an independent hasidic branch.[31]

After his death, Menahem Nahum was described by a fellow townswoman, then a high-school student, whose father was caretaker of the wing occupied by the rabbi and his family in the Shtefanesht hasidic court:

I remember Rabbi Nahumuni, a tall, majestic man, friendly when accosted, sharp-witted, knowledgeable, and experienced, able to dispense good advice to all who turned to him. At his disposal was a huge library, filled with holy tomes and scholarly works in several languages, mainly Latin. Learned individuals waited on his doorstep to consult with him. Behind his desk hung a picture of Herzl. Every year he received the emissaries of the Jewish National Fund, and would donate and solicit funds for them and show interest in the Zionist institutions. He looked favorably on the Zionist and pioneering youth and bestowed his blessing on every cultural and Zionist initiative. He took an interest in his fellow townspeople who immigrated to the land of Israel and gave me a personal present when I left for the land of Israel.[32]

Literary Legacy

Rabbi Menahem Nahum was no pampered descendant of a distinguished hasidic dynasty who simply rested on his ancestors' laurels; his personal world was far removed from the regal practices in the hasidic courts of his forefathers and other family members. Not simply an ardent hasid, he was ultra-Orthodox, a proud Jew, and a clever individual who possessed intense intellectual curiosity and erudition and was prepared to accept the truth no matter what its source. He left an unusual literary legacy: including traditional commentaries on scripture and Tractate *Avot*, and several responsa; as well as journalistic and philosophical essays surprising for their topics, content, and style.

To the best of my knowledge, no memoirs, dairies, or handwritten notes by Menahem Nahum have survived; recently, however, several personal letters written by him to the historian of Hasidism, Shmuel Abba Horodezky, have been found.[33] Nonetheless, his spiritual world is readily detected from the works published during his lifetime. A brief excursion through the books he composed, in chronological order of their publication, testifies to his broad horizons and daring.

Divrei Menahem

Friedman composed his first book, *Divrei Menahem* (The words of Menahem), just before World War I, while still serving as rabbi in Itscan. The book contains twenty-six expository homilies on different midrashic passages, grounded in the premise that "all the aggadic statements by the sages are directed to a desirable goal, to teach us wisdom and morality."[34] It appears likely that these were not public sermons, but rather theoretical chapters composed especially for this book.

Here Friedman already treats at length ethical issues that will later engage his intense interest: reward and punishment, good and evil, predestination and free will, the underlying rationale for the commandments, causality and miracles, human nature, and the like. Apart from his obvious expertise in Talmudic and midrashic sources—in addition to several quotations from halakhic literature and wide-ranging references to Jewish philosophical literature from the medieval period on[35]—Friedman also cites Socrates, Philo, Josephus,[36] and some German philosophers, though not by name here. Philosophy is not the only discipline that Friedman regards as worthy of profound consideration;[37] he also refers to the opinions of naturalists, chemists, and historians.[38] Inherent in his thought is the belief in Judaism's morality and sublimity, attributed to the divine desire for humankind's existence and vitality. Accordingly, all the commandments in the Torah, even those beyond human understanding, are intended for the good of humans and to teach them to perform meritorious deeds. Friedman repeats this principle on numerous occasions, and it appears that his aim in this collection was to prove it from different perspectives.[39]

Friedman's remarks do not overstep the bounds of Orthodoxy. Although they exhibit the influence of expository preaching as practiced in German Jewish neo-Orthodox circles, their tone and content are consistent with what a moderate rabbi would write. Thus, for example, Friedman attacks the false culture of his contemporaries, hasidic, rabbinic, and maskilic alike:

> To our regret, in our day falsehood has become so entwined with external garments that, if formerly, the word "hasid" meant someone who acted charitably, who acted toward others indulgently, now, what a pity! The garment makes a hasid, not deeds. And the same with the title "maskil." If we understood a maskil to be someone involved in wisdom and sciences, now he who curls his hair, wears long pants and short jackets, is called a maskil, even though he is actually an empty ignoramus and a crude fool . . . Our sages stated, "It is a disgrace for a scholar to go out with patched shoes into the market place" [BT *Shabbat* 114a] . . . but because of our manifold iniquities scholars are clearly recognizable by their much patched and stained apparel.[40]

Although drawing freely upon the classics of Western civilization, whether ancient Hellenistic or contemporary European, Friedman was nonetheless aware of their enticing, assimilatory power. But he did not fear a threat to the future of Judaism, neither from the European nations "that sought to forcibly swallow the Israelites by making them to accept their culture, religion, and manners," nor from those who thought to do so "by granting equal rights and freedom, through flattering remarks, by stating you are our brothers, our nation is your nation, our ways are your ways." Even if parts of the nation had left the path, "they have not yet come to total assimilation and loss of identity, for they are a stiff-necked people, whose religion, national identity, and holy Torah will not allow them to assimilate and be lost among the nations forever. Israel cannot be destroyed through troubles and persecution, nor can it be swallowed through freedom and glory!"[41]

Perush man

Friedman's profound interest in moral questions and in interpersonal relationships influenced the choice of his next exegetical project: *Perush man* (an acrostic for Menahem Nahum), a commentary on Tractate *Avot.* This 350-page, systematic commentary was published serially, chapter by chapter, from 1920 to 1928.[42] As Menahem Nahum moved from Itscan to Shtefanesht during the publication process, the title pages changed accordingly.

This book opens in a most unconventional fashion for a rabbinical work, by reporting a heated discussion between the author and a modern Jew in the course of a train trip from Ancona to Rome. The two chatted about current affairs, "but when I unwittingly let fall that I was a rabbi, he immediately pounced upon me with various questions relating to religion and the Torah." This traveler sought to prove that what appears in the Talmud is not attuned to "the spirit of the age," which is "an age of culture, knowledge, and developing industry, an age filled with wisdom and science." Just as astronomy refutes the sages' assumption that the sun and the stars orbit the Earth, so too anatomists have overturned their notions that the human body contains 248 organs, or that the male sexual organ has two orifices. Also, zoology invalidates the hypotheses regarding the pregnancies of various animals proffered by the Talmudic sages. Thus, as opposed to the Talmudic opinion, the snake has no lips, cannot drink from a barrel, and certainly cannot poison its contents. In short, the natural sciences show these statements to be grounded in ignorance. And if that did not suffice, what did the rabbi think of all those Talmudic absurdities, like the one about a man who developed breasts and breastfed his child, or about rain mixed with wheat?

Friedman patiently replied that it was unfair to cite absurdities alone; after all, Talmudic literature also contains statements compatible with current scientific knowledge. Accordingly, it was possible to cite these remarks and to praise the ancients for their acuity. But, truthfully, it is neither its embedded scientific and empiric knowledge, nor its authority as a source of information on the world and nature, that makes the Talmud praiseworthy. This is not the spirit of the Talmud. The sages never demanded acceptance of their verdict regarding such "external" matters, which "serve the Torah alone and nothing else." Their main interest was directed to abiding by the Torah and morality. *Avot*, for example, is a work that well articulates their overall aspiration: the inculcation of moral values and correct opinions rather than the teaching of the sciences or earthly wisdom.

In response, his interlocutor posed a further question: how is it possible to explain the unethical attitude toward non-Jews evidenced in Talmudic sources and Halakha? In reply, Friedman quoted a plethora of citations indicating the low moral level and barbarism of non-Jews during the Talmudic period, also noting that the sages treated decent non-Jews and non-Jewish scholars with respect, and moreover demanded fair treatment for them.

The conversation between the two unfolds over several pages, with the traveler posing thorny questions and the young rabbi providing apologetic answers. Friedman's companion complained of the sages' and the halakhists' overt racism toward non-Jews, which contradicted his interlocuter's claim regarding their intense humanity and morality. Behold, he noted, an animal can be saved from drowning, as the prevention of cruelty to animals is a pentateuchal command, but Maimonides rules that a non-Jew drowning in a river is not be rescued: "Is that love of humanity? Can such laws be considered ethical?" Menahem Nahum replied that this ruling was directed at ancient idolaters, who were baser than, and inferior to, animals. Because these bestial humans not only treated Jews with extreme cruelty but also saw their lives as forfeit, any ethical being would therefore agree that the principle of "if a man comes to kill you, rise early and kill him first" (BT *Berakhot* 58a) applies to them. But regarding non-Jews who are not suspected of spilling blood, the rabbis displayed a high moral attitude and required that they be treated equitably, like all Jews.

If that was indeed the case, his companion went on to ask, why do Jews despise the wisdom of non-Jews and loathe their books? Friedman replied that this was far from true. In fact, the Jewish sages not only determined that one should accept the truth from whoever states it, whether Jew or non-Jew, but also quoted non-Jewish sages and relied on their wisdom in a variety of matters. Talmudic literature is not the only place where non-Jewish sages are given recognition and cited; many medieval Jewish works ("and I believe attestation is superfluous") are replete with proofs and assumptions by philosophers, "and we even find the philosophical doctrines of world sages in the holy *Zohar*."

Clearly, the questions posed by the anonymous traveler were those that troubled the author, questions he had tried to answer at an earlier date, consulting the many Talmudic, halakhic, and philosophical sources mentioned in the course of this train conversation—whether real or imagined—and interpreting them in line with his apologetic needs. Meanwhile, the train arrived at its destination, and the conversation between the two passengers wound down. Recalling this, Menahem Nahum penned the following poetic remarks:

The steam engine emitted an elongated whistle as a sign of the approaching station and the conductor announced "Rome." When I set foot in Rome and looked around and pondered, observed and dreamed, memories of the past proceeded before my eyes. This was the city that laid waste to Jerusalem, destroying it to its very foundations! She stands on her hill, and the city of God is humiliated to the very depths. All the great Israelites and its sages walked this terrain to plead before the regime to overturn the evil decree. And when I came to ancient Rome, I and my companion, and we passed Titus's Arch . . . my eyes filled with tears, but I bit my lip and began to laugh. My companion asked in surprise why I was laughing. I replied as follows: "Look at the profound silence, the silence of the grave, that reigns here, graves and ruins, ruins and graves, nothing more. Is this the noisy city that roars like the sea, the city filled with life and movement, the center of the earth? . . . Where are Augustus Caesar and Hadrian? Where are Nero and crude Titus, and the other emperors who pridefully turned against the people of Israel? . . . Their hatred and jealousy shall be lost, they came in vain and walked in darkness and darkness shall cover their names. But "Jabneh and its sages" live on among the Jewish people![43]

This passage does not simply reflect Friedman's poetic sensitivity, but is a sophisticated literary device. Rome here is not just the capital of a powerful military and political empire, but is also a symbol of the intellectual power and continuity of European civilization, whose beginnings lie in ancient Greece. In Jewish tradition, on the other hand, Rome symbolizes idolatry and, later, Christianity. On entering the physical gates of Rome, Friedman could not ignore this associative baggage. As an individual who valued European philosophy and saw himself at home on its paths, he stresses from the outset that he is no pilgrim but a representative of the winning side in the historical battle between pagan, political Rome and spiritual Jabneh. It is therefore possible to fearlessly enter the gates not only of physical but also of cultural Rome. Its civilization no longer has the power to threaten, but can at most only contribute to, Jewish culture.

Moreover, the hasidic rabbi who wandered the streets of early-twentieth-century Rome bit his lip and began to laugh, in direct imitation of the second-century sage Rabbi Akiva. Every Torah scholar was familiar with the story of Rabbi Akiva's visit to Rome, accompanied by Rabban Gamliel, Rabbi Joshua, and Rabbi Eleazar ben Azariah. When they "heard the murmuring sound of the (great) city . . . they burst into tears, except for R. Akiva, who laughed." When Akiva asked them "'Why are you weeping?' They said, 'Should we not weep when these pagans, who sacrifice to idols and bow down to images dwell in security, peace, and serenity, while the House which is our God's footstool has been reduced to a charred ruin and a lair for the beasts of the field?' To which R. Akiva retorted, 'But this is exactly why I laughed—if this is what God has given to those who have angered Him, how much more so will He give to those who fulfill his will.'"[44]

The introduction to the book also hints at what motivated Friedman to write a commentary on *Avot*, which is explicitly stated later in the work: the centrality of moral values to Talmudic thought, their greater importance than universal moral doctrines, and their adaptation to the changing values in each generation, including the current one so estranged from God and the divine word. In *Avot*, Friedman states, the seeker will not find anything relating to geometry or astronomy, just moral sayings "unmatched in world literature." In order to understand them, "it is first necessary to understand the essence of human nature and of human life, their revelation and purpose, and the purpose of humanity, namely, its ultimate teleology."[45]

Friedman's fluently written, lucid commentary usually opens with a brief biographical entry on the sage whose sayings are cited in the Mishnah. Friedman then poses a series of questions based on a plain reading of the text, to which he immediately responds using other Talmudic sources (as well as the Apocrypha, Philo, and Josephus), common sense, and with reference to the period's historical and cultural background. Throughout, he depends on a variety of sources and does not hesitate to mention pagan beliefs or traditions derived from Greek, Buddhist, Scandinavian, and Slavic mythology.[46]

The questions Friedman poses serve as a springboard for exploration of his favorite topics: various philosophical doctrines, old and new, and their affinity to human ethics and spiritual awareness. What arises from this discussion is the superiority of divine morality—naturally, according to its Jewish interpretation. And to the observation that many religious functionaries, including religious Jews, do not follow the basic ethical norms and are caught performing corrupt, despicable acts, Friedman would reply that indeed formal observance of the commandments does not suffice: "We do not bring proof from hypocrites or fools"—even if such individuals keep the commandments in all their minutiae, they are not religious men but heretics.[47]

One example is his original interpretation of the well-known Mishnah regarding three things on which the world stands (*Avot* 1:2). He interprets "world" not as the universe but as the individual, in line with the Greek philosophers—Pythagoras, Plato, and Aristotle—who viewed humans as a "little universe." Human existence relies then on "Torah," the unceasing search for wisdom and erudition; on "avodah," not the sacrificial service as most exegetes explain, but "work, according to its plain meaning," whether physical or intellectual; and "on deeds of loving-kindness"—mutual assistance, "as there is no individual who does not require his fellow's assistance during his lifetime."[48]

The Mishnah "know what to reply to an Epicurean" (2:14) provides Friedman with an opportunity to trace the metamorphosis of *apikoros*, from the personal name of a Greek philosopher to a term used for a Jewish heretic. He recalls an unpleasant personal experience, used here to allude to his frustration with the contemporary Orthodox leadership's limited horizons.

During a visit to a hot springs resort frequented by zaddikim and rabbis, he was walking with a rabbi and a Protestant minister on the seashore when the minister asked the rabbi to explain the apocalyptic verse: "But I will fill the House of David and the inhabitants of Jerusalem with a spirit of pity and compassion; and they shall lament to Me about those who are slain, wailing over them as over a favorite son and showing bitter grief as over a first-born" (Zechariah 12:10). "Not only was the rabbi unable to provide a correct answer, he was unaware that such a verse appeared in the Minor Prophets. And when the minister began to interpret the verse as if the verb 'are slain' refers to Jesus, instead of 'blunting his teeth' the rabbi stood shamefacedly like a golem."

Friedman interprets this Mishnah in classic maskilic spirit: "A rabbi and leader of Israel must observe the commandment 'Let not [this Book of the Teaching] cease [from your lips]' [Joshua 1:8] and study God's Torah diligently day and night," but must also study "external wisdoms" so that he will know how to reply to an *apikoros*—whether Christians seeking to prove the verity of their religion from the Pentateuch, or Jewish heretics who deny the Torah. So it was in the Talmudic and the medieval ages, but "alas, in our day this is almost unheard of that an Eastern European ultra-Orthodox rabbi knows how to argue with opponents of the Torah or what to reply to an *apikoros*."[49]

Exegesis of the Mishnah "Pray for the welfare of the government" (3:2) opens the door to a discussion of the nature of government. Friedman divides governments into three types: constitutional, absolute, and welfare. After a discussion of each, he decides in favor of constitutional government, for absolutism is a form of idolatry; its leaders demand, and receive, personal adulation. Socialism is but a mirage, "a utopia and nothing more, as Bolshevism proves." Only a constitutional state enables "a strong government on the one hand and liberty and freedom on the other."[50]

The commentary ends with a short summary essay in ten chapters. In the absence of a title, we can call it "On Morality." In it, Friedman surveys the various definitions accepted in world philosophy for morality and then asks: "And what shall we, as believers, reply to this question: 'What is morality?' We shall give the old, but constantly new, answer: 'It is ours only to carry out the bidding of the son of Amram.'"[51]

Hahalom ufitrono

While engaged in working on his commentary on *Avot*, Menahem Nahum also began writing short philosophical essays intended to bridge the gap between Judaism and Western philosophy. The first of these four essays, *Hahalom ufitrono* (The dream and its interpretation), was published with neither an explanatory introduction nor a conclusion.[52] This is a philosophical and psychological discussion of the phenomenon of dreams, their varieties, and the predictability of their recurrence and content; hypnotic and psychotic states; insomnia; and somnambulant states. In it, Friedman attempts to discover why we forget dreams, but he focuses mainly on the question of the meaning or "interpretation" of dreams: are they a reflection of the psyche, which makes the attempt to understand them worthwhile, or are they devoid of value? Friedman naturally concludes that whereas some dreams are indeed of no significance, others have a prophetic, truth-revealing basis through symbols or riddles, whether direct or indirect.

As always, underpinning the discussion are opinions culled from the Bible, Talmudic literature, and medieval Jewish thought, alongside principles derived from German thought of the nineteenth and early twentieth-centuries (from Schleiermacher and Schopenhauer to Freud), in addition to examples drawn from encyclopedias, books, and newspapers. Friedman accepts Freud's psychoanalytical theory as put forth in his *Interpretation of Dreams*—namely, that the dream and the dreamer's past are linked—and, by way of demonstration, presents and interprets some of his own dreams. Friedman also notes his habit, for the past eight years, of recording his dreams every morning.[53] This apparently constitutes the first, and perhaps the only, positive rabbinic response of its kind to Freudian insights.[54]

What emerges from Friedman's essay is his inclination to accept the verity of a certain type of dream, arrived at through his internalization of general culture. "I call my offense to mind today," he admits. "I displayed childish impudence toward dreams, saying 'Dreams are of no effect, either one way or the other' and speak only falsehoods. Until something happened to show me my mistake, that it was wrong to name the dream a speaker of untruth and deception." Faced with a knotty personal dilemma, he decided to reach a rational, rather than a dream-based, resolution. To his amazement, shortly thereafter he discovered "that exactly what I saw in my dream was what transpired . . . to the very last detail." This prompted him to reconsider his stance on dreams: "And because mysterious things require greater care and moderation . . . I therefore act accordingly. If I dream at night, in the morning I record it precisely as I remember"—this to prevent him from both forgetting his dream and making imaginative additions. From time to time, he thumbed through his notebook in an attempt to arrive at the meaning of his dreams.[55]

Al ha'emet vehasheker

Friedman's next work, *Al ha'emet vehasheker* (On truth and falsehood),[56] was a sixteen-chapter exhortation on the supreme religious obligation to search for the truth wherever it is found, and to shun all manifestations of falsehood. The difference between a true and a false prophet, he notes in the introduction, does not lie in appearance or behavior. "How can one distinguish a truly God-fearing person from a false one?" he asks, alluding to the reality of his day, and answers that a true prophet does not hesitate to berate his people, whereas a false one always speaks well of and flatters them. Truth is the foundation on which divine kingship rests, and falsehood is "absolute evil" and "the ultimate impurity": "Truth is life, falsehood is death." "The spirit of truth" in all humankind, found alongside "the spirit of falsehood," is like the inescapable and unchangeable knowledge that resembles the reflection seen in a mirror "with all its blemishes and imperfections." Knowledge is what distinguishes between humans and animals: "the beacon overlooking the stormy sea of life that points the way to the shore," in the words of an "English philosopher." Knowledge is the source of morality and the divine voice. Its opposite, of course, is falsehood.[57]

Friedman classifies the common types of lies: polite lies, not seen as true falsehood; negative lies, or lies one is forced to tell for fear of the harsh consequences of revealing the truth; positive lies, the "progeny of passion" evoked by an evil heart and corruption; "white" lies; lies accepted in the political and diplomatic worlds; hyperbole or lies stemming from ignorance; and other categories.[58] He notes the relative nature of lies, and how they conflict with other moral values (such as "the paths of peace" or modesty), and states: "Falsehood is forbidden in any time, place, or situation."[59] As usual, in addition to surveying the opinions of Talmudic and medieval Jewish thinkers, he provides those of "their moralists," ranging from Pythagoras, Aristotle, Socrates, Plato, Plutarch, and Herodotus to Kant, Fichte, and von Hartmann; nor does he neglect to mention hasidic opinions or the practices of various zaddikim.[60]

For Friedman, the enemies of truth are found at opposite poles of the spectrum: at one end, there is heresy, the apperception that all is vanity; at the other, "superstition," the foolish belief in anything, even if nonsensical, the exaggerated faith that guides those who choose to keep their eyes shut and uproots any critical sense.[61] It was only natural that one focus of Friedman's condemnatory critique was the Orthodox camp:

> Those very lying, sanctimonious hypocrites who speak comforting words but have hearts of stone . . . they crawl like worms when confronted by the more powerful, and act crudely like snakes toward those under their dominion. Loudly sanctimonious and zealous for the Lord of Hosts, they hope thereby to hide their ignorance and crudity and all the evil things that they do privately, in secret.

No warnings suffice, he writes, to alert people to refrain from contact with such individuals, for the most corrupt person inflicts less damage than a liar or hypocrite:

Deceit and hypocrisy have become a widespread plague, so entrenched in society that people no longer recognize their evil corrupting influence . . . And this terrible tragicomedy evokes bitter laughter on seeing how these hypocritical, sanctimonious individuals have the nerve to chastise and rebuke their compatriots who are better than they.[62]

Friedman is angered by those who self-righteously state "that a person can be religious and God-fearing even if he throws off the yoke of proper social behavior (*derekh erets)*, and who do not wish to recognize that religion and morality are not just linked but are melded like a candle and its flame, for religion contains nothing but what is in morality." "These strange beings" rush to synagogue and at the same time "tell a thousand lies to, and flatter, the powerful and shamefully humiliate the weak."[63]

In addition, Friedman condemns diplomatic lies, attributing to their distortion the hegemony of falsehood in the world. Diplomats profess to reduce anger and establish order, and yet, "vexatiously, the opposite occurs."[64] He singles out the wealthy, for the amassing of wealth is the primary cause of corruption and falsehood in the world: "The wealthy are the golden idols, and they too use lies to their benefit and enjoyment." They established stock exchanges in order to suck the blood of the poor. They heap "lie on lie, deception on deception, raise and lower their net worth, or raise prices for their benefit, or lower them, as this lowering is for their future rising, and ostentatiously dazzle the eyes of society with their being great and honored merchants who faithfully help society (more likely, faithfully oppress it)." More than anything he finds distasteful the kowtowing to the rich, prevalent in all strata of society, even among the hasidim and the God-fearing: "And if some rich man comes among the learned and utters some worthless, meaningless Torah chatter, all the Torah scholars sitting there dissemble and say 'sweeter than honey,' 'fantastic' . . . And if he comes among hasidic businessmen, they too flatter him, calling him 'rabbi' and if he is named Yosef or Moshe they add *'le'* to his name, calling him 'Reb Yosele,' 'Reb Moshele,' even though they know him to be an ignoramus."

Friedman's critique of the capitalistic system is especially blunt: "The accursed earth now revolves not on its axis but on money. Everything is for money; the world was created only for wealth . . . there is but a single wisdom in the world, the wisdom of amassing money; everything else is worthless . . . How it is attained is of no import, the main thing is that it be attained, and on that account humans commit all the evils in the world, plundering and robbing, charging extortionate prices; they are willing to condemn the world to destruction because of their malicious desire for gains and to amass wealth."[65] Mark these words of a direct descendant of the zaddik Yisrael of Ruzhin, known for his wealth and amassing of worldly goods!

Al hayofi

Menahem Nahum Friedman's third philosophical treatise, *Al hayofi* (On beauty), is undoubtedly his boldest, most interesting work. The very treatment of the subject is surprising, as no ultra-Orthodox—certainly no hasidic—author had ever written about beauty before.[66] Indeed, the "Preface for the Reader" provides a manifesto-like statement of his outlook:

> The reason for my penning a book on this topic is grounded in the following episode. A group of us was arguing about the relationship between aesthetics and morality. Mr. S. stood up and proudly shouted: Cease your remarks! The ultra-Orthodox have no entrée to this discipline; aesthetics, which is for the entire world the essence, foundation, and purpose of life, has not even secondary importance among you. I replied, saying: You are mistaken. I will show you, God willing, that there is no contradiction between the doctrine of aesthetics and ultra-Orthodoxy. Indeed, not only our beauty, but even the chief beauty of Japheth [the non-Jewish world] can live among the tents of Shem [the Jewish tradition] in companionable brotherhood, and you will see how beauty and God-fearingness walk arm in arm without one excluding the other. And so Mr. S., here is your answer!

Friedman's treatise is a sincere, if apologetic, attempt to combine the assets of Western, secular culture and aesthetics ("the doctrine of beauty") with Jewish spirituality as interpreted according to selected Talmudic sources and Jewish thought over the ages. Once again, his writing recalls that of the early, moderate maskilim, such as Naftali Hirz Wessely and Yitshak Ber Levinsohn. Like them, he truly believed—and not just as a tactical ploy—that Enlightenment values were not foreign to Jewish tradition, but were rather neglected, blurred, or distorted over the generations, and that it was his task to unveil these hidden ideas. His stated aim was thus to relegitimize aspects of aesthetics through reliance on Jewish sources.

For Friedman, whoever despises or is indifferent to beauty is an unlettered ignoramus, for sensibility to beauty confers "spiritual form" on life, enhances the emotions, and purifies the soul. Moreover, "our ancestors knew the importance of beauty," and for the sages this word was synonymous with what they saw "as the ultimate good."[67] As usual, he surveys the opinions of non-Jewish sages and compares them to Talmudic thought. He treats such issues as the nature of beauty (physical and spiritual) and of ugliness; whether there is an objective standard for beauty, or is it all in the eye of the beholder; the difference between beauty and charm; the interdependence between the perception of beauty and the human senses and impulses; music and beauty; poetry and beauty; and graphic art and beauty—to mention just a few.

A special chapter at the end of the book, not organically linked to the preceding ones and, moreover, one with no parallel that I am able to recall in all of rabbinical writing, contains an autobiographical description of how Friedman was stirred by nature and natural vistas during his travels in Switzerland and Italy. "It is indeed wonderful," one reviewer wrote shortly after the book's appearance, "and truly a new, and almost unique, phenomenon, that a rabbi, an admor no less, teaches knowledge and comprehension of the discipline of aesthetics, and treats it in depth with all its details and minutiae."[68]

Al ha'adam

Friedman's final philosophical treatise, published a year before his death, is titled *Al ha'adam* (On humankind). This essay, like his previous ones, attempts to demonstrate that there is no contradiction between modern philosophical and Talmudic views—in this case, of the relationship between humans and the world, their surrounding environment. But it is extremely pessimistic in tone. Humankind, he writes, has shown itself to be innately ungrateful, stupid, and wicked.

Human ingratitude is manifested, for example, in the shameful treatment of great figures among the Jews and the nations by their compatriots. He provides a long, itemized list of personalities, ranging from Moses, David, Bar Kokhba, and Maimonides to Socrates, Columbus, Galileo, Gutenberg, Cromwell, and Cervantes, ending with Molière and Hugo, all of whom reaped humiliating scorn instead of honor: "This is the reward and recompense of the best, most honest, and excellent individuals among humankind, who sacrificed their blood and innards on the altar of spirituality. The people that walk in darkness throw stones at their finest and kill the most excellent among them. This has been their path in the past, the present, and so it will be forever."[69]

Stupidity is the only quality shared by all humans, exemplified not only by their faith in astrology, "as fragile as a spider web," but also by the absurd belief in superstition found in highly developed, cultured societies. The idolatry entrenched among the peoples of ancient Egypt, Babylonia, Persia, India, Tibet, and South America proves "there is no nonsensical thing, no strange creature or monster, that humans have not turned into an idol." And in Friedman's opinion, this applies not just to antiquity but also to modern Europe.[70]

For Friedman, it is knowledgeable, sensitive individuals who are the ones who reach the heights of human foolishness in their deeds. Although they recognize what is proper and what is moral, they do the opposite. Such is the nature of alcoholism, whose dangers are apparent to all, although people are still drawn to it; such is the lust for war, "in which the beast in humans entirely throws off moral constraints; what is forbidden becomes permissible, and not just permissible but obligatory."

Friedman's remarks on World War I, whose horrors he witnessed firsthand, are particularly incisive:

> And now hear what the statistics tell us: fifteen million of the best youth killed; twenty million injured, including those who have lost an arm or a leg, or have been blinded or lost the power of speech, or suffer from strange nervous disorders, the half-mad and the truly mad, and the terribly maimed, without arms or legs, without human shape . . . and a huge number of towns and cities destroyed and laid waste. How many fields were overrun and how many gardens trampled, how much sadness there was, bringing millions to madness; the dearest to parents and women, and ordinary relatives, became cannon fodder. More than twenty-four million were turned into refugees—Frenchmen, Poles, Belgians, and Serbs were expelled from their land and went into exile; more than six million prisoners of war were turned over to every overweening tyrant . . . and even though the rivers of blood in which humankind wallowed have not yet dried, notwithstanding, if the government were to declare war, the nation would rejoice and dance, for the beast in man lusts to murder, destroy, shed blood, and to sink its teeth into its fellows. Thus has it always been. There will always be war in the world![71]

It is instructive to compare these bleak remarks to the writings of another important contemporary Jewish thinker: Rabbi Avraham Yitshak Hakohen Kook (1865–1933), the chief rabbi of Palestine. In contrast to Menahem Nahum Friedman, who attributed the world catastrophe and horrors not to God but to human divergence from the laws of divine morality ("this can be compared to a fool who puts his hand in the fire and is then angry at God because he burned his hand"),[72] Rabbi Kook took an optimistic view of the world war, seeing in it the guiding hand of divine providence. For him, the war was an exalted, apocalyptic event that underpinned the foundations of the national revival and heralded the redemption soon to emerge from the ruins of the old, failed European culture. "When there is a great war in the world," Rabbi Kook wrote in a famous passage, "the power of the Messiah is aroused. *The time of song* (zamir) *has arrived*, the scything (*zemir*) of tyrants, the wicked perish from the world, and the world is invigorated *and the voice of the turtledove is heard in our land.* The individuals who are killed unjustly in the revolution of the flood of war participate in the concept, 'the death of the righteous atones' . . . The present world war is possessed of an awesome, great, and deep expectation."[73]

Like Friedman's other works, *Al ha'adam* incorporates a wide range of sources. For instance, in chapter three, Friedman takes the reader on a swift, three-page journey from Aristophanes and Diogenes to Frederick the Great, Goethe, and Schopenhauer, proceeding next to Dostoevsky, Adam Mickiewicz, Anatole France, and Oscar Wilde, among others. The book's two concluding chapters contain a long list of aphorisms on human nature and the human soul, its instability, attributes, and primarily its evil. "They say that man was created from the monkey," Friedman writes. "This is doubtful. But that man can become a monkey is certain, for we encounter such on a daily basis."[74]

"Religious Zeal Is a Plague Recounted in the Torah": Between Innovation and Conservatism

Traces of daring innovation are perceptible in Menahem Nahum Friedman's conservative world. Notwithstanding his unqualified loyalty to tradition and Halakha, here and there Friedman not only criticizes his contemporaries' strict halakhic approach,[75] he also takes a critical attitude toward statements by ancient authorities. He observes: "For some Talmudic statements we can arrive at their meaning only after intense study of the mores of the time and place in which they were uttered."[76] He consistently attempts to interpret difficult statements in Talmudic literature in light of the Greco-Roman historical, social, and political reality.[77] Yet, despite his wide horizons, his knowledge of languages, and his keen interest in the history of the Jews and their literature, nowhere in his writings does he refer to the emergent Hebrew or German literature in the field of Jewish studies (*Wissenschaft des Judentums*), let alone modern Hebrew or Yiddish literature.[78] This strange overlooking of the *Wissenschaft* characterizes Friedman's divided, selective world, in which he was more comfortable quoting world authorities such as Plato and Kant than Jewish heretics like Nahman Krochmal, Leopold Zunz, or Micha Yosef Berdyczewski.

In spite of Friedman's impressive knowledge of classical and contemporary philosophical literature, he cannot be considered a true philosopher, given his autodidactic, unsystematic training and, especially, his unwillingness to reach overarching conclusions. Essentially, he must be regarded as an enlightened Torah scholar. Like the eighteenth-century harbingers of Enlightenment,[79] he saw the medieval Jewish rationalistic tradition as the means by which Jews loyal to tradition and Halakha could make their way in a changing world, as providing intellectual enrichment and reinforcing their attachment to Judaism against the allure of secularization. Because he believed "that it was a fundamental principle in Jewish history, that there was no religious, philosophical, or political system in which Jews did not participate and take a leading role,"[80] he therefore found no fault with "external wisdom." But for our purposes it makes no difference whether he was a professional or an amateur philosopher, or whether his acquaintance with the books he cites was at first, second, or third hand. What is decisive is the fact that a hasidic rebbe mentions these sources at all, and does not deny their influence on his Torah outlook.

The basically apologetic and harmonistic nature of Friedman's writing is not surprising. He does not skim off the cream of world philosophy for its own sake, but rather in support of Judaism's worthiness (at least, the worthiness of some of its parts) and harmony with the achievements of modern Western thought. He interprets the Mishnah in *Avot* 3:18 as encouraging the acquisition of external disciplines (such as astronomy and geometry), "for every true Torah scholar must experience external wisdoms, for they are 'the after-courses to wisdom,' and bring honor to the Jews in the eyes of the nations . . . and in actuality, the Jewish sages of all generations, the Talmudic and the medieval sages were known for that. They had Torah at their right hands and all sorts of wisdom and sciences at their left."[81] The reader of his commentary cannot help but notice the omission of contemporary rabbinic figures.

Friedman's free-ranging thought remains within the confines of halakhic Judaism. As long as the remarks of world philosophers accord with aspects of Talmudic or Jewish philosophical thought, he draws upon them happily, weaving them into the continuum he denotes "the truth." But he summarily rejects any wisdom, whether ancient or modern, that contradicts Judaism's fundamental principles.

Entirely missing from his treatise on beauty, for example, is the world of Christian aesthetics, even though Friedman was certainly aware of its influence on large sectors of the artistic, poetic, and musical spheres. Likewise, he was not prepared to consider, and certainly not to accept, the Darwinian approach to evolution. "It is self-evident," he wrote, "that evolution was finished on the Sabbath, and from that time neither the created nor the creatures have changed, unlike those heretical philosophers who claim that evolution is still ongoing and will continue to the end of time, heaven forbid."[82]

The opinions scattered throughout his works undoubtedly showcase Friedman's personal worldview, developed through a process of selection that overlooks, or distracts attention from, large parts of Jewish culture that are inconsistent with, or even contradict, his doctrines. In itself, this selectivity is not surprising: it is the path of a thinker seeking to incorporate his personal truth into a multifaceted religious system. This naturally raises the question of how Friedman could ignore the obvious: that his stance did not represent the views of the society from which he came, and from which he derived his authority. The living social reality of hasidic Orthodoxy was predominantly that of a reclusive community, which saw modernity and its achievements as an opponent to be fought, and which had profound contempt for non-Jewish wisdom and anything smacking of secularization or general knowledge.

Surely Menahem Nahum Friedman was aware of the gap between the world of his personal thought and the conservative, ultra-Orthodox society in which he lived and acted. Was he simply naive, or perhaps self-deceiving? Did he really believe that his writings had the ability to convince the hasidic masses and their zaddikim to study foreign languages, look at Spinoza and Kant, read Dostoevsky's *The Insulted and Injured*, or at the very least internalize aesthetic or moral experiences drawn from the "beauty of Japheth"? What was his status within his own community; and more important, who were his presumed readers, and what, if any, reaction did his works evoke among this audience?

Evidently, his books had no real audience. Hasidim were not interested in them, nor were nonobservant Jews. As for traditional Jews—whether national religious or liberal—who had divorced themselves from the ultra-Orthodox environment and turned to secular education, they felt no need for this brand of apologetic writing "permitting" them to read general literature and proving the absence of contradiction between the traditional and the modern, aesthetic and moral ways of life.

Mention of his readership is largely absent from Friedman's writings, with the exception of a possible hint in the introduction to *Al ha'adam*. There he laments "the huge polarity" which afflicts the prophet: on the one hand, he stands before the transcendent divine holiness; on the other hand, he must descend to the corrupt, degenerate people. The prophet thus alternates between a supremely holy environment and one "of refuse and scum, filth and impurity." This contradiction embitters his life and leaves him with an existential choice: to flee God or the people. He has, however, no real choice: he must let out the fire confined within and speak his message even if no one pays attention to it. Perhaps Friedman refers here to the gap between his world and that of the surrounding hasidim, providing a glimpse of what motivated him to publish his treatises.

That Friedman imagined the hasidic public in Romania or Galicia as his natural audience is doubtful. To them, not only would his writings seem unintelligible, they would have evoked incredulity and even anger at the young rebbe for devoting his time and talents to such topics. Like any original thinker, Friedman felt impelled to record his thoughts without necessarily having an audience in mind (and, as noted, the audience for his works was virtually nonexistent). His acquisition of knowledge and his strong desire to impart his message evidently encouraged him to publish his works regardless of whether or not they found readers.

However, Friedman was certainly not blind to what was happening in his own camp, as evinced by his especially harsh outcry against religious fanaticism, of which I cite several lines here: "Religious zeal is a plague recounted in the Torah, as it is written: 'The Lord will strike you with madness, blindness, and dismay' [Deuteronomy 28:28]. This plague, or more correctly, the ultimate plague, has brought much destruction to the world in general and to the Jewish world in particular. The accursed Inquisition . . . is the fruit of religious zeal, as are the Crusades . . . but we too, the chosen people . . . can become entrapped in this pitfall, we too can be affected by the plague of religious zeal, even if to a lesser degree than other nations. Yet we also have sinned, sinned greatly; worse yet, we continue to sin."[83]

Friedman goes on to cite examples: the persecution of Maimonides and the attempt to destroy his works, the banning of the kabbalah and the *Zohar*, the persecution of Hasidism, Yaakov Emden's obsessive hounding of suspected Sabbateans—concluding with the statement that "religious zeal has sparked harsh battles among the Jews." To fanaticism, the sages opposed the ideal of tolerance, as exemplified by the midrash in which God conveys to the prophet Elijah that he does not desire his accusatory prophecies. "From the elite the sages demanded extreme tolerance," and indeed all the true zaddikim who followed in the footsteps of the Besht also practiced "extreme tolerance, even toward heretics and the truly evil." Religious zeal is therefore an outcome of jealousy and hypocrisy, "for generally speaking the zealot belongs to the type that knows in his heart that he too can be tarnished."[84]

Especially trenchant remarks appeared in early 1925, in an article published in a minor Romanian Torah journal.[85] As Friedman put it, this was a "public protest" against the behavior of some representatives of Judaism. The background to this article was the call by some Romanian rabbis to withdraw from the collective and found an autonomous representative body for the Orthodox congregations.[86]

Friedman first notes the religious renaissance ostensibly sweeping Europe: nearly every book or newspaper being published these days praises religion and its benefits. Indeed, some cast aspersions on this trend's authenticity (Friedman himself undoubtedly belonged to this camp), viewing it as an artificial creation aimed at masking one goal: the employment of religion by the ruling powers to forward their political interests and to preserve the desired old (or new) order. Authors and journalists are nurtured by the generosity of politicians and are at their beck and call, serving as their envoys: "With blood and fire and pillars of smoke, with wrath and indignation, [they] seek to force religion on the public . . . for their own good, so they can prevail and retain the reins of government." Sober observers point to "the religious movement in Hungary and its evil outcome, and to the religious movement of the swastika-bearers in Germany" as proof of this argument.

This conjoining of religion and politics, Friedman claims, causes greater damage to religion—any religion—than all the opposition of "dry rationalists." The responsibility for this damage lies with the bearers and representatives of religion: "Those who believe that scientific enlightenment brought the destruction of religion are mistaken. Only the Hophnis and Pinhases[87] in every generation, who use religion for some dark aim . . . are those who destroyed and destroy religion." Therefore everything depends on whether the leader is a fraud and a demagogue, or a righteous person of integrity: "I remember the negative impression made on me in Vienna, how in 1915 thousands and hundreds of thousands of people stood near the Parliament and how demagogic leaders stood and spoke the praises of the war and the people clapped their hands and called out: 'War! War! War to the last drop of blood!' And in 1924, people by the thousands and hundreds of thousands again occupied the very same spot near Parliament, and when some demagogues condemned the war, the people clapped their hands and shouted: 'No more war! No more war in the world!'" And that is the trouble, Friedman concludes: the masses always grant preeminence to those who mislead and flatter them.

By what means, then, can the masses be persuaded to cherish religion? The first requirement is to improve the image of the religious leader, through deeds, not talk. The God-fearing must "seek truth and justice even in monetary matters, act modestly and not chase after honor, not mix politics and religion, and behave with moral rectitude even when not observed." Moreover, the unity of the camp must be maintained. The separatist Orthodox communities created in Germany and Hungary, which some now seek to transfer to Romania, brought disaster on the nation.[88] Friedman mocks these rabbis, saying that they do not fear "pairs"—an ancient, popular prohibition against eating and drinking pairs—after all, "the sage Jerome says that Scripture does not state 'it was good' regarding the second day of Creation because the number two is unlucky." Moreover, was it not already decided in King Solomon's court "that she who says 'cut it in half' is not the mother, but a simple prostitute?" With bitter mockery, Friedman wonders whether the same rabbis would still call for separatism if promised the office of "chief rabbi of Romania." In actuality, he grants internal unity supremacy and concludes his essay with the following quote from the Midrash: "Great is peace, for even if Israel practice idolatry but maintain peace amongst themselves, the Holy One, blessed be He, says, as it were, 'I have no dominion over them'" (*Genesis Rabbah* 38:6).

Disregard or Polemic? *Hatov vehatakhlit*

Menahem Nahum Friedman's bold written and oral statements—most likely enunciated in conversations or sermons—seemingly evoked no debate or direct public condemnation. This contrasts with the response—mudslinging and accusations of heresy—to far less daring statements by other Orthodox writers. Thus, fifty years earlier, in 1865, Shtefanesht hasidim in the Romanian town of Siven had hounded a melamed for saying that Rabbi Hayyim ben Attar composed his commentaries to the Torah "through his wisdom and learning in the yeshiva" and not through the divine spirit. The hasidim, so the melamed recounted, denounced him to the zaddik Menahem Nahum of Shtefanesht (Menahem Nahum of Itscan's grandfather), "and told him what I said . . . as well as other matters of which I knew nothing. And the rabbi, the *ẓaddiq* R. Naḥum ordered that I be expelled from the town, for he said I am a heretic on this matter."[89] And now, a scant two generations later, not only was there no open censure of the rabbi of Itscan, but we even find several favorable critiques by Torah scholars, enthusiastically noting Friedman's talent, polished Hebrew, and broad horizons.[90]

Hasidic traditions, both oral and written, indicate the admiration of the Shtefanesht hasidim in Romania for Menahem Nahum, and their expectation that he would inherit his uncle's place. In his eulogy, Rabbi Nahum Shmaryahu Schechter of Hush termed Menahem Nahum "the great rabbi, the perfect scholar, a man of many accomplishments . . . composer of wise treatises . . . He was the nephew of the late admor of blessed memory, who considered him his successor . . . Great in Torah and wisdom and perfect in scholarship, he was a steadfast learner who studied constantly. To him may be applied the words of the Mishnah: 'When Ben Azzai died, diligent students came to an end [*Sotah* 9:15].'"[91] In contrast, the Ruzhiner hasidim of Galicia, mainly from the house of Chortkov, found his path less pleasing.[92] But because he was descended from a distinguished hasidic dynasty, and was moreover a fully observant Jew who dressed like a rebbe and enjoyed the backing of the Shtefanesht zaddik, whom he was expected to succeed, none dared criticize him.

For combating embarrassing phenomena, the most effective *haredi* weapon, then as now, was intentional disregard—not loudly proclaimed bans and denigration, but a still, small voice. Menahem Nahum Friedman's borderline status is also reflected in his marginality in Ruzhiner collective memory: although his name and memory were never rejected or totally hidden, at the same time his books are not reprinted,[93] nor are references to or citations from his works included in the vast hasidic anthological literature. Although buried in Vienna, his monument is not on the usual hasidic pilgrimage itinerary.

But, as no foreign implant but a part and parcel of hasidic Orthodoxy, Menahem Nahum of Itscan could not be entirely overlooked. Testimony to the ambivalent hasidic attitude toward Friedman comes from the booklet *Hatov vehatakhlit* (The good and the goal). Evidently written in response to his literary activity, it was authored by none other than Menahem Nahum's brother-in-law, Rabbi Zvi Aryeh Twersky of Zlatopol (1890–1968)![94]

Published in Vienna in 1933, probably before Friedman's death in that year, nowhere does this unusual treatise mention Menahem Nahum, or any other individuals or authorities, by name.[95] To all appearances, this is a conceptual essay in the ethical, homiletical spirit. Written in a fluent, flowing style, it aims "to clarify the purpose of human life, what is truth, and what is the good . . . to separate food from refuse, truth from illusion, good from evil."[96] But this booklet has covert aims too: a polemic against Menahem Nahum's doctrines alongside the enhancement of the ultra-Orthodox Jew's faith and self-image in the face of secular modernity.

It is the remarks of a later hasidic writer that reveal this book's polemical cast. He claims that the booklet was written at the request of their mutual father-in-law, Yisrael of Chortkov: "The doctrine of our holy rabbi *Tiferet Yisrael* [Yisrael of Chortkov] that one should not deal with philosophy and critical studies touching on faith is widely known . . . one should follow the path of simple faith without in-depth examination and certainly not engage in investigations and studies derived from foreign sources. Accordingly, *when books stemming from* haredi *circles on matters of faith and human nature based on foreign sources were published*, Rabbi Zvi Aryeh was summoned to the inner chambers and his holy father-in-law commanded him to write a series of essays displaying the paths of pure faith transmitted from generation to generation, from the Torah viewpoint alone."[97] The rabbi of Zlatopol fulfilled his set task and composed a treatise addressing emotion and morality, imagination and reality, body and soul, joy and sorrow, and the like.

In its opening, the treatise's author denies any link between knowledge and a high moral standard. Indeed, at times the very converse is true: "many men of science lack morals, and ordinary people have high standards of morality. This leads many to conclude that knowledge alone corrupts." But this is a superficial viewpoint, for "there is no doubt that science itself benefits humans and the world . . . the catch is that science is used for evil, converting good to bad." Thus, for example, the airplane: in wartime it sows destruction and damage; at the same time it has the ability to bring great benefit, and this is the case for every scientific innovation. If so, the question remains: why do many men of science "have worse morals than those with no part in science?" And the answer? The more learned and sophisticated a person is, the greater his cunning, which enables him to conceal, and rationalize, sin and moral failure. The distinction between Moses and Balaam is the difference between "true wisdom" and "cunning, which is the wisdom directed to evil purposes."[98]

And from this biblical comparison he swiftly moves to contemporary homiletics: "And in our day many are the disciples of wicked Balaam . . . these are the writers and poets of our generation, who in their hearts fear neither God nor sin. They exhort like prophets, preaching morality to the masses in their books and poems. Despite their gifted, alarming exposure of the refuse and scum of human society, nonetheless, this leaves no lasting impression. Namely, it does not cause people to be so ashamed of their deeds or embarrassed by their sins that they change their ways with respect to morality."[99] "And why is this the case?" The answer is simple: secular writers or poets possess solely artistic aims and do not really seek to spark moral correction: "They focus on high art; it and nothing else is their aim. 'Art for art's sake.'" In any event, none take their words or their writings seriously. Moreover, they themselves sin and contravene the moral principles preached in their writings, "for doctrine is one thing and deeds another." How, then, can one possess wisdom and erudition and still be a person of moral rectitude? The advice offered is to pay attention to those with experience, to those who have succeeded in both. One should be guided by the Psalmist: "The beginning of wisdom is the fear of the Lord, all who practice it gain sound understanding" (Psalm 111:10). "Before entering the hall of science, a person's fear of sin should precede wisdom," for good deeds are what matter, "and neither poetry nor literature, nor science and art, are the goal."[100]

With the exception of these subtly worded remarks, the reader is hard put to identify other polemical elements in this work. Outwardly, these statements contain nothing that Menahem Nahum would have found objectionable. Evidently then, Zvi Aryeh of Zlatopol's main goal was to provide an alternative model of writing: an easily accessible, moral and homiletic work, a sort of Orthodox psychology that does not require the wisdom of the nations and is firmly planted in Torah tradition.

A Humanist among Hasidim?

In early 1924, Shmuel Abba Horodezky, the scholar of Hasidism, published a brief article surveying the first parts of Friedman's *Perush man* on *Avot.* He found impressive the fact that a zaddik could compose and publish a commentary "containing quotations from Aristotle, Plato, Epicurus, Kant, and Humboldt, among others, and that no one objects or questions this zaddik. Nor is the world of Hasidism terror-stricken." He continues to lead his hasidim comfortably, and his followers believe that the angel Gabriel taught him seventy languages and the seven wisdoms. "How times have changed!" Horodezky ended in amazement. In his eyes, the rabbi of Itscan was a sort of "modern zaddik," markedly different from his ancestors—the Maggid Dov Ber of Mezhirech, Avraham Hamalakh, Yisrael of Ruzhin, or Bernyu of Leova.

Though "he walks his path among his fellow zaddikim, he is unique and alone among them, even if ostensibly sharing their mores and living their life."[101]

But had times really changed? Perhaps Horodezky, who was evidently not personally acquainted with Menahem Nahum Friedman,[102] hoped that this surprising phenomenon heralded a change in the future development of hasidic Orthodoxy. But, as we well know, this hope had no chance of realization. Friedman's path—almost unlimited intellectual horizons, receptiveness to the best of world literature and thought and their integration into Judaism, internalization of aesthetic and artistic experiences, sensitivity to broad humanistic questions—had almost no sequel in Hasidism.[103] His uniqueness lies not in a new, coherent conceptual or public agenda, but in his daring to diverge from mainstream hasidic writing and thought. Apart from the amazement that this phenomenon evoked, mainly outside the hasidic camp, Friedman's writings kindled little reaction, either pro or con. In every respect, the rabbi of Itscan was and remained a marginal figure with no lasting impact; his historical importance rests in the fact of his existence.

Moreover, as was its habit, hasidic apologetics obscured his unique innovativeness and distorted his personality. In 1987, for example, Yitshak Hakham, a veteran Shtefanesht hasid who had met Menahem Nahum on several occasions in his youth, published a facsimile edition of three of Friedman's "less problematic" books. After describing Friedman's sanctity, greatness, and burning love of truth, the editor then noted: "He was famed as a great opponent against the various 'innovators' and the 'maskilim,' who had proliferated frighteningly in his day. He was a man of truth . . . therefore he argued with those 'reformers' and 'maskilim' and naturally, always bested them. Sometimes he had to use 'their language' in order to expose the contradictory nature of their arguments. But as an adept in Torah, science, and kabbalah, he always succeeded in overcoming the various 'reformers.'"[104]

Compare this apologetic description by a simple admiring hasid—who could not distinguish new from old, to whom the opening of the gates of knowledge was not only foreign but also served as a tactic in Orthodoxy's war on maskilim and secularists—to the eulogy by Friedman's friend, the essayist Avraham Kahana (whose pen name was Avrech):

> If we place this zaddik on a pedestal, it is because he was not just one of the thousands of zaddikim . . . familiar to us from the dawn of time, but because he was an outstanding exception, an impressive individual whose like is hard to find. Wonder of wonders, he did not deal with esoteric matters, with obscure acronyms, with combinations of holy names, but operated in the "exoteric" and "the real worlds," looking at and observing the world and its human inhabitants, especially the Jewish one and its members, identifying in it hypocrisy and falsehood, and fighting these negative phenom-

ena. Within his own camp, the camp of zaddikim . . . he found much of this malignant leprosy, due to our manifold sins, and he fought it with all his strength and all his might . . . and he rested not for a moment. Several months ago he informed me of all manner of tasks and treatises that, due to weakness and infirmity, do not reach completion. But who could have expected that the true zaddik of the generation and this veteran thinker would be so swiftly torn from us before his time? He will not be quickly replaced.[105]

"What Befell the Rebbes' Grandchildren Who Left the Fold"?

Even if Menahem Nahum Friedman of Itscan exerted minimal influence on the development of Hasidism, within his own family context, he was neither odd nor strikingly different. He constitutes yet another example of that distinct, elite group of scions of hasidic rebbes who differed from other hasidim by virtue of upbringing, education, and the brunt of internal and external pressures. Well aware of the deep spiritual crisis affecting traditional society, its members were directly and indirectly exposed to various manifestations of modernity; they responded in different, even contradictory ways to its spiritual challenges.[106]

From this perspective, Menahem Nahum was not anomalous. Perhaps more than for any other hasidic dynasty, among the descendants of Yisrael of Ruzhin we can identify individuals who, in search of new horizons, boldly stepped outside the restrictive bounds of the hasidic court. It is therefore illuminating to glance at his contemporaries who also did not tread the hasidic highway. The two individuals discussed below belonged to Menahem Nahum's immediate family circle.

Aharon Matityahu (Matesl) Friedman

The first figure is Aharon Matityahu (Matesl) Friedman (1892–1917), Menahem Nahum's talented younger brother, who died young and whose memory has been entirely obscured in hasidic writing.[107] Raised in Adjud, Romania, where their father, Avraham Yehoshua Heschel, served as zaddik, Matesl left his father's court upon reaching adulthood and moved to Pashkan, and later to Chernovtsy. The move to Chernovtsy was not fortuitous. Rather, it was a gesture of sorts to his relative Dov Ber (Bernyu) of Leova, Yisrael of Ruzhin's favored son, who was the first of the Ruzhiner zaddikim who had dared, fifty years earlier (in 1869), to rebel against his dynastic legacy and, for a short time, join forces with this town's maskilim.[108]

Exposed to socialist ideas (he was even active in Romanian socialist circles), Zionism, and the Jewish revival from a very young age, Matesl viewed himself as following in Ahad ha-Am's path, and even served as secretary of the Federation for Hebrew Language and Culture in Romania. He published articles in Hebrew, Yiddish, and Romanian, including in such secular forums as *Hatikvah* (a Zionist periodical published in Galats), *Der hamer* (Brila), and *Licht* (Iasi, 1915), the first literary compendium in Romania to attract a circle of modern Yiddish writers.

As a learned individual of distinguished lineage, who had turned his back on the hasidic court, Matesl was something of a sensation among his friends, by and large unfamiliar with the hasidic experience.[109] Despite the dramatic shift in his lifestyle, Matesl's friends testified that he took care not to hurt his family members; to prevent his father's followers from identifying him, he therefore wrote under a pseudonym.[110] Although we know nothing specific regarding the ties between the two brothers, it appears likely that they did maintain contact. In any event, following Matesl's death during a typhus epidemic, his relatives, who apparently found his writings not to their liking, burned all his remaining manuscripts, including a drama titled *Der rebe Reb Ber*.[111] This final scrap of information fits Matityahu's anomalous world, for Reb Ber was none other than the above-mentioned Bernyu of Leova, whose tragic, twisted path was a source of inspiration for the confused, Matityahu especially, who spoke of this explicitly.[112]

Yaakov Friedman

Another close relative was Yaakov Friedman (1910–72). The son of the zaddik Shalom Yosef of Mielnica (Galicia) and a great-great-grandson of Yisrael of Ruzhin,[113] Friedman acquired his fame as a talented Yiddish poet.[114] Although the hasidim wanted him to succeed his father (d. 1927), he refused in favor of his younger brother, Aharon Moshe, who reestablished the Mielnica court in Kolomea. Shortly thereafter, Yaakov began to publish poems in the Yiddish press. Yaakov, his widowed mother, and his remaining siblings moved to Warsaw, where he slowly left the hasidic path. By the time he returned to Chernovtsy in 1932, he was in every respect a modern poet.[115] He moved to Israel in 1949, after suffering terribly during the Holocaust and spending two years in a Cyprus detention camp. He settled in Bet Dagan and became a writer and farmer. His last years were spent in Tel Aviv.[116]

In his introduction to selected translations of Friedman's poems from Yiddish to Hebrew, Dov Sadan noted that this poet's life mirrors those of a group of poets and artists, the sons or grandsons of eminent zaddikim, who preferred the "kingdom of the spirit and artistic freedom" to "the kingdom of their fathers and the tradition of faith." Among this group's members, Sadan listed such researchers, journalists, writers, and poets as Shmuel Abba Horodezky, Avraham Yehoshua Heschel, Menashe Unger,[117] Uri Zvi Greenberg,

S. Shalom, Barukh Hager, and the above-mentioned Yaakov Friedman. To this list, which is by no means exhaustive, we can add the names of other prominent figures such as Moshe Bornstein,[118] Fischel Schneersohn,[119] Yosef Hager, Yohanan Twersky, and Yehiel Yeshaya Trunk. Sadan concluded his remarks: "But the question of what befell the rebbes' grandchildren who left the fold is a serious one."[120]

Sadan even remarked on the unique character of the Ruzhin dynasty and its descendants' earth-shattering, at times tragic, encounter with modernity: "The crises of the past generations affected this hasidic dynasty more than others—there too [among the other hasidic dynasties] there were brief sallies outside the way, but no tragedies like the episode of Reb Bernyu of Leova or that of Matityahu Friedman; it was shaken more strongly by the shifts in the past generations than other dynasties . . . and the principle we can derive is that internal tragedy and external shocks enhanced the sensitivity and sensibilities of the members of the house of Ruzhin, that its descendants who entered the fields of poetry inherited and ultimately intensified this sensitivity, just as they inherited and refined its sensibilities to the utmost."[121]

Concealed in the folds of Hasidism and Jewish Orthodoxy are additional figures similar to the ones described here. Due to the difficulty of dealing with these anomalous "princes," Orthodox historiography ignored them and expunged them from the roster of exemplary individuals. Liberating them from the oblivion to which they have been consigned and describing their original, complex spiritual worlds is not just a historical and investigative challenge, but it also adds delicate shading to the intricate portrait of the rich, multifaceted world of Eastern European Jewry in a stormy period of change.[122]

"It Is Forbidden to Uphold This Book"

Shortly before Rosh Hashanah 2001, the following letter appeared in the *haredi* newspaper *Yated ne'eman.* Titled "Hayav nipui" (Requires screening), it was written by Yisrael Lieberman: "I have seen in some hasidic households in Bnei Brak a book titled *Divrei Menahem,* which includes three books[123] authored by a descendant of the Shtefanesht admorim. I wish to announce that this book contains things that it is forbidden to publish, such as the use of idolatrous notions in order to explicate the importance of certain concepts, and other matters not in the spirit of the Torah and the Halakha. I showed this book to one of the greatest halakhic authorities and he simply said that *it is forbidden to uphold this book without first screening it.* And even screening and censoring are insufficient."[124]

Thus, Menahem Nahum Friedman's book traveled a long, obstacle-ridden path: from early-twentieth-century Chernovtsy and Kishinev to present-day fanatical Bnei Brak. The rabbi of Itscan's honest, engaging attempt to disseminate religious humanism among the hasidim, and to harmonize general and Torah knowledge, has evidently reached its terminus. If his enterprise initially sparked raised eyebrows, and mainly prompted intentional disregard, it has currently been condemned by "one of the greatest halakhic authorities" of the day to harsh censorship and "screening" in order to expunge its heretical and idolatrous foundations, which "it is forbidden to publish."

7 "Confession of My Tortured, Afflicted Soul"

The World of Rabbi Yitshak Nahum Twersky of Shpikov

> "How old are you?" I asked.
> "Sixteen. But this isn't the only idea I've had. You must understand that every rabbinical family is distinguished by a special talent. We are the philosophers and the rhetoricians among the rabbis. We like to speculate. It's a marvelous game, but it's also a trial. It's like walking on a narrow bridge. One false step, and you fall into heresy. But if the Lord is with you, if you don't stumble and can keep your Jewishness intact, you cherish your idea doubly . . . I like to take walks by myself and think about Hasidism. Faithful to my theory, I try to grasp ideas that will occur to me years later. That is why my eyes look so much older than I really am. I want to discover things. I do not like my grandfather's way, nor my father's . . . I told Father that I was not very satisfied with his way . . . he then confided in me that he himself was even less satisfied than I."
> —Jacob Glatstein, *Homecoming at Twilight*[1]

Shpikov Hasidism

The confession at the heart of this chapter—and, in the words of its author, "the confession of my life, withered and faded before its time, the

---

This chapter is an expanded version of my article "'My Tiny, Ugly World': The Confession of Rabbi Yitzhak Nahum Twersky of Shpikov," *Contemporary Jewry* 26 (2006): 1–34. Used here with kind permission of Springer Science and Business Media.

confession of my tortured, afflicted soul, the confession of my squandered talents"—is one of the more moving literary documents in the history of Hasidism. Indeed, it is almost unique. In this self-assessment, Yitshak Nahum (Nakhum'l) Twersky of Shpikov (1888–1942) takes stock of his life, courageously exposing his "duplicity," his "two-facedness," and "the cleft" in his troubled soul to a complete stranger.

Mailed in early 1910, when its author was but twenty-two years old, the confession was addressed to the Yiddish writer Yaakov Dineson (1858–1919), then living in Warsaw. Filling twenty-seven notebook pages, and written in rich, fluent Hebrew, with hardly any erasures, this letter was preserved in the Dineson Collection.[2] From its pages emerges the riveting figure of a sensitive, intelligent young man, an aesthete of poetic bent. Weary of life in the hasidic court, he laments his wasted youth and talents, and expresses his fear of the future and his despair at his inability to change his fate.

Yitshak Nahum was a scion of a branch of the Twersky family, whose members founded the Chernobyl dynasty and its many branches. He was raised in his birthplace, Shpikov, a small town in Podolia Province that is fifty-six kilometers south of Vinnitsa, and near Nemirov, Bratslav, and Tulchin.

Shpikov Hasidism was then a new, small offshoot of an existing hasidic dynasty, just established in 1885 by Yitshak's grandfather, Menahem Nahum (Nakhumchi), after the death of his father, the zaddik Yitshak of Skvira, forced his sons to divide not only his assets but also his followers among them.[3] Following the practice by hasidic dynastic elites of marrying within their extended illustrious families, Nakhumchi married his cousin Sheyndl, the daughter of the zaddik David of Talne. Like her husband, Sheyndl was also a grandchild of the dynasty founder Mordekhai (Motl) of Chernobyl.

Nakhumchi had barely managed to establish his new court in Shpikov before his death in 1886. He was succeeded by his only son, Mordekhai (Motele), then twenty-five years old. Like his father before him, Motele also married within the extended family. His wife was Chava (Chaveleh), the youngest daughter of the zaddik Yohanan of Rachmistrivke, who was Mordekhai of Chernobyl's youngest son. The writer of the confession and the subject of this chapter, Yitshak Nahum, was their child.[4]

Biography

In March or April 1910,[5] shortly after writing his confession, young Yitshak Nahum married Sheve (Batsheva), the daughter of Yisakhar Dov Rokeah (1854–1926), the revered leader of the Belz dynasty in eastern Galicia.[6] This rebbe himself had family ties to the Chernobyl dynasty; his wife was a granddaughter of Aharon of Chernobyl, Mordekhai of Chernobyl's oldest son. Having remained in the Chernobyl court for about a decade after his marriage,

Yisakhar Dov of Belz not only came to admire the Chernobyl branch of Hasidism but also considered it a great privilege to have married into this family; thus he later encouraged matches between his descendants and members of this dynasty.[7] At the time he wrote his confession, Yitshak Nahum of Shpikov had already been engaged to Yisakhar Dov's daughter for six years but had yet to see his future bride's face; rumor was his sole source of information about her. His confession clearly reflects his trepidation concerning this arranged match and his future life at the Belz court.

The wedding took place in Belz;[8] afterward, Yitshak Nahum lived with his in-laws, who supported the young couple, as was customary.[9] Given the Belzer rebbe's reputation as an extreme conservative and a harsh opponent of any traces of modernity, and the famed Belz bastion, which ostensibly protected its thousands of adherents, we can only guess at how Yitshak Nahum endured his first days within this hasidic court of which he had been so wary.[10] Evidently, his youthful rebellion, so forcefully expressed in his confession, subsided—outwardly, at least. Also, contrary to his expectations, the match was apparently a success; it seems that he and his wife developed a mutual affection.[11] According to hasidic tradition, Yitshak Nahum quickly acclimated to the Belz way of life and was esteemed by the Belz hasidim "for his nobility and sensitivity, his majestic appearance and the cleanliness of his clothes, his moderate speech, his respect for others, and his hospitality."[12] "Non-Belzer rabbis who come to Belz," a late Belz source states, "are brought to Reb Yitshak Nahum, in order to show them that besides Hasidism, there is also Torah scholarship in Belz. Prominent guests, anxious to 'get a whiff' of Belz, find interest in his home, as he is conversant with all the problems that have emerged, from time to time, in the life of the Jews of Poland."[13]

Four years later, Yitshak Nahum returned to Shpikov to visit his ailing father. When the father died during Passover 1914, his adherents immediately crowned Yitshak Nahum as their new rebbe, preventing him from returning to Belz, where his family had remained. Several months later, World War I broke out. As was the case for other Jewish communities in the Ukraine and Galicia, the disasters accompanying the war—raging civil conflict, raids by soldiers and brigands, and the terrible typhus outbreaks that ravaged many Ukrainian towns—did not bypass the hasidic court of Shpikov. Notwithstanding these and other hardships, Yitshak Nahum, his mother, and his sisters miraculously survived this catastrophic period.[14]

Like Shpikov, Austrian Belz was not spared. The Russian army also conquered Belz, destroying the town and setting fire to the rebbe's court. The Jews of Belz, along with the rebbe and his entourage, including Yitshak Nahum's wife and children, abandoned the town. Initially, the Belzer court relocated in Ratsfert, Hungary, where it remained for the duration of the war.[15]

FIG. 7.1. The Belzer rebbe, Yisakhar Dov Rokeah, being driven in a horse-drawn carriage, in a 1916 photograph

Only in the summer of 1918, after four years of separation, was Yitshak Nahum reunited with his family in Hungary.[16] Just a year later, in April 1919, the members of the Belz court were once again forced to move, this time, making for Munkatsh in the Carpathians. There they clashed with the Munkatsh hasidim; this controversy rapidly escalated into a war of denunciations, slander, and intrigue.[17] In 1922 the Belzer rebbe and his family, including Yitshak Nahum and his family, returned to Galicia, but not to Belz. As Belz had not yet been rebuilt, the rebbe and his court settled temporarily in nearby Oleszyce.[18] Only in 1925 did the Belz court return to its hometown.

In 1926 Yitshak Nahum left Belz for the town of Rawa Ruska (about thirty-five kilometers from Belz), where he was appointed town rabbi with his father-in-law's backing.[19] Large numbers of Belz hasidim lived there, and the Belz court dominated this town.[20] Although Yitshak Nahum could easily have continued his tenure as an admor, he preferred—as he also states in his confession—to be a rabbi, not a rebbe. In Rawa Ruska, "he embodied the glorious role of the aristocratic hasidic rabbi, who sanctifies God's name in all his ways."[21] He and his family met their deaths in early 1942 at the hands of the Nazis and their henchmen, apparently at the Belzec death camp.[22]

"Freedom, Freedom!" The Twersky Sisters

What prompted young Yitshak Nahum, the rebbe's son, to send his confession to Dineson, whose literary star was already on the wane? Although famed as a sensitive, sentimental writer, Dineson was not very productive in his later years: at that point, he devoted his literary energies mainly to his function as Y. L. Peretz's secretary and loyal assistant. We must look to Yitshak Nahum's older sisters for the surprising Dineson connection.

The first son after four daughters,[23] Yitshak Nahum had three married sisters at the time he wrote his confession, and it appears that all three were living in Shpikov. The oldest sister, Feige, married Shalom Yosef Friedman of Buhush (1868–1920) in the summer of 1897. Her husband, the only admor from the Ruzhin dynasty in Russia, set up an independent hasidic court in Shpikov, which attracted the Ruzhiners living in Russia. To the best of our knowledge, the two courts, his and that of his father-in-law, coexisted harmoniously.[24]

The second sister, Haya (Haykeleh), married a relative, Menahem Nahum Twersky (1874–1942); he was the grandson of the zaddik Avraham of Trisk (Volhynia), another of Mordekhai of Chernobyl's sons. Famous for her erudition, Haya was from a young age drawn to Haskalah literature and a life of sensibility and imagination.[25] Her marriage was not particularly happy—her husband, interested in continuing the lifestyle of a hasidic rebbe, never came to terms with his wife's free spirit—and they divorced after years of mutual discontent and separation. Haya, who retained custody of their children, lived briefly in Warsaw, where she became acquainted with Y. L. Peretz and Yaakov Dineson.[26] She apparently returned to Shpikov before the outbreak of World War I.[27] After the war, she and her children lived in Berlin for five years (1921–26); she then immigrated to New York.[28] Her ex-husband, Menahem Nahum, returned to Trisk and began to wander between various towns, trailing the followers of his father, who died in 1918. He later remarried and settled in Warsaw. After the Nazi invasion, he evidently came back to Trisk, where he was murdered in the summer of 1942.[29]

Of the three married sisters, Mirl, the youngest, was also the most exceptional. It was she who forged the link between her brother and Dineson. Drawn to the world of literature and Haskalah like her sister Haya, she forwarded some of her poems to Dineson, who encouraged and nurtured her talents.[30] In 1902, she was married to Asher Perlow (1885–1942),[31] the oldest son of the zaddik Yisrael of Stolin (Byelorussia). Reb Asher (Asherke) never became a rebbe. Musically talented like the other members of his family,[32] at his wife's urging he enrolled in the Berlin conservatory of music, certainly an unusual step for a member of the conservative hasidic world. Asherke left for Germany without asking his family's permission, and they, disconcerted by the scandal, used every means to bring him home. It seems that in Mirl's case, too, she was unable to bend her free spirit to societal pressures and her husband's hasidic upbringing: Asherke returned to Stolin, divorced Mirl, and remarried.[33] Hasidic lore recounts that, after Asherke's return, his father confiscated his violin and decreed that because this holy instrument had been desecrated, it must never again be played in his court. From that time on, there was no instrumental accompaniment to the singing at the Saturday night repasts in the Stolin hasidic court.[34]

After her divorce, Mirl stayed in the Shpikov court. The letter that she wrote her sister Haya, when the latter was finally awarded her long-awaited divorce, reflects not only their unique spirit but also their closeness with Yitshak Nahum: "Hurrah! You have won, my dearest! Who could have dreamed that this joyfully fortunate moment would arrive? Freedom, freedom! Praises for your bravery, that you have traversed this dark hell with your head high! How we danced, went out of our minds, Haykeleh, we were like crazy people. I don't exaggerate. We kissed, laughed, jumped, ran from one room to another."[35]

Mirl and Dineson began to correspond in 1909, at least a year before Yitshak Nahum wrote his confession. In alluding to this correspondence at the outset of his letter, Yitshak Nahum nowhere mentions his sister Mirl by name; nonetheless, it is undoubtedly she to whom he refers. It appears that Mirl had revealed her younger brother's doubts to Dineson in one of her letters. And, despite Dineson's explicit request that she refrain from sharing his response with her brother for fear of Yitshak Nahum's negative reaction, Mirl did show Yitshak Nahum this letter. Evidently, it sparked his impulse to make a direct connection with the Warsaw author. Before sending his confession, however, Twersky first mailed Dineson his photograph, so that the famous writer could see for himself the glaring disparity between his external appearance and his internal world.

It is worth noting the place of his sisters in Yitshak Nahum's world. He testifies that his sisters' rooms, where he can discuss "life and literature" with them and other youthful friends, serve as his refuge from the suffocating atmosphere of the court. Indeed, it should not surprise us that women were the first to absorb modernity and secular values in traditional society. Tutored privately in foreign languages by teachers with maskilic leanings; women were allowed to read for pleasure in their spare time, including French and Russian literature. Also, in general, girls were more laxly supervised than boys.[36] In his memoirs, the writer Yohanan Twersky, Yitshak Nahum's nephew, recounts that the women of the Shpikov court, including Yitshak Nahum's mother, the rebbetzin Chava,[37] used to read secular books acquired from a traveling bookseller. His wares included novels by Nahum Meir Shaykevitsh (Shomer), Ozer Blaustein, Yitshak Yoel Linetski, and Ayzik

FIG. 7.2. Yitshak Nahum Twersky during his tenure as rabbi of Rawa Ruska

Meir Dik.[38] Given the amount of time that Yitshak Nahum reported spending with his sisters, he too was probably familiar with these and other books.

Despite his clearly enunciated sense of distress and isolation, which emerges unequivocally from his confession, Yitshak Nahum was no recluse. Apart from his sisters, his faithful partners in his dual existence, he mentions a group of "young friends and acquaintances" with whom he meets often, to read and converse. Although they do not perhaps fully comprehend the complicated depths of his soul, they are aware of and identify with his yearnings.

In addition, Yitshak Nahum was unable to totally conceal his inclinations. Tales were spread in the town that, alongside his Torah studies, "he also studied secular works—during the twilight hours."[39] One reliable witness reports that the Shpikov court housed a four-thousand-volume library, bequeathed by Yitshak of Skvira to his son Nakhumchi. In addition to biblical, Talmudic, and classic halakhic works, this library contained many old manuscripts, kabbalistic and philosophical works, and even some maskilic books such as Yitshak Ayzik Benjacob's *Otsar hasefarim*. Mordekhai Glubman, who tutored Yitshak Nahum for a time, recounted that it took him and his pupil an entire year to properly catalog and shelve the books. The hours spent on this task must have widened Yitshak Nahum's intellectual horizons, transporting him to new spheres.[40]

Even after settling in Belz and taming his rebellious spirit (outwardly, at least), he continued to correspond with his sisters. Thus we know, for example, that while en route to Marienbad, the popular spa of the Galician rebbes, he detoured to Berlin to visit his sister Haya and her children. Her son Yohanan was then studying philosophy and psychology at the University of Berlin, and Yitshak Nahum quizzed him about his studies and the innovative theories of Sigmund Freud, Alfred Adler, and Kurt Lewin.[41]

"A Sacrifice on My Mother's Altar": Taking Stock of the Confession

The importance of Twersky's confession lies primarily in its literary and psychological content. As a historical document, its value for the study of Hasidism and its history is limited, even problematic.

Indeed, Yitshak Nahum's critique of the petty shopkeeper mentality of contemporary Hasidism, and of its traditional dress, fanaticism, conservatism, and indolence, is forthrightly harsh. It almost seems as if Yitshak Nahum had read and absorbed the satiric voice of the nineteenth-century maskilim and their followers, the first generation of students of Hasidism, with their animosity for what they perceived as the vulgar manifestations of contemporary Hasidism. His wittily mocking description of the dress and behavior of the Belz hasidim in Galicia, as well as his description of the atrophied hasidic courts in the Ukraine, might have originated from the caustic pens of Yosef Perl or Yitshak Ber Levinsohn. Even his terminology—"idiotic costume," "hallucinations and nonsense," "wild motions and customs," "degeneration," "atrophy"—comes from the maskilic, antihasidic lexicon.[42] His critique of the institution of matchmaking—which required him to marry a woman he had never even seen—as not in tune with the twentieth century could have been lifted verbatim from many items in nineteenth-century Haskalah literature.

However, missing from Yitshak Nahum's criticism of Hasidism is a systematic ideological dimension. Although the intimate genre of confession does not lend itself to a coherent ideological or historical doctrine, nevertheless, the overall impression is that Yitshak Nahum's debate with Hasidism remains at the personal and experiential level. Nowhere in his anguished letter do we find echoes of principled criticism of Hasidism's religious or ideological foundations, or of the doctrine of the zaddik. Nor does he suggest an alternative to hasidic ways, or a cure for its ailments. Beyond general reflections, with an emphasis on aesthetics in particular, he fails to pinpoint his aspirations. Greatly troubled by the problem of external appearances, he repeatedly expresses his views about the ugliness of traditional hasidic dress; he also returns time and again to natural beauty, which he believes Hasidism ignores. Yet, justified as this criticism may be, does it go to the core of the actual problems facing Hasidism in the early twentieth century? Despite loud protestations of its degeneration, he makes no real attempt to get to the root of Hasidism's circumstances at the time.

Note, moreover, the absence of a mature historical perspective (after all, he was then but twenty-two years old), as typified by his approach to the mythic past of Hasidism in general, and of his family in particular.[43] As a product of traditional society, Yitshak Nahum looked at history through apologetic glasses of self-disparaging awe of the past, in the spirit of the famous Talmudic dictum: "If the earlier [scholars] were sons of angels, we are sons of men; and if the earlier [scholars] were sons of men, we are like donkeys" (BT *Shabbat* 112b). Accordingly, he did not link Hasidism's current crisis to the founders of the movement—the Besht and his disciples—or to his immediate forebears, the founders of the Chernobyl dynasty to which he belonged. He attributed the breakdown to the 1890s, to his father's day: "For some twenty years, since my grandfathers, the famed zaddikim of Skvira, Talne, and Rachmistrivka[44] . . . and their brothers, the standard-bearers of Hasidism in our province, who commanded thousands of faithful hasidim, died . . . Since then, the light of Hasidism has dimmed and its glory has gone into exile, and it has atrophied until it is now little more than a debased coin, a name entirely devoid of content."[45]

And the main reason for this degeneration was indeed connected to the decline of the generations' concept: "My ancestors did not leave after them sons like themselves, men of understanding and intelligence, who might influence and impart of their spirit to the flock of hasidim." This historiographical theory, however, derives from Yitshak Nahum's perception of his conflicted family's internal world, and not from historical reality as we know it. After all, rightfully so or not, nineteenth-century critics of Hasidism considered Mordekhai of Chernobyl's eight sons, Yitshak Nahum's forebears, as prime representatives of the "degeneration" plaguing Hasidism. If many maskilim mocked this dynasty, which for them symbolized the establishment of courtly rule in Hasidism, the lust for wealth and glory, and neglect of Hasidism's original values, Yitshak Nahum took pride in his lineage, laying the blame for Hasidism's ossification at the door of the zaddikim of his own generation.

This is not the place for a profound psychological analysis of Yitshak Nahum's relationship with his parents. Unsurprisingly, his "cold-tempered" father is barely mentioned in the confession and plays no significant role in his considerations. It is with his mother that he has a close relationship; only his warm feelings for her prevent him from breaking his shackles and altering his fate. But in the confession, his open love and compassion for his mother become an oblique indictment that feeds his sense of victimhood: "I shall bare my soul, explaining the obvious truth to you: a sacrifice am I, a sacrifice on my mother's altar." This blaming of his mother for his inability to take his fate in his own hands brings to an apex his sense of self-deprecation and dependence on his parents. At this dramatic moment in his life, when he feels that he has been deprived of free will, he imputes his impotence to his love for his mother and his responsibility for her fate. "My compassion for my beloved mother" must be interpreted as self-pity.[46]

It is noteworthy that Yitshak Nahum neither sees himself as a heretic, nor considers secularism as a solution to his existential crisis. He is not plagued by religious doubts, although we cannot ignore the surprising fact that the name of God appears only in passing in the letter.[47] Although Yitshak Nahum wishes to remain in traditional Jewish society, he seeks to break free of what he sees as the constraints of ossified, degenerate hasidic society, which no longer meets his needs.

Yitshak Nahum's troubled soul, his spirit that yearns to be free, is trapped in the confines of the oppressive hasidic fellowship. He views all his attempts to break out of the circle in order to build a fresh self-identity as predestined to failure. Like a lamb led to the slaughter, he is unable to change his fate. His escape from his detested hasidic identity is prevented not just by his emotional commitment to his beloved mother's fate and his fear of the embarrassment his actions would cause her, but also by his inability to detach himself from his self-awareness as the son of a zaddik, as a leader on whom many hasidim hang their own hopes: "What is this? What am I? Is it possible that I am naught but a hypocrite, a sham? Am I permitted thus to deceive people? . . . And besides, that step would be final proof that I am dissolute, a long-standing unbeliever, and that in vain I have misled all those who know me, letting them think me faithful to God and to His holy ones."

This sincere statement is reminiscent of the famous scene in Y. L. Peretz's 1903 drama *Hurban beit tsadik* (Collapse of the zaddik's house), known also in its later Yiddish version *Di goldene keyt* (1907), where Peretz places the following heart-rending cry in the mouth of the zaddik's son, who stands before the open Torah ark: "I am the last link of the chain. I am the last one here . . . show yourselves, reveal yourselves, give me a sign that I am not deceiving and cheating the people. Because if you will not show or reveal yourself or give a sign, then—I am a swindler . . . And if I am a swindler—my father was a swindler too . . . Also my father, my grandfather, my great-grandfather too . . . The entire dynasty, the entire chain!"[48] Indeed, Yitshak Nahum consoles himself with the thought that he may minimize the damage, if he takes the crucial step of crossing the line after he marries and settles in Belz. But, as we know, this step was never taken.

Of special interest is his indirect criticism of the nascent neo-Romantic orientation toward Hasidism, represented mainly by such writers as Y. L. Peretz, Micha Yosef Berdyczewski, Yehuda Steinberg, and Martin Buber, among others. Already described as Romantic in their day, their approach ostensibly viewed Hasidism and its values as a source of inspiration that might illuminate and revive Jewish national life, even for those outside the hasidic camp.

But this viewpoint is erroneous: the complex approach of these authors (at least some of them) to Hasidism is better described as patronizing, more grounded in the mitnagedic and maskilic perspectives than in the hasidic world. Thus Yitshak Nahum accurately characterizes Berdyczewski's double standard: he appreciates the hasidic world, its beliefs, and way of life as long as he does not have to live with them:

> Well I remember what I read in Dr. Berdyczewski's book *The Hasidim*,[49] where, after heaping copious praises on the hasidic doctrine, he concludes with a heartfelt cry, "May I be so lucky as to share their portion!"[50] . . . And, recalling that exclamation, I cannot hold back my laughter. Indeed, *Herr Doktor*! How right you are! But how convenient it was for you to utter this exclamation, on your lofty chair at Heidelberg University,[51] far removed from the hasidim and their masses. But what would you say if it really fell to your lot to be among them always? Methinks you would have spoken differently then, a very different call would have issued from your heart, and together with me you would have cried, "May I be so lucky as *not* to share their portion."

Even this criticism is not unique to Twersky. His remarks, spoken from a profound familiarity with the daily reality so different from the convivial descriptions of the hasidic courts, share much with the mocking comments of other contemporary condemnations of the Romantics; for example, the following statement by the Galician maskil Mordekhai David Brandstetter (1844–1928):

> What does Peretz know of the hasidim? And how familiar are Berdyczewski and Steinberg with hasidic life? Did they live among them as I did? Do they know of their persecution of their opponents, of any who dare to diverge somewhat from their lifestyle? I saw all this firsthand. I lived among them. I resided with them and got to know them inside out! If the hasidim were still in power—we would walk in darkness to the present! And to this day I still converse with them and hear their talk! Hasidism is based on superstition, on zaddik worship—blind worship! The majesty and glory of the contemporary zaddik has departed and his teachings are but a deception. The zaddik uses clever trickery and his followers are reactionaries who harshly persecute any who "leave the path." Peretz, Berdyczewski, and Steinberg's stories are poetry, and the best of poetry is its falsity. There is no connection between the "Hallelujah" of this poetry and the reality. They see what their hearts desire.[52]

"The Spirit of the Times": The Confession's Historical Context

The literary passion with which this young, gifted zaddik poured out his heart, and its rich, engaging Hebrew (notwithstanding its flowery language and repetitiveness),[53] could have made his letter a manifesto, a voice for the many refined, sensitive young men who, growing up in the lap of Hasidism, had tortured themselves in an hour of soul-searching. But their inner battles with their tormented souls, and their attempts to escape from the hasidic world, did not always succeed. It was, moreover, never Yitshak Nahum's intention to be a mouthpiece for his peers to the public. What he wrote was an intimate confession, intended to remain confidential between him and his correspondent, the writer Yaakov Dineson.

In many respects, Yitshak Nahum belongs to that identifiable group of anomalous scions of zaddikim (*benehem shel kedoshim*) endowed with intense poetic sensitivity, some of whose biographies have been examined in previous chapters of this book. Growing up, like them, in the aristocratic hasidic courts during a period of dramatic change, he is another example of a young man profoundly affected by the deep rupture within traditional society. Exposed to the varied manifestations of modernity that managed to infiltrate the supposedly sealed gates of the hasidic court, these youths were unable to remain indifferent to change or to the intellectual and spiritual temptations of Haskalah, modern literature, nationalism, aesthetics, Romanticism, philosophy, and the *Wissenschaft des Judentums*. All these possessed not only both destructive and constructive aspects, but also formidable seductive powers.[54] The range of reactions to modernity by these scions of zaddikim resembles that of other members of the Eastern European Jewish Orthodox elites: fanatical opposition, confusion and despair, attempts to bridge the gap between Orthodoxy and the enticing world outside the hasidic courts,[55] or escape to that wider world. Repelled by Hasidism, some were drawn to communism[56] or to Zionism; naturally, others of these sons and daughters took the extreme step of leaving the fold, abandoning their families and religion, and completely casting off Jewish observance.[57] Not surprisingly, internal hasidic historiography downplays or obscures these crisis-driven phenomena. Aaron Ze'ev Aescoly strikingly summed up these little-researched phenomena in his essay on Hasidism in Poland at that time:

> Not a house remained whose sons and daughters were not swept up in the current of that generation . . . Moreover, in conjunction with the transfer of hasidic courts to the cities, this phenomenon did not skip over the families of the zaddikim. Against the background of city life, and the conjoining of atrophy and indolence, the families of the zaddikim could not resist the spirit of the times. *The sons and daughters of the zaddikim were the first to sense that their fathers' path had no future*, and they grazed in other fields—from Hamizrachi to the Communist Party, from the hasidic perspective all negative to the same degree. An intriguing principle may be established regarding this generation: in all the hasidic dynasties the eldest son, the *heir*, continued in the

path of faith, but the remainder of the family, who had no hold on the horns of the altar, left Hasidism and the ancestral path.[58]

Rabbi Yitshak Nahum Twersky clearly illustrates the searing bewilderment and despair experienced by many of his contemporaries—the children of hasidic rabbis growing up at the turn of the twentieth century. Awareness of the deep spiritual crisis facing Jewish Orthodoxy in general, and Hasidism in particular; the immense attraction of modern Jewish culture, which broke through the self-imposed barriers of the faithful; the helplessness of the individual seeking self-definition, who finds himself confronting powerful familial and social pressures, both visible and invisible, which block his extrication from the old world—all exemplify this model, which also comprises a building block of modern Jewish identity.

"My Tiny, Ugly World": The Text of the Confession[59]

Sunday, [the week of parashat] Terumah, January 24, 1910,[60] Shpikov

Dear friend and beloved author, Mr. Yaakov Dineson!

For a whole year now I have been endeavoring with all my will and strength to write your honor a letter. For there is none other to whom I can lay bare my mind and reveal the secrets of my life or, better, the gloomy life of my environment; and there is none other who possesses a warm, sensitive, feeling heart, that might fittingly resonate to all the spasms and tremors of my soul. For behold, throughout that whole year, since becoming acquainted with you and your gentle, delicate soul, I have been consumed by an innermost need to correspond with you, to reveal to you all that is hidden in my heart, to unburden before you all that is concealed and confined in my soul. I imagine always that my soul will then find solace, unburdened of a heavy load of stones. My stifled thoughts and unspoken words will find proper expression in my letter, and they will surely achieve their object, for in your honor they will find a person who will understand them and sense them.

Thus I thought, and thus I desired all year. But not merely one thought and one desire do I harbor in my heart, hollowing out for them a deep grave therein. Much have I experienced in such matters. All my life is one long chain of suppressed desires, concealed ideas, shattered cravings and wishes. And indeed I was forced to do so with this particular desire as well. Thus dictated the circumstances of my accursed life, and who shall oppose them.

But now the opportunity has beckoned, and I have sent you my portrait; far be it from me to deny that, apart from sending my portrait to you—a person whom I think of as a dear and highly respected friend, deeming it a great honor for myself if my portrait should be in your possession—apart from that, I had another, covert, intention. I wished you to see and recognize all the duality and two-facedness of my world, to apprehend the great difference and distance between my inner world and my outer world. I thought, therefore, to let your honor gaze at my portrait, see all the wretchedness and ugliness in my clothing, and by logical analogy infer the whole picture, all the external trappings of my life. I wished you to recognize all the darkness and gloom around me, to inspect at a glance my external appearance, in all its fearful darkness. I will then approach your honor in my letter—for I felt that, despite all the obstacles, it will no longer brook any delay; for as lava bursts forth from a volcano, so shall my letter burst forth from the conflagration of my blazing soul, surging forth and carrying all obstacles before it—then shall I stand before you in the fullness of my inner portrait, remove the veil and discard the black mask from my face; I shall reveal to you the depths of my soul, its hidden light. And then a new world will open before your eyes, a world full of song, a world full of light and radiance, a world full of sublime aspirations and lofty hopes. In contrast, I shall also picture for you my second, other, outer world, in all its blackness—the blackness of the portrait is naught in comparison. I shall not use many colors, nor heap words one upon another. Only a window shall I breach into that terrible, awful gloom, to enable its darkness to be seen in all its horror; and then, against the radiance and brilliance of my soul, the darkness in my outer world shall be seen in all its terrible obscurity; and against the background of this awful, gloomy darkness, the light of my inner world shall shine forth in all its radiant loveliness. And then, when your honor should perceive the terror in that darkness, and the magnificence and magic in that light, in all its fullness and depth, then shall you understand the extent of the sorrow and the pain of that welter and chaos of light and darkness or, better, of the light that is usurped by darkness; and then shall you apprehend the whole depth of the rift in my soul.

Such was my intention in sending you my portrait, and that is what I planned and wished to do. How great then, was my amazement that your honor had truly understood, or better, sensed, all this even before I had time to write you my letter, and perceptively expressed this in such fitting words in your letter to my sister.[61] Nevertheless, there is much, very much, that remains locked away and concealed from you in my soul, concerning which you wish to know, and you address this question to my sister. These words and questions of yours have further fanned the flames of my craving to write your honor a detailed letter, in which I shall present myself whole and all of my environment without embellishment. That I shall do in this present letter.

But before proceeding to the main body of my letter, let me forestall your complaint to my sister that she disregarded your warning and admonishment not to show me your letter. Presumably, your honor thought and supposed that your words would pierce my heart like daggers, and was therefore loath to distress me. Please believe, then, what I am now telling you, that, quite the opposite, the impression your words made upon me was the reverse of what you might have anticipated. Your words could not distress me, because they in no wise surprised me. I might have been aggrieved only by words that surprised me, by new words, the like of which I had never heard before, new ideas the like of which had never occurred to me. For example, had I been calm and composed, stoical about the conditions of my life, finding nothing amiss with them, and your honor had addressed me with sharp words and proved the opposite to me, then surely would the pain have been great and awful, the distress deep and profound. For with such words your honor would then have been demolishing all the lovely castles and magnificent towers that I had erected in my mind, evicting me from my own world where I had already found myself a good place and thought it calm and restful, by showing me that my own world is not good and not beautiful, that there is another, more beautiful world, more fascinating and appealing. Like a man sitting in the dark, never having seen light in his life, the thought never having occurred to him that darkness is not good but harmful, and suddenly another person appears and opens up for him a window into the light, to show him its goodness and beauty—would he ever be able to reconcile himself to his darkness?

But that is not my situation. Never have I been content with my narrow, dark, gloomy world, and always am I aware of the contrast between the wide, beautiful world and my tiny, ugly world. And always I say, "*The place is too crowded for me.*"[62] Could your words astonish me, of all people!? Could they cause me grief and pain!? On the contrary, I felt myself consoled by your words, realizing that a great man like yourself sympathizes with me and feels the wretchedness of my world. The very opposite—had your honor not told me such things, had you proved to me that even a life like that which I am living is not bad, then should I have felt myself wretched and depressed. Could there possibly be any person who would say of such a terrible life that it is good?—So let your honor's mind be at rest. You have not caused me any grief; on the contrary, I owe you thanks for your letter and your sympathy. Therefore, my sister, who knows me well and who well understood your honor's intention in your admonition, knew that there was no need here for such concern, and allowed me to read the letter. And that is, then, my answer to your letter.

Does your honor know the state of Hasidism in our time and in our country?—In our country in particular! For in Poland and Galicia the situation is very different. Do you know its essence, its content, and its nature? I shall not be far wrong, I believe, if I answer in your name: "No!" Perhaps your honor is familiar with the state of Hasidism in the early days of its flowering and its growth, in the time of the Besht and his disciples, and later too, in its heyday, in the previous generation, when Hasidism itself was still a kind of "system," and the zaddikim who bore its banner aloft were still imbued with the spirit of Hasidism, and still exerted considerable influence on the people.

As to Hasidism and its standard-bearers in those days, surely your honor has read the many monographs that have been written about them in our literature. Surely your honor has personally perused the books of Hasidism and extracted the precious pearls scattered here and there in that literature, among the heaps of ashes of hallucinations and nonsense. Thus your honor surely knows about the origin of Hasidism and its state in the first and second period [of its existence], although your knowledge is not perfect but involves some errors and misconceptions; for hearsay is quite different from eyewitness evidence, and a person who has been reared and educated in the innermost circle of Hasidism, with masters of the movement all around him, familiar with the development of the movement from its beginnings to this day, with all its faults and merits, cannot be compared with a person born and reared in an environment foreign to Hasidism, all of whose knowledge is derived from books alone, from legends, not from life itself. And most of the books, in particular those of our latest authors, who have begun to deal in recent years with Hasidism as a system and a movement, are so remote from life and from reality; they are so openly tendentious that a person consulting them in order to trace the roots of Hasidism from them alone, be it only through popular legends which are mostly very beautiful but far from the truth, might liken the false luster of rotten wood to a brilliantly glittering gem, and an ugly sight in this movement to a splendid, charming revelation. But nevertheless you have at least some idea concerning the Hasidism of those times. But as to the Hasidism of our times and our provinces, surely you have heard nothing, for the literature makes no reference to it at all, and in life your honor is very, very remote from us. Your honor resides in Warsaw, the capital of Poland, where Hasidism still has all its power and its influence is still tremendous. So let me describe for you, quite briefly, the state of Hasidism here, in our province, the province of Ukraine.

In saying here "Hasidism," I use a metaphorical name, for that name is entirely inappropriate to present-day Hasidism and has been so for some twenty years, since my grandfathers, the famed zaddikim of Skvira, Talne, and Rachmistrivke—all my ancestors—and their brothers, the standard-bearers of Hasidism in our province, who commanded thousands of faithful hasidim, died or, as the hasidim say, departed this world. Since then, the light of Hasidism has dimmed and its glory has gone into exile, and it has atrophied, continually declining, continually diminishing from day to day, until it is now little more than a debased coin, a name entirely devoid of content.

The reasons for this are many, more than can be listed here, for in order to explain them one would be obliged to delve deeply into the history of its development from its beginnings until today. But such is not my object here, for I have not come to tell the story of Hasidism, but only that which affects my person, my life history. Nevertheless, there are two main reasons: first, my ancestors did not leave after them sons like themselves, men of understanding and intelligence, who might influence and impart of their spirit to the flock of hasidim. [Their sons were] either men who, though indeed great masters of Torah and pious, proficient in the works of kabbalah and Hasidism, were weak, exhausted, and uncivilized in all their ways. Little knowledge have they of the world and of men, they lack any sense of beauty; ugliness rules all their doings, their clothing, their speech, all their motions; or they were common men, faceless and nondescript, neither masters of Torah nor knowledgeable and virtuous in the ways of the world, their only claim to fame being their ancestry. That is one reason.

The second is the intellectual development of our province. In the last twenty years, our part of the world has taken such enormous steps forward that it has almost overtaken even Lithuania.[63] A new generation has arisen, a generation that knows not—and does not want to know—its old ancestral traditions, a generation that thirsts for [secular] education and longs for freedom. This young generation has influenced the older generation and imbued them with its spirit. The generation looks completely different. The old type, the pious, patriarchal Jew of the previous generation is no more, has almost completely disappeared, displaced either by the completely freethinking Jew, or by the simple, bourgeois Jew, neither very pious nor freethinking, just an ordinary Jew, no longer with the perfect, simple faith of the Jew of the previous generation. While many old people from the former generation still remain, they are but solitary remnants, few in number in every town, with no influence on the march of life, a few lost souls. They sit, each in his own corner and shaking their heads in disgust, heap their curses upon the new generation that has left them behind, advancing far, far beyond them. Upon such arid ground, of course, Hasidism cannot possibly bear fruit, and so it has gradually degenerated, until there is almost no trace of it here.

Those old hasidim, in whose hearts the memory of the first zaddikim, the forerunners, still lives, could not communicate with the sons who succeeded them. Sorrowfully they look and gaze from afar upon those who have come to occupy the throne of their masters and teachers. In their grief, they have retreated into themselves, delving deeply at least into the books of the zaddikim, contenting themselves with tales and memories of the good old days, that they tell each other upon meeting. And a new generation of hasidim, who do not recall the "founding fathers" and will make do with the sons, has not arisen, for the new generation is far removed from Hasidism.

In short, that first Hasidism, whose name at least was fitting, has wholly perished. Instead, a new Hasidism, which might more precisely be termed "wheeling and dealing," has appeared. For the new Hasidism is little more than shopkeeping.[64] A Jew who enters the rebbe's house does not come to be admonished, to learn some virtue, to hear a good word, for such hasidim are no more; they come to the rebbe in his capacity as a wonder worker, begging him to demonstrate his miracles for them, to save them from misfortune, in exchange for the money they pay him for the miracle.

And it is self-evident that such people are most brutish people, whose very boorishness is their Hasidism. For lo, the great legacy our ancestors bequeathed us, all the virtues of that heritage—for those who considered these qualities virtues—all its splendor and magic, have been totally swept away. And this alone the house of the rebbe in our parts retains as a heritage from our ancestors—all the refuse left over from its ancestral customs. All the wretchedness and ugliness, the idiotic costume, all the wild motions and customs, these alone remain to them, they are sacred and untouchable to this very day. Such is the state of Hasidism in our time and in our province, such are the hasidim, and such is the image of the house of the "rebbe." And in such a time, in such a house, was I lucky enough to be born.

I imbibed piety with my mother's milk, I was reared on the wellsprings of Torah and Hasidism, and no foreign spirit penetrated our home to dislodge me, God forbid, from my place. But nevertheless, since the day I attained maturity I was imbued with a different spirit, I was different from all around me. Of course, that was within the hidden depths of my mind; outwardly—the less said, the better. I felt that my world was small and tiny, constricted, choking and strangling me; and in my innermost being I longed so much for a different world, a beautiful, wide world, that would give me enough air to breathe. I despised the people around me, loathed their way of life, and was drawn upward as if by a hidden force. There, in the infinite expanse, above the swamp in which I was immersed.

How did such ideas occur to me even in my infancy? What moved me to despise my surroundings, to hunger with all my heart for a different world? I myself know not, for who knows the way of the spirit? But one thing I do know: I have a delicate, poetic soul. A yearning soul, that could never reconcile itself to its gloomy, dark condition, but has always longed and pined for another life, more beautiful and far more interesting.

I remember the impression made upon me by my frequent hikes, when in my youth I would go out in the summer, with my teacher,[65] to the forest outside the town, along a path meandering between green meadows. Leaving the house, with its pervasive stifling air and stifling spiritual atmosphere, and my encounter with nature. Free, living, blooming, nature; the enormous contrast between our house—our house in particular—and Creation. All these had such an enormous influence upon me that in the first moments I felt drunk, intoxicated with life and its joy, intoxicated by the magnificence and magic of nature. I forgot the whole world, forgot the house and its duties that I had left behind, the narrow surroundings and everything that I hated, and was seized by only one strong sensation—a sensation of pleasure and life. All those sleeping life powers within me, that had flickered deep within my heart, burst forth with overwhelming force. I desired then to embrace the whole world, to kiss the world—the fields, the forest, the birds flying over my head—with one kiss. To satiate my burning, life-desiring soul.

But this mental state was not long-lived. Slowly but surely, the joyful feelings began to evaporate, to be replaced by muted sorrow. My memory began to resurrect my duties at home, my way of life, the chains that shackle my spirit. I remembered that no son of nature am I, to rejoice in nature's joy is not my lot. I remembered how far I am from nature—the very opposite, I am far removed from free, honest, and simple nature, which knows no cunning or falsehood; for I, hypocrite that I am, dissemble and deny. I do what I desire not to do, say what I think not, and I am entirely unnatural. I love nature, all that is good and beautiful, but I myself, in my dress, my actions, my movements, embody the antithesis of both good and beautiful. Such sorrowful thoughts and bitter feelings filled my mind as I ended my outdoor walks, returning home always with pain in my heart to discharge my "duties" and to live my "life."

Thus I grew up and thus I lost my way, my heart a burning hell and fiery furnace, but outwardly behaving as if everything was as it should be, a child of my environment. And so I became what I am now.

Much Torah have I studied in my life. Much have I racked my brains over weighty volumes of Talmud and legal codes. I have also pondered books of our philosophers, kabbalists, and hasidim. Thereby have I earned a place of honor among the Torah scholars of my town, and acquired a "name" throughout my neighborhood. And all the Torah scholars and the hasidim—of the old type, proficient in the books of the early hasidim, who served under the old zaddikim—come daily to visit me. One comes to me troubled by a weighty problem in the Talmudic text that he wishes to discuss with me and hear my opinion of the matter; another comes with a perplexing passage from Maimonides; and yet another wishes just to sit with me, regaling me with his tales and recollections of the early zaddikim, to hear a pleasing adage from such-and-such a book that I have seen, and to tell me something of what he has read and seen. What shall I tell your honor? The sufferings of the dead in the grave, if such indeed exist—as the faithful tell us—are naught compared with the mental anguish and heaviness of heart that these visits occasion me.

I am young in years, bursting with youthful energy and life forces. My ideas are ideas of life, and my ambitions, ambitions of life. But my bitter, harsh fate forces me to spend most of my days among old men—whether old in years or in attitudes, what matter?—mummified, dismal, whose God is not my God, their views not my views, all their thoughts, goals, and desires foreign to me.[66] In such circles am I obliged to spend my days, to partake of their rejoicing, to sympathize with them in their sorrow and grief, to be considered as one of them.

Imagine, if you will, your honor, the scene: a beautiful, clear, summer's day, the sun bathing the whole universe and world in its rays. Waves of light stream through the wide window into my room, and I am seated at my table, the thick tomes open before me, but my thoughts and feelings are not for those tomes at all. I glance outside, I see the blue sky above my head and the abundance of light outside; and hushed, secret longings seize me. I pine for, dream of a beautiful, magical world, under a pristine pure, blue sky, its brilliance unmarred by the smallest cloud, radiant with brilliant light, not the slightest shadow darkening its expanses. Thus I sit pining and dreaming, my imagination bearing me on its wings to the farthest reaches. Suddenly—a knock at the door. I open, and there before me stands the local rabbi . . . [67] He wishes to delight me with a novel point that he has made in his Torah studies. And immediately I am torn away from my pleasant dreams. It is as if I had fallen all of a sudden from the heights of magical imagination to the depths of bitter, black reality. And then the sharp, hair-splitting, discussion begins, objections and solutions flying back and forth. An onlooker might believe me wholly engrossed in this give-and-take; but how bitterly is my heart weeping in secret, for the ruin of my world, for the theft of my youthful dreams, that I am forced to exercise the best of my powers and talents in empty, dry, casuistry about the minutiae of the dietary laws, in conversation with hasidim about the Divine Presence in exile—by God! do they understand, feel, the meaning of "Divine Presence"? and what is "exile"?!—or about so-and-so the zaddik who performed such-and-such a miracle, and some rebbe or another who worked some kind of wonder.

Well I remember what I read in Dr. Berdyczewski's book *The Hasidim*, where, after heaping copious praises on the hasidic doctrine, he concludes with a heartfelt cry, "May I be so lucky as to share their portion!"—that is, that of the hasidim. And, recalling that exclamation, I cannot hold back my laughter. Indeed, *Herr Doktor*! How right you are! But how convenient it was for you to utter this exclamation, on your lofty chair at Heidelberg University, far removed from the hasidim and their masses. But what would you say if it really fell to your lot to be among them always? Methinks you would have spoken differently then, a very different call would have issued from your heart, and together with me you would have cried, "May I be so lucky as *not* to share their portion."

Duplicity, two-facedness, the cleft in my soul—whoever has never experienced them cannot possibly imagine their bitterness. Is there any greater sorrow, stronger pain, than the need to constantly strangle one's dearest thoughts, one's most sacred feelings, lest they be detected outwardly, God forbid, and some harm come to one? To constantly see one's most cherished hallowed ideas trampled by others, and to profess happiness, as if in agreement with them?

I constantly have free thoughts, but I am obliged to observe my ancestors' most minute stringencies of observance; I have good taste and love beauty, but I am obliged to wear the clothing of the uncivilized: a long silk *kapota* down to my feet, a *shtrayml* of fur tails[68]—that is the "badge of shame" imposed upon us by our enemies for generations, which has become holy to us Jews, enamored of the hand that beats us—with a skullcap beneath it, and other such "ornaments" as well. What would your honor say, were you to come suddenly, not knowing me, and see me standing among the praying congregation, clad in this tawdry finery, swaying and praying, what would you think of me then? Surely you would hold me to be ultra-Orthodox, a devout fanatic. Never would it occur to you that I am different from all around me, and that under this showy trumpery of clothes hides a beautiful soul, dreaming, longing, and pining, just as it would never occur to any of those who know me—with the exception of those of my young friends of like mind—and who consider me to be a *haredi*. And how my heart aches when perchance I hear my praises sung, whether in my presence or otherwise, that I am a God-fearing, perfect person. A terrible thought pierces and gnaws my mind: What is this? What am I? Is it possible that I am naught but a hypocrite, a sham? Am I permitted thus to deceive people?

Thus do I live out my life here, a dark, gloomy life, without a spark of light, without a shadow of hope, all darkness about me. Nevertheless, even in my life here, despite the all-pervading darkness, sometimes a glimmer of light breaks through. At times of leisure, free of my environment and its obligations, I repair to the "left wing" of our home, to my sisters.[69] Then does a new world open up to me. I cast off the dust covering me, distance myself from the filth, from the grime in which I am immersed all day. Some freedom indeed reigns there, in contrast to the chains and shackles in our home, freedom that my sisters have earned "with their sword and with their bow," freedom from that fine company that surrounds me all day. There I meet young friends and acquaintances, and we read and speak of life and literature. In brief, there I live my real life, there I remove the mask from my face, to be what I really am, without dissembling. Although even there the shadows overcome the light—as you already know well of this "life" from my sister's letters—and even there I cannot breathe freely, even there the air is full of sorrow and grief. But in comparison with my own "life" in my room, that too may be called a life. So here there is still a gleam of light illuminating me within the darkness.

But what a terrible thought, to think now where I am going. To the blessed town of Belz in Galicia! For I have to settle there, in their "harem." I underline that word to emphasize my intention, that I am being married by coercion, against my will. For me [to marry] a woman from there—my gloomy life here, with all its black darkness, will pale in comparison with the life awaiting me there. First, I am marrying a woman from there, a woman who has been destined these six years to be my bride, but even so I have never ever had sight of her face and I have not the slightest idea of her, her beauty, intelligence, and understanding. And with such a maid, of whom I know absolutely nothing, I am now being led to the bridal canopy!

Can your honor, a cultured person, living in the twentieth century, possibly understand and conceive of this? When I think on it—and when do I not?!—I am seized by trembling. I am entering a new period in my life, the most important period in human life—and whom have they given me as a life partner, to be my wife, with whom I am to spend the rest of my life, sharing my happiness and my sorrow, my joy and my woes? I know not. One thing only do I know, that there is a certain town somewhere, Belz by name, and there lives a young maiden, as unattractive as can be—this I have indeed been told by people who have been sent to see her visage—and she is "my bride." What is the sign that she is "my bride"—that I know not, but that is what people are saying, and there is the proof, for now I am being led to the bridal canopy with her. What is the nature of this maid? That I know not, and neither do all those who have gone there to see her and have tried to investigate her character. For how much can be determined from fragmentary information, acquired in a few days, and moreover by a stranger, who knows not what to say and what to ask, and I cannot extract from him a proper sentence about her? Having now to approach her to make her my life's partner, I am relying on accident. Perhaps accident has indeed ordained a suitable match for me. And it is equally possible, very easily, that it has matched me with my very opposite. At best, however, what might I expect of a "Belzian" maid? What spiritual development could she have had in such an environment, in such an atmosphere, where such a simple, innocent thing as learning to write is a serious offense in a young maid, at most a luxury. "A woman's wisdom is confined to the spindle" . . . ![70] What hope is there for me, why should I delay any longer? The greatest fortune would be if, at least, she were not already entirely imbued with the usual Belzian ideas and desires, if her heart were still lively and open to other human ideas and desires as well. And if the saplings of humanism that I shall try to plant in the soil of her heart, bear fruit and do not find arid ground—that would be my greatest happiness.

That is one of the "good" things awaiting me in the near future. That is the central point, and if the center is naught, what could the circumference be?—even less than naught.

And the circumference, the environment, what of it? If ten measures of extreme religious fanaticism, ignorance, and vulgar stupidity came down to the world, Belz has received nine, and the rest of the world one. If your honor should wonder at my nonmodern dress, being so remote from this ancient world, he will marvel a thousandfold at the Belz customs and will despair of even understanding them with his mind. Let me tell you now a little of their capers, a drop in the sea of their deplorable ways of life, for my feeble pen is powerless to provide a faithful, complete picture of their doings. That would be a task worthy of a witty belletrist's pen. May your honor gaze and marvel, hear and not understand, and you will think that I am leading you far, far away, from the cultured lands of Europe to the uncivilized lands of China or India, for there, only there, can one view other pictures like these.

In addition to the stringent and precautionary measures that surround every Jew, Belzers have adopted further such restrictions that have no sanctified source, nor have they issued from the legal decisors, they originate solely in "ancestral" customs. Left and right, upon one's every step, one finds and stumbles over a custom established by "the ancestors." So uncivilized, so obstructing and disturbing the free course of life are these customs, that one cannot imagine how a person—even a person like myself, accustomed to strange life practices and precautions, but who thinks always of one way of life—could survive in such a stifling atmosphere, in which every move, every wink of an eyelid, every innocent thought, any action, the most proper action imaginable, in line with Jewish law, will be met with ponderous objections, on account of "custom."

Here are some examples. The bridegroom on his wedding day must shave his head with a razor. And the bride? That goes without saying, for all women there have shaved heads, for that has been decreed by custom.[71] And a wig—which in our provinces is the custom even of saints and pious people, and most women go about with their hair uncovered—is considered there a greater abomination than swine. In all the town of Belz you will not find even one woman wearing a wig on her head, but all wrap their shaved heads in a kerchief.[72] And on Sabbath days and festivals they wear a kind of old-fashioned veil, which, if I am not mistaken, is the very veil with which the Matriarch Rebecca covered her head. [The veil] must conform to this fashion, it cannot be otherwise, and all according to the custom and decree ordained by the ancestors of my future father-in-law,[73] the zaddikim, the leaders of the town and its environs; and he—my future father-in-law-being their representative, enforces them, and by virtue of his tremendous influence not one tittle of them may be omitted.

Picture, your honor, if you will, the following scene. Imagine that myself and my "intended" are being pictured. A young couple—"He" has his head shaven, and "She" has her head shaven. He wears a *shtrayml* and a skullcap on his head, with all the other finery—as you will see later—and she wears a magnificent scarf on her head with all other female trumpery from Chmielnitzki's times.

A nice caricature! Good candidates for a museum of antiquities! Were it not that this matter concerns myself, I could laugh most heartily at the sight of such a picture. Unfortunately, however, the matter is so close to me, so relevant to me, that it may arouse in me not laughter but only tears, tears over my ill fortune, the fortune that fate has declared for me in this inhospitable land.

Trousers are now fashionable, but anything fashionable is strictly forbidden there. So the men wear long *kapotas* down to the ground, and the *kapotas* must be sewn from a single piece of fabric, and they may be from any kind of fabric, from silk to choice linen. But not a woolen weave, which is forbidden for fear of *sha'atnez.*[74] And under that long uniform they wear their long winter underwear visibly, white as a "pavement of sapphire."[75] And their sidelocks are long, O how long—down to the navel and more, for that is an immutable decree: "It is forbidden to cut the sidelocks of the head and to shorten them, from day of birth till day of death!" And those long, thick, sidelocks, spread over the face and swaying here and there, wherever the wind blows them, and they seem as if attached by glue to the white, shaven, head—and why is that?—To mar man's handsome visage, "God's image." And in this beautiful costume one has to go about all day, not only during prayers, girded with a sash.[76]

No lamp will you find in their houses, only candlelight to illuminate the dark. Now in this generation of ours, a generation of great technical discoveries, a generation served by electricity in daily life, when the human spirit, unsated, is blazing new trails and new paths, striving hard to find new inventions. In this generation, at this time, there is a dark corner, in the heart of Europe, where even a simple kerosene lamp is not yet used, even one that might today be considered an antique, and the dark light of a tallow candle satisfies them.[77] O, people who live in darkness! Beautiful furniture and household utensils are a luxury. A mirror is considered as leaven [on Passover], to be banished from the house. Galoshes over the shoes are an abomination—"Everything that walks on four is an abomination," an explicit proof from the Bible![78] A newspaper, even in Hebrew, or in Yiddish—not to speak of a volume of the new literature—is condemned to be removed and banished.

Those are some of the uncivilized customs that prevail there, a few small details, which your honor will be able to put together and thus to conceive a full, accurate idea of all their ways of life there. And these customs are supervised by my future father-in-law, the Grand Inquisitor,[79] who watches over the slightest move of the members of his family, his town, and his hasidim in general. And woe to any person who dares to infringe even one of all these "customs," who deliberately disregards one of them. He will be pursued and beaten with cruel wrath, with all their burning, wild, fanaticism. They have one refrain: "Eat and drink, study and sleep," for that is the whole man!

They are far from the world and from life. The voice of the sun's orb, traversing the heavens and announcing that time is passing and will not stand still, that the times are changing and with them man too—they hear not that voice. They are frozen, fossilized, standing constantly on the same level as our ancestors in Poland three hundred years ago. And if they have developed, if they have taken a step forward and gone farther than their ancestors, they have done so only in the sense that they have heaped more restrictions on their ancestors' restrictions and added stupidity to their stupidity. That is the blessed Belz, such is its visage, in miniature. In that Belz, in that locality, am I to settle now.

And if all the happy things in store for me there were not enough, my father-in-law-to-be is a strong, hard man, one who likes everything to proceed according to his will, strict, intimidating all those around him, à la Stolin—your honor is surely acquainted with the picture of Stolin through my sister.[80] I shall have to submit to him and bow to his authority, suppressing my will in favor of his. And I am so enamored of freedom—I do not speak anymore of freedom in its broad sense, but at the very least freedom for myself, in my innermost soul, not that another person should trample my soul with his coarse sandals—I am so unable to relent, to submit, to bow to authority! Those are my great prospects for the nearest future. Even now I drown in mud up to my neck, and now I am being dragged to drown entirely in mire, in a pool of sewage. Indeed, a terrible idea, and the reality is seven times worse!

I know that, upon reading this confessional letter of mine, your honor will think of many questions that you will labor to solve, and first and foremost, one central question that pervades the whole letter: "If you are so remote from and abominate the life that you live; if you so feel and understand how terrible the new life that is awaiting you, if you so understand the depth of its tragedy—who is it, what is it, that forces you to persist in that miserable life? Sever, in one blow, the bond that binds you to it, break out into the great, wide, world, that you so love, for which you so yearn and pine!"

Yes, yes, your honor is absolutely right in asking that question. That is the question I am asked by many of my young friends, who cannot understand my mind, to whom my psychology is foreign, who only see the terrors of my outer life. They, not knowing my mind, ask me such a question; I dismiss them with a brief answer that says nothing, and they retreat. But before your honor I shall bare my soul, explaining the obvious truth to you: a sacrifice am I, a sacrifice on my mother's altar.

As difficult as it is for me to sever the thread of my life, as helpless as I am in that respect, nothing would hold me back, nothing would withstand my burning passion, the fire of my aching soul, and I would indeed have taken such a step. With my last remaining strength I would cast off these shackles, abandon my home, my family, my place of birth, all the habits I have accumulated since my youth, and travel to a big city, to study there, complete my education, to live another life. I would reconcile myself indifferently to poverty, sorrow, and suffering. I would accept everything in love, provided only that I could save my soul. Nothing would prevent me—save just one hidden power in my soul which is stronger than all these combined, which holds me back with tremendous force and will not loosen its grip—the power of compassion. This feeling, which I have to a high degree, is what will not allow me to carry out my plan—my compassion for my beloved mother.

This wretched soul, who has had nothing in her life, all of whose life is one terrible tragedy, and I, I alone, am her only hope, her heart's desire, I am her comforting salve. My sisters have never given her much pleasure, only in me does she put her trust; I am her sole support in her life. So how could I bear to see the evil that would befall my mother, how could I, with my own hands, shatter her only hope and cause her such overpowering disappointment, such great sorrow and grief? I shall not investigate the question logically, whether that is how things must indeed be, if I must indeed abandon my future world, which is still beyond my reach, for her world which is already old and withered, for her life which is already behind her.

I shall not investigate—because I cannot investigate. Where emotion reigns, there is no logic; everything is molded by instinct. That is why I have suffered in silence till now, and that is what now forces me to take this new step of marrying into Belz and settling there. Why do I have to settle there, of all places? Why can I not live here even after my marriage? For a very simple reason: My parents lack the means to support me, to sustain me and my wife in their home, to supply all our needs. So I have no choice but to live there.

To think of the possibility of leaving there and making my own way, that too I cannot do, for if so there are only two roads open to me: To be a [hasidic] rebbe, or to be a rabbi. The first alternative is of course out of the question. And the second alternative too, apart from the fact that it is not to my liking, could never be realized, because to be a rabbi I would need authorization from my future father-in-law-who by then would be my father-in-law—and if he were opposed, I could of course do nothing to oppose him, for he is stronger and more influential than I, and no community would accept me against his will. But I would never receive such authorization, because he wishes to keep me under his wing for a few years, who knows how many? And even were he to grant me authorization, I would then have to be a "rabbi" according to the Belz style, so what would I gain? Once again the same slavery, the same wretchedness, and the same ugliness.

So I have absolutely nothing to hope for, there is not a single glimmer to light my way, the way of my future, only darkness, awful darkness, profound gloom await me. And when I throw myself into the waves, the angry, flowing, current of life, where shall they carry me as they flow? I know not. I hope that at long last the waves may bring me to some shore, for if not for that hope, how terrible life would be! I hope that this Belz will be no more than a way station, a stopover on the way to a more beautiful, better life, to that life that I so desire and yearn for! Indeed a difficult stopover, but nevertheless only a stopover. One cannot reach paradise without first passing through the departments of hell.

Belz as a way station—how is that to be? Listen and I shall tell you. As long as I am here under my mother's authority I can do nothing. I stress, always *my mother*, not my father, for my father is cold-tempered and will not feel such pain. But my mother—she is a warm, feeling, person, and I must take her into consideration. Were I to take such a step as I intend to take—to depart from here, from her, before my wedding, she would be burdened with all the responsibility; all the "What will people say?"—the questions she fears so much—would fall upon her. The noise, the public commotion, would be too much. Here I was, and all of a sudden—I am gone. The embarrassment, the uproar, the questions all around, from all the townspeople, all our acquaintances, the talk, the gibes, the wagging of heads, how shall she bear all these? And besides, that step would be final proof that I am dissolute, a longstanding unbeliever, and that in vain I have misled all those who know me, letting them think me faithful to God and to His holy ones. Why else should I have taken such a sudden step? This proof, which would be public knowledge, would be difficult for my mother, most difficult. So everything would be lost, everything: "This one too, my son, in whom I have put all my hope, he too has become a disappointment, and so what is left for me in my life?"

So I cannot possibly take that step from here, it being so abrupt and so public. Not so if that were done from there, from Belz. My mother herself knows and senses the great difference between myself and Belz, and however much she does not know me in all respects, she knows me more than others and is therefore aware, how different I am from Belz and its life. Moreover, she is worried lest I dislike my bride, since she is not very good-looking and may also not be to my taste in other respects, and so think many other townspeople as well. She is therefore apprehensive and worried, lest I be unable to reconcile myself with Belz, and go to war there; and she, instinctively, realizes the possible results of that war . . . And more than once she has told me of her fears. Nevertheless, she comforts herself, in the hope that perhaps that will not happen, and I will accustom myself to Belz ways; and perhaps I shall like my bride and things will turn out for the best. But all the same, she fears the other side, the other aspect, and that step would not come to her as a surprise. And any pain, strong as it might be, would therefore not be new, it would be expected and foreseen, and so less acute, not so painful and stinging. The public aspect would also not be so obvious here [in Shpikov], for only an echo of that step would be heard here. Only fragmentary information, wrapped in secrecy, would reach our town here, insufficient to arouse such a commotion. And moreover people might find some justification for my action—"Who knows what forced him to take such a step, surely he could no longer bear it." And the shame would not be so great, and above all, responsibility for my action would not rest with her, my mother, because I shall already have left her home. Therefore, her pain would not be so unbearable, and that would make it easier for me to take the step.

So in the final analysis, every cloud has a silver lining. Perhaps through Belz I shall be able more easily to achieve my goal, my long-standing heart's desire, and perhaps, taking the step from there, I shall have better means at my disposal.

Such is the situation now, that is what I am doing and thus I think. Darkness surrounds me, but one spark glimmers in the darkness. I intend to fan the spark and ignite a great fire that will light my way in life; but possibly, before I am able to make it into a flame, it will flicker and die out completely, and I shall remain standing alone, solitary in the darkness. I fear that possibility, but find strength in the hope that it will not go out, that I will be able to make it into a great light, an illuminating light.

I hope, for without hope what worth is life? And out of that hope I am now about to take the first, difficult, step, of marrying into Belz.

That is my confession, the confession of my life, withered and faded before its time, the confession of my tortured, afflicted soul, the confession of my squandered talents. I began to write it several weeks ago, but could not complete it until now. The harsh conditions of my life have brought me to this. I have been writing it for a very long time, one quarter-hour each day, and upon beginning to write I have been forced to stop midway, obliged to hide the letter for fear it might be seen by someone. Your honor will realize from my unclear writing in what state it has been written. A word here, a word there, page by page, until the letter was complete. Were I able to write my letter with the requisite peace of mind, it would be different, more solid and coherent, from beginning to end, one continuous narrative. But since I have not been able to do so, it consists only of disconnected ideas, fragments,

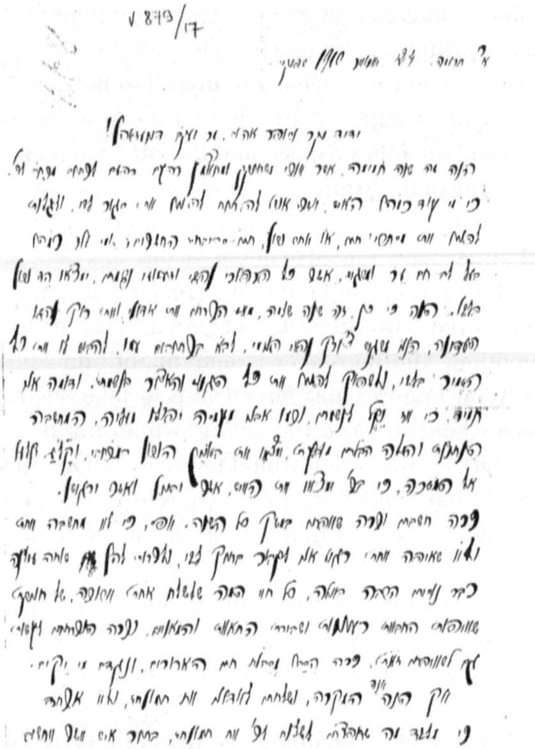

FIG. 7.3. The first and last pages of the confession

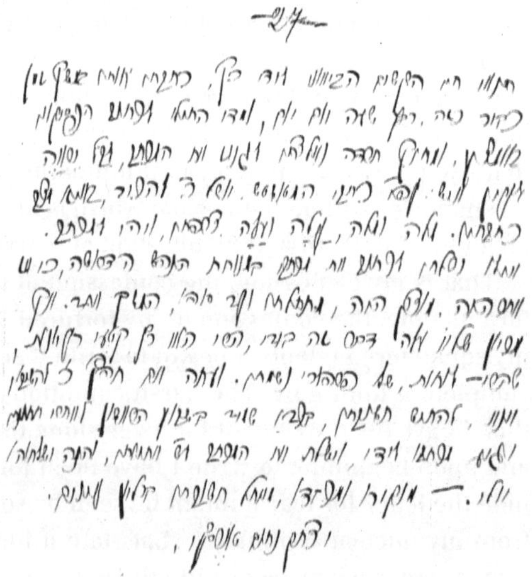

convulsions of my mind. And now, if your honor should wish to reply, I beg you to reply quickly, to reach me immediately during the first week after my wedding. You may send the letter care of my sisters, and they will send it on to me.

With admiration and respect, hoping against hope for your answer,

Yitshak Nahum Twersky

Notes

Preface to the English-language Edition

1. Yaacov Shavit, "The Detective as an Optimist Historian," *Zmanim* 16 (1984): 76 (Hebrew).

2. L.Z., "Mipi hashemu'ah," *Reshumot* 1 (1918): 414. For reports on the event itself, in which the case of Bernyu of Leova was evidently incorporated, see Abraham Joshua Heschel, *Kotzk: The Struggle for Integrity*, vol. 2 (Tel Aviv: Hamenorah, 1973), 564–73 (Yiddish); Morris M. Faierstein, "The Friday Night Incident in Kotsk: History of a Legend," *Journal of Jewish Studies* 34 (1983): 179–89.

3. Assaf, "The Clash over *Or Ha-Hayyim*."

Introduction

1. Sadan, "Ro'eh vetson marito," 7–8. Elsewhere, Sadan notes that Martin Buber drew his attention to this phenomenon (*Orhot ushvilim*, 28).

2. Sadan, *Orhot ushvilim*, 28–29. See also ibid., 313–14; Sadan, *Hadashim gam yeshanim*, 3:201; Twersky, "Ha'otsar shebeShpikov."

Chapter 1. "Lies My Teacher Told Me": Hasidic History as a Battlefield

1. *Beit Rabbi*, 1:5. A similar anecdote is related in the name of Rabbi Avraham Shimon Halevi Horowitz of Zelichov, a unique hasidic figure who died during the Holocaust and whose writings have only recently been published: "The students began to ask about the rift between . . . the great Kohen of Kalisk . . . and the holy rabbi of Lyady . . . and he refused to expand on it. He only said jokingly, 'What do these matters have to do with our work . . . *of these and similar matters, nothing more should be said.* But we must understand that all were beloved, all were mighty, and all were holy'" (*Neharei esh*, "Likutei diburim," 217, no. 167).

2. New York: New Press. See also James W. Loewen, *Lies across America: What Our Historic Sites Get Wrong* (New York: Touchstone, 1999).

3. Assaf, *Regal Way*, 37–40 (unless otherwise specified, citations to this work are to the English edition).

4. See chapter 2, note 3, where a long list of descendants of zaddikim and rabbis who embarrassed their parents is provided.

5. *Shivhei haBesht*, 135.

6. Liberman, *Ohel Rahel*, 1:1. In a 1997 letter, Liberman acknowledged his use of sharp language but claimed that "the times required it." He noted in addition: "Habad members here [in Brooklyn] begged me on several occasions to allow them to publish these four essays in a special booklet titled 'How Hasidism Is Studied in Israel' . . . and I refused because I feared that such a booklet would give me a quarrelsome reputation." For this letter, along with other examples of this polemic, see Assaf and Liebes, *The Latest Phase*, 82–90.

7. Including Joseph Weiss himself, who admitted in a letter to Gershom Scholem in 1953: "The trouble is, of course, that he is correct *at least* regarding the Baal Shem, that this version appears in *Yalkut shimoni*, of which I was unaware." Nonetheless, Weiss cynically attacked his critic: "And I regret greatly having brought shame upon Scholem's Bet Midrash. But it is not Reb Haim's aim to correct what I do not know concerning *Yalkut shimoni* but to announce 'by all rights this topic should be handled by the experts: namely, the hasidim themselves.' If so, this bottom line also requires that those dealing with Mexican culture should also be the experts, namely, the Aztecs; with Greek culture, the ancient Greeks; etc." See Assaf and Liebes, *The Latest Phase*, 88–89.

8. For example, Rapoport-Albert, "Hagiography"; Bartal, "Shimon ha-Kofer"; Israel Bartal, "True Knowledge and Wisdom: On Orthodox Historiography," *Studies in Contemporary Jewry* 10 (1994): 178–92; Assaf, *Regal Way*, 8–28; Assaf, "*Yesod ha-Ma'ala*"; Etkes, *Gaon of Vilna*, 96–150; Karlinsky, *Counter History*; among many others.

9. *Teshuva hanora'ah vehanifla'ah . . . odot havurata kadishta hanikra'im beshem hasidim* (Bnei Brak: Mekhon Mareh Yehezkel, 1991). Rabbi Panet's epistle appeared in his responsa collection, *Mar'eh Yehezkel* (Sighet, 1875), no. 104.

10. *Kovets mishkenot Yaakov* 4 (Kislev 1995): 121.

11. *Other People's Money and How the Bankers Use It*, quoted in http://colorsinsidemyworld.wordpress.com/2007/06/04/sunlight-is-said-to-be-the-best-of-disinfectants/ (accessed 17 November 2009).

12. This book is devoted to hasidic figures, but there are many examples of individuals from prominent Lithuanian mitnagedic families made to disappear from the collective memory of the world of Lithuanian yeshivas because they grazed in foreign pastures, as the saying has it. For some examples, see Assaf, *Ne'ehaz basevakh*, 24–25, note 15.

13. Hayyim Elazar Shapira, *Divrei torah tinyanah* (Munkatsh: Kalisch, 1929), 11a, no. 24. The "above-mentioned book" is Shlomo Zalman Breitstein's *Sihot hayyim* (Piotrkov: 1914).

14. On this term, see Kimmy Caplan, *Internal Popular Discourse in Israeli Haredi Society* (Jerusalem: Shazar, 2007), 273–74 (Hebrew); and the other works cited in note 8 above.

15. *Nes lehitnoses: Hatsava'ah hakedoshah "hamekorit" . . .* (Jerusalem: Makhon Leheker Tsava'at Rabbenu, 2000), 8–9. Interestingly, this book claims that the refusal of the opposing side to allow the original will to be tested by experts was grounded

in "the twisted argument that no impure secular person should touch the holy will" (14).

16. This was not the first instance of mutual accusations of forging a zaddik's will. The same claim was made regarding the will of the third Lubavitcher rebbe, Tsemah Tsedek, who died in 1866. See chapter 2, note 146.

17. *Amitat pesak beit din: Berur devarim . . .* (Jerusalem: Tevet, 2000), 106–9.

18. There are many *haredi* forums, but the most popular one is "Behadrei haredim." Another site that deserves mention is "Atsor, kan hoshvim" (Halt, we're thinking here). The discussion of the Hebrew edition of this book (http://hydepark.hevre.co.il/topic.asp?topic_id=1948392&forum_id=1364) was up to that time the longest and most accessed in this forum's history. See also chapter 2, note 223. For an interesting article on *haredim* and the Internet, including a comprehensive discussion of the forums on the Hebrew edition of this book, see Rose, "Haharedim veha'internet."

19. For a review of this book, see Neriah Gutel, "'HaGaon' bemivhan haredi-hasidi," *Hatsofeh*, 15 February 2002, 11, 15. For another accusatory review, see Yaakov Perlov, "Al sefer 'HaGaon,'" *Yeshurun* 10 (2002): 831–42, which blames the author of "burrowing and publicly picking at past internecine hatreds" (831). For the raging internal *haredi* polemic sparked by the appearance of the book's second edition (2005), see http://hydepark.hevre.co.il/topic.asp?topic_id=506334&forum_id=1364, accessed 3 November 2009. On Eliach's ideological bias in a different context, see later in this chapter.

20. See Eliach, *HaGaon*, 3:930, 937.

21. Etkes, *Gaon of Vilna*, 150.

22. On the book and the accompanying storm, see, for example, Joseph Berger, "Rabbis Who Were Sages, Not Saints," *The New York Times*, 23 April 2003; Aaron Rakeffet-Rothkoff, "Favoring History over Storytelling: *Making of a Godol*," *Jewish Action*, Summer 2003 (http://www.ou.org/publications/ja/5763/5763summer/MAKINGOF.PDF), accessed 6 October 2009; Marc B. Shapiro, "Of Books and Bans," *The Edah Journal* 3/2 (Elul 5763), http://www.edah.org/backend/coldfusion/search/document.cfm?title=Of%20Books%20and%20Bans&hyperlink=3_2_shapiro.htm&type=JournalArticle&category=Jewish%20Diversity%2FRelating%20to%20the%20Non-Orthodox&authortitle=Dr.&firstname=Marc%20B.&lastname=Shapiro&pubsource=not%20available&authorid=350&pdfattachment=3_2_Shapiro.pdf (accessed 3 November 2009).

23. Unconfirmed rumors reported the burning of copies of the book at the Lakewood Yeshiva, in New Jersey, under the aegis of descendants of the yeshiva's founder Rabbi Aharon Kotler (1892–1962), who deemed the book detrimental to his honored personality.

24. Quoted from the English translation of the ban: http://www.canonist.com/?p=189. *Haredi* extremists banned a second, "improved" edition of this book, issued in 2004 (Jerusalem: PP Publishers). Nathan Kamenetsky, its author, documented the entire affair of the ban on the first edition in a separate book: *Anatomy of a Ban: The Story of the Ban on the Book "Making of a Godol"* (Jerusalem: PP Publishers, 2003).

25. Nosson Slifkin, *The Science of Torah: The Reflection of Torah in the Laws of Science, the Creation of the Universe, and the Development of Life* (Southfield, Mich.: Targum/Feldheim 2001); Slifkin, *Mysterious Creatures: Intriguing Torah Enigmas of Natural and Unnatural History* (Southfield, Mich.: Zoo Torah and Targum, 2003);

Slifkin, *The Camel, the Hare, and the Hyrax: A Study of the Laws of Animals . . . in Light of Modern Zoölogy* (Jerusalem: Zoo Torah and Targum/Feldheim, 2004). A copy of the ban was published in *Yated ne'eman*, supplement, 26 Tevet 2005, 25.

26. See Alex Mindlin, "Religion and Natural History Clash among the Ultra-Orthodox," *The New York Times*, 22 March 2005. For many sources covering the stages of the controversy, see Slifkin's website: http://www.zootorah.com/controversy/controversy.html (accessed 7 October 2009).

27. Indeed, the single copy of this work housed in the National Library of Israel has been cataloged as a rare book.

28. *She'erit yisrael*, 4. See also Assaf, *Regal Way*, 14.

29. See chapter 4, note 64.

30. Assaf, *Regal Way*, 13–15.

31. For a general treatment of this phenomenon, see Assaf, "*Yesod ha-Ma'ala*," 61–63. A more recent example is Yitshak Alfasi's *Me'orot me'olam hatorah* (Jerusalem: Shem, 2005). One of the more prolific writers in the fields of the history of Hasidism and the rabbinate, Alfasi consistently uses various means to avoid mention of or to conceal negative phenomena. Thus, he will never provide information on descendants of the personality in question who have strayed from the ancestral path. Regarding the great-grandchildren of the Hafetz Hayyim, who abandoned the world of Judaism, he writes: "Many of the Hafetz Hayyim's descendants survived, but I will not go into detail, as not all are worthy of being mentioned by name and 'it is the glory of God to conceal a matter'" (164).

32. Mondshine, *Migdal oz*, 595; *Igrot kodesh*, 1:351; Yehoshua Mondshine, "Authenticity of Hasidic Letters (Part Two)," *Cathedra* 64 (1992): 89–90 (Hebrew).

33. For an instructive analysis of the use of censorship, forgery, and suppression in the Soviet Union, see David King, *The Commissar Vanishes: The Falsification of Photographs and Art in Stalin's Russia* (New York: Owl, 1999).

34. For details, see chapter 3. For a bibliographical discussion of the early editions of this book, see Assaf, *Ne'ehaz basevakh*, 37 note 39.

35. *Eser orot*, 72, no. 22.

36. Wunder, *Meorei Galicia*, vol. 4, introduction.

37. Ibid., 2:448, 5:164.

38. For example, "During the 1869 storm he signed for Rabbi Hayyim." See ibid., 2:367, 743; 3:180, 617, 976.

39. Ibid., 1:328–29. In his introduction to volume 5, Wunder, who relies heavily on oral family traditions, attacks the "phenomenon of implanting false data in order to glorify the family," and hints at the pressures he faced: "There are those unable to accept what is printed in the book and seek to reinvestigate each and every detail recorded there. Some promised heaven and earth if I would insert someone they favored even if objectively he did not belong there" (ibid., 5:7).

40. Yosef David Weisberg, *Rabenu hakadosh miTsanz*, 3 vols. (Jerusalem: Keset Shelomoh, 1976–80), 1:7 (translation from Assaf, *Regal Way*, 14).

41. Jacob Katz, "Kavim lidmuto shel HaHatam Sofer," in *Halakhah and Kabbalah*, 355.

42. Moshe Hanokh Greenfield, *Ateret hayyim* (New York: Nehmad, 1980), 2:17. A

similar phenomenon is revealed in Aharon Surasky, *Yesod hama'alah* (Bnei Brak: Zivtanim, 1991). All the letters relating to the dispute between Avraham of Kalisk and Shneur Zalman of Lyady were omitted in this collection of nineteenth-century hasidic letters from Eretz-Israel. See Assaf, "*Yesod ha-Ma'ala.*"

43. Assaf, *Regal Way*, 198–202. Further evidence of these family ties comes from an 1847 letter sent by the zaddik Avraham Twersky of Trisk to Levinsohn, in which he respectfully refers to him as "my relative" (David Ber Nathanson, *Sefer hazikhronot . . . divrei yemei . . . Yitshak Ber Levinsohn* [Warsaw, 1876], 81). Avraham of Trisk's father, Rabbi Mordekhai of Chernobyl, was Yisrael of Ruzhin's uncle.

44. In contrast, Nahman of Bratslav's disciples were forced to develop various explanations for their rebbe's connections with the Uman maskilim. See Piekarz, *Braslav Hasidism*, 21–55.

45. Eliach, *HaGaon*, 3:1305–6. Eliach's sole supporting evidence ostensibly comes from Shmuel Yaakov Yatzkan, *Rabenu Eliyahu miVilna: Hayyav, zemano, korotav umifalav* (Warsaw, 1900), 119. Yatzkan, the editor of the daily *Heynt*, cites this as nonsense, however. According to him, Rabbi Abele's approbation was indeed a wondrous thing, on which "the Lithuanian elders heaped legends," each with its own bent. Note that this approbation also appears in maskilic folklore. The approbation was not printed in subsequent editions of *Te'udah beyisrael*, and was only mentioned by the editor David Ber Nathanson. He related that, after the book's publication, the Vilna notables asked Rabbi Abele: "What is this book? What is its nature? And what are its faults?" Rabbi Abele replied: "Its only fault is that it was not composed by our great rabbi, Rabbi Eliyahu Hehasid of Vilna."

46. His approbation appeared in the book *Gelot ha'erets hahadasha al yedei Kristof Kolumbus* (Vilna and Grodno, 1823), the Hebrew translation of Joachim Campe's book on the discovery of the New World by the Vilna maskil Mordekhai Aharon Guenzburg. Another approbation was appended to *Kneh hokhmah* (Vilna and Grodno, 1829), a work on algebra by Nissan ben Avraham of Deliatitz, and another to *Mosdei hokhmah* (Vilna and Grodno, 1834) by the well-known maskil Hayyim Selig Slonimski (Hazas), which also treated algebra and mathematics (Rabbi Abele appeared on the subscribers' list to this book, alongside other well-known maskilim such as Adam Hakohen and Levinsohn). See Yehoshua Mondshine's remarks in *Kerem Chabad* 155, where he makes polemical use of this fact to show that it was the mitnagedim and not the hasidim who were guilty of wasting time better devoted to Torah study.

47. The claim that Dubno's separation from Mendelssohn was grounded in his reservations regarding lax religious observance by Mendelssohn's students is based on a 1789 letter from Dubno to Wolf Heidenheim. Of doubtful authenticity, it has been argued that this letter was forged for internal Orthodox consumption. For the view that "fear of heaven" had nothing to do with their parting, see Moshe Samet, *Chapters in the History of Orthodoxy* (Jerusalem: Dinur, 2005), 70 (Hebrew); and Mondshine, "Haskamot shtukot," 151.

48. Fuenn, *Kiryah ne'emanah*, 159–60, 197–98. For the complete version, see Shmuel Yosef Fuenn, *Safah lane'emanim* (Vilna, 1881), 135–37.

49. With respect to the historiographical trends regarding the image of the Gaon as exhibiting a favorable attitude toward Haskalah, see Etkes, *Gaon of Vilna*, 37–72.

50. Mondshine, "Haskamot shtukot," 154.

51. Eliach, *HaGaon*, 3:1300, 1305. See also a series of articles by David Kamenetsky, "Haskamoteyhem shel gedolei harabanim lahumashim shel Rabbi Shlomo miDubno," *Jeshurun* 8 (2001): 718–59; 9 (2001): 711–55; 10 (2002): 751–75.

52. Eliach, *HaGaon*, 3:1305. Actually, Fuenn, who did not seek to publish all the approbations, did refer specifically to Rabbi Shmuel's approbation in his *Kiryah ne'emanah*, 131.

53. Eliach, *HaGaon*, 3:1297. See also his apologetic comment: "Until recently, only a limited amount of material was available regarding the approbations to Dubno's work . . . The only source for the approbations . . . was Fuenn's books. It is then clear why the approbation of Rabbi Hayyim of Volozhin was not added to the list . . . when the sole source speaking of it (which does not cite it in full) is that of a prejudiced maskil, and I have not yet found time to undertake an independent study" (1305, note). Needless to say, he makes no mention of Mondshine, "Haskamot shtukot."

54. *Olam hahasidut* 88, Shevat 2002, 52.

55. Krauss, *Birkhot hahayyim*, 22–23.

56. Ibid., 32. Krauss also treats other maskilim, such as Yehuda Leib Ben-Zeev, David Friedlaender, Yitshak Euchel, and Zvi Hirsch Levin (38–42).

57. Shaul Rosenberg, *Responsa hemdat Shaul* (Jerusalem: Hamaarav, 1969), no. 19, p. 39.

58. Sar Shalom Marzel, *Kuntres mashiv haru'ah . . . lekayem et haminhag hakadum lomar mashiv haru'ah umorid hagashem bekamats tahat hagimel* (Jerusalem: privately printed, 1981), 10–11 (emphasis in original).

59. For additional bibliographical references, see Assaf, *Ne'ehaz basevakh*, 47 note 63.

60. Another maskil who underwent "conversion" was Menahem Mendel Lefin (1749–1826). Also from Satanow, his book *Heshbon hanefesh* (Vilna, 1844) was studied in the Lithuanian *musar* movement yeshivot. The many *haredi* editions of this book present the author as a God-fearing Jew. See Etkes, *Salanter*, 123–34; Yaakov Gershon Weiss, *Kuntres bo'u heshbon* (Jerusalem: Hamosad Leidud Limud Hatorah, 1998), which contains a detailed introduction praising the book and its author. Weiss treats, and unhesitatingly relies on, academic research in the introduction.

61. Yehoshua Mondshine, *Kerem Chabad*, 221. This "confession" was omitted from an abridged version of this article that appeared in Assaf, *Zaddik and Devotees*, 297–331.

62. Etkes, *Gaon of Vilna*, 138.

63. An anecdote regarding the Habad bibliographer Rabbi Haim Liberman highlights the dialectical framework in which the hasidic researcher who also attempts to be a critical historian functions. It is well known that the sixth Habad rebbe, Yosef Yitshak Schneersohn, was among the leading proponents for the authenticity of the "Kherson genizah" documents, whose status as a forgery has been decisively proven and is now axiomatic in the study of Hasidism (see Assaf, *Regal Way* [Hebrew ed.], 202–3). Liberman, who was the rebbe's secretary, did not like to discuss these letters. But once, when asked, "Rabbi Haim told them that he had known the forger well, and that he was in need of money and forged the letters in order to make a living. One of those present inquired that if that was so, how did the rebbe Yosef Yitshak of blessed

memory say that these letters were the word of the living God? Rabbi Haim did not miss a beat and replied: 'He who doubts his rebbe is like one who doubts the Shekhinah. I have no questions with respect to the rebbe on this score. *Although I know the letters are forged, having known the forger personally, but who or what am I, a fly without wings, to say why the rebbe did so and said what he said.* The rebbe devoted himself to God every single moment. *If he said this, then that is a sign that it had to be said*, and that these are the words of the living God'" (*Sefer hazikaron leRabbi Moshe Lipshitz*, edited by Rafael Rosenbaum [New York: Lipshitz, 1996], 140).

64. See Kimmy Caplan, "'Absolutely Intellectually Honest': A Case Study of American Jewish Modern Orthodox Historiography," in *Creation and Re-Creation in Jewish Thought: Festschrift in Honor of Joseph Dan*, edited by Rachel Elior and Peter Schäfer (Tübingen: Mohr Siebeck, 2005), 339–61. This article describes historiographical dilemmas and similar phenomena in the American modern Orthodox context.

Chapter 2. Apostate or Saint? In the Footsteps of Moshe, the Son of Rabbi Shneur Zalman of Lyady

1. Sadan, *Ke'arat tsimukim*, 116. Ahron Marcus (Verus) also pointed out the similarity between Bernyu and Moshe (*Der Chassidismus*, 374).

2. On Bernyu, see Yitshak Ewen, *Mahloket Tsanz veSadigura: Kol korot hapulmus mithilato ve'ad sofo . . .* (New York: Rosenberg, 1916); Litvin, "A drame in rebn's hoyf," in *Yudishe neshomes* 6; Horodezky, *Hahasidut vehahasidim*, 3:124–54; Shaul M. Ginsburg, *Ketavim historiyyim* (Tel Aviv: Dvir, 1944), 74–95; Raphael, *Hasidut vehasidim*, 248–60; Assaf, *Regal Way*, 13–15 [English ed.], 458–59 [Hebrew ed.].

3. One was Kalman Kalonymus, the son of Hayyim Tyrer of Chernovsty and son-in-law of Avraham Yehoshua Heschel of Apta, who became a heretic. Kalman Kalonymus reportedly frequented inns, played cards, and ate nonkosher food; he was eventually forced to divorce his wife, Yokheved. Yosef Perl claimed that he incorporated his personality in *Megaleh temirin* (*Hashahar* 1 [1869]: 9). For a detailed bibliography, see Assaf, *Ne'ehaz basevakh*, 52 note 2. Another was Yehezkel, a disciple of the Seer of Lublin and the son of the Maggid Aryeh Leib of Kuzmir, who converted to Christianity and became a scholar and a censor, and called himself Stanislaus Hoga. On Hoga, see Assaf, *Ne'ehaz basevakh*, 52 note 3. Yet another was Yaakov Yokl Horowitz (1773–1832), the brother of the zaddik Naftali of Ropshits, who became a maskil. Regarding Yaakov Yokl, hasidic sources relate that "while in Berdichev he was exposed to the Berlin circle when students of Mendelssohn came there and he followed them, and his father regretted this greatly" (*Ohel Naftali*, 72, no. 227). There was also Meir, the son of the Hungarian zaddik Yitshak Ayzik of Kalov, of whom it was said that after his father's death, "he followed an evil path. And none of the reproaches of those close to his holy father availed" (*Eser tsahtsahot*, 73, no. 21; Tuvia L. Szilágyi-Windt, *Hatsadik miKalov ukehilato* [Tel Aviv: Neographika, 1975], 40). And there were many others like them.

4. Stories regarding repentance by the figures mentioned here were also current: Of Kalman Kalonymus, it was said that his father did not break off relations with him

even when he left the path. He later "repented" and moved to Safed like his father, "where he was as one of the great zaddikim" (Barukh Yashar [Schlichter], *Beit Komarno* [Jerusalem: Ha'ivri, 1965], 17). On Yehezkel of Kuzmir, see Zederbaum, *Keter kehunah*, 124; on Bernyu of Leova, see Marcus, *Hahasidut* (1954), 264; on Yaakov Yokl Horowitz, see Wunder, *Meorei Galicia*, 2:235–36; and on Meir of Kalov, see *Eser tsahtsahot*, 73, no. 21.

5. For a rare example of the dual life of a zaddik's son who despised the hasidic court and longed for freedom (though he dared not fulfill his longings), see the final chapter of this book. On the pressures experienced by rabbi's sons in the United States, see Irving N. Levitz, "Children of Rabbis," *Tradition* 23/2 (1988): 76–87.

6. Yehuda Leib Levin [Yehalel], *Zikhronot vehegyonot* (Jerusalem: Bialik Institute, 1968), 45–46; Sadan, *Hadashim gam yeshanim*, 1:204–6. Memoir literature is replete with many such descriptions. See, for example, Kotik, *Journey*, 68–69, 364–72.

7. *Hamagid*, 15 February 1865, 49; 15 March 1865, 83. Translation from Etkes, *Salanter*, 314–15. On this episode, and that of the grandson of Yisrael Salanter, who also studied in Germany and did not observe kashrut strictly, see the penetrating insights of Dov Katz, *The Musar Movement: Its History, Leading Personalities and Doctrines*, translated by Leonard Oschry (Tel Aviv: Orly, 1975), 1:313–15; Etkes, *Salanter*, 314–16. On Lipkin, see *Hatsefirah*, 17 March 1875, 87–88; *Heasif* 1 (1885), "Otsar hasifrut," 259–62.

8. All of these cases are described by Remba, *Banim akhlu boser*, 75–226. See also Katz, *Zikhronot*, 38, 182–83. I mention but a few of the many converts, such as the daughter of Shmuel Yosef Fuenn, the editor of *Hakarmel* and a well-known representative of Vilna Haskalah, or the descendants of Alexander Zederbaum, the editor of *Hamelits*, including his grandson Julius Martov, leader of the Russian Mensheviks. For further details, see Assaf, *Ne'ehaz basevakh*, 55 note 13.

9. Perets Hirschbein, *Bemahalakh hahayyim: Pirkei 1900–1910* (Tel Aviv: Sifriat Poalim, 1971), 94–95; see also Remba, *Banim akhlu boser*, 98–123.

10. Thus, four of Moses Mendelssohn's five children converted (but only after their father's death!). See Michael A. Meyer, *The Origins of the Modern Jew: Jewish Identity and European Culture in Germany, 1749–1824* (Detroit, Mich.: Wayne State University Press, 1967), 85–114. Although his sons did not see conversion as a betrayal of their father's path, for outside observers it symbolized the failure of the Berlin Haskalah. On the fierce debate between Avraham Ber Gottlober and Perets Smolenskin regarding the implications of the conversion of Mendelssohn's students and children, see below.

11. Many cases are detailed in Assaf, *Ne'ehaz basevakh*, 56 note 16.

12. Sholem Aleichem, *Tevye the Dairyman and the Railroad Stories*, translated by Hillel Halkin (New York: Schocken, 1987), 78. The story of Chava served as a starting point for Chaeran Freeze's study of the ramifications of conversion for family structure, both for the Jewish family "left behind" and the new Christian one, and for husband-wife and parent-child relationships ("When Chava Left Home: Gender, Conversion, and the Jewish Family in Tsarist Russia," *Polin* 18 [2005]: 153–88).

13. "The Lottery Ticket" also describes a Jewish family sitting *shiva* for a son who converted—in that case, a symbolic *shiva* lasting only an hour. See Sholom Aleichem,

The Old Country, translated by Frances and Julius Butwin (London: Vallentine, Mitchell, 1946), 367. An intriguing manifestation of the misery experienced by the families of converts and their desperate hope for the convert's return was preserved in the custom of the *shmad-tsigl*, in which a burned brick containing the following inscription was placed on the grave of a famous zaddik: "Just as this brick burns, so too should the heart of so-and-so who has moved to an evil culture be turned toward heaven, for good." See Rechtman, *Yidishe etnografye*, 120–22.

14. Aqiva Ben-Ezra, "Jewish Apostates," *Yeda-'Am* 20/47–48 (1980): 73–75 (Hebrew).

15. According to the statistics compiled by German missionaries, 204,540 Jews converted during the nineteenth century, the largest group (74,500) in Russia. See J. de le Roi, "Judentaufen im 19. Jahrhundert, ein statistischer Versuch," *Nathanael: Zeitschrift für die Arbeit der Evangelischen Kirche an Israel* (Berlin), 15/3–4 (1899): 111–13. De le Roi gives a breakdown by the different churches (93–94, 102–7). According to the data of the Holy Synod, in nineteenth-century Russia, 69,400 Jews converted (to which we must add 12,000 Polish Jews who converted to Catholicism, and some 3,100 who converted to Protestantism). See Stanislawski, "Jewish Apostasy in Russia," 190. Even if exaggerated, the numbers suggest that most of the conversions took place in the latter half of the nineteenth century. For a list of Jews baptized in Warsaw from 1804 to 1903, see Teodor Jeske-Choiński, *Neofici Polscy: Materyały historyczne* (Warsaw, 1904). This book sought to unveil "hidden" Jews (mainly descendants of followers of the false messiah Jacob Frank) who had infiltrated noble Polish families. See Todd Endelman, "Jewish Converts in Nineteenth-Century Warsaw: A Quantitative Analysis," *Jewish Social Studies* 4/1 (1997): 28–59.

16. The responsa literature treating the personal status of converts and their family members clearly reflects an understanding of the missionizing aim of Nicholas I's conscription policy; Western European missionary societies in Russia also enjoyed government support. Although not its stated aim, everyone was aware that conversion of the Jews was indeed the conscription legislation's intent. See, for example, Ginsburg, *Historishe verk*, 3:62ff.; Salo W. Baron, *The Russian Jew under Tsars and Soviets* (New York: Macmillan, 1976), 29–31; Michael Stanislawski, *Tsar Nicholas I and the Jews: The Transformation of Jewish Society in Russia, 1825–1855* (Philadelphia: Jewish Publication Society, 1983), 22–25. For a reflection of the problem in memoir literature, see Kotik, *Journey*, 233–36. There are no firm data on the number of cantonists who converted; but contrary to Kotik's estimation, their numbers were large. In Stanislawski's opinion, about half of the seventy thousand Jews forcibly conscripted to Nicholas I's army from 1827 to 1855 converted, including some twenty-five thousand children under the age of eighteen (*Tsar Nicholas I and the Jews*, 25; Stanislawski, "Jewish Apostasy in Russia," 193–94). See the probably exaggerated testimony by the leaders of the Vilna Jewish community in a memorandum to Moses Montefiore (1846): "Of the children taken into the army, the majority converts, leaving their parents, who die before their time, in eternal mourning" (Ginsburg, *Historishe verk*, 2:294).

17. This motivation was not limited to the impoverished—undoubtedly the majority of apostates (Stanislawski, "Jewish Apostasy in Russia," 199–202)—but also existed among the criminal element, whose conversion lightened their sentences (ibid., 195, 197). Stanislawski notes the scholarly emphasis on the intelligentsia and bourgeoisie,

which ignored conversion's widespread dimensions among Russian Jewry's lower and artisan classes.

18. See Hadassah Assouline and Benyamin Lukin, "The Apostate Dmitry Blank Writes to Tsar Nikolai I," *Gal-Ed* 20 (1996): 125–34 (Hebrew). Although some converts claimed that they had discovered the "true faith," in actuality, they converted because of conflict with communal institutions, as was the case for Yaakov Brafman of Minsk. See J. Levitaz, "The Authenticity of Brafman's 'Book of the Kahal,'" *Zion* 3 (1938): 170–78 (Hebrew); John D. Klier, *Imperial Russia's Jewish Question, 1855–1881* (Cambridge: Cambridge University Press, 1995), 263–83.

19. Stanislawski, "Jewish Apostasy in Russia," 197–99. This "positive" motive was generally concealed in memoir literature and in scholarship. Shimon Dubnow related the story of his fellow townsman from Mstislavl, who "converted voluntarily and not forcibly," was filled with admiration for crucifixes, and latched onto Russian monks who missionized among Jews (*Sefer hahayyim*, translated by M. Ben-Eliezer [Tel Aviv: Dvir, 1936], 1:58).

20. One example is the poet and photographer Konstantin Abba Shapiro, who fell in love with a Russian woman but retained lifelong ties to Judaism, Zionism, and his mitnagedic roots. See Freid, *Yamim veshanim*, 2:206–20; *Kitvei Hillel Zlatopolsky: Sefer hafelitonim* (Tel Aviv: Omanut, 1943), 220. The erotic attraction of the Christian "other" was particularly strong in small towns, where there was daily contact between Jews and non-Jews, and it became a favorite literary subject (an outstanding example is Hayyim Nahman Bialik's story "Behind the Fence," in *Random Harvest: The Novellas of Bialik*, translated by David Patterson and Ezra Spicehandler [Boulder, Colo.: Westview, 1999], 81–131). On some of its manifestations in belles-lettres and journalism, see the bibliographical references in Assaf, *Ne'ehaz basevakh*, 59 note 25.

21. For a typology of converts (according to the files of the Lithuanian Consistory of the Russian Orthodox Church, which relate to the conversion of 244 so-called ordinary Jews from 1819 to 1911), see Stanislawski, "Jewish Apostasy in Russia," 191ff. The extensive literature on apostates and their reasons for conversion is mostly popular and anecdotal in nature, rather than analytical or historical. Most of this material was published serially in the Yiddish daily press between the two world wars. See, especially, Azriel Nathan Frenk, *Meshumodim in Polyn in 19ten yahr-hundert* (Warsaw: Fried, 1923–24); Zitron, *Meshumodim*; Ginsburg, *Meshumodim* (and many articles by him published in the Sunday edition of the New York *Forverts* [Forward] from December 1934 to March 1935, not all of which are included in his collected writings); Katz, *Zikhronot*, 35–39, 51–53, 56–60; Yaakov Shatzky, *In shotn fun over* (Buenos Aires, 1947), 64–68. For converts in Poland, see Jacob Goldberg, *Converted Jews in the Polish Commonwealth* (Jerusalem: Shazar, 1985; Hebrew); Magdalena Teter, "Jewish Conversions to Catholicism in the Polish-Lithuanian Commonwealth of the Seventeenth and Eighteenth Centuries," *Jewish History* 17 (2003): 257–83; Aleksander Gutterman, "Three Generations of Warsaw Assimilationists and Their Attitudes towards Conversion, 1820–1918," *Gal-Ed* 12 (1991): 57–77 (Hebrew).

22. Todd Endelman notes how, as opposed to their Western counterparts, Eastern European converts remained more aware of, and connected to, their Jewishness even after their conversion. The leap made by these converts, many of whom came from

traditional Jewish society, was greater than that made by Western ones ("Memories of Jewishness," 322–23).

23. The maskilic attitude toward apostates has yet to be studied fully. Undoubtedly fundamentally negative, the maskilic explanation differed greatly from that of traditional society. Jacob Katz alludes to this in his discussion of the transfer of the expression "even though he has sinned, he remains a Jew" from converts to the freethinking maskil (*Halakhah and Kabbalah*, 268–69). Alongside the loathing and disgust voiced by maskilim for apostates (e.g., their comparison to "feces and excrement" [Hirsch Seidel, *Sefer toldot . . . Yehoshua Heschel Schorr . . .* (Drohobych, 1898), 9]), there was an ambivalent dialectical attitude toward "good" converts, such as the famous Russian-Jewish orientalist Daniel Chwolson (converted in 1855), who acted against blood libel accusations and even earned the admiration of Orthodox Jews (Freid, *Yamim veshanim*, 2:205–6). See Endelman, "Memories of Jewishness," 323.

24. See, for example, Shmarya Levin, *Mizikhronot hayyai* (Tel Aviv, 1939), 3:173–74; Nurit Govrin, *"The Brenner Affair": The Fight for Free Speech (1910–1913)* (Jerusalem: Yad Izhak Ben-Zvi, 1985; Hebrew).

25. Alexander Ziskind Rabinowitz, "Toldot mishpahat Schneersohn," *Heasif* 5 (1889): 163–80.

26. Among those "few," we must mention Yisrael Landau, a Habad hasid who converted and became well-known in St. Petersburg as a censor of Hebrew books, but nevertheless continued to live as an "enthusiastic hasid." See Ginsburg, *Meshumodim*, 222–34; Ginsburg, *Amolike Peterburg*, 224–28; Zitron, *Avek fun folk*, 3:255–60; Freid, *Yamim veshanim*, 2:220–25; Katz, *Zikhronot*, 36–38, 126, 134–35; Zvi Kasdai, *Hamityahadim* (Haifa: Warhaftig, 1930), 220–27; *Kitvei Hillel Zlatopolsky: Sefer hafelitonim* (Tel Aviv: Omanut, 1943), 220; Ben-Zion Dinur, *Beolam sheshaka* (Jerusalem: Bialik Institute, 1958), 13. The apostate Asher Temkin of Vitebsk—the author of a missionizing pamphlet, *Derekh selulah liyedi'at amitiyut ha'emunah* (Petersburg, 1835)—was evidently a Lubavitch hasid in his youth. On Temkin, see Zitron, *Avek fun folk*, 3:261–65; Shaul Ginsburg, *Forverts*, 27 January 1935, B, 3; Klausner, *Historiyah*, 3:7, 53. Habad leaders, by the way, had no difficulty maintaining contact with apostates as long they found them helpful. An example comes from their battle against the maskil Moshe Berlin in 1856, in which they were aided by a convert by the name of Rosen. See Lurie and Zeltser, "Moses Berlin and the Lubavich Hasidim," 52–53.

27. Moshe's date of birth is extrapolated from the date of his marriage (1797; see below); Rashaz's family members usually married at fourteen. Moshe's date of death is also uncertain, but in 1853, the maskil Moshe Berlin already knew of Moshe's death (see below). However, one Habad tradition sets the date of his death as 1855 (see below). More problematic are the dates of birth and death suggested by the sixth Habad rebbe, Yosef Yitshak Schneersohn (Rayyats), who sets Moshe's birth in 1784 and his death in 1878 (*Igrot kodesh: Moharayyats*, 7:16). It appears unlikely that Moshe lived to the age of ninety-four, spending nearly seventy years in absolute anonymity. More confusing is yet another, earlier date of birth supplied elsewhere by Yosef Yitshak Schneersohn in his grandfather Shmuel Schneersohn's name: Tammuz 1779 (*Sefer hasihot, 5704*, 150; *Sefer hatoladot: Moharash*, 134; *Sefer hatoladot: Moharashab*, 13; see also Hillman, *Igrot ba'al haTanya*, 213, no. 119), making Moshe's life span nearly

ninety-nine years! Yet another version penned by Rayyats places Moshe's date of birth as Adar 1780 (*Divrei hayamim hahem*, 91; see the notes in *Sefer hatoladot: Moharash* [New York, 1997], 106).

28. For praises penned by his brother Dov Ber (perhaps in 1825), see *Igrot kodesh*, 1:177–78. See also *Beit Rabbi*, 1:112–13.

29. *Beit Rabbi*, 1:114–16. Detailed information on the Schneersohns is concentrated in intramural genealogical texts, such as *Mishpahat haRav miLiadi* (for Shneur Zalman's children, see 45–51), and *Sefer hatse'etsa'im*.

30. Herein lies the explanation for the rumor noted in *Beit Rabbi*, 1:76: "One of our rabbi's grandchildren reported that, even after our rabbi was entirely free to return home, our rabbi remained in St. Petersburg for the entire summer until just before Rosh Hashanah 1801. Not forced, he did so of his own good will. But we do not know why he was there."

31. *Be'oholei Habad*, 1:38.

32. *Igrot kodesh*, 1:427; *Kerem Chabad* 4 (1992): 361 note 4.

33. See *Mishpahat haRav miLiadi*, 46, 57; *Sefer hatse'etsa'im*, 93–94. As we shall see below (note 61), Shifra moved to Palestine in 1843, died on 7 Tevet 1849, and was buried on the Mount of Olives. On the discovery of her gravesite, see Yitshak Alfasi, *Hamishim tsadikim* (Jerusalem: Karmel, 1997), 265–66.

34. On Moshe's father-in-law's family and his brothers-in-law, see *Beit Rabbi*, 1:113, 143. On Shneur Zalman's visits to Ule in 1804 and 1812, see *Kerem Chabad* 4 (1992): 380, 411; *Ma'amar inyan vehithalakhti betokhekhem (1812)* (New York: Kehot, 2005), 3, note.

35. Although hasidic sources make no mention of his serving in the rabbinate in Ule, this is borne out by Ribal's letter, cited below, and by archival documents.

36. *Beit Rabbi*, 1:113. For a discussion of the term *hozer* to refer to those individuals who repeated the rebbe's talks, and when this function was institutionalized, see Assaf, *Ne'ehaz basevakh*, 64 note 44. Moshe does not appear on the "official" list of *hozrim* appointed by Shneur Zalman, as recorded by Rayyats (*Divrei yemei hahozrim*, 2).

37. On the term *meniah* for someone who records the rebbe's talks, see *Divrei yemei hahozrim*, 1. Parts of his father's Torah teachings recorded by Moshe between 1802 and 1808 were preserved in the Chabad-Lubavitch library. Rayyats stated: "The writings of Rabbi Moshe . . . are in my possession in his holy handwriting and they fill seven volumes" (*Igrot kodesh: Moharayyats*, 2:321, letter 520 [1931], 321). See also ibid., 2:496 and 4:79; *Kerem Chabad* 4 (1992): 351 (see that page and 377 for photographs of Moshe's handwriting); Shalom Duber Levin, *Sifriyat Lubavitsh: Sekirat toldoteha al pi mikhtavim, te'udot vezikhronot* (New York: Kehot, 1993), 15, 27. Some of Moshe's *hanahot* were published from his handwriting in *Sefer ma'amarei Admor Hazaken al Maarzal (Shas, Zohar, utfilah)* (New York: Kehot, 1984), 342–426. See Fig. 2.1 for a sample of Moshe's handwriting.

38. Rayyats refers to Moshe's notes or memoirs on several occasions. See *Sefer hasihot, 5704*, 59, and *5705*, 78; *Sefer hatoladot: Admor Hazaken*, 11. Note that the many *toladot* (descendants, in Hebrew) books edited by the Habad writer Avraham Hanokh Glizenstein are not critical, historical works but primarily slanted selections from the talks and writings of Rayyats that are closer in nature to light fiction. See, for

example, his descriptions of Moshe (*Sefer hatoladot: Admor Hazaken*, 101, 173, 209, 231–32).

39. Rashaz despised the French and viewed Napoleon's regime as endangering the future of traditional Jewish society. His son Dov Ber quoted him: "'This is a great evil for the Jews, for not one will retain his Jewishness or his property. I hate him [Napoleon] so much, for he is the devil' . . . and because of this hatred he decided to flee, saying that it would be better to die than to live under him . . . he absolutely did not want to be under his regime for even a single day" (*Igrot kodesh*, 1:238–40).

40. Ibid., 237–47, 489–90 (which includes a map). Parts of this letter, which is extant in several versions, were evidently written in 1813, as they mention prayers recited at Rashaz's gravesite before the previous Rosh Hashanah (245). Incidentally, this letter was first published by Rodkinson, *Toldot amudei haHabad*, 84–94 (this was deliberately omitted from the notes to the version published in *Igrot kodesh*), who reported that he copied it at the home of one of "our rabbi's grandsons in Warsaw" (83–84)—namely, Shmaryahu Schneersohn, who will be mentioned below. See Schneersohn's complaint in a letter to Dubnow (Dubnow Collection, no. 77539, YIVO Institute for Jewish Research, New York). For further details on the family's flight, see Levin, *Ma'asar*, 41–43.

41. *Igrot kodesh*, 1:243–44.

42. Ibid., 1:234.

43. Dov Ber's description of the flight notes his father's reluctance to remain in Lyady for even another day, notwithstanding his advanced age and weakness, and the fact that he was burdened with four families—himself and his wife, Dov Ber's family, Hayyim Avraham's family, and the family of his son-in-law, the Tsemah Tsedek. Twenty-eight people fled in two wagons (ibid., 1:240). Moshe's absence is also confirmed by Rayyats's version: "The Admor Hazaken took with him all the family members living with him, except for his youngest son Moshe who was then living with his in-laws in Ule . . . [later Moshe] moved . . . temporarily to Druya, where the French army was encamped" (*Divrei hayamim hahem*, 106–7; *Sefer hatoladot: Admor Hazaken* [1986], 1028–29; see also *Igrot kodesh: Moharayyats*, 14:167). Druya is 180 kilometers northwest of Vitebsk. Habad historiography ascribed heroic motives to Moshe's move to Druya, placing it in the framework of Rashaz's network of spies against the Napoleonic army. See *Be'oholei Habad*, 1:61.

44. This letter, whose contents are discussed below, appeared in Hebrew translation in Assaf, *Ne'ehaz basevakh*, 133–34.

45. Havlin, *Hamashpi'a*, 177; *Igrot kodesh* 2:73. In another letter, Dov Ber notes that, because of his father's death, he has taken it upon himself "to keep a compassionate eye on my mother, the rebbetzin . . . and my brother, and my brothers-in-law, and their households, as they are in darkness and great sorrow" (*Igrot kodesh*, 1:235). Note the use of "brother" in the singular.

46. *Beit Rabbi*, 1:102.

47. On this controversy, which, like many such, combined personal rivalry and theological dispute on the essence of Hasidism, see *Beit Rabbi*, 2, chapter 2; Louis Jacobs, *Seeker of Unity: The Life and Works of Aaron of Starosselje* (London: Vallentine Mitchell, 1966), 12–13, 23–25, 159–62; Elior, "Habad Movement"; Rachel Elior, *Theory*

of Divinity of Hasidut Habad: Second Generation (Jerusalem: Magnes, 1982), 3–21 (Hebrew); Naftali Loewenthal, *Communicating the Infinite: The Emergence of the Habad School* (Chicago: University of Chicago Press, 1990), 100–38; Rosman, *Founder of Hasidism*, 189ff.

48. See *Igrot kodesh*, 1:235.

49. Levin, *Ma'asar*, 19. This document was delivered to the interrogators by the informer Simha Kissin, who took it from the estate of the hasid Pinhas Schick of Shklov, who was the campaign treasurer.

50. Ibid., 18.

51. Ibid., 14. Later the document says this was: "because of the vow he took upon himself in the above-mentioned secret circumstances, and a hint is sufficient" (19).

52. The approbation by Rashaz's sons to the *Tanya* was signed on 22 Iyyar 1814 and published in the 1814 Shklov edition. See A. M. Haberman, "Sha'arei Habad," in *Alei Ayin: The Salman Schocken Jubilee Volume* (Jerusalem, 1948–52), 309–10 (Hebrew); Yehoshua Mondshine, *Likutei amarim hu sefer haTanya: Mahadurotav, tirgumav ube'urav* (Kfar Habad: Kehot, 1982), 60–62. The sons' introduction to *Shulhan arukh haRav: Hilkhot pesah* also appeared in the 1814 Shklov edition. See Yehoshua Mondshine, *Sifrei hahalakhah shel Admor Hazaken: Bibliografiyah* (Kfar Habad: Kehot, 1984), 20–25. In some copies of these books, the line containing Moshe's name was deliberately erased; in others, the entire page was ripped out.

53. Rosman alludes to this possibility (*Founder of Hasidism*, 191), but the facts do not support this supposition—which, as we shall see, has maskilic origins. All the uncontested facts, including the Habad tradition (e.g., *Beit Rabbi*, 2:6–11) indicate that the succession quarrel was between Dov Ber (the oldest son) and Aharon of Staroselye (the disciple), and that Dov Ber's brothers were not parties to the dispute. No proof exists that Moshe saw himself as a candidate for the leadership. It was the partial data and the attempt to uncover Moshe's motivation for converting that fostered the creation of a link between his surprising act and the succession dispute close to the time of these events, as seen from Ribal's letter, discussed below. For further details on the role of the brothers (or lack thereof) and the elimination of Moshe's signatures, see Assaf, *Ne'ehaz basevakh*, 67–68 note 60.

54. "Mibeit hagnazim," *Bita'on Habad* 15–16 [34–35] (Av 1971): 10; see also the notes by Yehoshua Mondshine, ibid., 11, where he remarks that this letter contradicts Rayyats's statement that Moshe had gone into exile by 1816.

55. See the letter by his brothers, in Assaf, *Ne'ehaz basevakh*, 133–34. This letter also indicates the high costs of medical treatment, which occasioned significant financial losses not only to Moshe's family but also to his brothers, who had to cover these expenses.

56. The use of "etc." is a stylistic feature of Dov Ber's writing and does not necessarily indicate an omission. Here, however, it apparently reflects his exercise of self-restraint in refraining from use of more condemnatory language. For the full quotation, see Levin, *Ma'asar*, 26; and Assaf, *Ne'ehaz basevakh*, 68.

57. See *Beit Rabbi*, 1:151; Havlin, *Hamashpi'a*, 180–81; *Igrot kodesh*, 1:260–61. Levin (*Ma'asar*, 26) suggests that the words "our well-known brother" refer to Aharon of Staroselye (Dov Ber indeed sometimes called his friends "brother"), and that the ref-

erence to a "greater difficulty" means "a greater fear than the rabbinate of Rabbi Aharon, namely, the hasidim who state that no one can take our great rabbi's place."

58. A copy of the files from the investigation of Dov Ber, including much material not published by Levin (*Ma'asar*), has been preserved in CAHJP, HMF 925. The letter in question is numbered as pp. 20–23. I thank Benjamin Lukin for bringing this document to my attention.

59. Levin, *Ma'asar*, 72–73.

60. CAHJP, HMF 925, 18b.

61. *Beit Rabbi* (1:113) implies that the members of the family were "sent" to Palestine as result of this episode, but the presence of other family members, including the Mitteler Rebbe's daughter Menuha Rachel and her husband, Yaakov, blurs the link between the supposed punishment and the crime. Also among the immigrants were Moshe's wife, Shifra, and their two daughters: Sarah Rivka with her husband, Nahum Yosef Schneersohn, and Rachel with her husband, Moshe Zvi Fundaminski. See *Mishpahat haRav miLiadi*, 54–57; Shalom Duber Levin, *History of Chabad in the Holy Land, 1777–1950* (New York: Kehot, 1988), 78 (Hebrew), and the additional bibliography there. Moshe's wife, Shifra, died in 1849; his daughters died in 1861 (Rachel) and 1864 (Sarah Rivka).

62. David Assaf, "Convert or Saint? In the Footsteps of Moshe, the Son of Rabbi Shneur Zalman of Lyady," *Zion* 65 (2000): 463 (Hebrew). See also ibid., 483.

63. See Shaul Ginsburg, *Forverts*, 11 August 1940, B, p. 5. Dubnow remarked on this in a letter to Horodezky. See Horodezky, *Zikhronot*, 120; Shmuel Abba Horodezky, "Letters of Shimeon Dubnov," *He'avar* 8 (1961): 130 (Hebrew).

64. He is identified as "Mowsze Sznejer" in the Polish documents. Shneur Zalman's brother and son Dov Ber called themselves Shneyer or Schneuri. Only from the days of the Tsemah Tsedek did the Habad dynasty adopt the surname Schneersohn. See Levin, *Ma'asar*, 4–5. Dov Ber and Hayyim Avraham signed their letter regarding Moshe (Assaf, *Ne'ehaz basevakh*, 134–35) with the name Shner (in Hebrew).

65. The documents are located in the collection of the Catholic consistory of Mogilev, 1781/2/271, 1781/3/51 (a copy is in CAHJP, inv. 8651). I again stress the preliminary nature of the data presented below. I thank Benjamin Lukin for his invaluable assistance in deciphering the documents.

66. According to the Julian calendar (13 July in the Gregorian calendar currently in use; the Jewish date was 2 Av 5580). Where relevant, all subsequent dates are according to the Julian calendar; the Gregorian date is supplied in square brackets.

67. Beginning in 1819, the deacon of Ule was Antony Suszyński, who also served as the deacon of Polotsk. See *Słownik geograficzny Królestwa Polskiego* (Warsaw, 1892), 12:789. In a letter to Stanisłav Bohusz (on Bohusz, see below) dated 16 July 1820, Suszyński noted that the Jews watched over "Rabbi Moshe" for two years.

68. A copy of the affidavit (the original was either stored in the church in Ule or lost) and its translation into Hebrew appears in Assaf, *Ne'ehaz basevakh*, 131–32.

69. In general, the Jewish *kahal* appointed special quartermasters for this purpose, whose job was to expropriate apartments as temporary quarters for soldiers. See Levinsohn, *Emek refa'im*, 10, 21.

70. Born into a poor Lithuanian family, Bohusz (1731–1826) was an ambitious priest

who also engaged in historical and linguistic study. After the first partition of Poland (1772), Catherine the Great founded the Catholic bishopric of White Russia in Mogilev without consulting the pope and appointed Bohusz, until then vice bishop of Vilna, as bishop. In 1782, when she converted the bishopric into an archbishropic, Bohusz was promoted accordingly. During his tenure, Bohusz cooperated with the authorities. He did not protest the persecution of Jesuit monks, and he tyrannized his underlings.

71. See Assaf, *Ne'ehaz basevakh*, 131–32.

72. Joining the Russian Orthodox Church had certain prerequisites: a personal interview with a priest in order to determine the potential convert's sincerity, study of the faith's tenets, and baptism in a church according to the Russian Orthodox rite. Baptism had to take place in the presence of a pair of godparents, who served as adoptive parents and whose job was to ensure the new convert's religious devotion. See Stanislawski, "Jewish Apostasy in Russia."

73. By virtue of his office, Golitsyn (1773–1844) was responsible for the Holy Synod and for all foreign religious denominations in the Russian Empire. He also supervised the activity of the Society of Israelitish Christians, founded by imperial decree in 1817 (and closed in 1833) in order to missionize among the Jews and to support converts. Golitsyn was removed from his office in 1824. On Golitsyn, see Dubnow, *Jews in Russia and Poland*, 1:392–404; Katz, "Igrot maskilim," 268; Mahler, "Hamisyonerim bePolin," 169.

74. The letter by Moshe's brothers was presented to Bohusz by the "representative of the Vitebsk *kahal*, the communal deputy Beinish Levkovskii." Even though Jews were not permitted to reside in St. Petersburg, a small community, mainly merchants and contractors, had existed there since the early nineteenth century (on its early days, see Ginsburg, *Amolike Peterburg*, 13–25). The deputies were members of the Deputation of the Jewish People, founded in 1818 by order of Alexander I, which had twenty-two representatives from eleven provinces. From among themselves, the deputies chose three delegates and three vice delegates (Levkovskii was one), who answered to Golitsyn. In actuality, the deputies functioned not as an advisory body to the regime, but as intercessors on behalf of Jews. See Dubnow, *Jews in Russia and Poland*, 1:392–96; Moshe Zinowitz, *Ets hayyim: Toldot yeshivat Volozhin* (Tel Aviv: Mor, 1972), 1:66–77.

75. Gossner (d. 1858) lived in St. Petersburg from 1820 to 1824 and maintained close ties with Golitsyn during this period. His success as a rousing preacher angered the Orthodox Church, and the church leadership persuaded the czar to expel him from Russia. See Hans Brandenburg, *The Meek and the Mighty: The Emergence of the Evangelical Movement in Russia* (New York: Oxford University Press, 1977).

76. Sholom Aleichem, "The Lottery Ticket," in *The Old Country*, translated by Frances and Julius Butwin (London: Vallentine Mitchell, 1946), 363.

77. Shaul Yisrael Ish-Horowitz, "Misefer hayyai," *Hashiloah* 40 (1923): 6.

78. The relationship was through Beyle, the Mitteler Rebbe's daughter, who married Yekutiel Zalman, the grandson of Levi Yitshak of Berdichev (*Beit Rabbi*, 2:25).

79. Berdichev had a cluster of Habad hasidim as early as Shneur Zalman's day, and he even visited there in 1810. See *Kerem Chabad* 4 (1992): 403–4; Menahem Mendel Schneersohn, *Tsemah Tsedek: Piskei dinim min shulhan arukh: Orah hayyim, hilkhot tefilat arvit* (New York: Kehot, 1992), 17.

80. Katz, "Igrot maskilim," 269; see also 267–68. The original manuscript has been

preserved in the Schwadron Collection, Manuscripts Department and IMHM, NLIS (Autographs, Levinsohn files).

81. Mordekhai Shapira of Brody's name appears on the list of advance subscribers (*prenumerantn*) to Ribal's *Te'udah beyisrael* (Vilna and Grodno, 1828). I was unable to find any data on Yosef Landau. Perhaps the manuscript reads Yudl. Yudl (Leibush) Landau (1788–1841), son of the well-known Brody notable Yakovke Landau and grandson of Yehezkel Landau of Prague, the author of *Noda biyehuda*, is known to have been Ribal's friend. See *Arim veimahot beyisrael*, 6:174.

82. Yosef Perl, *Bohen tsadik* (Prague, 1838), 67–68.

83. On Perl's methods of disguising names in his satirical writings, see Chone Shmeruk, *The Call for a Prophet*, edited by Israel Bartal (Jerusalem: Shazar, 1999), 144–55 (Hebrew); Avraham Rubinstein, "The Midrashic Exegesis of Names in the Writings of Joseph Perl," *Tarbiz* 43 (1973–74): 205–216 (Hebrew); Jonatan Meir, "New Readings in Joseph Perl's *Bohen Zaddik*," *Tarbiz* 76 (2007): 557–90 (Hebrew). See also Assaf, *Ne'ehaz basevakh*, 79 note 89.

84. Moshe Berlin, "Istoria Hasidisma," RGIA [Russian State Historical Archive, St. Petersburg]: F. 821, op. 8, D. 331, pp. 31b–32a. For a partial translation of this source into Hebrew, see Ilia Lurie, "Hasidut Habad beRusiyah bein hashanim 1827–1882: Hebetim historiyyim vehevratiyyim" (master's thesis, Hebrew University, 1998), 106 note 2; Lurie, *The Habad Movement in Czarist Russia, 1828–1882* (Jerusalem: Magnes, 2006), 1 note 2 (Hebrew).

85. See Lurie and Zeltser, "Moses Berlin and the Lubavich Hasidim." Other sources indicate that it was Berlin who assisted the Tsemah Tsedek in overturning accusations made by informers. See Klausner, *Historiyah*, 5:31. For further information on Berlin, see Yehoshua Ben-Yaakov Sirkin, "Partsufim," *Reshumot* 1 (1918): 198; Ginsburg, *Historishe verk*, 1:287–95.

86. *Hashahar* 1 (1869): 9–11. Although the poem is unsigned, Smolenskin undoubtedly authored it.

87. See Smolenskin, *Hato'eh bedarkhei hahayyim*, vol. 3 (Warsaw, 1910), 62–80; David Yeshayahu Zilberbush, *Mipinkas zikhronotai* (Tel Aviv: Hapoel Hatsair, 1936), 109–13; Klausner, *Historiyah*, 5:28–31, 217–27.

88. Shneur Zalman had three daughters but, as noted above (see note 29), two died during his lifetime.

89. Pesah Ruderman, "Hashkafah kelalit al hatsadikim ve'al hahasidim," *Hashahar* 6 (1875): 101–2.

90. See his series of satirical articles, "Tsror mikhtavim me'et mi shehayah hasid," *Hashahar* 7 (1876): 124–35, 180–87, 311–19. For more on Ruderman, see Assaf, *Ne'ehaz basevakh*, 83 note 96.

91. In the words of Alexander Zederbaum, who rejected the notion that Bernyu, the son of Yisrael of Ruzhin, fell in love with a non-Jew: "And it is even more improbable in our eyes that such a man, already elderly, would have have had an affair. Where would he have had the opportunity to be caught in the palm of a strange woman who would steal his heart to betray his ancestral faith and follow her?" ("Lo dubim velo ya'ar," *Hamelits*, 26 July 1869, 191). Shaul Ginsburg rejected this possibility on the same ground; see Ginsburg, "Di legende," 61–62.

92. In his famous essay "Et lata'at" (A time to plant), Smolenskin blamed Mendelssohn for the conversion of most of his sons, grandsons, and disciples (*Hashahar* 6 [1875]: 346).

93. *Haboker or* 1 (1876): 8.

94. Chernyakhov is located in Volhynia Province, thirty kilometers north of Zhitomir.

95. *Haboker or* 5 (1880): 246–47, reprinting, with additions, Gottlober, *Memoires and Travels* 1:151. It is difficult to date the writing of these memoirs exactly, but they probably originated during the 1860s. See Reuven Goldberg's introduction to Gottlober, *Memoires and Travels*, 1:32–33.

96. He named his son, born in 1827, Shneur. On his positive attitude toward Habad, see Gottlober, *Memoires and Travels*, 1:122, 128–30, 149–52, 166–72.

97. This event took place sometime between 1824 (when Gottlober came to Chernyakhov, upon his marriage at the age of thirteen) and 1828 (when his father died). Gottlober left Chernyakhov in 1829, after the admor Avraham Dov of Ovruch (then residing in Zhitomir) forced him to divorce his wife.

98. Gottlober also mentions elsewhere that his father was acquainted with Shneur Zalman and recalled his appearance (Gottlober, *Memoires and Travels*, 1:130). Note that, in Habad tradition, Moshe's brother Hayyim Avraham was also said to resemble their father. See Shmuel Krauss, "Gilguleha shel tmunah," *Beit mashiah* 67, 29 Kislev 1995, 26.

99. Deinard, *Zikhronot bat ami*, 2:3–20. He writes that he visited Lubavitch around Rosh Hashanah 1861 (3). In another work, he states that this took place in 1862 (*Herev hadah* [Kearny, N.J.: Deinard, 1904], 8).

100. Deinard, *Zikhronot bat ami*, 2:16.

101. Deinard, *Mashgei ivrim: Chassidism and Bolshevism in Modern Hebrew Literature* (St. Louis, Mo.: Moinester, 1919), 3–4 (Hebrew); reprinted in Deinard, *Zikhronot bat ami*, 2:26–27.

102. *Beit Rabbi*, 2:22–24.

103. Deinard, *Alata*, 29, 68–69, 82 ("And I heard already in 1862 that the hasidim killed him").

104. *The Library of Gershom Scholem on Jewish Mysticism: Catalogue*, edited by Joseph Dan and Esther Liebes (Jerusalem: Jewish National and University Library Press, 1999), 1:38, no. 569 (Hebrew).

105. On missionizing activity among Eastern European Jewry, especially in Poland, during the reign of Alexander I, see Thomas D. Halsted, *Our Missions: Being a History of the Principal Missionary Transactions* (London, 1866), 95–128; Gidney, *At Home and Abroad*, 94–118; Samuel H. Wilkinson, *In the Land of the North: The Evangelization of the Jews in Russia* (London, 1905), 89–91; Dubnow, *Jews in Russia and Poland*, 1:392–404; Fein, "Di londoner misyonern-geselshaft"; Mahler, "Hamisyonerim bePolin"; Mahler, *Modern Times*, 5:59–60; John D. Klier, *Russia Gathers Her Jews: The Origins of the "Jewish Question" in Russia, 1722–1825* (De Kalb: Northern Illinois University Press, 1986), 164–67; Arie Morgenstern, *Redemption through Return: Vilna Gaon's Disciples in Eretz Israel, 1800–1840* (Jerusalem: Maor, 1997), 108–10 (Hebrew).

106. Way, one of the leading figures in the London Society for Promoting Christian-

ity amongst the Jews (founded in 1809), was granted an audience with the czar in 1818. McCaul, Way's close associate and one of the heads of the London Society, was also active among Polish Jewry. In 1825 he presented to the czar a detailed proposal for converting the Jews (see note 115 below). The background for English missionary activity has received broad treatment: for a bibliography on the subject, see Assaf, *Ne'ehaz basevakh*, 88 note 111.

107. I thank Professor Shnayer Zalman (Sid) Leiman for bringing Lazarus, *Ebenezer*, to my attention. Regarding Lazarus's history after his book's publication, we know only that he served in the London Society in Liverpool and Manchester. See Gidney, *At Home and Abroad*, 57–58; William T. Gidney, *The History of the London Society for Promoting Christianity amongst the Jews (from 1809 to 1908)* (London: London Society for Promoting Christianity amongst the Jews, 1908), 161, 282, 334; Aaron Bernstein, *Some Jewish Witnesses for Christ* (London, 1909), 328.

108. Little attention has been devoted to autobiographies of Jewish apostates, either as a defined literary genre or as a source for the history of Eastern European Jewry. On this genre's problematic nature, see Yaakov Ariel, "From Judaism to Christianity: The Autobiographies of Jewish Converts to Christianity in the Twentieth Century," *Proceedings of the Eleventh World Congress of Jewish Studies*, Division B, Vol. 2 (Jerusalem: World Union of Jewish Studies, 1994), 123–29 (Hebrew); Samuel Z. Klausner, "How to Think about Mass Religious Conversion: Toward an Explanation of the Conversion of American Jews to Christianity," *Contemporary Jewry* 18 (1997): 108–15.

109. See the anonymous introduction to Lazarus, *Ebenezer*, xiii. McCaul's book, *Old Paths* (London, 1838) was translated into German in 1839, and into Hebrew in 1851 (by the apostate Stanislaus Hoga in London; see note 3 above). In 1841 Ribal wrote *Ahiyah hashiloni hahozeh* (published postmortem, Leipzig, 1863) in response to this work. See Klausner, *Historiyah*, 3:53–54; Israel Zinberg, *A History of Jewish Literature*, translated and edited by Bernard Martin, vol. 11: *The Haskalah Movement in Russia* (Cincinnati, Ohio: Hebrew Union College Press, 1978), 69–72.

110. Thus, Lazarus devotes an entire chapter to a description of Jewish marriage customs (*Ebenezer*, 36–52). Another example of this genre, which contains much valuable historical and folkloristic information, is a book by two Scottish missionaries who traveled among Eastern European Jews in 1839. See Bonar and M'Cheyne, *Mission of Inquiry to the Jews*.

111. Lazarus, *Ebenezer*, 74, 78–80. At a later date, after he had divorced his wife, Lazarus again encountered Dov Ber, when the latter was visiting his followers in the northeastern Lithuanian town of Ponedel (139–42). Lazarus also published a brief, serial survey of Hasidism in an American missionary newspaper. See Joshua George Lazarus, "The Sect of Khasidim in the North of Europe," *The Israelite* (Cincinnati, Ohio) 5/47–48, 27 May–3 June 1859, 375, 382.

112. Lazarus, *Ebenezer*, 77.

113. Czarist law permitted conversion from Judaism to Christianity only after the convert demonstrated familiarity with basic Christian tenets and was publicly baptized in an urban, not a rural, church. See Stanislawski, "Jewish Apostasy in Russia," 192. As noted above, the archival material related to Moshe shows awareness of, but not full adherence to, these rules.

114. Lazarus, *Ebenezer*, 75–77 (emphasis in original). Two years after its publication, we find pieces of Lazarus's remarks on Moshe copied by another convert, Moses Margoliouth, in his *The Fundamental Principles of Modern Judaism Investigated* (London, 1843), 220. On Margoliouth, see Assaf, *Ne'ehaz basevakh*, 90 note 119.

115. Lazarus's statement contains implicit criticism of McCaul, who in 1825 sent a memorandum to the czar, in which he submitted that the Jews in general, "with the exception of the hasidic sect," show interest in missionary propaganda. See Mahler, "Hamisyonerim bePolin," 176. McCaul devoted detailed attention to Polish hasidim in his *Sketches of Judaism and the Jews* (London, 1838), 17–42. The chapter, titled "The Chasidim, a Fanatical Jewish Sect," contains several interesting vignettes (23–24) on meetings between McCaul and various zaddikim (the zaddik of Mezhibozh is certainly Avraham Yehoshua Heschel of Apta; the zaddik of Kishinev is probably Aryeh Leib of Lantzut, a disciple of the Seer of Lublin, both of whom died in 1825).

116. See William James, *The Varieties of Religious Experience: A Study in Human Nature* (London: Longmans, Green, 1928), 189–258. The literature on the sources, motivations, and ramifications of conversion is vast. See Lewis R. Rambo, *Understanding Religious Conversion* (New Haven, Conn.: Yale University Press, 1993) and the detailed bibliography there.

117. Mayer, *Die Juden unserer Zeit*. Mayer, whose descriptions are generally reliable, also met Yisrael of Ruzhin. See Assaf, *Regal Way*, 81–84, 120–21.

118. Mayer, *Die Juden unserer Zeit*, 17–18.

119. Shimon Dubnow, *Fun "zhargon" tsu yidish un andere artiklen: Literarishe zikhroynes* (Vilna, 1929), 64–65.

120. Leeser Rosenthal, *Yode'a sefer*, entry titled "Sefer likutei amarim," in M. Roest, *Catalog der Hebraica und Judaica aus der L. Rosenthal'schen Bibliothek*, (Amsterdam, 1875), 2:164, no. 866.

121. For his son Dov Ber's description of the gravesite, see *Igrot kodesh*, 1:244–45.

122. Reports by the London Society indicate that Anglican missionaries had little impact on Jewish apostasy. Thus, for example, from 1841 to 1842, only 153 Jews converted. See Fein, "Di londoner misyonern-geselshaft," 41–42.

123. In the hasidic context, the ostensible conversion of the zaddik Menahem Mendel of Kotsk to Christianity is noteworthy. For details, see Assaf, *Ne'ehaz basevakh*, 93 note 128.

124. Shmaryahu was the son of Levi Yitshak, the grandson of Barukh Shmuel, and the great-grandson of Shneur Zalman's son Hayyim Avraham (*Mishpahat haRav mi-Liadi*, 97), and it was he who published Teitelbaum's *HaRav miLiadi*. See Schneersohn's introduction to vol. 1. Schneersohn's letters are housed in the Simon Dubnow Collection, nos. 77539–77544, YIVO Institute for Jewish Research, New York, and have appeared in English translation (Deutsch, "Letters by Shmaryahu Schneersohn"). It was Yaakov Dineson, then living in Warsaw, who introduced Dubnow to Schneersohn. Dubnow sent Schneersohn a list of questions regarding Shneur Zalman and his descendants, which Schneersohn willingly agreed to answer in hopes that the truth behind the legends would be revealed (31 May 1890, no. 77542). Dubnow mentions Schneersohn in his *Toldot hahasidut*, 379.

125. See *Ne'ehaz basevakh*, 95 note 130.

126. Dubnow Collection, no. 77543, YIVO Institute.

127. Dubnow Collection, no. 77539 (15 March 1891), YIVO Institute. A page appended to the letter (no. 77540) indicates that it was not posted until 13 April.

128. Dubnow Collection, no. 77541 (29 April 1891), YIVO Institute. Parts of this letter (not including the last lines, in which Schneersohn voices doubts regarding the accuracy of the rumors) were also cited by Krauss, "Chaikin," 27.

129. Dubnow Collection, no. 77540, YIVO Institute. The notes are in Dubnow's handwriting and initialed S.D. In his translation of the letter (which contains many inaccuracies), Deutsch attributes these remarks to Schneersohn ("Letters by Shmaryahu Schneersohn").

130. The basis of this antihasidic joke lies in various witticisms; see, for example, Alter Druyanov, *Habedihah vehahidud* (Jerusalem: Dvir, 1939–50), vol. 1, no. 561.

131. Examination of Dov Ber's literary corpus reveals the falsity of his characterization as an ignoramus. In fact, the standards "ignoramus" or "scholar" come from the mitnagedic and maskilic worlds and have no relevance for the choice of the person who sits on a particular hasidic throne.

132. Novakovski (1879–1933), a Yiddish author and activist, was initially a territorialist and then a communist. See *Leksikon*, 6:144–45. Two of his letters to Dubnow, which treat Shneur Zalman's children Moshe and Freyde, are located in the Central State Historical Archive of St. Petersburg (TsGIA SPb 2129/3/198). Copies are housed in Jerusalem, CAHJP, HM2/9446.9.

133. According to Novakovski's tale, Shneur Zalman visited Avraham Hamalakh in Tulchin! When he tried to enter the Besht's grave (which is actually located in Mezhibozh), Avraham Hamalakh accused him of heresy and tried to block his entry. Due to this quarrel, Avraham's daughter died (in fact, he had no daughters). In return, he cursed Shneur Zalman so that he would also lose a son. Clearly, either Novakovski, his mother, or his grandfather confused Rabbi Avraham (the son of the Maggid of Mezhirech and Shneur Zalman's friend), who had nothing to do with Moshe, and Barukh of Tulchin (the Besht's grandson) with whom Shneur Zalman was involved in a dispute. According to other hasidic sources—to be discussed below (see note 150)—Barukh tried to prevent Shneur Zalman from visiting the Besht's grave and cursed him that one of his sons would convert.

134. Horodezky, *Zikhronot*, 201 (reprinted in *He'avar* 8 [1961]: 130).

135. Dubnow, *Toldot hahasidut*, 402–3, no. 161.

136. Ginsburg, "Di legende." This was reprinted in a series of articles on converts in *Forverts*, 30 December 1934, Section B, 2, where Ginsburg added new data provided by Litvin (see below). In an additional article published in *Forverts*, 11 August 1940, Section B, 5, Ginsburg added the new information culled from Ribal's letter, published by Katz, "Igrot maskilim," 267–69.

137. In his 1940 article (see the previous note), Ginsburg retracted this dating and, based on Ribal's letter, suggested 1821 as the year of Moshe's conversion. Nevertheless, this did not alter his view linking the motivation for the conversion to the family's flight from Napoleon eight years earlier.

138. Copies of the original Hebrew letters were in Ginsburg's possession. These copies are housed in Saul Ginsburg Collection, 4° 1281A/25, Manuscripts Department

and IMHM, NLIS. They were first published in the Hebrew original in *Ohalei Lubavitsh* 2 (1995): 55–59.

139. Evidently, Levi Yitshak Schneersohn of Nezhin, the Mitteler Rebbe's grandson. See Krauss, "Chaikin," 25, 27.

140. Fastov was the residence and gravesite of Avraham Hamalakh, according to Habad tradition Shneur Zalman's friend and his instructor in Hasidism and esoteric lore (see Assaf, *Regal Way* [Hebrew ed.], 52). This town is located southwest of Kiev, in the region associated with Chernobyl Hasidism (which has marital ties with Habad). As we shall see below, geography played an important role in the development of hagiography.

141. The poorhouse (*hekdesh*, in Hebrew) provided free housing for the indigent and sick and was communally funded. Usually located at the edge of the town, it was seen as both threatening and contaminated. See Kotik, *Journey*, 152–53.

142. This is a reference to the four legs of the heavenly chariot (Ezekiel 1). Other Habad traditions, cited below (see note 216), also ascribe exegetical remarks on the legs of the chariot to Moshe.

143. *Ohalei Lubavitsh* 2 (1995): 58–59.

144. For details, see Krauss, "Chaikin." Zvi Hirsh Chaikin (d. 1883) and his son Yoel Meir (d. 1898) came to Palestine and were buried on the Mount of Olives. The letter's editor (*Ohalei Lubavitsh* 2 [1995], 55) correctly surmised that Chaikin was the father of Menahem Mendel [Chaikin?] of England, with whom Yosef Yitshak Schneersohn (Rayyats) corresponded in 1921: "Apparently I am not acquainted with his honor, and what you write regarding the investigation in Radomyshl that was undertaken by your father of blessed memory; I know nothing about it. Is this the investigation undertaken by the Admor Moharash [Shmuel] . . . in 1873, a copy of whose opinion I found among the old letters? If possible, please clarify. For I am fond of the memory of my forebears" (*Igrot kodesh: Moharayyats*, vol. 1, letter 97, 200). The contradiction between the dating of the "investigation"—1873 here and 1877 in Chaikin's letter—indicates Rayyats's carelessness in recording dates.

145. Note also that Mordekhai of Chernobyl is associated with a number of tales treating hidden saints, to the extent that some considered it heretical not to believe that Rabbi Mordekhai supported the thirty-six hidden saints with redemption money. See Yisrael Klapholtz and Nathan Ortner, *Hagadah shel pesah im midrash behidush . . . venilveh alav imrei kodesh* (Bnei Brak, 1965), 20. Regarding a family tradition of his encounter with the prophet Elijah, see Yeshayahu Asher Zelig Margoliot, "Or zaru'a latsadik," in Zvi Hirsh of Zhidachov, *Tsvi latsadik* (Jerusalem: [Hatehiyah], 1959), 79b.

146. Apparently, the greater scholarly interest in the writings of the sixth Habad rebbe, Rayyats, has diverted attention from the unusual personality of the fourth rebbe, Shmuel Schneersohn, who saw Habad split among the Tsemah Tsedek's six sons and the founding of the Kopust (Kopys) dynasty. Shmuel was also involved in the publication of his father's will, which, thought to be a forgery, sparked a tempest. For additional bibliographical references, see Assaf, *Ne'ehaz basevakh*, 103 note 154.

147. See notes 27 and 144 above.

148. *Di tsukunft* 36/3 (March 1931): 206–8. Litvin was the pen name of Shmuel Horowitz (1862–1943).

149. Fischel Schneersohn (1895–1958) composed profound books on Hasidism in general as well as on the Habad world. Of these, the most outstanding is the 1922–26 *Hayyim Gravitser* (translated into Hebrew by Avraham Shlonski, 2 vols. [Tel Aviv, 1939–40]); this book tells the story of a Habad hasid (perhaps the author himself), who undergoes a severe crisis of faith. See also Kressel, *Cyclopedia*, 2:961.

150. For the background to the dispute between Shneur Zalman and Barukh, see Gottlober, *Memoires and Travels*, 1:166–74; *Igrot kodesh*, 1:141–42. Although Gottlober knew of the sharp exchange between the two regarding the phylacteries—and of Moshe's conversion—he had no knowledge of Barukh's prophetic curse (*Memoires and Travels*, 172). Other sources recount the entire story, even if they do not explain how the prophecy was realized. The first was Rodkinson, *Toldot amudei haHabad*, 82, note. See also Novakovski's above-cited letter to Dubnow; Rechtman, *Yidishe etnografye*, 344–48 (a tale he heard in Vinitsa in 1910); Kahana, *Sefer hahasidut*, 217; Rapoport-Albert, "Hasidism after 1772," 111–14. Surprisingly, Habad sources also preserved this pseudo-prophecy (see below).

151. On Yehuda Leib Smolenskin (1836–1928), who was overshadowed by his younger brother, see *Die Hebräische Publizistik in Wien* (Vienna, 1930), vol. 3, edited by Alexander Kristianpoller, 73–74. Although Klausner criticized the reliability of his writing (see, for example, Klausner, *Historiyah*, 5:98–99, 199, and passim), Yehuda Leib's essay "Eleh toldot perets" (*Davar*, Sabbath and holiday supplement, 25 January 1935, 3–8) is a biographical source of inestimable value.

152. See Israel J. Yuval, "Vengeance and Damnation, Blood and Defamation: From Jewish Martyrdom to Blood Libel Accusations," *Zion* 58 (1993): 84–85 (Hebrew).

153. Litvin described their meeting, which took place in Vienna before World War I, in his sketch "Der zeelen-bezorger" (*Yudishe neshomes* 5).

154. Litvin expressed this theory in relation to Galician Hasidism in his sketch "A tselm in rebn's kloyz" (*Yudishe neshomes* 6). Intensely interested in missionaries and converts, Litvin published many brief reports of their activity in various places, such as Vilna, Warsaw, and Hungary. For further details, see Assaf, *Ne'ehaz basevakh*, 105 note 163.

155. On Grünwald (1889–1955), see *Leksikon*, 2:409; Assaf, *Ne'ehaz basevakh*, 106 note 164.

156. This is the town of Nagyszöllös—present-day Vynohradiv—located in the Ukraine, in the Transcarpathian region, some forty kilometers southeast of Munkatsh. On this town, see Samuel Weingarten, *A Memorial to the Jewish Community of Sevlus (Nagyszöllös) & District* (Tel Aviv: Olei Nagyszöllös in Israel, 1976; Hebrew), (on Barukh, see 23–24).

157. Yekutiel Yehuda Grünwald, "Lekorot hahasidut beUngariyah," *Hatsofeh me'erets Hagar* 5 (1921): 270–71. Ten years earlier, Grünwald had accepted the stance of *Beit Rabbi* (see below). See Grünwald, *Pe'erei hakhmei medinatenu* (Sighet: Kaufman and Sons, 1910), 60. See also Grünwald, *Mekorot lekorot yisrael* (Berehovo, 1934), 91; Shmuel Weingarten, "Harav Rabbi Barukh avi 'haTanya,'" *Bamishor* 7/269–270 (Erev

Sukkot 1945): 8; Yitshak Yosef Cohen, "Darkhei hahadirah shel hahasidut leHungariyah," *Yehudei Hungariyah: Mehkarim historiyyim* ([Tel Aviv], 1980), 26–27; Yosef ha-Glili, *Ha-shomrim laboker* (Meron: privately printed, 1992), 357.

158. *Beit Rabbi*, 1:107. See also Hillman, *Igrot ba'al haTanya*, 1 note; *Igrot kodesh*, 1:8–10. For another explanation for Reb Barukh's wanderings, penned by Rayyats, see *Kerem Chabad* 4 (1992): 8–9 (see note 170 below). From remarks made by Menahem Mendel Schneersohn, the last rebbe, recorded on 19 Kislev 1932, we learn that Ramam suggested to his father-in-law Rayyats that Barukh had acted in accord with Rabbi Meir of Rothenberg's dictum, as related by his pupil Asher ben Yehiel (the Rosh): "Once he achieved prominence he did not welcome his father nor did he want his father to come to him" (Asher ben Yehiel on *Kidushin*, chap. 1, no. 57). Rayyats's sincere reply was: "We have no data. Indeed, the Admor Hazaken was rarely at home; and of this, we also have almost no knowledge" (*Kfar Habad* 825 [1998]: 18). For further information on Barukh's final years, see Shaul S. Deutsch, "The Last Years of Reb Boruch: The Alter Rebbe's Father," *Chasidic Historical Review* 1/2 (February 1996): 4–7.

159. Regarding the rumors of Reb Barukh's death, Teitelbaum commented: "The various legends circulating among the hasidim are simply the products of fantasy" (*HaRav miLiadi*, 2:250).

160. Regarding Moshe, Heilman states this explicitly: "Before his death they inquired as to his name and his father's name, so as to know what to write on the headstone. He answered: 'Write Moshe on the stone and *that his father's name is not known to you*, write thus'" (*Beit Rabbi*, 1:113–14); the tale of the "old man" from Radomyshl contains similar events. Chaikin's letter, cited above, presents an opposite tradition. It recounts that the wayfarer answered, "I am Moshe, the son of the Gaon Rabbi Shneur Zalman of Lyady" (*Ohalei Lubavitsh* 2 [1995]: 57).

161. For brief treatments of the episode of Moshe, see Elior, "Habad Movement," 166–68; Rosman, *Founder of Hasidism*, 191–92; Louis Jacobs, *Tract of Ecstasy/Dobh Baer of Lubavitch* (London: Vallentine, Mitchell, 1963), 54 note 74; Avrum M. Ehrlich, *Leadership in the HaBaD Movement: A Critical Evaluation of HaBaD Leadership, History and Succession* (Northvale, N.J.: J. Aronson, 2000), 162–63, 189–90. Elior and Rosman, who rely on a small number of sources, adopt the maskilic version linking events to the succession war; Ehrlich avoids the issue by stating that it has no relevance to his study. Naturally, hasidim who study Habad neither mention nor treat the conversion in their works. Shmuel Krauss notes that he has written down little-known information about Moshe (Krauss, "Chaikin," 26), but the little he published there contains not a word on the subject (27). Deutsch, "Letters by Shmaryahu Schneersohn," is to date the only Habad hasid to explicitly confirm Moshe's conversion in his writings.

162. Yisrael Klausner, *Rabbi Hayyim Tsvi Schneersohn* (Jerusalem, 1943), 5 note 1 (Hebrew). Klausner relies on *Beit Rabbi* and on the *Evreiskaya entsiklopediia*, vol. 16 (St. Petersburg, 1915), 59. The entry from the latter contributes nothing new; it only briefly notes that Moshe converted and then repented.

163. "With one of the rebbe's sons . . . there was a disaster. His family was sent to Palestine" (Yisrael Klausner, *Rabbi Hayyim Tsvi Schneersohn: Mimevasrei medinat yis-*

rael [Jerusalem: Mossad Harav Kook, 1973], 9). Even the title of Shaul Ginsburg's article was changed when reprinted; it was shortened and omitted the reference to conversion. A similar approach is exemplified by David Margalit's *Hakhmei yisrael kerofim* (Jerusalem: Mossad Harav Kook, 1962), 189, where he refers to "Rabbi Moshe, the son of Shneur Zalman (*the well-known affair*)."

164. On historiographical trends in Habad writing, and its overt and covert polemic with the maskilim through pseudohistorical treatises, see Rapoport-Albert, "Hagiography," 137ff.; Zeev Gries, *The Book in Early Hasidism* (Tel Aviv: Hakibbutz Hameuchad, 1992), 32–33, 69, 118–19 (Hebrew); Bartal, "Shimon Ha-Kofer"; Etkes, *Gaon of Vilna*, 116–30. On Heilman, see Nahum Karlinsky, "The Dawn of Hasidic-*Haredi* Historiography," *Modern Judaism* 27 (2007): 20–46; Karlinsky, *Counter History*, 109–65. Note that comparing *Beit Rabbi* with the writings of Rayyats does not do justice to Heilman, whose historical value and reliability far outweigh those of Rayyats.

165. Heilman was probably familiar with Gottlober's memoirs (see note 95 above), in which he relates his father's testimony regarding the resemblance between Moshe and Shneur Zalman, but Heilman uses Gottlober's memoirs without mentioning his source.

166. This is Yaakov Yisrael Twersky (1794–1876), Mordekhai of Chernobyl's son, who married Devorah Leah, the daughter of Dov Ber (the Mitteler Rebbe), in 1811.

167. Aharon Twersky of Chernobyl (1787–1871) was Mordekhai of Chernobyl's oldest son.

168. *Beit Rabbi*, 1:113–14. An abridged version appeared in the Yiddish translation (Vilna, 1904, 90).

169. *Beit Rabbi*, 1:4–5.

170. The similarity to Rayyats's account of Barukh's death is striking: "The members of the burial society came before his death . . . and inquired as to his name, whether he had sons, and where they resided so that they could be informed. And he replied, 'On my grave, place a stone marked "Here lies Barukh"; nothing more. And as for your inquiry regarding my sons, I do have sons. I have one son who will know of my death without being informed, and he will tell his brothers'" (*Kerem Chabad* 4 [1992]: 8).

171. Rapoport-Albert, "Hasidism after 1772," 125; see also Etkes, *Gaon of Vilna*, 122; and the items cited in note 164 above. Also of interest are the recent remarks by David Zvi Hillman (who edited *Igrot ba'al haTanya*): "Rabbi Haim Liberman (the dean of the bibliographers and Rayyats's secretary and confidante) told Shlomo Zalman Havlin that Rayyats's memoirs fall into the category of 'belles lettres' . . . He further stated that whatever Rayyats wrote in *Divrei hayamim hahem* is tendentious, motivated by the desire to blame the Vilna Gaon and his circle for the Haskalah's penetration into Russia" (in David Kamenetsky, "Haskamot gedolei harabanim lehumshei Rabbi Shlomo Dubno," *Yeshurun* 10 [2002]: 762, addition to note 35; for more on *Divrei hayamim hahem*, see ibid. 9 [2001]: 714–15; and below).

172. Mondshine, *Migdal oz*, 174. Fastov is located in Vilna Province.

173. This evidently refers to the above-mentioned hasidic *hanahot*. See notes 37 and 205.

174. See *Hatamim* (Warsaw) 1 (Tammuz 1935): 81–83.

175. Not only was Rayyats familiar with Ginsburg's writings, he even made polemical and historiographical use of them. See Bartal, "Shimon ha-Kofer," 248–55.

176. Babinovichi is a district town located twenty-five kilometers west of Lubavitch (Mogilev Province). The czar's visit to this town was preserved in another Habad tradition cited by Rayyats. See *Sefer hatoladot: Moharashab*, 105 (according to *Sefer hasihot, 5701*, 51). See also below.

177. Vyazma is located 145 kilometers northeast of Smolensk, which is 120 kilometers southeast of Vitebsk.

178. Orsha is eighty kilometers south of Vitebsk.

179. *Igrot kodesh: Moharayyats*, 14:167.

180. The linguistic expertise of Habad hasidim was also noted by Bonaventura Mayer (see above), but Rayyats's version not only endowed Moshe with knowledge of Russian but also attributed to him the ability to "speak French elegantly." See *Sefer hatoladot: Admor Hazaken*, 209, 232, 262; *Sefer hatoladot: Admor Hazaken* (1986), 3:702.

181. Jarcevo is located forty kilometers northeast of Smolensk.

182. Here Rayyats became confused. Smolensk and Tula are names of provinces; Nezhin is a town in Chernigov Province, the burial site of the Mitteler Rebbe. Perhaps he was referring to Riazan Province, near Tula Province.

183. Vladimir, the ancient capital of Kievan Russia and an important religious center, is 180 kilometers northeast of Moscow.

184. The synod was the supreme body of the Russian Orthodox Church; its members included three metropolitans (from Kiev, Moscow, and St. Petersburg), and five or six bishops and abbots (archimandrites) appointed by the czar.

185. Oryol is 120 kilometers southeast of Bryansk, and 370 kilometers southwest of Moscow.

186. Pogar is a town in Chernigov Province, 105 kilometers southwest of Bryansk.

187. This letter was first published in *Sefer hatoladot: Admor Hazaken*, 356–57. As that version is corrupt, this translation is based on the edited Hebrew version, "according to the copy held by the secretary," published in *Igrot kodesh: Moharayyats*, vol. 7 (1943), letter no. 1881, 15–16. See also ibid., letter no. 1889, 28, 30. The letter was reprinted in *Sefer hatoladot: Admor Hazaken* (1986), 4:1191–92; *Shmu'ot vesipurim*, 2:26–27.

188. In a recently published talk from 1938, Rayyats once again makes peripheral mention of the story of the debate which ended with Moshe's arrest, his escape "through a window," and exile. One of the hasidim observed: "But he had nothing for which to do penitence." The rebbe replied: "Correct. He had nothing for which to do penitence, but he acted in the ways of penitence" (from a letter by Rabbi Yehezkel Feigin, http://www.shturem.net/index.php?section=artdays&id=1303, accessed 4 November 2009).

189. This point is given prominence in Kaminetsky, *Ta'arikhim bedivrei yemei Habad* (Kfar Habad: Kehot, 1994), 67–68. He stresses that Moshe was "redeemed from the priests on 19 Kislev 1815."

190. See Rabbi Dov Ber's letter in *Igrot kodesh*, 1:243. Rayyats was familiar with this letter, which was originally published in *Beit Rabbi*, 1:95–103.

191. See above.

192. Rayyats did not adhere to this chronology in his other works. For example, in *Divrei yemei hahozrim*, 9, he places Moshe with his brothers on Lag baOmer 1816, some five months after his ostensible flight. Elsewhere, Rayyats refers to Moshe's knowledge and love of argument (*Igrot kodesh: Moharayyats*, 14:167), and his sharp mind and organizational ability (*Sefer hatoladot: Moharayyats*, 2:56; *Sefer hatoladot: Moharash*, 148). He also tells how Shneur Zalman appointed Moshe to be his general manager, and how Moshe consequently traveled to St. Petersburg on several occasions (*Sefer hatoladot: Admor Hazaken*, 249), and refers to Moshe's assistance in spying on the French (ibid., 262). For more on Moshe, see *Sefer hasihot, 5701*, 40, 52, 54–55. Rayyats further recounts that Moshe, "whose talents were immense," asked permission to travel to St. Petersburg because he was "convinced that his arguments would effect his father's release from prison" (*Divrei hayamim hahem*, 91, 94–97).

193. Rachel Elior, "The Minsk Debate," *Jerusalem Studies in Jewish Thought* 1/4 (1982): 234 (Hebrew). Recently, a different version of this source came to light; see *Beit mashiah* 212 (1999): 26–29. On this work's unreliable nature, see Etkes, *Gaon of Vilna*, 121–27.

194. Here, as well, Rayyats mixes reality and fiction. The archival testimony substantiates his claim that Moshe accompanied his father, Rashaz, on his trip to St. Petersburg; this was, however, to find a cure for his mental illness. Another of Rayyats's pseudohistorical works links Prince Golitsyn to the Moshe story. According to this version, after the rabbinical convention of 1843, Golitsyn, then old and far from the centers of power, but full of admiration for the Habad zaddikim, "recalled his debates . . . some forty-four years earlier, and the impression he made on all, and on him especially" (*Admor haTsemah Tsedek utenu'at hahaskalah* [New York: Kehot, 1946], 29, 51–52.

195. *Divrei hayamim hahem*, 95–97. A censored form of this story appears in *Sefer hatoladot: Admor Hazaken* (1986), 3:744–46. On *Divrei hayamim hahem* as a fictional source, see note 171 above.

196. This evidently refers to Arkadii Suvarov (1783–1811), son of the famed general Alexander Suvarov. Arkadii also served in the military but was not known either as a thinker or theologian. I thank Uriah Sack for the identification.

197. *Divrei hayamim hahem*, 95–97.

198. Mordekhai was one of Rashaz's first followers, and "lived permanently in St. Petersburg for his business affairs and was close to the great princes in the upper echelons of the regime" (*Beit Rabbi*, 1:60, 65–66, 147).

199. We know of no ban issued in Vilna in 1783.

200. *Divrei hayamim hahem*, 98–102. These remarks were penned as early as 1922, in a letter sent to Menahem Mendel [Chaikin] of London. This letter has only recently been published. See *Igrot kodesh: Moharayyats*, 14:164–68. Support for the purported hasidic excommunication of the Vilna Gaon comes from David of Makov's *Zmir aritsim* (Warsaw, 1798): "And who could be more eminent in Torah and God-fearingness than our teacher Elijah of blessed memory, whom those evildoers excommunicated, as is known" (quoted in Wilensky, *Hasidim and Mitnaggedim*, 2:217). Heilman also de-

scribes an attempt by the Maggid's disciples to excommunicate the mitnagedim, but he frames it as a response to the ban of 1772 (*Beit Rabbi*, 1:9).

201. See note 150 above.

202. The two disciples of the Maggid who approached Shneur Zalman with the request that he join in the ban were evidently Shlomo of Karlin and Barukh of Mezhibozh. For additional references, see Assaf, *Ne'ehaz basevakh*, 119 note 210.

203. Yisrael Rapoport, *Divrei David* (Husiatyn, 1904), 59.

204. *Igrot kodesh: Moharayyats*, 7(1943):16–18.

205. Rafael Nahman Hakohen, one of the Habad elders, reported: "In 1908 an exceedingly old man named Reb Nahum of Radomyshl came to Lubavitch . . . He was close to the admor Tsemah Tsedek . . . He related many tales to the admor Rashab and to his son the admor Rayyats who wrote these stories down, stating *that he investigated and found that all of his stories were accurate*" (*Shmu'ot vesipurim*, 3:254). According to another Habad tradition, Reb Nahum met privately with Rayyats for three hours and told him of Moshe's asceticism. On that occasion, Reb Nahum also gave Rayyats "writings" by Moshe (Shneur Zalman Duchman, *Leshema ozen* [Brooklyn, 1963], 112). For additional stories recounted by the "graybeard" and his identification, see *Yagdil torah* 3/6 (1979): 227–29; *Heikhal haBesht* 12 [2006]: 140 (including note).

206. This represents a 300 square-kilometer triangle, which crosses the borders of three provinces. Two of the towns mentioned are linked to Habad Hasidism: although Chernobyl (Kiev Province), 100 kilometers southeast of Mozyr (Minsk Province), was the center of the Twersky dynasty, the zaddik Yaakov Yisrael (later of Hornistopol and Cherkas), the son of Mordekhai of Chernobyl, married the Mitteler Rebbe's daughter, and two of his daughters married other scions of the Schneersohn dynasty. One of these, Yosef Yitshak Schneersohn (1819–75), the son of the Tsemah Tsedek, married Yaakov Yisrael Twersky's daughter Hannah and moved to Ovruch in Volhynia Province, eighty kilometers southwest of Mozyr. See Yehoshua Mondshine, "Beshulei hagnazim," *Bita'on Habad* 19–20/38–39 (Shevat 1973): 12–13.

207. See note 160 above for Heilman's version of these events.

208. The hasid Hayyim Mordekhai Perlow noted that, in 1907 or 1908, he heard this old man state that he was already ninety-two. See Perlow, *Likutei sipurim* (New York: S. Z. Perlow, 1992), 132.

209. There are many examples, especially in hasidic courts, of "the silent," who took vows of silence for lengthy periods. For a detailed bibliography, see Assaf, *Ne'ehaz basevakh*, 121 note 217.

210. Rechtman, *Yidishe etnografye*, 127–29; *Kovets siftei tsadikim* 3 (1991): 71–73. Zeev Wolf's gravestone has also been identified in Zhitomir. See Michael Greenberg, *Graves of Tzaddikim in Russia* (Jerusalem: Shamir, 1989), 41. Another tradition places his burial site in Ivnytsia, thirty kilometers southeast of Zhitomir. See *Kitvei R. Yoshe Shuv* (Jerusalem,[1980?]), 176, no. 9.

211. For additional examples of Habad traditions on Moshe in oral stories, see Assaf, *Ne'ehaz basevakh*, 122 note 219.

212. *Sefer hatse'etsa'im*, 93–94.

213. The rabbi and dayyan Avraham Abba Kosovsky of Volkovysk, Lithuania, emi-

grated to Palestine and died there in 1898 (see Aryeh Leib Frumkin and Eliezer Rivlin, *Toldot hakhmei Yerushalayim* [Jerusalem, 1929], 3:262). His descendants—particularly his son Hayyim Yehoshua Kosovsky (1862–1960)—specialized in the compilation of concordances of rabbinic literature.

214. *Sefer hatse'etsa'im*, 94.

215. Mondshine, *Migdal oz*, 257. On Horowitz (1883–1978), see Wunder, *Meorei Galicia*, 2:247–49.

216. *Sefer hatoladot: Admor Hazaken*, 357–58 (1986 edition, 4:1192–93); *Shmu'ot vesipurim*, 2:27–28.

217. *Ohev yisrael* (Zhitomir, 1863), 215–16 ("Likutim, parashat vayikra"); translation quoted from Assaf, *Regal Way*, 56 (see the discussion there and Mark, *Mysticism and Madness*, 47–48). For more on hasidim and madness, see Assaf, *Ne'ehaz basevakh*, 127 note 226.

218. The inherent potential of the Russian archives extends well beyond the material on Moshe, to include fascinating archival documentation on the arrest and interrogation of Shneur Zalman (*Kerem Chabad* 4 [1992]) and of his son Dov Ber (Levin, *Ma'asar*), as well as the memorandum by Moshe Berlin discussed above.

219. Gedalya Oberlander, *Kfar Habad* 391 (1989): 34–35.

220. See Yitshak Alfasi's letter, *Kfar Habad* 395 (1989): 34, where he backs his praise of Oberlander by citing remarks that he attributes to the last Habad rebbe, regarding "the high estimation of Rabbi Moshe, of blessed memory, of whom falsehoods were put about." An additional example of Alfasi's art of concealment comes from another book he wrote (*Hamishim tsadikim* [Jerusalem: Karmel, 1997]),where he states: "Rabbi Moshe left home after his father's death and wandered among various places, thereby enabling the creation of a halo of legend, for better or for worse" (265). Moshe is missing from Alfasi's two genealogical works, *Hahasidut* (Tel Aviv: Sifriyat Maariv, 1977) and *Hahasidut midor ledor*, 2 vols. (Jerusalem: Makhon Da'at Yosef, 1995–98). There is an entry on "Moshe Schneersohn of Lyady" in the third and final volume of *Entsiklopediyah lehasidut*, edited by Alfasi (322–23). On the one hand, this entry is characterized by the usual flowery language ("a figure wrapped in mystery") and contains not a word of the "grief" Moshe caused. On the other hand, there is a reference (with reservations) to my article "In the Footsteps of Moshe, the Son of Rabbi Shneur Zalman of Lyady," which appeared in *Zion* 65 (2000). Sharp-eyed readers will certainly note that Alfasi omits the reference to conversion in title's first part, which reads "Convert or Saint."

221. Anshel Pfeffer, "Ha'av, haben veru'ah hakodesh," *Kol ha'ir*, 13 October 2000, 82–85.

222. Yair Sheleg, "Haben ha'oved shel Habad," *Ha-aretz*, 26 December 2002, 5. (For an English version, see http://failedmessiah.typepad.com/failed_messiahcom/2004/10/chabads_lost_so.html, accessed 9 October 2009.)

223. http://hydepark.hevre.co.il/topic.asp?topic_id=1948392&forum_id=1364, accessed 5 November 2009.

224. See ibid., 6ff. For Internet forums on *Ne'ehaz basevakh*, see Rose, "Haharedim veha'internet," 45–46; Yossi Chajes, "David Assaf: *Caught in the Thicket: Chapters of Crisis and Discontent in the History of Hasidism*," *Zion* 73 (2008): 89 (Hebrew).

Chapter 3. One Event, Multiple Interpretations: The Fall of the Seer of Lublin

1. Although the reason for this epithet (which was not used during his lifetime; see note 65 below) is not clear, it evidently relates to his spiritual and magical qualities, as reported by his disciples. For example, Zvi Elimelekh of Dinov wrote: "With my own eyes, I saw that when he read the name of a person who sent him a letter he would use his holy spirit to discern this person's characteristics, whether he is pure and acts honestly, or the opposite, heaven forfend" (*Igra depirka* [Lemberg, 1858], 5a, no. 25; see Zvi Elimelekh, *Igra dekalah* [Lemberg, 1868], "Parashat pekudei," 26b). Late hasidic hagiography supplies additional explanations, like "because he used to look from one end of the earth to the other" (*Eser orot*, 83, no. 1; additional explanations follow). One of the explanations was more "realistic": "When he was ten years old he covered his eyes so that he could see nothing, removing the covering only to study the Torah. He acted thus for fifteen years. And that was why he merited glory in his old age, that he had the ability to see what was happening all over the world" (letter from Rabbi Yosef Lowenstein of Serotsk to Avraham Kahana, *Nahalat Tsvi* 15 [1997]: 201); see also Yitshak Landau: "For several years he tied a covering over his eyes and did not look at all; for his entire life he did not look outside his immediate surroundings" (*Zikaron tov* [Piotrkov, 1892], 18); "in his youth he kept his eyes closed for seven years lest he see shameful things, except for when he prayed and studied, for he had to peruse the book in which he read or prayed. Because of this his eyes dimmed and he became short-sighted" (*Eser orot*, 89, no. 22). On the power of sight as a feature of holy men, see Haviva Pedaya, "The Baal Shem Tov, R. Jacob Joseph of Polonnoye, and the Maggid of Mezhirech: Outlines for a Religious Typology," *Daat* 45 (2000): 27–28 (Hebrew).

2. An Aramaic text from the *Zohar* recited on Friday nights in the hasidic prayer rite.

3. *Eser kedushot*, 89, no. 22. See Yitshak Yehuda Yehiel Safrin, *Megilat setarim*, edited by Naftali Ben-Menahem (Jerusalem: Mossad Harav Kook, 1944), 11.

4. *Nifle'ot harabbi*, 87, no. 290.

5. Aaron Ze'ev Aescoly states: "The court of the Seer was the nursery of Hasidism in its Polish version, but it did not acquire its form there" (Aescoly, *Hasidism in Poland*, 49). In his opinion, the Polish version of Hasidism was actually set in Pshishkha. See my introduction to Aescoly's book, 16–17. Although much has been written on the Seer, a definitive biographical study is still a desideratum. See, for now, Bromberg, *Hahozeh;* Alfasi, *Hahozeh*; Tsvi Meir Rabinowicz, *Beyn Pshishkha leLublin: Ishim veshitot behasidut Polin* (Jerusalem: Kesharim, 1997), 103–58; *Entsiklopediyah lehasidut*, 2:282–91. On the Seer's theoretical writings (which some researchers, such as Dubnow and Aescoly tend to ignore), see Mendel Piekarz, *Between Ideology and Reality: Humility, Ayin, Self-Negation and Devekut in the Hasidic Thought* (Jerusalem: Bialik Institute, 1994), 130–41 (Hebrew); Rachel Elior, "The Innovation of Polish Hasidism," *Tarbiz* 62 (1992–93): 381–432 (Hebrew); Elior, "Between *Yesh* and *Ayin*," 393–455. For an additional bibliography, see Assaf, "Hasidut Polin bame'ah ha19," 364–65.

6. For a critical, annotated edition of this text, see Assaf, *Ne'ehaz basevakh*, 166–78.

7. According to hasidic sources, the Seer had great reservations about Napoleon (as

opposed to Menahem Mendel of Rimanov, who prayed for his victory; see *Eser tsahtsahot*, 87, no. 17). But the Seer's messianic views and the attempts to bring redemption associated with his name in and around hasidic legend only indirectly concern this study. Some writers express doubts regarding the purported connection between the Seer and attempts to usher in the messianic age. See Alfasi, *Bisdeh hahasidut*, 411; Mendel Piekarz, "Hasidism as Reflected in the Collection *Tif'eret Shlomo* by Rabbi Shlomo of Radomsk," *Gal-Ed* 14 (1995): 37–38 (Hebrew). Note, however, that the extant writings of the Seer are early, dating from the late eighteenth century (see Elior, "Between *Yesh* and *Ayin*," 397–98), and do not reflect his thinking and spiritual world as these crystallized in his Lublin period. In addition, the messianic image was linked to the Seer shortly after his death, as seen in the satirical work *Gilgul nefesh*. See below.

8. For the effects of the Napoleonic wars on Polish Jewry and the Duchy of Warsaw, see Azriel N. Frenk, *Yehudei Polin biyemei milhemet Napoleon* (Warsaw: Hatsfirah, 1913); Artur Eisenbach, *The Emancipation of the Jews in Poland, 1780–1870* (Oxford: Basil Blackwell, 1991); Mahler, *Modern Times*, 3:61–94 (abridged English edition, 347–68); Mevorakh, *Napoleon utekufato*, 173–75; "Hahasidut veyahasah leNapoleon," in Alfasi, *Bisdeh hahasidut*, 249–60.

9. For the German, see Verus [Ahron Marcus], *Der Chassidismus*, 163–65; for the Hebrew, see Marcus, *Hahasidut* (1980), 120–21. Alfasi noted that Marcus was the source for the story of the Seer's fall; he also noted Marcus's questionable reliability as a source and called the story an invention (*Bisdeh hahasidut*, 412).

10. An expert in the history of Hasidism, Rabbi Yosef Lowenstein of Serotsk preserved important traditions, especially those regarding Polish Hasidism. See Shlomo Shrebrek, *Zikhronot hamotsi la'or Shlomo Shrebrek* (Tel Aviv: Shrebrek, 1955), 139; Wilensky, *Hasidim and Mitnaggedim*, 2:350–60; "Kitvei hagaon hahasid Rabbi Yosef miSerotsk," *Nahalat Tsvi* 14 (1997): 170–83; 15 (1997): 198–213. Nonetheless, Lowenstein was not always precise, and his remarks and writings contain many mistakes.

11. Napoleon was not taken captive; this apparently refers to his exile to Elba in April 1814.

12. This is Kalonymus Kalman Epstein of Krakow (d. 1823), an outstanding disciple of Elimelekh of Lyzhansk and the Seer of Lublin. His *Ma'or vashemesh* (Breslau, 1842) is a basic tract of hasidic teachings. At the time, he was living in Nowe Miasto. On him, see Mahler, *Modern Times*, 6:40–42; Wunder, *Meorei Galicia*, 1:276–78; Mendel Piekarz, *The Hasidic Leadership: Authority and Faith in Zaddikim as Reflected in the Hasidic Literature* (Jerusalem: Bialik Institute, 1999), 213–19 (Hebrew).

13. Yehuda Leib of Zaklikov and of Zawichost was also a disciple of Elimelekh of Lyzhansk and the Seer, and a leading opponent of the "Holy Jew" of Pshishkha.

14. Apparently Rabbi Zvi Yehezkel Michelsohn of Plonsk, who lived in Zaklikov in his youth.

15. The square brackets appear in the original; emphasis mine. Evidently either Michelsohn or Yisrael Berger added these bracketed sentences. The last sentence appears only in the first edition of *Eser orot* (Piotrkov, 1907) and was omitted in all subsequent editions. See also below.

16. The seemingly grotesque description of the lottery taking place while the Seer

was groaning with pain is more properly viewed as a projection of his funeral; it was the practice to announce that only disciples could carry the coffin at the funeral of an eminent rabbi. It may also allude to the story of the Besht's death: "He showed them [the members of the burial society] the signs on each of the members of his own body, and he explained how the soul emanates from this member and from that member" (*Shivhei haBesht*, 256). This motif was explicitly incorporated into the fictional funeral of the Maggid of Mezhirech: "There was a feud between the disciples and the members of the Mezhirech burial society, for the burial society members argued that it was their business to bury the rabbi, whereas the disciples said that since they had served him during his lifetime it would be inappropriate for strangers to do so upon his death. And they reached a compromise . . . and afterwards *the disciples who were members of the burial society cast lots for the members of the Maggid's body* and the rabbi [Shneur Zalman of Lyady] received the golden head (Michael Frumkin, *Shivhei haRav* [Lemberg, 1864], 13 [my numbering]); Frumkin, *Kehal hasidim* [Lemberg (1870?)], 77). The description of the lottery is also reminiscent of the Temple lottery for who would place what parts of the daily sacrifice on the altar (Mishnah *Tamid*, 3:1) and may reflect a perception of the zaddik's body as a sacrifice.

17. Reb Shmuel of Kuriv was a disciple of Elimelekh of Lyzhansk and the Seer. From 1815 on, he was the admor of Kuriv in Galicia, and later of Sokolow and Wengrow, in the Lublin district, where he died in 1820 (see Alfasi, *Hahozeh*, 283; Granatstein, *Hashvil vehaderekh*).

18. Part of *Tikun hatsot, Tikun Leah* consists mainly of biblical, Talmudic, and zoharic passages recited at midnight. See Gershom Scholem, *Elements of the Kabbalah and Its Symbolism* (Jerusalem: Bialik Institute, 1976), 144–45 (Hebrew).

19. *Eser orot*, 91, no. 27. Minor reworkings of this story appear in additional hasidic sources, such as *Nifle'ot harabbi*, 51–52, no. 108; Yehuda Aryeh Frankl Te'omim, *Ohalei shem* (Bilgoray: Zeilingold, 1911), 49–50; *Siah sarfei kodesh* (Rakats), 5:103, no. 43; *Darkhei hayyim veshalom*, 143–46; Granatstein, *Hashvil vehaderekh*, 93–95 (his addition is of interest: "To the greatness of the joy . . . testified the empty mead bottles that the associates of the Seer drank in his presence, which remained on the windowsill of the small window"—accordingly, it was his associates who drank, and not the Seer); *Beit tsadikim ya'amod*, 2:141.

20. The Seer's study house was located at 28 Szeroka Street. This is how the historian Majer Balaban described it in the second decade of the twentieth century: "The courtyard, which is entered through a narrow corridor, has a large room with a wooden roof and many windows: this is the *kloiz* where the Seer prayed and where he spent most of the day. The Seer's living quarters were in the front of the house, on the first floor. The *kloiz* is a large room, plastered, with a roof of wooden beams. At the entrance to the *kloiz* there is a small room in the shape of a cage: this is where the women pray . . . At present, on weekdays the *kloiz* serves as lodging for the poor and crippled, who spend most of their days and nights here and warm themselves at the large stove in the winter" ("Tiyul begeto Lublin," in *Lublin*, 244–45; see also below). On the granting of permission to the Seer to found a prayer house in his private home, see Assaf, *Ne'ehaz basevakh*, 142 note 19.

21. For some data on Bernhard, see Assaf, "Hasidut Polin bame'ah ha19," 365–66.

22. Note the explicit messianic overtones connected with the conversion of Tisha beAv into a joyful day, which was also a central facet of Sabbateanism. See Gershom Scholem, *Sabbatai Sevi: The Mystical Messiah, 1626–1676*, translated by R. J. Zwi Werblowsky (Princeton, N.J.: Princeton University Press, 1973), 615–20, 629–32. The irony of the hasidic interpretation of the Seer's fall (traditionally, the Messiah was to be born on Tisha beAv, and the Seer died on that date) was noted by Aescoly, *Hasidism in Poland*, 62.

23. Marcus, *Hahasidut* (1980), 120. The rabbi of Sosnovits is David Pardes of Stashev, who came to that town in 1900. See Meir S. Geshuri, ed., *Sefer Sosnovits vehasvivah beZaglambiya*, vol. 1 (Tel Aviv, 1973), 64, 504–5.

24. It is possible that the folk etymology equating Napoleon with *nefilah* played some role in shaping the myth. See the hagiographic story regarding Napoleon, who came to the Maggid of Kozhenits dressed as a simple man. Upon his departure, the Maggid called out after him, "You shall surely fall, Napoleon will fall" (*Eser tsahtsahot*, 87, no. 17; Avraham Hayyim Michelsohn, *Ateret Menahem* [Bilgoray, 1910], 38, no. 125. The language used refers to Esther 6:13).

25. For the possibility that the Seer tried to commit suicide, see the end of this chapter.

26. See chapter 1.

27. This tradition's polemical nature is firmly established by the very existence of another hasidic tradition which sees it as a "joke," and connects these remarks to an entirely different set of circumstances. In 1911, when Moshe Menahem Walden of Warsaw expressed an interest in printing an anthology of stories about the Seer and his teachings, Rabbi Zvi Yehezkel Michelsohn of Plonsk sent him a letter containing an anecdote that he had found in the Lithuanian preacher Binyamin Lewin's *Hamesh yadot* (Vilna, 1904), 2:354. This anecdote related the Seer's chastisement of the members of the burial society for drinking vodka at funerals. When one of them replied that it "is the time-honored custom . . . that the burial society members drink copious amounts of vodka while arranging the funeral and, in a hundred years hence, when his [the Seer's] time to leave the world comes, then too we will take a glass of vodka without diverging from established custom. The holy rabbi immediately countered: Be certain that when my time comes I will not even allow you a spoonful of cold water. And so it came to pass." In response to this story, Walden wrote that he had heard it "from trustworthy informants in a different version," surmising that it was the author of *Hamesh yadot* who was mistaken (*Nifle'ot harabbi*, 9).

Furthermore, the hasidic tradition of mitnagedic joy on the day of the Seer's fall echoes the mitnagedic tradition about hasidic rejoicing at the Gaon of Vilna's death (Sukkot 1797): "Immediately after his death the hasidim gathered and made a joyful feast . . . they drank to inebriation . . . and danced the whole night long" (Wilensky, *Hasidim and Mitnaggedim*, 2:95; see also Dubnow, *Toldot hahasidut*, 254–55; *Kerem Chabad* 4/1 [1992], 212–13).

Ironically, Yosef Perl, the avowed enemy of Hasidism, also died on Simhat Torah, in 1839. Rumor had it that the "hasidim danced wildly" on his grave, a rumor strongly denied by the friends of the deceased (see *Kerem hemed* 5 [Prague, 1841]: 163, 167). Polemically speaking, the spreading of such rumors, even if baseless, was equivalent to desecration of the grave itself; see Mahler, *Hasidism and the Jewish Enlightenment*, 148. Another unnoticed source also reports hasidic joy at Perl's death. This was a report written by two Scottish missionaries, who happened to be in Tarnopol on the day of Perl's funeral. They visited the school that Perl had founded and run, and observed: "There is great mutual contempt between the Jews of the Old and those of the New School. They told us that the rabbi who founded the New School in Tarnapol had died there that very day, and all the Chasidim were rejoicing at the news" (Bonar and M'Cheyne, *Mission of Inquiry to the Jews*, 444; see also 448–49).

28. Shlomo Gabriel Rosenthal, *Hitgalut hatsadikim* (Warsaw, 1905), 21; *Eser orot*, 90, no. 26. The continuation contains a typical hagiographic description of how the Lublin mitnagedim underwent a change of heart; upon realizing the Seer's spirituality, the Lubliners invited him to reside in their city. The suburb of Czechov is located northeast of Lublin and is also called Wieniawa. During the nineteenth century, this area was *juridica*—namely, it belonged to the nobility and had an independent legal status. See Rosenthal, *Hitgalut hatsadikim*, 20; Balaban, *Die Judenstadt von Lublin*, 80; *Pinkas Hakehillot: Lublin*, 13. On the Seer's move from Czechov to the heart of Lublin's Jewish quarter, see Wilensky, *Hasidim and Mitnaggedim*, 2:356. See also Marcin Wodziński, "How Should We Count Hasidim in Congress Poland?" *Gal-Ed* 20 (2006): 111.

29. *Nifle'ot harabbi*, 44, no. 79; 86, no. 283.

30. Shmuel of Shinova, *Tanna devei Eliyahu im . . . ramatayim tsofim* (Warsaw, 1881), "Seder Eliyahu zuta," 110, chap. 24, no. 22 ("It was his way to constantly pester the Rabbi of Lublin with questions"); *Devarim arevim*, 1:36b, no. 3; *Eser orot*, 93, no. 38. On Rabbi Azriel, see also Zederbaum, *Keter kehunah*, 124–25; Shmuel Barukh Nissenbaum, *Lekorot hayehudim beLublin* (Lublin, 1900), 95–96, 136; Bromberg, *Hahozeh*, 87–95.

31. *Devarim arevim*, 1:37b, no. 10 (and also in the errata in the beginning of the book); *Nifle'ot harabbi*, 29–30, no. 46. Hasidic hagiography relates that, on his deathbed, Rabbi Azriel voiced regret for having persecuted the Seer (ibid. 84, no. 261). Another prominent figure involved in this campaign was the Lithuanian rabbi Dov Berish Hielpern-Szwerdszarf, who preached in Lublin (d. Tevet 1823). On his opposition to the Seer, see Zederbaum, *Keter kehunah*, 124–25. This mitnaged received polite treatment in a hagiographic hasidic work by his relative Avraham Hayyim Michelsohn, which even includes a long quote from Zederbaum's antihasidic work! See *Ohel Naftali*, 117–20. See also Moses Jacob Szwerdszarf, *Da'at linevonim* (Munkatsh, 1899), "Megilat yuhasin hakatsar," 3; Bromberg, *Hahozeh*, 82–87.

32. This is a paraphrase of Genesis 10:8–9. These verses treat Nimrod, in rabbinic tradition considered a great evildoer. The hint is obvious.

33. The image of "flocks upon flocks" may create the impression that many hundreds of hasidim attended the Seer's court, also alluded to in later sources: "*Thousands of people* traveled from near and far to the holy one of Lublin" (Zederbaum, *Keter kehunah*, 124). But this is evidently far from the truth. Recently Marcin Wodziński argued that the number of hasidim in Congress Poland during the Seer's lifetime (until 1815) was marginal, and much lower than the impression its opponents tried to create. Between the Seer's death and 1830, there was a moderate increase in the num-

ber of adherents of Hasidism; nonetheless, they comprised no more than a tenth of the Jewish population. See Marcin Wodziński, "How Many Hasidim Were There in Congress Poland? On the Demographics of the Hasidic Movement in Poland during the First Half of the Nineteenth Century," *Gal-Ed* 19 (2004): 37–40, 46–47; and the ensuing debate in *Gal-Ed* 20 (2006), including Wodziński, "How Should We Count Hasidim in Congress Poland?" *Gal-Ed* 20 (2006): 111.

34. Quoted in Wilensky, *Hasidim and Mitnaggedim*, 2:195.

35. From this point on, David of Makov mocks the Seer according to Habakkuk 2:19: "Ah, you who say, 'Wake up' to wood/'Awaken' to inert stone!/Can that give an oracle?/Why, it is encased in gold and silver,/But there is no breath inside it."

36. Here the author bases his mockery of the Seer on Hosea 7:6: "For they have made ready their heart like an oven, while they lie in wait/Through the night their baker has slept/In the morning it flares up/Like a blazing fire."

37. At night, the Seer ostensibly must cease extorting money from his followers, according to Isaiah 14:4: "How is the taskmaster vanished, How is oppression ended."

38. This part is based on Micah 3:6–7: "It shall be night for you/So that you cannot prophesy/And it shall be dark for you/So that you cannot divine . . . The seers shall be shamed/And the diviners confounded." For the text, see Wilensky, *Hasidim and Mitnaggedim*, 2:208; Dubnow, *Toldot hahasidut*, 216–17, 326–27.

39. Quoted in Wilensky, *Hasidim and Mitnaggedim*, 2:313. It is not clear exactly when the Seer moved from Lantzut to Lublin; various legends are attached to different dates (compounding the difficulty is the fact that the Seer continued to sign his approbations "Yaakov Yitshak Halevi Horowitz of Lantzut" even after he was living in Lublin). See Alfasi, *Hahozeh*, 42–43, 48–49. Loebl's *Sefer vikuah* was first published in Warsaw in 1798; if he was telling the truth, then he visited Lantzut in the winter of 1796–97. Accordingly, the Seer did not leave Lantzut for Czechov before 1798.

40. Deinard, *Zmir aritsim harishon*. The book *Zmir aritsim veharvot tsurim* (Wicked shears and flint knives) was first published in Oleksiniec, near Brody, in 1772. For a detailed discussion of the contents of the book and its editions, see Wilensky, *Hasidim and Mitnaggedim*, 1:27–69. On Landesberg and Deinard, see ibid., 32.

41. Deinard, *Zmir aritsim harishon*, 1–5 (second pagination). Landesberg, the scion of a wealthy family of leaseholders, collected rare books. Ribal, a private tutor at his home and apparently also a relative, quarreled with him and wrote two sharp satires about him. See "Dor yashar," *Hamelits* 6, 15 February 1866, 72–73; Gottlober, *Memoires and Travels*, 2:116; Klausner, *Historiyah*, 3:65; Shmuel Ettinger and Chone Shmeruk, "The History of the Jews in Kremenets," in *On the History of the Jews in Poland and Russia: Shmuel Ettinger Collected Essays* (Jerusalem: Shazar, 1994), 351, 355 (Hebrew); Yehuda Friedlander, *Bemisterei hasatira: Hebrew Satire in Europe in the Eighteenth and Nineteenth Centuries*, (Ramat Gan: Bar-Ilan University Press, 1989), 2:116–17 (Hebrew).

42. In his introduction, Landesberg noted that he gave his original copy of *Zmir aritsim* to Yosef Perl as a gift through Mendel Lefin (second pagination, 3), and retained a copy for himself. Deinard used this second copy; accordingly, his edition has many corruptions, and one document has been omitted altogether. See Wilensky, *Hasidim and Mitnaggedim*, 1:35.

43. Deinard, *Zmir aritsim harishon*, 5 (second pagination). For the text of *Ma'asei harav*, see ibid., 5–11. The reference to *Emek refa'im* is not fortuitous. Landesberg made a copy of this work from a manuscript and evidently planned to publish it together with *Zmir aritsim*, *Ma'asei harav*, and *Megilah afah* (see below). This plan never came to fruition. For a comprehensive discussion, see the introduction to the forthcoming critical, annotated edition of *Emek refa'im* that I am currently preparing with Jonatan Meir.

44. There is no reason to doubt this date, which appears in the manuscript as the day on which the narrator arrived in Lublin. The satire was evidently written not long thereafter.

45. Although not printed until 1819 in Vienna, *Megaleh temirin* was submitted to the Austrian censor in 1816. See I. Vaynlez, "Yosef Perl—Zeyn lebn un shafn," *Yosef Perls yidishe ksovim* (Vilna, 1937), xxvii. For polemical antihasidic texts written before 1815 that probably influenced Perl's *Megaleh temirin*, see Shmuel Werses, "Hidden Polemical Letters on the Nature of Hasidism," in *Jerusalem Studies in Jewish Thought* 13, *Rivka Shatz-Uffenheimer Memorial Volume* 2 (1996): 447–93 (Hebrew); Werses, "An Unknown Maskilic Polemical Tractate against the Hasidism," in *Studies in Hasidism*, 65–88 (Hebrew).

46. For a description of the transmission of Landesberg's collection after its purchase by Deinard, see Assaf, *Ne'ehaz basevakh*, 148 note 49.

47. See Katz, "Igrot maskilim," 268. Deinard's version was also noted by Klausner, *Historiyah*, 2:329 note 28; and Werses, *From Language to Language*, 200 note 91. See Rubinstein's introduction to his edition of Perl's *Al mahut kat hahasidim*, 18–19, 53–54. Rubinstein surmised that the manuscript had been copied in 1815 or 1816, and mistakenly viewed it as part of a larger work titled *Shivhei Alekse*. As we shall see below, other than their shared author, there is no link between the two works.

48. Perl Collection, 4° 1153, folder 110a, Manuscripts Department and IMHM, NLIS. See also Assaf, "Hasidut Polin bame'ah ha19," 373.

49. Katz, "Igrot maskilim," 268 note 8; Shmuel Werses, "Ginzei Yosef Perl biYerushalayim vegilguleyhem," *Hauniversitah* 19/1 (March 1974): 43–45.

50. This letter was published by Katz, "Igrot maskilim," 273; see also below.

51. Katz's comment was partially and faultily copied by Rubinstein (Perl, *Al mahut kat hahasidim*, 54). The manuscript is torn in several places and my reconstructions appear in curly brackets. Boldface in original.

52. Philip Koffler's itemization of the contents of the Perl Collection is housed in the Perl Collection, Appendix B. This item is recorded as no. 26 (no. 41 in the list Katz used). Note that Koffler neither mentions authorship, nor attributes it to Landesberg. As recorded by Koffler, the date, taken from Isaiah 46:1, has no significance because he did not copy the supralinear dots that indicate the exact date. The mentions of the press at Charny Ostra (which had no Hebrew press) and Sudlikov perhaps hint that the writer was close to the coterie of Hayyim Malage of Bar (Podolia), who authored the antihasidic satire "Gedulat R. Wolf miTsharny-Ostraha" (published in *Perls yidishe ksovim*, 221–44, and mistakenly attributed to Perl; see the introduction by Z. Kalmanovitch, lxxxvi ff.).

53. "Is he not the well-known man named Reb Itsik Lantzuter, who at present sits

firmly on the throne of Hasidism in the big city of Lublin" (Deinard, *Zmir aritsim harishon*, 6; see also below).

54. Vols. 1–2 (Zholkva, 1822–28); vol. 3 (Lemberg, 1853). For further details on Bloch and his works, see Assaf, *Ne'ehaz basevakh*, 150–51 note 59.

55. Katz, "Igrot maskilim," 273; the letter is housed in the Schwadron Collection, "Bloch, Shimshon Halevi," Manuscripts Department and IMHM, NLIS.

56. *Shivhei haBesht* (Rubinstein), 237–38.

57. See, for example *Shivhei haBesht* (Rubinstein), 153–54, 177, 192, 215, 230, 270–71; *Keter shem tov* (1795; reprint, Brooklyn, 1987), 2:124–25, no. 464. The fact that the Besht had a permanent coachman is of interest, because only the wealthy had personal coachmen; ordinary people hired one for specific journeys only.

58. Perl, *Al mahut kat hahasidim*, 71; see also 151. Perl's remarks are based on a story found in *Shivhei haBesht* (Rubinstein), 153–54, but the original dubs him the "servant." See also the version in the manuscript edition of *Shivhei haBesht* (Yehoshua Mondshine, ed., *Shivhei ha-Baal Shem Tov: A Facsimile of a Unique Manuscript, Variant Versions and Appendices* [Jerusalem: Mondshine, 1982], 103, 177).

59. The name Aleksey first appears in *Sefer mifalot hatsadikim* (Lemberg [1866?]), 44; see Gedalyah Nigal, ed., *Menachem Mendel Bodek: Hasidic Tales: Critical Edition with Introduction and Indices* (Tel Aviv: Golan, 1990), 105–9 (Hebrew). For further details on the appearance of the name Aleksey in hasidic sources, see Assaf, *Ne'ehaz basevakh*, 152 note 65.

60. For details, see Assaf, *Ne'ehaz basevakh*, 152 note 66.

61. In his introduction to Perl's *Al mahut kat hahasidim*, 18–19, Rubinstein speculatively attributes the absence of a portrait of the Seer in the mire to lack of funds; however, Perl clearly spoke only in jest. Rubinstein correctly links this picture and the picture of the author that was supposedly to be published at the beginning of Perl's *Megaleh temirin* ("in case the author's name isn't written in the *bukh*, maybe it contains the author's picture, the way the sinners print their picture at the beginning of their trashy books"—Perl, *Megaleh temirin*, letter 1; idem, *Al mahut kat hahasidim*, 16–19). Rubinstein argues that Bloch's satire influenced Perl in this regard, but it is also possible to argue the converse, that the idea of the portrait originated with Perl, who incorporated it here and there. See Letter 1 in *Megaleh temirin*, in which Perl refers to the Seer of Lublin: "Last *Shabes* there was here by our *rebe* a visitor from Galicia from the Lubliner's people and he brought our *rebe* greetings from the *tsadek* of Lublin with some *nigunim*. Our *rebe* added a few sections to them and made them whole" (English edition, 23). Is it possible that this hints that the "visitor from Galicia" was none other than Bloch, and that "our *rebe*" was none other than Perl? But this remains speculative. In addition, Ribal's satire *Divrei tsadikim*, which Perl edited, makes it clear that the fictional author of *Megaleh temirin*, the hasid Ovadya ben Petahya, was a disciple of the Seer. See Meir, *Words of the Righteous*, 76. Meir's speculation that Perl himself (who is identified with Ovadya) was a student of the Seer has no basis.

62. It was Perl's practice to intervene in and edit works sent to him, and to make additions of his own. See Klausner, *Historiyah*, 3:37–38; Meir, *Words of the Righteous*, 24–25.

63. Explanatory notes are a known satiric device for the "initiated," intended to award "canonical" or "scientific" status to the text so annotated. On the significance of maskilic satiric notes and their definition as "hostile documentation," see Shmuel Werses, *Story and Source: Studies in the Development of Hebrew Prose* (Ramat Gan: Massada, 1971), 21–22 (Hebrew); Ben 'Ami Feingold, "*Zifronah:* A.M. Dick's Neglected Satire," *Jerusalem Studies in Hebrew Literature* 9 (1986): 254–57 (Hebrew).

64. On Perl's disciples and friends whom he employed in copying works intended for publication, see Abraham Meir Habermann, *K'vusei Yahad: Essays and Notes on Jewish Culture and Literature* (Jerusalem: Rubin Mass, 1980), 144 (Hebrew); Meir, *Words of the Righteous*, 25.

65. This satire may preserve the Seer's original appellation, "Haroeh." The appellation "Hahozeh" is late and does not appear in print before the 1860s. See Bromberg, *Hahozeh*, 119–20; Alfasi, *Hahozeh*, 58. David of Makov's remark (cited above), that "the seers shall be shamed and the diviners confounded," probably refers to this appellation.

66. Examples decrying hasidic drunkenness are legion, and Perl consistently refers to it in his satiric oeuvre, in *Megaleh temirin* in particular. For additional examples, see Assaf, *Ne'ehaz basevakh*, 155 note 73.

67. See BT *Avodah Zarah* 20b (for a variant, see Mishnah *Sotah* 9:15). See also Moses Hayyim Luzzatto, *Mesillat Yesharim: The Path of the Upright* (Philadelphia: Jewish Publication Society, 1936), chaps. 10–12 ("Cleanness," "Details as to the Quality of Cleanness," and "How to Acquire the Trait of Spiritual Cleanness").

68. On another vulgar work by Perl, which was concealed and never published, see Shmuel Werses, "An Unknown Satirical Work by Joseph Perl: The Periodical *Kerem Hemed* and Its Contributors as Seen by a Hassid," *Hasifrut* 1 (1968): 224 note 68 (Hebrew). Perl evidently erased a crass sentence.

69. Assaf, *Ne'ehaz basevakh*, 171–73 (English translation quoted, slightly revised, from David Assaf, "One Event, Two Interpretations: The Fall of the Seer of Lublin in Hasidic Memory and Maskilic Satire," *Polin* 15 [2002] 200–203).

70. Mass inebriety on Simhat Torah night also appears as a motif in Dick's satire *Zifronah* (see above). However, this is not just literary, but also realistic. See, for example, Kotik, *Journey*, 362–64; Yisrael Isser Kasovich, *Shishim shnot hayyim: Zikhronot hayyai vehayyei dori biyisrael (1859–1919)* (Berlin: Dvir, 1923), 139–40.

71. Erter, *Hatsofeh leveit yisrael*, 156–58. On the satire *Gilgul nefesh*, first published in Leipzig, 1845, see Klausner, *Historiyah*, 2:327–30; Moshe Pelli, "Satiric Techniques in *Gilgul Nefesh* by Erter," *Proceedings of the Sixth World Congress of Jewish Studies* (Jerusalem: World Union of Jewish Studies, 1977), 3:337–48 (Hebrew); Pelli, "Erter's Storytelling Technique in his Satire 'Transmigration of a Soul,'" *Criticism and Interpretation* 11–12 (1978): 121–39 (Hebrew); Shmeruk, *Yiddish Literature*, 234–36; Werses, *From Language to Language*, 211–31. Friedlander's comment in his introduction that, apart from the allusion to Shlomo Kopler (who initiated a tax on candles in Galicia), the character who transmogrifies in this satire "is a stereotypical character without any individual characteristics" (Erter, *Hatsofeh leveit yisrael*, introduction, 40) is not precisely correct. The first to identify this rebbe with the Seer was Dov Sadan, who noted that Erter's remarks are a "maskilic mirror of the hasidic legend on . . . the Seer of Lublin and his famous fall on Simhat Torah. Comparison of these two perspec-

tives is a separate topic" ("Gilgulo shel gilgul," *Betseitkha uveohalekha*, 73). Mahler as well noted this identification (*Modern Times*, 6:123). For another identification, see note 74 below.

72. Erter may refer to the Seer of Lublin and his love of wine in another satire (see *Hatsofeh leveit yisrael*, 89–90). Perhaps Erter's "watchman," who observes the injustices of his contemporary society, is a foil for the drunken Seer who sees false angels with his spirit? (See also Simon Halkin, *Trends and Forms in Modern Hebrew Literature* [Jerusalem: Bialik Institute, 1984], 1:178 [Hebrew]).

73. The statement "and from drunkenness and heavy-headedness I fell through the lattice, breaking my neck" alludes to the killing of King Eglon of Moab by Ehud (Judges 3:23–24), to Sisera's fall (Judges 5:27–28), and to Ahaziah (2 Kings 1:2) and Eli (1 Samuel 4:18).

74. Thus his mockery of the zaddik who lives in a "spacious house," "a royal palace," which houses the "Messiah's palace" (Erter, *Hatsofeh leveit yisrael*, 152) clearly alludes to Yisrael of Ruzhin (see Assaf, *Regal Way*, 275). Erter was definitely familiar with Ribal's *Emek refa'im*, written in the early 1820s and disseminated in manuscript copies, as Erter's *Gilgul nefesh* contains a scene from *Emek refa'im*: the episode of the zaddik placing a grain of barley in the child's rectum (Erter, *Hatsofeh leveit yisrael*, 151–52; Levinsohn, *Emek refa'im*, 12–13). See Sadan, *Betseitkha uveohalekha*, 65–68; Shmeruk, *Yiddish Literature*, 193. Note too that the scene in which the zaddik invites heavenly guests on Simhat Torah also derives from *Emek refa'im*, 10–11.

75. The tendency to demean the hasidic world and to emphasize the hasidic concern with excretion is characteristic of antihasidic satire. It is not fortuitous that the plot of *Megaleh temirin* opens with the zaddik being on his way to the outhouse (Letter 1) and concludes with his death there (Letter 147). This satiric portrayal of the zaddik in the outhouse is drawn from the description of the Besht's death (*Shivhei haBesht*, 255–57), where it says that the Besht was "sick with diarrhea" and relates that he "went to the toilet" before his death.

76. See note 27 above. Dov Sadan noted this matter (*Betseitkha uveohalekha*, 73) but interpreted it as Erter's mistake.

77. The Seer lived on Szeroka Street (*szeroka* means "wide" in Polish).

78. An allusion to the fall of the wicked king of Israel, Ahaziah ben Ahab, who was injured when he fell through the lattice of his upper chamber (2 Kings 1:2).

79. Zederbaum, *Keter kehunah*, 125.

80. *Hashahar* 8 (1877): 418. On this satire and its author, see Assaf, *Ne'ehaz basevakh*, 160 note 90.

81. *Pardes* 1 (1892): 221–42. It was also published in typescript in Odessa, 1892.

82. Dubnow, *Toldot hahasidut*, 380. Shapiro's letters have been preserved in the Dubnow Collection, YIVO Institute, New York. Eight of the letters were published by Edelbaum, "Letters," but Edelbaum's edition is faulty and contains many errors of transcription and interpretation.

83. Edelbaum, "Letters," *Tagim* 2:55. The letter is dated 5 Elul 1891. The original document is housed in the Dubnow Collection (file 949, no. 73985). Shapiro returned to this matter in a letter to Dubnow, dated 15 Av 1893 (Dubnow Collection, file 1032, no. 77551).

84. Dubnow, *Toldot hahasidut*, 330.

85. The other three were Yisrael the Maggid of Kozhinets (d. on Erev Sukkot 1814), Menahem Mendel of Rimanov (d. Iyyar 1815), and the Seer's disciple Rabbi Yaakov Yitshak, "the Holy Jew" of Pshishkha (d. Sukkot 1813). Dubnow viewed 1815 as a turning point in hasidic history, and his study of Hasidism terminates with that year. See Dubnow, *Toldot hahasidut*, viii, 37, 332. See Mahler, *Modern Times*, 3:307.

86. "The hasid, the rabbi Moshe Meir Shmerler, related that he heard from elderly hasidim that it never happened, as many think, that the rabbi of Lublin stubbornly desired to bring the Messiah. Rather, he sought some secret knowledge that was hidden from the heavenly seraphim and that resulted in the well-known event" (Mordekhai Hakohen Blum, *Sefer otsar yisrael* [Jerusalem: privately printed, 1991], 1:141, no. 13); "one disciple asked that our rabbi inform us of the details of what happened to the Seer of Lublin on the night of Simhat Torah, and he refused to go on at length" (*Neharei esh*, "Likutei diburim," 215, no. 161).

87. Granatstein, *Hashvil vehaderekh*, 200.

88. *Darkhei hayyim veshalom*, 146. On the condition of the site in the early twentieth century, see *Neharei esh*, "Likutei diburim," 216, no. 162; and note 20 above.

89. According to Gruenbaum's memoirs (housed in the Central Zionist Archives in Jerusalem), A A127/355. A reworked version of the memoirs appeared as "Yalduti" in *Sefer Plonsk vehasvivah*, edited by Shlomo Tsemakh and Mordekhai Halamish (Tel Aviv: Yotsei Plonsk, 1963), 86–95 (on the Seer, see 92), and in a toned-down version in the *Encyclopaedia of the Jewish Diaspora*, vol. 12 (*Warsaw*, vol. 3) (Jerusalem: Encyclopaedia of the Jewish Diaspora, 1973), 53, 67. I thank Dr. Marcos Silber for the reference.

90. Rabbi Yehuda Leib Maimon moved the spectacle of the Seer's fall to the study house: "The 'Seer' mounted the *bimah*, a Torah scroll in his right hand and communed with his thoughts. The hasidim as well purified their thoughts—and suddenly an enormous groan was heard. The frightened hasidim followed the noise . . . and lo and behold, alas, the Seer was lying in the street in his white festival clothes" (*Sarei hame'ah: Reshumot vezikhronot* [Jerusalem: Mossad Harav Kook, 1961], 4:87–88). For additional reworkings, see Assaf, *Ne'ehaz basevakh*, 163 note 99.

91. For example, Balaban, *Die Judenstadt von Lublin*, 83–84; Dubnow, *Toldot hahasidut*, 329–30; Mahler, *Modern Times*, 3:302–3; Mevorakh, *Napoleon utekufato*, 188–89.

92. Aescoly, *Hasidism in Poland*, 55–62. Aescoly commented that, notwithstanding the massive amount of information on the Seer, "this is one of the more cryptic episodes in hasidic history in Poland" (46).

93. This book first appeared in Hebrew in 1944. On its transmigrations and influence, see Werses, *From Language to Language*, 317–56. Alongside his own additions, Buber's description of the Seer's fall incorporates traditions derived from Ahron Marcus and Rabbi Lowenstein of Serotsk. See Buber, *For the Sake of Heaven*, 298–302; Werses, *From Language to Language*, 349.

94. *Nifle'ot harabbi*, 27, no. 37 (translation quoted from Zvi Mark, "Madness, Melancholy and Suicide in Early Hasidism," *Kabbalah* 12 [2004]: 31–32; see also 27–44). See Mark, *Mysticism and Madness*, 50–51. For some data on Reb Zelke, see *Entsiklope-*

diyah lehasidut, 1:531–32. Additional allusions to the Seer's tendency to depression exist. Thus the Seer confessed to the zaddik Mordekhai of Chernobyl "that he undertook a self-accounting of what he had done over the years, months, days, and hours; how he angered the Creator, and how his soul finds no solace, only by remembering that he will die . . . will he then not anger God" (Yoets Kim Kadish Rakats, *Tiferet hayehudi* [Piotrkov, 1912], 23, no. 26).

95. For additional examples of indirect maskilic polemical dialogues with hasidic hagiography, see Shmeruk, *Yiddish Literature*, 234–60; Israel Bartal, *Exile in the Homeland: Essays* (Jerusalem: Mossad Bialik, 1994), 28–29 (Hebrew). See also Immanuel Etkes's reservations in *Ba'al Hashem: The Besht—Magic, Mysticism, Leadership* (Waltham, Mass.: Brandeis University Press, 2005), 217–18; David Assaf, "Enemies—A Love Story? Research on the Interrelationship between Hasidism and Haskalah," in *The Varieties of Haskalah*, edited by Shmuel Feiner and Israel Bartal (Jerusalem: Magnes, 2005), 193–94 (Hebrew).

Chapter 4. "Happy Are the Persecuted": The Opposition to Bratslav Hasidism

1. For bibliographical evidence of the impact of Bratslav Hasidism, both internal and external, see the more than 1,100 entries in Assaf, *Bibliography*. The update, containing some 350 additional entries, can be accessed online from my homepage: www.tau.ac.il/~dassaf.

2. See, for example, Horodezky, *Hahasidut vehahasidim*, 3:28–30; Weiss, *Braslav*, 5–57 and passim; Ada Rapoport-Albert, "Self-Depreciation (*qaṭnuth, peshiṭuth*) and Disavowal of Knowledge (*'eyni yodea'*) in Naḥman of Braslav," in *Studies in Jewish Religious and Intellectual History Presented to Alexander Altmann*, edited by Siegfried Stein and Raphael Loewe (University, Alabama: University of Alabama Press, 1979), 13 (Hebrew section); Green, *Tormented Master*, 94–134. For the debate about whether Rabbi Nahman was influenced by Sabbatean ideas, and whether this constituted one of the reasons for the fierce opposition to him, see the exchange of opinions between Yehuda Liebes and Yehoshua Mondshine in *Zion* 45 (1980): 201–45; 47 (1982): 198–223, 224–31. See also Zvi Mark, "'The Tale of the Bread': A Hidden Story of R. Naḥman of Braslav," *Tarbiz* 72 (2003): 415–52.

3. Mahler, *Modern Times*, 6:32.

4. It has recently been suggested that one of the reasons for the controversy was Nathan's interference with the Savraner's desire to marry Rabbi Nahman's daughter. Naturally, this possibility appears only in Bratslav sources and could not alone be responsible for so harsh a controversy. See Zvi Mark, "Why Did R. Moses Zvi of Savran Persecute R. Nathan of Nemirov and Bratslav Hasidim?" *Zion* 69 (2004): 487–500 (Hebrew).

5. *Yemei hatela'ot*, 20.

6. On this dispute, see Horodezky, *Hahasidut vehahasidim*, 3:79–80; Weiss, *Braslav*, 38–39 notes 6, 9; 235 note 41; Piekarz, *Braslav Hasidism*, 209–11. Although Piekarz states that the Savraner accused Rabbi Nahman's disciples of "Sabbatean-Frankist

heresy" (76, 210), as Green (*Tormented Master*, 128 note 26; 130 note 48) notes, the events accompanying this controversy have yet to receive worthy critical examination. See the more recent treatment by Mendel Piekarz, "The Lessons of the Composition *Liqutei Halakhot* by R. Nathan of Nemirov," *Zion* 69 (2004): 203–38 (Hebrew). In addition to the letters of Nathan of Nemirov from the years of the controversy, collected in the various editions of *Alim litrufah mikhtavei Moharnat* (see Assaf, *Bibliography*, nos. 226–27), Bratslav sources of information include *Yemei hatela'ot*, which presents the later Bratslav perspective on this controversy; *Tovot zikhronot*; *Neveh tsadikim*, 91–105; Chaim Kramer, *Through Fire and Water: The Life of Reb Noson of Breslov* (Jerusalem: Breslov Research Institute, 1992). For considerable new data on the history of this controversy, based on oral traditions culled by Levi Yitshak Bender (Avraham Hazan's disciple), see *Siah sarfei kodesh.*

7. Piekarz argues that no Bratslav sources attest to a leadership role for Nahman of Tulchin (see Piekarz's comments to Weiss, *Braslav*, 212–13 note 36). But Avraham Hazan's remarks indicate that Nahman of Tulchin did assume a leadership role, though not of the same magnitude as Nahman of Nemirov's (*Sihot vesipurim*, 146–47; Assaf, *Ne'ehaz basevakh*, 181 note 7). Nonetheless, note that Hazan was Nahman of Tulchin's son, and his writing attests to his desire to strengthen his father's role in the Bratslav historical continuum.

8. Nathan of Nemirov's leadership was contested, particularly by Nahman of Bratslav's veteran disciples. Nathan's acceptance as leader was gradual and developed concurrently with his taking charge of Nahman's written legacy. In any event, reservations regarding his leadership continued to be voiced throughout the entire period. See Weiss, *Braslav*, 222, 236–41; Piekarz, *Braslav Hasidism*, 203–8; Green, *Tormented Master*, 149–50.

9. On opposition to Nahman of Tulchin's leadership, see *Sihot vesipurim*, 147. On Nahman ben Pesah's attempt to lead the group, see *Avaneha barzel*, 91–93; *Gidulei hanahal*, 78–79. From Avraham Hazan's apologetic remarks on his father's attributes as compared to the failings of other disciples of Nathan of Nemirov, it appears that the brothers Moshe and Zanwill in Chyhryn also opposed his leadership. See *Sihot vesipurim*, 131–32. Evidently, Nathan of Nemirov's son Yitshak accepted Nahman of Tulchin's leadership and even gave him redemption money (*Alim litrufah*, 210a). For additional information on Nahman of Tulchin, see *Gidulei hanahal*, 74–75.

10. For an impressive literary description of a band of Bratslav hasidim in Berdichev in the 1870s, see the Yiddish Russian-Jewish author Pinkhes Kahanovitsh (Der Nister)'s *The Family Mashber*, translated by Leonard Wolf (London: Flamingo, 1989), especially 92–118. On this book and its familial and historical context, see Assaf, *Bibliography*, no. 856.

11. The Chernobyl zaddikim became much more powerful after the zaddik Yisrael of Ruzhin fled Russia (1841) and settled in Sadigura, in Austrian Bukovina. For the most recent survey of Chernobyl Hasidism, see Sagiv, "Chernobyl Dynasty."

12. These are evidently stereotypical initials (the first and last letters of the alphabet) and do not stand for the author's name.

13. In spite of Zederbaum's antihasidic image, this was not the sole instance in which he tried to prevent publication of harsh criticism of zaddikim. Another case

concerned an article on the appointment of an unsuitable rabbi in Mezhibozh (who turned out to be an army deserter) by the zaddikim of Chernobyl and Zinkov. See *Hamelits*, 4 February 1864, 56–58; see especially the editor's comment, 58.

14. Ibid., 25 February 1864, 105–6.

15. On the curse "Bratslaver dog," see also below, and *Siah sarfei kodesh*, 5:98. The negative image of dogs in Eastern European folklore is common knowledge; in addition, dogs symbolized satanic forces and impudence.

16. "Hasidei Braslav ve'ir Uman," 106.

17. See below.

18. "Hasidei Braslav ve'ir Uman," 127.

19. On the complex interaction between the Uman maskilim and Nahman of Bratslav and Nathan of Nemirov, see Gottlober, *Memoires and Travels*, 2:74–75; Ginsburg, *Historishe verk*, 2:71–81; Liberman, *Ohel Rahel*, 3:310–28 and 1:71–73; Piekarz, *Braslav Hasidism*, 21–55; Green, *Tormented Master*, 253–66. On the confrontation between Enlightenment and Orthodoxy in Uman in the latter half of the nineteenth century, see Assaf, *Ne'ehaz basevakh*, 184 note 20.

20. "Hasidei Braslav ve'ir Uman," 127–28.

21. Ibid., 140.

22. Primarily Nathan of Nemirov's *Kin'at hashem tseva'ot* and *Makhnia zedim*. On these works and the identification of their author, see Piekarz, *Braslav Hasidism*, 23–24, 197–202; Shmuel Feiner, "*Sola fide!* The Polemic of Rabbi Nathan of Nemirov against Atheism and Haskalah," in *Studies in Hasidism*, 89–124 (Hebrew); Assaf, *Bibliography*, nos. 13, 16.

23. "Hasidei Braslav ve'ir Uman," 141.

24. Zederbaum, *Keter kehunah*, 168.

25. Gottlober, "Zikhronot miyemei ne'urai," *Haboker or* 6 (1881): 75; Gottlober, *Memoires and Travels*, 1:202–3. Gottlober's memoirs were penned in 1865 (see *Haboker or* 6 [1881]: 5, note). Gottlober devoted a generous amount of space to Rabbi Nahman in his memoirs (1:193–203).

26. For examples of interest by nineteenth-century maskilim, as well by as nonhasidic writers to the present, see Assaf, *Bibliography*, 124–29, 197–213.

27. On Perl's attitude toward Rabbi Nahman of Bratslav, see Assaf, *Ne'ehaz basevakh*, 187 note 28.

28. The remarks of the author from Chyhryn are instructive in this regard. He alludes to an ostensible reforming basis in Nahman's thought: "The customs of the Bratslav hasidim differ for the better from those of other hasidim, and the new regulations that Rabbi Nahman made on which the reformers in Germany worked so hard for many days . . ." ("Hasidei Braslav ve'ir Uman," 107). Alef-Tav did not recognize that this contradicted his earlier remarks, that "these people are at one with our written and oral Torah, and do not depart right or left from the stipulations of the *Shulhan arukh*" (ibid., 106).

29. Talne is thirty-eight kilometers northeast of Uman. Memoir literature contains much information on David of Talne (also called Duvidl or Duvidnyu), on his royal court ("like a small city within a large city"), and on his harshness toward those who did not bow to his authority. For bibliographical references, see Assaf, *Ne'ehaz base-*

vakh, 187–88 note 30. See also below, especially chapter 5. On David of Talne, see Radensky, "Biography of David Twersky"; Sagiv, "Chernobyl Dynasty."

30. Spektor, *Mayn lebn*, 1:133–55, 3:117–48. On Spektor, see *Leksikon*, 6:518–27.

31. Ish-Naomi, "Mitehom haneshiyah," 1:173. The Naftali in question is Naftali Weinberg of Nemirov, Nathan of Nemirov's contemporary and friend. He lived in Uman, in close proximity to Nahman's gravesite, for some fifty years until his death in 1860. On him, see *Gidulei hanahal*, 81; *Siah sarfei kodesh*, 3:81–86. Intriguingly, Bratslav tradition confirms Wexler's memoirs: "At Rabbi Naftali's funeral, when they passed the large synagogue of Uman, which was near the synagogue of their opponents [the Talne hasidim], a bottle was thrown at his bier from this synagogue. And our compatriots said that this disgrace would be transformed into great honor in the world to come" (*Siah sarfei kodesh*, 3:82).

32. *Siah sarfei kodesh*, 5:70. Another hint of David of Talne's negative image in Bratslav tradition comes from the following source: "Once Rabbi Nathan was in Bratslav and shared the same inn with David of Talne. And Rabbi Nathan did not eat there. Afterward, it became known that the ritual slaughterers were murderers" (*Avaneha barzel*, 60).

33. Rzhishchev is on the banks of the Dnieper, sixty-two kilometers southeast of Kiev.

34. *Hamelits*, 19 January 1865, 22–24.

35. Kasdai, "Kit'ei zikhronot," 217. See Mordekhai Lipson, *Midor dor* (Tel Aviv: Dorot, 1929), 1:52. Regarding Kasdai and his memoirs' reliability, see chapter 5.

36. Kressel, *Cyclopedia*, 2:154–55, mistakenly notes Kasdai's birthdate as 1862, whereas Kasdai himself states in his memoirs ("Kit'ei zikhronot," 216) that he was born in 1865.

37. Little is known of this great-grandson of Yaakov Yosef of Ostra, known as Reb Yivi. For additional references, see Assaf, *Ne'ehaz basevakh*, 191 note 37.

38. See Gottlober, *Memoires and Travels*, 1:191; Horodezky, *Hahasidut vehahasidim*, 3:91–97.

39. 12 October, according to the Gregorian calendar now in use. All the dates in the Russian documents below are cited according to the Julian calendar that was in use in the nineteenth century, in which the dates are twelve days earlier.

40. Important archival documents shedding light on this episode and on the Russian regime's attitude to Hasidism in the 1860s can be found in Galant, *Zbirnik*. For further references, see Assaf, *Ne'ehaz basevakh*, 191 note 40. Note that, alongside harsh words regarding Reb David and his negative influence, the Russian reports also contain positive comments. Thus, for example, in his reply to the governor general in 1864 regarding suspicions that David of Talne supported Polish nationalism, the military governor of Kiev Province wrote: "The chief of police in the Uman district reported at my request that Rabbi David Twersky who resides in Talne takes no part in the Polish revolutionary movement. He engages in no despicable acts, behaves modestly, and busies himself only with advising his coreligionists who approach him concerning religious or family matters and show him respect and have trust in him." Nonetheless, David of Talne was not allowed to travel to other provinces. See Galant, *Zbirnik*, 325. Regarding the "edict concerning the zaddikim," see Zederbaum, *Keter kehunah*, 145; Radensky, "Biography of David Twersky," 126–44, and below.

41. Some of the Russian documents cited by Galant note that one of the zaddikim active in Kiev Province is a "merchant by the name of Yos Mendel who resides in the town of Rzhishchev" (*Zbirnik*, 319, 328). It was also reported that this was the name of the local rabbi in Rzhishchev whom David tried to depose (336, 342). Indeed, on the envelope that he used to send his moving letter to the *Hakham bashi* Yakir Ghiron in thanks for rescuing him from the Turks on his return journey from Palestine, Yaakov Yosef of Ostra wrote his return address and signed the letter "Yaakov Yosef Mendel" (see Gerson Cohen, "A Letter of R. Jacob Joseph of Iržiščev to R. Yaḳḳir Ghiron," *Kiryat Sefer* 42 [1966–67]: 503–6 [Hebrew]).

42. Galant, *Zbirnik*, 335–37.

43. Tarashcha is ninety-four kilometers north of Uman.

44. The article was written on 9 Heshvan 1864; the author was therefore referring to mid-Tishri 1864, and to the persecution of the Bratslavers in Uman during the High Holidays.

45. "Erev rav," *Hacarmel* 5, 10 February 1865, 126 (see 98–99, 109–10 for other parts of this article).

46. Further confirmation comes from an article published in the Russian newspaper *Kievlianin*, 14 December 1864. See Radensky, "Biography of David Twersky," 129–30.

47. For further details on the consecration of cemeteries by zaddikim and some of the accompanying controversies, see Assaf, *Ne'ehaz basevakh*, 194 note 47.

48. Zederbaum, *Keter kehunah*, 147–48. See his remarks in *Hamelits*, 18 January 1866, 7, where he comments on the events at Rzhishchev as exemplifying the despicable acts that occur among hasidim on a daily basis, even though his newspaper refrains from publishing information about them so as not to distress its readers. For more on the Rzhishchev affair, see *Hamelits*, 24 February 1887, 389.

49. Zederbaum, *Keter kehunah*, 147–48. At the time (1862–65) the governor general of Kiev Province was Nikolai Annenkov. The landlord of Talne and Reb David's patron was Count Piotr Pavelovich Shuvalov. For a hasidic reworking of this story, see *Netsah shebanetsah*, 70–74.

50. Zederbaum, *Keter kehunah*, 147–48. The enmity between the hasidim of Talne and of Rzhishchev continued long thereafter and spread to other issues. For details, see Assaf, *Ne'ehaz basevakh*, 195 note 50.

51. For a similar case, see Kotik, *Wanderer*, 184.

52. Quoted in Tishby, *Studies in Kabbalah*, 2:549–51. Shapira evidently wrote this satire in 1866 or 1867. Comparison to a similar, more sympathetic description of a rebbe's visit to a Lithuanian town is instructive. See Kotik, *Wanderer*, 44–49.

53. Y. L. Gordon describes a similar takeover of a Lithuanian community against the background of a quarrel between two zaddikim, one of whom was Aharon (the second) of Karlin. See *Kitvei Yehudah Leib Gordon: Prozah* (Tel Aviv: Dvir, 1960), 17–77. For the historical background to this story, see Tishby, *Studies in Kabbalah*, 2:544 note 101; Israel Bartal, "Pinsk in Heaven and Pinsk on Earth: *Hasidim* and *Maskilim*, History and Fiction," in *Studies in East European Jewish History and Culture in Honor of Professor Shmuel Werses*, edited by David Assaf et al. (Jerusalem: Magnes, 2002), 259–83 (Hebrew).

54. Quoted in Assaf, *Ne'ehaz basevakh*, 223.

55. In a responsum, the hasidic rabbi Moshe Nahum Jerusalimski noted the *magidut* contract as a custom unique to the Ukrainian provinces and among the Chernobyl zaddikim. See *Be'er Moshe* (Warsaw, 1901), no. 26.

56. Glubman, *Ketavim*, 21–22.

57. For further details on the *ma'amadot* tax, see Assaf, *Regal Way*, 299–303.

58. Zederbaum, *Keter kehunah*, 134–35. Translation (slightly revised) quoted from Assaf, *Regal Way*, 304–5. The final line alludes to the above-mentioned "edict concerning the zaddikim." For a more comprehensive discussion of the *magidut* contract and its signification, see Assaf, *Regal Way*, 303–7; Sagiv, "Chernobyl Dynasty," 140–46.

59. The mainly impoverished members of this group lived a cooperative life and shared their property and money, donating all profits to charity. That, at any rate, is their portrayal in the idealizing Bratslav tradition. See *Siah sarfei kodesh*, 4:79–81.

60. According to *Gidulei hanahal*, 87, Sender moved into Bratslav circles in 1854 under Nahman of Tulchin's influence. In 1865 he funded the renovation of the Bratslav *kloiz* in Uman. For additional sources on Sender, see *Kaftor vaferah*, 2:22–26; *Siah sarfei kodesh*, 4:80–81, 103; 5:87–89.

61. *Siah sarfei kodesh*, 4:80–81.

62. Further evidence of David of Talne's animosity toward Bratslav has been preserved in a story concerning an individual who consulted him before marrying a Bratslaver. The zaddik viewed that as "a calamity" and compared the Bratslav pilgrimage to Uman to a Christian pilgrimage to Kiev (Kahana, *Sefer hahasidut*, 336).

63. The High Holidays of 1865 apparently also saw almost no significant outbursts against the Bratslav hasidim in Uman. This is alluded to in a report on how fanatical hasidim sought a means of combating the sins to which they attributed an outbreak of cholera in the town: they attacked a woman suspected of sexual licentiousness, and fought the fashion of wearing crinolines that had spread among the women of Uman. The writer commented: "There was an outcry in the town unseen from the days when they stopped striking the Bratslaver Hasidim until the present." See *Hamelits*, 12 July 1866, 383–84. See also ibid., 9 January 1862, 204–5. On the combined struggle against the Bratslaver Hasidim and crinolines in Uman, see also Spektor, *Mayn lebn*, 1:141–42. A Russian report from 1862 recounted that the followers of Rabbi Yohanan of Rachmistrivke beat women found wearing crinolines when the zaddik visited Berdichev. See Galant, *Zbirnik*, 323.

64. MS X893.19 K71, nos. 183–85, Columbia University, New York (IMHM-NLIS, no. 16504). A corrupt, censored version (the main censorship is the omission of Yitshak Twersky of Skvira's name) of the letter was published by the Bratslavers in *Nahalei emunah* (edited by Nosson Zvi Kenig and Shmuel Tuktsinski), 17–22. For further details, see Assaf, *Ne'ehaz basevakh*, 200 note 64. Interestingly, we find a parallel phenomenon among the Skvirer hasidim. Yitshak Twersky of Skvira's letters appeared in the journal *Mishkenot Yaakov* 1 (Kislev 1994): 67–69, where they were taken out of context and do not specify their opponents, the Bratslavers, by name. For a complete edition of this correspondence, see Assaf, *Ne'ehaz basevakh*, 222–28.

65. Yitshak of Skvira left no writings, and only a few stories about him and scraps of his teachings have survived, such as the stories compiled by his disciple Yeshayahu

Wolf Tzikernik (see Gedalyah Nigal, ed., *Czarnobil Hasidism Tales* [Jerusalem: Carmel, 1994; Hebrew]). For an interesting report by the Russian police regarding his visit to his father's grave in 1865 and his participation in a family wedding in Makarov, see Galant, *Zbirnik*, 339–41. For bibliographical references that reflect the divergent, even opposite, reactions that Yitshak of Skvira aroused, see Assaf, *Ne'ehaz basevakh*, 200 note 65. See also Sagiv, "Chernobyl Dynasty."

66. *Hamelits*, 18 January 1866, 8–10. For the annotated text, see Assaf, *Ne'ehaz basevakh*, 228–31.

67. There are several places by this name in the Ukraine, making its precise identification uncertain.

68. *Kol mevaser*, 18 January 1866, 1–4 (for an annotated Hebrew translation, see Assaf, *Ne'ehaz basevakh*, 231–34). An editorial comment, undoubtedly written by Alexander Zederbaum (*Kol mevaser*, 18 January 1866, 4–7) notes the arrival of the article a few weeks earlier and recalls Feingold's article published in *Hamelits*, noting that they were not contradictory.

69. See Weiss, *Braslav*, 204 note 25. According to the article in *Kol mevaser* (Assaf, *Ne'ehaz basevakh*, 231–34), Teplik had slightly more than thirty Bratslav families in the 1860s.

70. For another example in which the parties turned to Kluger to mediate an internal hasidic quarrel, see Assaf, "The Clash over *Or Ha-Hayyim*." See also Assaf, *Regal Way*, 154–56; Gertner, "Kluger."

71. Like the Bratslavers, the Bershad hasidim apparently refused to appoint a successor to their zaddik Rafael (d. 1826), as Feingold relates: "They as well do not believe in any zaddikim, not even former ones, with the exception of their dead zaddik" (see Assaf, *Ne'ehaz basevakh*, 228). Perhaps this similarity enhanced the hatred between these two groups.

72. Quoted in Assaf, *Ne'ehaz basevakh*, 228–29. See Spektor, *Mayn lebn*, 3:131; Mahler, *Modern Times*, 6:29.

73. Assaf, *Ne'ehaz basevakh*, 230.

74. See Shmeruk, "Hashehitah hahasidit." See also Jacob Katz, *Tradition and Crisis: Jewish Society at the End of the Middle Ages* (New York: New York University Press, 1993), 208 and note 15 there; Wilensky, *Hasidim and Mitnaggedim*, 1:144; Isaiah Kuperstein, "Inquiry at Polaniec: A Case Study of a Hassidic Controversy in 18th Century Galicia," *Bar-Ilan: Annual of Bar-Ilan University* 24–25 (1989): 25–40 (English section).

75. Shaul Stampfer, "The Dispute over Polished Knives and Hasidic *Schechita*," *Studies in Hasidism*, 197–210 (Hebrew).

76. "It is well known and an explicit ruling in their [the hasidim's] *Shulhan arukh* that the shehitah of a shohet who does not obey his rabbi is invalid" (*Hamelits*, 4 February 1864, 57). For a description of the typical takeover by zaddikim of appointments of all communal functionaries, see *Kol mevaser*, 23 December 1870, 342; Shochat, "Leadership of the Jewish Communities," 182. See also Assaf, *Regal Way*, 181–87. This phenomenon was also noted by the maskilim. See, for example, Mahler, *Hasidism and the Jewish Enlightenment*, 143; Raphael Mahler, "Tazkir shel Yosef Perl lashiltonot bidvar shitat minui rabanim, shohatim umohalim," in *Sefer hayovel likhvod N. M. Gelber*, ed. Yisrael Klausner, Raphael Mahler, and Dov Sadan (Tel Aviv: Olameinu, 1963), 85–104.

77. On the importance of the meat tax to the Jewish communal budget, see Shmeruk, "Hashehitah hahasidit." For a consideration of the meat tax in Russia after the *kahal* was abolished, and of its overt and covert aims, see Shochat, "Leadership of the Jewish Communities," 195–97; Mahler, *Modern Times*, 5:106–7, 121–22.

78. For a detailed discussion of how this was accomplished, and specific examples, see Assaf, "The Clash over *Or Ha-Hayyim.*" Note, however, that the Bratslavers themselves were not untainted. See the Yiddish memoirs of Rabbi Levi Glickman (b. 1859), the son of a Savraner hasid who served as a shohet in Bratslav, in which he describes a dispute when the Bratslav hasidim libelously defamed his father's shehitah as unkosher (*Zikhroynes beys levi* [Kishinev, 1934], 55ff.).

79. "Hasidei Braslav ve'ir Uman," 127. This statement, attributed to the Savraner zaddik, is missing from hasidic sources, and its only witness is Alef-Tav of Chyhryn, who recalled it from memory and not from written notes. See Piekarz, *Braslav Hasidism*, 209–11. Horodezky (*Lekorot hahasidut* [Berdichev, 1906], 74) testified that he saw a letter in which the zaddik of Savran ordered one of his adherents to cease employing a Bratslav melamed, even though he was a truly God-fearing person, and that the man complied with the zaddik's request. We must distinguish, however, between a prohibition of, or a recommendation not to employ, Bratslav slaughterers, melamedim, or cantors and the formal halakhic ramifications of a ban. But hasidim did use these methods in their internal disputes. Not surprisingly, Hayyim Halberstam of Sandz's campaign against Sadigura began by declaring the meat slaughtered by their shohatim nonkosher, and by forbidding the employment of Sadigura melamedim. See, for example, *Kneset hagedolah vedivrei hakhamim* (Lvov, 1869), 20–21.

80. Assaf, *Ne'ehaz basevakh*, 225.

81. See the summary in Menahem Elon, *Jewish Law: History, Sources, Principles* (Philadelphia: Jewish Publication Society, 1994), 2:935–36.

82. For more on this issue, see Assaf, "The Clash over *Or Ha-Hayyim.*" Piekarz (*Braslav Hasidism*, 198) notes that even though hasidic literature puts forth many solutions for the contradiction between the "belief in zaddikim" and the fact that the zaddikim are themselves divided as to the proper way of worship, these solutions were not applied in the case of the active opposition to the Bratslavers' belief in their zaddik. This perhaps inheres in the distinction between a live zaddik and a dead one, and may underlie the derogatory name for the Bratslavers: *di toyte hasidim* (the dead hasidim). See Assaf, *Bibliography*, xiii. Alef-Tav of Chyhryn also attributed opposition to Bratslav "to their unwillingness to place their faith in the contemporary zaddikim living among us today" ("Hasidei Braslav ve'ir Uman," 128). See Zederbaum's remarks: "And after his name [Rabbi Nahman's] a sect of Bratslaver hasidim was founded *who mock the contemporary zaddikim* and only go to the grave of their zaddik in Uman, and they are the target of angry bolts directed at them by the other hasidic sects" (*Keter kehunah*, 109).

83. See, for example, David of Talne's accusatory remarks that the Bratslaver hasidim "bait me and my people" (discussed earlier).

84. For further indications that "belief in the zaddik" was the crux of the controversy with Bratslav, see Assaf, *Ne'ehaz basevakh*, 208 note 83.

85. On the printing of *Likutei Moharan*, see Weiss, *Braslav*, 251–77.

86. *Hayyei Moharan* (Jerusalem: Makhon Torat Hanetsah Braslav, 1976), 2:33 no. 7; and many other similar statements.

87. Among those granting approbations were Efraim Zalman Margoliouth of Brody, the maggid Yisrael of Kozhenits, and Yaakov Yitshak Horowitz, the Seer of Lublin. On the authenticity of these approbations (printed only in the second edition and therefore suspect), see Weiss, *Braslav*, 262–63. Even after its publication and the raising of doubts concerning its contents, some zaddikim still displayed a positive attitude toward this book. For a detailed list of these zaddikim, see Assaf, *Ne'ehaz basevakh*, 210 note 86.

88. *Alim litrufah*, 78a.

89. Ibid., 82a, no. 181; see also nos. 164–67.

90. *Siah sarfei kodesh*, 5:92; see also 4:83: "Rabbi Pinhas of Kublich . . . was revered by all the important Talne hasidim before he came close to our rebbe, so much so that the Talne rebbe appointed him to guide the young hasidim in divine worship and fear." On Pinhas of Kublich, see *Gidulei hanahal*, 90; *Kaftor vaferah*, 26–33. Kublich is fifty kilometers west of Uman. On the ripping up of copies of *Likutei Moharan* by "one of the opponents," probably in the early twentieth century, see *Siah sarfei kodesh*, 6:78.

91. See, for example, Wilensky, *Hasidim and Mitnaggedim*, index, "*serefat ketavim hasidiyyim*" and "*serefat ketavim mitnagdiyyim.*"

92. Kluger bemoaned the condition of shehitah and of the shohatim in his day, attributing it to moral and economic corruption. See his responsa to the community of Zalishtshik, *Shut tuv ta'am vada'at, mahadurah telita'i* (Lvov, 1884), *Yoreh de'ah*, no. 33.

93. "From 1865 on he [Kluger] did not even speak with anyone and sat alone" (Yehuda Aharon Kluger, *Toldot Shlomo* [Lemberg, 1888], 145). See also Wunder, *Meorei Galicia*, 4:485.

94. *Siah sarfei kodesh*, 4:92. In the continuation, this source mistakenly claims that Dov settled in Tiberias and became a melamed; see the following note. According to Asher Leml Feingold (Assaf, *Ne'ehaz basevakh*, 229), Dov was the grandson of the ritual slaughterer Dov Ber of Linitz (in Kiev Province), who was well known as the compiler of the main body of the stories comprising *Shivhei haBesht.*

95. See *Gidulei hanahal*, 22, no. 9. From the letters of the Bratslav hasid Nathan ben Yehuda (*Netiv tsadik*), it appears that by 1875 at the latest, Dov and his son Henokh were living in Safed. Dov continues to be mentioned in these letters until 1884. See, for example, *Netiv tsadik*, 19, 265–66.

96. Aharon's daughter Haya Sara married Yisrael, Nahman of Bratslav's grandson (through his daughter Sara) in 1819. See *Yemei Moharnat* (Bnei Brak, 1956), 2:169, no. 6. In the story of the wedding found in *Yemei hatela'ot*, 48–50, we can detect hints of anger among the Chernobyl hasidim because of the coarse behavior of one of the Bratslavers, Ozer of Uman.

97. See Nosson Zvi Kenig, *Yekara dehayyei* (appended to *She'erit yisrael*), 156; *Siah sarfei kodesh*, 3:133–34. On Nahman of Chyhryn and his literary oeuvre, see Weiss, *Braslav*, index; Piekarz, *Braslav Hasidism*, index; *Neveh tsadikim*, 161–73; *Gidulei hanahal*, 74.

98. *Siah sarfei kodesh*, 4:90.

99. As Avraham Kokhav Lev states in relating the miraculous circumstances for the cessation of the controversy on the Savraner rebbe's part; see his *Tovot zikhronot*, 147.

100. *Netiv tsadik*, 190. Bratslav tradition over the generations, from Nahman of Bratslav on, stresses the moral value of passivity in face of controversy and the need to accept humiliation with joy (*Likutei Moharan*, Torah 6:20). The letters of Nathan ben Yehuda from the 1880s contain many examples of the typical Bratslav moralizing approach that sets persecution and insults in a positive light (for examples, see *Netiv tsadik*, 137–38, 146–47, 153–54). See also Ariel Burger, "Hasidic Nonviolence: R. Noson of Bratzlav's Hermeneutics of Conflict Transformation" (Ph.D. diss., Boston University, 2008).

101. For a list of the collections containing Bratslav correspondence, mostly edited by Nosson Zvi Kenig, see Piekarz, *Braslav Hasidism*, 201; Assaf, *Bibliography*, section 2.

102. *Likutei Moharan*, Torah 57:145. See also Piekarz, *Braslav Hasidism*, 10–16; Zvi Mark, *Scroll of Secrets: The Hidden Messianic Vision of R. Nahman of Bratslav* (Ramat Gan: Bar-Ilan University Press, 2006; Hebrew).

103. Exceptional in scope and momentum is the spiritual, organizational, and publishing activity of Rabbi Eliezer Shlomo Schick, a contemporary leader of a Bratslav faction of the newly repentant. See Assaf, *Bibliography*, index. Schick's views and their affinity to the original ideas of Bratslav Hasidism are treated by Piekarz, *Braslav Hasidism*, 199–218.

104. *Siah sarfei kodesh*, 3:144–45.

105. *Parpera'ot lehokhmah* (Lemberg, 1876), "Tik'u emunah," 5b, no. 5.

106. *Netiv tsadik*, 173.

107. The letters of Nathan ben Yehuda (ibid., 146–47, 187–94, among others) present a strong picture of harsh persecution of the Safed Bratslavers, which culminated with their expulsion from the Ari synagogue in 1883. See also *Mabu'ei hanahal* 54 (1982): 14–17. The persecution of the Bratslavers in Safed and Jerusalem continued into the first quarter of the twentieth century, as shown in the memoirs of the Bratslav hasid Shmuel Horowitz, *Yemei Shmuel*, vols. 1–2 (Jerusalem: privately printed, 1992).

108. *Hamelits*, 1 July 1868, 177.

109. Rodkinson, *Toldot ba'alei shem tov* (Königsberg, 1876), 40.

110. See, for example, *Netiv tsadik*, 137–38, 146–47, 153–54.

111. *Hamelits*, 24 March 1884, 365.

112. Ephraim Deinard, *Kitot beyisrael* (New York, 1899), 25.

113. *Arim veimahot beyisrael*, 2:277.

114. Yehuda Yudl Rosenberg, *Tiferet maharal miShpoli* (Piotrkov: Fellman, 1912), 94.

115. Micha Yosef Berdyczewski,"Garei rehov," *Hatekufah* 5 (1920): 13–16; Berdyczewski, *Sipurim*, 263–64.

116. Rechtman, *Yidishe etnografye*, 253.

117. *Der freynd: Yuvileums-beylage* 35 (supplement to no. 198), 29 September 1912, 2–3.

118. Alter Druyanov, "Shurah shel pega'im," *Reshumot* 3 (1923): 132–40 (for the Bratslaver hasidim, see especially 137).

119. The gathering took place at Yeshivat Hakhmei Lublin (with the permission

and participation of the head of the yeshiva, Rabbi Meir Shapira) and at the gravesite of the Seer of Lublin. The choice of Lublin was not based only on the number of Bratslav hasidim there, but also on its convenient location, and because of the Seer's favorable attitude toward Rabbi Nahman (see note 87 above). Regarding this matter, see the memoirs of my late father, Moshe Krone, *Morai verabotai, ahai vere'ai* (Tel Aviv: Moreshet, 1987), 39–44; and his letter cited by Moshe Zvi Neriah, "Batei hamidrash 'Bet Avraham' bePolin," in *Iturim: Pirkei iyun vehagut likhvod Moshe Krone* (Jerusalem: Sifriyat Elinar, 1986), 161–62. The strong desire of Bratslav hasidim in Poland to reach Uman emerges from the letters and prayers of their leaders—among whom the most prominent were Aharon Leib Ziegelman and Yitshak Breiter—compiled by Nosson Zvi Kenig in his *Nahalei emunah* and *Or tsadikim* (Bnei Brak: N. S. Kenig, 1972). Bratslav Hasidism in Poland during the period between the two world wars has barely been described. For a bibliography on this topic, see Assaf, *Bibliography*, section 13.

120. For Bratslav suffering under the Communists before the Holocaust, see Menashe Unger, "Mikhtavim shel hasidei Braslav beVrit Hamo'atsot," *Mahanayim* 74 (1963): 68–79; A. E. Gershuni, "Hasidei Braslav beRusiyah haSovyetit," in his *Yehudim veyahadut beVrit Hamo'atsot* (Jerusalem: Feldheim, 1970), 129–34; Altshuler, "Braslaw *Ḥassidim*," 129–34. See also David Ettinger, "This is Uman (memortes)," *He'avar* 3 (1955), 118 (Hebrew).

121. Dubnow, *Toldot hahasidut*, ix–x. The Soviet regime closed down the Bratslav *kloiz* and ritual bath in Uman but did not destroy Nahman's grave. See Altshuler, "Braslaw *Ḥassidim*," 39–40.

122. Regarding the destruction of the Jews of Uman and the surrounding area by the Nazis and their collaborators, see "The Extermination of Two Ukrainian Jewish Communities: Testimony of a German Army Officer," *Yad Vashem Studies* 3 (1959): 303–20; Altshuler, "Braslaw *Ḥassidim*," 38 note 4.

123. On this group, admirers of Yisrael Dov Odesser, see Assaf, *Bibliography*, 233–39.

124. Most of the Skvirer hasidim in the United States live in the hasidic town of New Square, in New York State. See Jerome R. Mintz, *Hasidic People: A Place in the New World* (Cambridge, Mass.: Harvard University Press, 1992), 198–205, 392–94; Allan L. Nadler, *The Hasidim in America* (New York: American Jewish Committee, 1994), 20–21.

125. This undated proclamation is signed by the "friends and family of the yeshiva student." It bears no indication of where it was printed; we do know, however, that the student's name was Avraham Marmelstein. For the full Hebrew text, see Assaf, *Ne'ehaz basevakh*, 220–21.

Chapter 5. "Excitement of the Soul": The World of Rabbi Akiva Shalom Chajes of Tulchin

1. On his death in 1868, see Berdyczewski, "Tsiyun lenefesh," 72. Binyamin Horowitz, Chajes's son-in-law, wrote: "He lived for 53 years and died in 1868" (*Ikvei shalom*,

"Hakdamah aharonah"); thus he was born around 1815. His sister's grandson wrote: "Uncle Akiva died in 1868, when he was fifty-two years old" (Glubman, *Ketavim*, 16).

2. Dubova is in Kiev Province, twenty-five kilometers southeast of Uman. In 1888, Berdyczewski described it "as a small town with few residents; they number about one hundred and eighty householders." According to him, Jews settled in this town only in the early nineteenth century; Akiva Chajes's activity sums up the only thing of importance that happened there (Berdyczewski, "Dubova"). Later descriptions also emphasized its wretchedness; for the references, see Assaf, *Ne'ehaz basevakh*, 255 note 2.

3. *Zera Yitshak al hamishnayot* (Frankfurt am Oder, 1732); *Zera Yitshak al tehilim* (Jerusalem, 1945). On Yitshak Chajes and the transmission of his works, see Wunder, *Meorei Galicia*, 2:1034–36.

4. *Yesod datenu* is first mentioned in I. A. Benjacob, *Otsar hasefarim* (Vilna, 1880), 224. For further bibliographical details, including the mistaken dating of the book to before Chajes's birth, see Assaf, *Ne'ehaz basevakh*, 257 note 5.

5. Berdyczewski, for example, who was familiar with Chajes's literary heritage, did not include this work among those printed during Chajes's lifetime; nor do other memoirists mention this book. The sole hint comes from the Bratslav tradition treated below: "That he composed some book making mockery of the zaddikim of the generation" (*Avaneha barzel*, 84–85); however, this does not necessarily imply that the book was ever published.

6. Berdyczewski, "Dubova."

7. *Ikvei shalom*, "Hakdamah aharonah." Chajes himself mentions writing a work on *Midrash Rabbah* (ibid., 119). According to Rabbi Hayyim Berlin of Volozhin's approbation to *Ikvei shalom*, "many written works [by Akiva Chajes] have survived, both novellae on Talmudic tractates, especially to Tractate *Shekalim*, and responsa setting the Halakhah." Thus, Chajes's literary estate apparently contained a commentary on PT *Shekalim*.

8. In the second introduction (to the commentary on "Avinu malkenu"), Chajes noted that he had named the book *Nishmat hayah* "for a clandestine personal reason"; in any event, it appears that the word *hayah* also alludes to his Hebrew surname Hayot.

9. Chajes's later works also highlight the topics of repentance, confession, and the *al het* and *Avinu malkenu* prayers; however, nowhere do we find any autobiographical details, nor does he mention Hasidism anywhere. I found only one reference to a hasidic work: *Sefer toldot Yaakov Yosef* (*Ikvei shalom*, 114).

10. On Frumkin (1845–1903), see Jonatan Meir, "Mikhael Levi Rodkinson: Between Hasidism and Haskalah," *Kabbalah* 18 (2008): 229–86 (Hebrew).

11. Berdyczewski, "Tsiyun lenefesh," 72.

12. Although its title page bears 1896 as the date of publication in Lublin, it was not published until 1898. This emerges from the Russian imprint and Horowitz's introduction, which attributes the delay to a fire at the printers. For additional bibliographical details, see *Ne'ehaz basevakh*, 258–59 note 13.

13. In his introduction ("Hakdamah aharonah"), Horowitz complains of his great poverty and expresses his hope that the prayer book will sell well. The list of presubscribers appended to the book numbered in the hundreds, from Lithuania in the north to Bessarabia in the south; this alone should have ensured the sale of the entire run.

14. For bibliographical details, see Assaf, *Ne'ehaz basevakh*, 259 notes16–20.

15. According to Berdyczewski's father's testimony. See *Ginzei Micha Yosef* 5 (1988): 26, 30; Avner Holtzman, *Towards the Tear in the Heart* (Jerusalem: Bialik Institute, 1995), 298 (Hebrew). Evidently, in the interim following Chajes's death, the post of town rabbi in Dubova remained unfilled. Incidentally, Berdyczewski's father's name, Moshe Aharon, headed the list of presubscribers from Dubova to *Siddur ikvei shalom.*

16. Berdyczewski, "Tsiyun lenefesh," 71–72. The expression "stab him" is an ironic reference to the Talmudic jest that it is permissible to stab an ignoramus on the Day of Atonement that falls on a Sabbath (BT *Pesahim* 49b).

17. Other sources to be mentioned below indicate that Chajes earned a living by lending money at interest. We know very little of his family members: his daughter married Binyamin Halevi Horowitz of Tulchin; and two sons (Aharon and Yitshak Aryeh) are mentioned in Horowitz's acknowledgements in his introduction to *Siddur ikvei shalom* (16).

18. Berdyczewski, "Dubova." It is obvious that both of Berdyczewski's pieces were written at the same time. They differ somewhat in content because of their audiences. "Tsiyun lenefesh," which appeared in *Bet hamidrash*, is entirely devoted to Chajes's Torah personality; "Dubova," which appeared in the daily *Hatsefirah*—like other "correspondence" submitted to the contemporary press—is devoted to a general depiction of the town, and Chajes is mentioned only in its first part.

19. In 1886, upon completing his studies at the Volozhin yeshiva, Berdyczewski returned to his parental home in Dubova. He remained there for about a year until his second marriage and his move to Bershad in early 1887. Some months later, Berdyczewski published his well-known articles on Volozhin ("Olam ha'atsilut" and "Tsror mikhtavim me'et bar-be-rav"), in which he traced the portrait of the diligent Talmud student. Note that his piece "Tsiyun lenefesh" heightens the myth of Chajes as a prodigy, inflates the number of years of study, and attributes to Chajes some twenty hours of daily study.

20. Berdyczewski, "Dubova."

21. Berdyczewski notes this zaddik's name in both pieces. On the problematic nature of this identification and on the Savran dynasty, see below.

22. Per the statement in the Babylonian Talmud: "If two disciples of the Sages reside in the same city and do not support each other in [the study of] the law, one dies and the other goes into exile" (*Sotah* 49a). The same anecdote is cited by Mordekhai Lipson in his anthology *Midor ledor* (Tel Aviv, 1938), 3:278, no. 2620; there, however, it is aimed at Moshe Zvi of Savran, Shimon Shlomo's father. As we shall see, this was impossible. For many additional uses of this witticism in other contexts, see Assaf, *Ne'ehaz basevakh*, 261 note 28.

23. Note that the Berdyczewski family also had ties to the zaddik David of Talne. Around 1851, Micha Yosef's grandfather, Zvi Hirsh (d. 1894), was appointed rabbi of the town Ternovka by David of Talne (see *Ginzei Micha Yosef* 5 [1988]; 26–27, 30; A. Gad [Gedalyahu Amitai], "The Townlet Ternovka," *He'avar* 17 [1970; Hebrew]: 238; G. Bar-Zevi [Gedalyahu Amitai], *Ayarateynu Ternovka* [Tel Aviv 1978], 12). It is likely that David of Talne also appointed his father to the rabbinate in Dubova. Berdyczewski's complex relationship to the Talne dynasty is also embedded in his story "Hahafsakah"

(*Sipurim*, 154–57), which describes David of Talne's grandson's visit to Ternovka. See Zvi Mark, "Hasidut vehefkerut: Tashtiyot historiyot ve'otobiografiyot lasipur 'Hahafsakah' leM.Y. Berdyczewski, *Tsafon* 7 (2004): 219–37.

24. These largely standard approbations, which praise the author and his work, contain no new biographical data. For further details on the hasidic and nonhasidic rabbis who granted approbations, see Assaf, *Ne'ehaz basevakh*, 262 note 30.

25. Horowitz notes that he saw "his biography written in a book in *Bet hamidrash* and he therefore refrained from writing it and only cited two or three pages of what appears there" (*Ikvei shalom*, "Hakdamah aharonah"). The unsuspecting reader who was unfamiliar with Berdyczewski's anthology, which was titled *Bet hamidrash*, would simply assume that this was a book that the author came across during his studies in the bet midrash (study house).

26. *Ikvei shalom*, "Hakdamah aharonah."

27. *Eyn dim'ah, hame'ir eynei hamehakim lislihato* (Zholkva, 1850). See also Yehoshua Mondshine, *Nahalat Tsvi* 4 (1991): 71–83 (for Akiva Chajes, see 74); Gertner, "Kluger."

28. See Zvi Hakohen Schwadron, "Ohel shem," in Shalom Mordekhai Hakohen Schwadron, *Darkhei shalom* (Bilgoray, 1929), 4; see also Assaf, *Regal Way*, 119–20.

29. Kasdai, "Kit'ei zikhronot," 216–19. On Kasdai and his memoirs, see chapter 4 and below; David Cohen, *Shpole: Masekhet hayyei yehudim be'ayarah* (Haifa: Irgun Yotsei Shpole Beyisrael, 1965), 189–92; Kressel, *Cyclopedia*, 2:154–55.

30. Savran is located in the Balta district of Podolia Province, seventy-five kilometers south of Uman.

31. "Even his opponents admit that he was expert in Torah and had wisdom in everyday matters . . . but for all his wisdom and acuity and expertise in the ways of the world, he was a harsh enemy of Haskalah" (Zederbaum, *Keter kehunah*, 136–38). For further descriptions of his combination of Torah and secular wisdom, including his assistance to a Brody maskil whom a Savraner hasid tried to cheat, see ibid.; for a different, more detailed version, see Gottlober, *Memoires and Travels*, 1:271–78.

32. On the tension between him and the zaddik Yisrael of Ruzhin and its ramifications, see Assaf, *Regal Way*, 94–95. On his anti-Bratslav campaign, see chapter 4, notes 3–6.

33. Chechelnik is eighty-eight kilometers southwest of Uman. The reasons for this move are not known; some suggest that he moved because of an epidemic.

34. Zederbaum, *Keter kehunah*, 138; Gottlober, *Memoires and Travels*, 1:190–91. See also Yosef Yeruham Fishl Hager, *Heikhal haBesht* 9 (2005): 111–28; 10 (2005): 177–78; 12 (2006): 85–94, 162–65.

35. In his book Chajes cites remarks that he heard on several occasions from Yitshak Yaakov, who headed the Tomashpol rabbinical court (*Nishmat hayah* [Vilna, 1846], 20; *Ikvei shalom*, 257; see also note 41 below), a disciple and close associate of Moshe Zvi of Savran who assisted him in his anti-Bratslav campaign (see *Yemei hatela'ot*, 6–7). This perhaps implies that Chajes's relationship with the Savraner hasidim worsened only after Moshe Zvi's death.

36. Traditional Jews negatively identified the maskilim with the Berlin center of Haskalah.

37. The mention of Berdichev is not accidental. Of all of Kluger's addressed responsa from 1832–63, some sixty were intended for Berdichev; this is the largest number of responsa that he sent to any town in the Ukraine and they evidently paid close attention to his decisions. See Haim Gertner, "Gevulot hahashpa'ah shel rabanut Galitsiyah bemahatsit harishonah shel hame'ah ha-19: R. Shelomoh Kluger kemikreh mivhan" (master's thesis, Hebrew University, 1996) where he notes that another city that approached this number of responsa from Kluger was Tulchin (44).

38. In line with the midrash cited in the Passover Haggadah: "I and no other (*aher*). "Aher" (other) is, of course, the name assigned to the tanna Elisha ben Abuyah, who became a heretic. For similar hasidic stories concerning the abuse of the term "I," see Assaf, *Ne'ehaz basevakh*, 265 note 44.

39. Kasdai, "Kit'ei zikhronot," 216–19.

40. See below. Mekler, whose remarks will be treated below, copied his traditions directly from Kasdai's memoirs.

41. For references to exchanges between Kluger and Chajes, see Assaf, *Ne'ehaz basevakh*, 266 note 46.

42. This possibility is suggested by their correspondence. See Assaf, *Ne'ehaz basevakh*, 266–67 note 47.

43. Chajes's name does not appear either in *Toldot yehudei Brody* (vol. 6 of *Arim veimahot beyisrael*), by Nathan M. Gelber, or in Wunder's *Meorei Galicia*; even if not definitive proof, this is telling.

44. See the responsa collections *To'afot re'em* (Zholkva, 1855) and *Imrei ash* (Ungvar, 1864). Known in Hebrew sources as Orhayuv, the town of Orhei is seventy-six kilometers north of Kishinev. See *Pinkas Hakehillot: Rumania*, 2:327–31; *Entsiklopediyah shel galuyot: Yahadut Besarabia* (Jerusalem, 1971), index. Chajes's as yet unexplained stay in Orhayuv (perhaps he was offered a rabbinical post there?) is linked to his marginality in the historiography of the rabbinic world. One survey places him among the rabbis whose names mean nothing to us (ibid., 93).

45. See Assaf, *Ne'ehaz basevakh*, 259 notes 16, 20.

46. Glubman's memoirs, titled *Shishim shnot hayyim* (Sixty years of life), were written in Jerusalem in 1933 but have only recently been published by his family. An interesting source for the history of the branches of Chernobyl Hasidism in the late nineteenth century, these memoirs will be referred to again in chapter 7. On Chajes, see Glubman, *Ketavim*, 13–21. Chajes was much admired in Glubman's family circle, and Glubman even named one of his sons for Chajes. This son, Akiva Govrin (1902–80) held a ministerial post in the Israeli government in the 1960s. The history of the Glubman-Chajes family has recently been covered in Michal Govrin's biographical appendixes to the memoirs of her father, Pinchas Govrin, *We Were as Dreamers* (Hebrew).

47. Glubman, *Ketavim*, 13.

48. Ibid., 14.

49. Ibid., 19.

50. Ibid., 14. Binyamin Horowitz also noted Chajes's involvement in moneylending and praised him for doing so in line with halakhic norms and for teaching him to act accordingly (*Ikvei shalom*, "Hakdamah aharonah").

51. Glubman, *Ketavim*, 14–15.

52. Ibid., 15.

53. Berdyczewski, "Tsiyun lenefesh," 72.

54. Glubman, *Ketavim*, 21–22. On the *maggidut* contract and its socioeconomic implications, see chapter 4; Assaf, *Regal Way*, 303–7.

55. Glubman, *Ketavim*, 15–16.

56. Ibid., 21.

57. Mekler, *Fun rebns hoyf*, 1:9–10 (where he provides the names of his informants). Mekler was an Orthodox Zionist journalist. Born in Lithuania, he immigrated to the United States in 1907. Although not a hasid, he was close to the leaders of hasidic courts in New York, especially Lubavitch. On Mekler, see David Tidhar, *Entsiklopediyah lehalutsei hayishuv uvonav*, vol. 11 (Tel Aviv: Hitahadut Bnei Hayishuv, 1961), 3726–27; *Leksikon*, 6:81–82.

58. Mekler, *Fun rebns hoyf*, 2:64.

59. For a mild caveat about Mekler's reliability issued by the last Talne rebbe, see *Kerem hahasidut* 2 (1985): 137 note 2. This, however, is recent. The Talne admorim were the main transmitters of the traditions used by Mekler in his book. Especially noteworthy are the Yiddish memoirs of Rabbi David Mordekhai Twersky (1888–1956), "Fun Talne biz Nyu-york," published in 1951 as a series in *Der morgen zhurnal*, under Mekler's editorship.

60. Mekler, *Fun rebns hoyf*, 2:70–76.

61. *Netsah shebanetsah*, 91.

62. This perhaps alludes to his lost work *Yesod datenu*. See above.

63. *Avaneha barzel*, 84–85. Regarding the special circumstances under which this work was written (by hasidim from Palestine who spent time at Rabbi Nahman's gravesite in Uman, and recorded traditions they heard from Avraham Hazan), see the introduction by the publisher Shmuel Horowitz, and Assaf, *Bibliography*, no. 57. Avraham Hazan (1849–1918) was one of the more important preservers of Bratslav traditions. As the son of Nahman of Tulchin (a disciple of Nathan of Nemirov), he must have absorbed traditions relating to his fellow townsman Akiva Chajes. Chajes appears among the other hasidim and disciples listed in the lexicon *Gidulei hanahal* (89); however, the sole supporting evidence that he was a disciple of Nathan of Nemirov is *Avaneha barzel*.

64. This is a common polemical motif in hasidic tales: a maskil comes to a zaddik in order to test or to embarrass him, but the zaddik in his wisdom foresees this and entraps him. For a comprehensive treatment, see David Assaf, "The Encounter between Yitzhak Baer Levinsohn (RIBAL) and Rabbi Abraham Joshua Heschel of Apt: A Study in Polemic Memorial Traditions," in *A Festschrift for Professor Chava Turniansky* (forthcoming; Hebrew).

65. The manuscript was written by Shmuel Meir Anshin; the proofreader was evidently Avraham Hazan. For a reproduction, see Assaf, *Ne'ehaz basevakh*, 275.

66. Deinard, *Alata*, 92–93 (regarding this book's doubtful value, see chapter 2). According to Deinard, Zvi Lifschitz showed him a letter in which the admor asked him to explain a difficult passage in his "own" book.

67. *Magen David* was first published in Zhitomir in 1852. For details on the homi-

letic nature of this book, which was based on sermons delivered orally on Sabbaths and holidays and copied by an anonymous disciple, and its delayed publication, see Assaf, *Ne'ehaz basevakh*, 274–76 note 74.

68. The table illustrates the different texts of the *Kedushah*. The disputed words are italicized.

Ashkenaz and Habad	Sefarad and Ha-Ari
Na'aritskha venakdishkha kesod siah sarfei kodesh hamakdishim shimkha bakodesh, *kakatuv* al yad nevi'ekha [*as it is written by your prophet*] . . . Kadosh, kadosh, kadosh . . .	Keter yitnu lekha . . . malakhim hamonei ma'alah im amkha yisrael kevutsei matah. Yahad kulam kedushah lekha yeshaleshu, *kadavar ha'amur* al yad nevi'ekha [*as was said by your prophet*] . . . Kadosh, kadosh, kadosh. . .

69. See *Hamelits*, 5 April 1881, 235–36.

70. Mekler, *Fun rebns hoyf*, 2:58 (evidently Mekler converted the mockery of opponents of Talne into praise). Although today most hasidic groups recite *kadavar* (except Habad, as noted earlier), during the nineteenth century, this was a contested matter, as the zaddik Avraham David of Buchach (1771–1840) attests in his commentary *Tefilah leDavid* on his prayer book *Da'at kedoshim* (Pshemyshl, 1892), 83b–84a. Apart from his remarks, which describe the change as having preceded David of Talne, I found no echoes of the *kadavar* controversy in hasidic literature. It is possible that this controversy was blown out of proportion in the Jewish press and memoir literature.

71. *Hamelits*, 9 November 1885, 1298. For further references to this controversy, see Assaf, *Ne'ehaz basevakh*, 277 note 77.

72. The reference is to Gedalya Aharon Rabinowitz of Sokolivka; see below.

73. Kasdai, "Kit'ei zikhronot," 217. J. Bokstein, "Recollections," *He'avar* 13 (1966): 172 (Hebrew) also relates a similar event of flogging by the authorities over the *kadavar* faith.

74. Kasdai, "Kit'ei zikhronot," 218–19.

75. Sokolivka is thirty-eight kilometers northwest of Uman; Gedalya Aharon lived there from 1852. For further details on this dynasty, see Assaf, *Ne'ehaz basevakh*, 278 note 81.

76. Mekler, *Fun rebns hoyf*, 2:67–69.

77. As noted in the last chapter, Kasdai gives his birth date as 1865.

78. Hasidic tradition ascribes this move to 1852. See *Netsah shebanetsah*, 61, 65; Radensky, "Biography of David Twersky," 80. However, the list of presubscribers to the book *Bat ayin* (Jerusalem, 1847) mentions "the study house of the rabbi of Talne" in Safed; accordingly, he moved to Talne before 1847. David of Talne evidently alternated between these two towns.

79. Kasdai, "Kit'ei zikhronot," 216–17; Mekler, *Fun rebns hoyf*, 2:61–62 (according to Mekler, David of Talne himself intervened in lightening Yitshak Yoel's sentence).

80. Gedalya Aharon (1815–78) lived in Sokolivka from 1852 to 1867. On the eve of Sukkot 1867, after learning of the denunciations made against him, he fled this town. Russian documents indicate that the authorities wished to punish him for his refusal to promise in writing not to travel from his hometown without prior permission. See

Radensky, "Biography of David Twersky," 142. In 1869, Gedalya Aharon settled in Podul-Iloaei in Rumania, where he remained until his death (*Ivri anokhi*, 20 Nisan 1869, no. 25, 195–96; "Erekh avot," 12–13). His son, Yitshak Yoel (1840–85), served as the rabbi of Linitz, beginning in 1863. Because of a denunciation, he was arrested in 1869 and sentenced to exile in Siberia. En route, his sentence was lightened in varied and strange ways. He lived in various towns in eastern Russia, was released in 1874, and settled in Kantakuzova in Kherson Province. See "Erekh avot," 10–12; Radensky, "Biography of David Twersky," 142–43.

81. *Kovets siftei tsadikim* 1 (1989): 21–22; "Erekh avot," 10. For further discussion of this affair, see Assaf, *Ne'ehaz basevakh*, 279–80 notes 89–90.

82. *Hamelits* (5 April 1881, 235–36) reported an incident involving the *kadavar* controversy between Talner and Savraner hasidim in the town of Hashchuvate in Podolia Province. The author wrote: "*Just because of this one word* our town has become a battlefield" (emphasis in original). For quarrels between Savran and Talne hasidim, see also *Hamelits*, 8 November 1882, 847–50.

83. In 1862, his daughter, Yochebed, married Mordekhai (1848–76), David of Talne's only son, who died young, during his father's lifetime. According to Talne tradition, only one of his eleven children survived childhood. See *Netsah shebanetsah*, 169–78.

84. Reb Moshe, who eventually succeeded his father in Chechelnik, was the son-in-law of Rabbi Yohanan of Rachmistrivke: "This was Moshe, who sat on his grandfather's throne in Chechelnik, while he was still a youth [*na'ar*], and graybeards stood before him and the elderly bowed to him and licked the dust of his boots" (Gottlober, *Memoires and Travels*, 1:191; the use of the word *na'ar* may be a word play on the Yiddish *nar* [fool]). On Reb Moshe (d. 1876?; some date his death to 1871), see also Wigdermann, "Kevurat hamor"; Samuel Kaufman, *Zikhronot ("Toldot yemei hayyei")* (Tel Aviv: privately printed, 1955), 15–16; *Heikhal haBesht* 12 (2006): 86–90. Reb David (d. 1912)—known as David Hakatan (the small) of Savran, to distinguish him from his uncle "the great" of Talne—married Aharon of Chernobyl's granddaughter. He was the last admor of the Savran dynasty. In his memoirs, Barukh Schwartz describes him as a quarrelsome person who loved controversy (*Hayyai: Toldotai vezikhronotai* [Jerusalem: Darom, 1930], 129–30, 174–79). For additional details on his family, see ibid., 209–22. See also *Hamelits*, 9 November 1885, 1297–1300; Wigdermann, "Kevurat hamor"; Zederbaum, *Keter kehunah*, 138. For a dispute between Savran and Bershad hasidim over the recitation of *kegavna* in the Friday night prayers, which culminated in denunciations to the authorities, see Ish-Naomi, "Mitehom haneshiyah," 1:166.

85. For examples of these clashes, see Assaf, *Ne'ehaz basevakh*, 280–81 note 95.

86. "And there was a drawn-out controversy, this is the famous controversy known in our parts as the '*kadavar* controversy,' which is how the Talne hasidim start the *Kedushah* . . . and this young zaddik [of Savran] went against the opinion of the ruling elder and transferred his camp from *kadavar* to *kadosh*" (*Hamelits*, 9 November 1885, 1298).

87. For a comprehensive treatment of nineteenth-century maskilim in Brody, see *Arim veimahot beyisrael*, 6:173–221.

88. In Akiva Chajes's day, an outstanding family figure was the maskil Zvi Hirsh

Chajes (1805–55), who served in the rabbinate in Zholkva. See *Arim veimahot beyisrael*, 6:201; Meir Hershkowitz, *Maharats Hayot: Toldot Rabbi Tsvi Hirsh Hayot umishnato* (Jerusalem: Mossad Harav Kook, 1972).

89. David of Talne apparently moved to Brody in 1877. See Yitshak Ewen, *Funem rebns hoyf: Zikhroynes un mayses, gezehn, gehert un nokhdertselt* (New York, 1922), 137–43; *Netsah shebanetsah*, 181–91.

90. Kasdai, "Kit'ei zikhronot," 217.

91. On the doubtful authenticity of Kasdai's memoirs, their tendentiousness (settling accounts with his childhood friend Micha Yosef Berdyczewski), and his unreliability in other matters, see Assaf, *Ne'ehaz basevakh*, 282 note 101.

Chapter 6. "How Times Have Changed": The World of Rabbi Menahem Nahum Friedman of Itscan

1. This book (1893–1900) is a reworking of a German historical novel by Hermann Reckendorf, *Die Geheimnisse der Juden* (Of the secrets of the Jews; 1856), which tells the tale of the descendants of King David throughout Jewish history. It was very popular with teenagers and appeared in many editions.

2. Sadan, *Ke'arat tsimukim*, 83 no. 150.

3. On Orthodoxy's generally negative attitude toward modernity and secular culture at that time, see Luz, *Parallels Meet*, chapter 1; Benjamin Brown, "Orthodox Judaism," *The Blackwell Companion to Judaism*, edited by Jacob Neusner and Alan J. Avery-Peck (Oxford: Blackwell, 2000), 311–33.

4. In his memoirs, Asher Korekh of Glina, in eastern Galicia, related: "In my day pagination with Roman numerals was still a sign of a secular book; such a book was called a Perets'l (for Perets Smolenskin) and it was condemned to burning" (*Bagolah uvamoledet* [Jerusalem: Gazit, 1941], 53).

5. *Al hayofi*, 45–48.

6. He mentions works by Michelangelo, Raphael, Rembrandt, Dürer, and Titian, among others (ibid., 34–37).

7. He refers to Beethoven's *Pastoral* and Ninth Symphonies, Handel's *Israel in Egypt* and *Judas Maccabeus*, Chopin's nocturnes, and some of Schubert's lieder (ibid., 26, 42).

8. An exception is a long note explaining the "true doctrine of the Besht" (directed against neo-Romantic maskilim who, in Friedman's opinion, distorted Hasidism; see note 78 below).

9. This responsum was published by Raphael, *Hasidut vehasidim*, 314–19.

10. For brief entries on Friedman, see Reisen, *Lexicon*, 3:186–87; Kressel, *Cyclopedia*, 2:663; *Leksikon*, 7:484–85; *Entsiklopediyah shel hatsiyonut hadatit*, vol. 4 (Jerusalem: Mossad Harav Kook, 1972), 424–28; Wunder, *Meorei Galicia*, 4:205–6; *Ner yisrael*, 6:11–12. Recently a four-page letter written after 1927 and containing biographical information on Menahem Nahum was offered for sale at a public auction (Jerusalem Judaica, April 2008 catalog, lot 601). This letter was written on the rebbe's formal stationary by Menahem Nahum's secretary, Rabbi Shlomo Eliyahu Schwemmer.

11. For further information on this dynasty, see Assaf, "The Clash over *Or Ha-Hayyim*," 219 note 30.

12. Yehiel Mekhl Hibner, *Nahalah leyisrael* (Lemberg, 1876), no. 9, fol. 9b; *Ner yisrael*, 3:21.

13. The history of Hasidism in Romania has yet to receive systematic, critical study. For a relatively recent study, see Lucian Zeev Herşovici, "An Outline of the History of Hasidism in Romania," in *The History of the Jews in Romania*, vol. 2: *The Nineteenth Century*, edited by Liviu Rotman and Carol Iancu (Tel Aviv: Tel Aviv University, 2001), 185–203 (Hebrew).

14. Friedman dedicated his first book, *Divrei Menahem*, to his mother's memory. His father (1858?–1940) remarried and lived in Buhush until 1896. He then moved to Adjud, Romania, where he established a hasidic court. During World War I, he moved to Galats, where he died. See Wunder, *Meorei Galicia*, 4:147–48.

15. For letters of invitation to this impressive wedding, see *Nahalat Tsvi* 15 (1997): 175–76. For a description, see Hakham, Introduction to *Sefarim niftahim*, 6–7. On Yisrael of Chortkov, see Wunder, *Meorei Galicia*, 4:188–94; *Entsiklopediyah lehasidut*, 2:562–64. For an admiring, hagiographic treatment of this figure, see *Madbarna de'umtei*. For an intriguing memoir account of Rabbi Yisrael, see Yaakov ben Yeshayahu Masie, *Zikhronot* (Tel Aviv: Yalkut, 1936), 3:50–56.

16. This is according to oral hasidic traditions, which I was unable to verify in written material.

17. Itscan is located near Suceava, in present-day Romania.

18. According to one of his admirers, who was also personally acquainted with him, Menahem Nahum served as an admor in Itscan, but this is not attested to in any other sources. See Brayer, "Admorei Romaniyah," 215–16.

19. *Hahalom ufitrono*, 23–24.

20. With the outbreak of World War I, nearly all of the zaddikim from the various branches of the Ruzhin dynasty in Romania, Galicia, and Bukovina left their towns and established their courts in large cities, especially Vienna. This intriguing sociological and geographical phenomenon of the wholesale transplantation of hasidic courts has yet to be studied. See Assaf, *Regal Way*, 308–9; *Madbarna de'umtei*, 1:189–212.

21. Raphael, *Hasidut vehasidim*, 316.

22. He signed these articles with the pen name Peli. For the editor's comment on the first of these articles, and other articles on this topic, see Assaf, *Ne'ehaz basevakh*, 287 note 23. For Peli's identification as Friedman, see Shaul Chajes, *Pseudonymen-Lexikon der Hebräischen und Jiddischen Literatur* (Vienna: Glanz, 1933), no. 5133 (Hebrew).

23. *Madbarna de'umtei*, 2:15–74.

24. On his suggested compromise to a quarrel between ritual slaughterers, in which one of the parties breached the zaddik of Shtefanesht's wishes, see Betsalel Zeev Shafran, *She'elot uteshuvot haRabaz* (Warsaw: Levin-Epstein, 1930), vol. 1: *Yoreh de'ah*, no. 116. A eulogy for both figures, published by their disciple Rabbi Nahum Shmaryahu Schechter in 1936, consistently refers to Menahem Nahum as the rebbe's deputy (see *Aniyat amen*). See also Brayer, "Admorei Romaniyah," 216.

25. Hakham, Introduction to *Sefarim niftahim*, 10–11; *Ner yisrael*, 6:13; *Madbarna de'umtei*, 2:460.

26. Brayer, "Admorei Romaniyah," 216; Raphael, *Hasidut vehasidim*, 316; Yitshak Alfasi, *Hassidism and the Return to Zion* (Tel Aviv: Sifriyat Maariv, 1986), 137 (Hebrew).

27. This emerges in a letter by his uncle Avraham Matityahu, dated 5 Av 1924. See Hakham, Introduction to *Sefarim niftahim*, 19.

28. The evidence for his trips abroad is undated. Based on its mention in *Divrei Menahem*, 9, his trip to Italy took place before 1913, and based on a reference in *Halalom ufitrono*, 21, his trip to France took place around 1920.

29. On his journey to the sanatorium, see *Aniyat amen*, 9, 13–14, 18. His wife, Miriam, died in Paris in 1963 and was buried in Givatayim. Their only daughter, Feige, lived in Paris with her husband and son; they died during the Holocaust.

30. According to Nahum Shmaryahu Schechter, in order to avert distressing the sick rebbe, the hasidim did not inform him of his nephew's death (*Aniyat amen*, 18).

31. After their rebbe's death, most of the Shtefanesht hasidim affiliated themselves with the zaddik Moshe Leib of Pashkan, Yitshak of Buhush's son. For details as to how Rabbi Avraham Matityahu was buried in Israel in 1968, and how his gravesite came to be associated with miracles, see Assaf, *Ne'ehaz basevakh*, 288 note 32.

32. Cited in Yehudah Evron-Nachberg, *MiShtefaneshti leErets Yisrael* (Beersheba, 1989), 125–26. The author, Hannah (Schwemmer) Morgenstern, somewhat overenthusiastically described Rabbi Menahem Nahum as having studied at the University of Vienna and as possessing doctoral degrees in literature and philosophy (32–39, 118–126).

33. The letters are housed in the Horodezky Collection (no. 23) at the Gnazim Institute in Tel Aviv. Among other matters, Friedman thanks Horodezky for an article praising him. For that article, see Shmuel Abba Horodezky, "Tsadik meyuhad bemino," *Hadoar* 3 (27 Tevet 1924): 9–10 (reprinted in his *Hahasidut vehahasidim* [1951], 4:179–81). See also Horodezky, "Mishulhan hasefarim," *Hayom* (Warsaw), 14 Iyyar 1925, 4. I thank Gad Sagiv for this reference.

34. *Divrei Menahem*, 49.

35. This literature included not just philosophical classics like Saadya Gaon's *Book of Beliefs and Opinions*, Judah Halevi's *Kuzari*, or Maimonides' *Guide for the Perplexed*, but also less well-known works like Gersonides' *Milhamot hashem*, Hasdai Crescas's *Or hashem*, or Hillel of Verona's *Tagmulei hanefesh*.

36. Even though these works had been translated into Hebrew in the nineteenth century, he was evidently familiar with Philo and Josephus in their German translations.

37. See, for example, *Divrei Menahem*, 133; *Perush man*, 75–76.

38. See, for example, *Divrei Menahem*, 131–32, 138, 149.

39. Ibid., 10, 103, 109; see also *Perush man*, for example, preface, 8 ("For morality is the heart of religion, its soul, its pulse and focus").

40. *Divrei Menahem*, 148.

41. Ibid., 59–60.

42. The commentary itself was composed prior to the publication of his first book (see the conclusion of *Divrei Menahem*, 186). He also notes in the first part of the commentary (Vienna, 1920) that "my book *Perush man* on all of tractate *Avot* is complete" (54) and cites technical reasons for why it was published serially.

43. *Perush man*, preface, 13–14.

44. *Sifre Deuteronomy*, piska 43 (translation quoted from *Sifre: A Tannaitic Commentary on the Book of Deuteronomy*, translated and edited by Reuven Hammer [New Haven, Conn.: Yale University Press, 1986], 91); BT *Makkot* 24a–b.

45. *Perush man*, 1.

46. See, for example, ibid., 243ff. (which includes a reference to the Christian belief in the Trinity).

47. Ibid., 9. Friedman's comment to *Avot* 3:13, "Tradition is a fence for the Torah," is of interest. He notes that the sixteenth-century rabbi Yosef Ashkenazi emended the text "in the name of a certain book to 'morality is a fence for the Torah' . . . for without morality there is no Torah . . . and without Torah there is no morality" (167, 169). Note the orthographic similarity between tradition and morality (*masoret* and *musariyut*, respectively, in Hebrew).

48. Ibid., 15–17. The notion of the individual as a "little universe" is not foreign to hasidic thought. It appears in the works of Yaakov Yosef of Polonnoye (*Toldot Yaakov Yosef* [Lemberg, 1858], "Parashat aharei," 95a); in the name of the Besht (*Keter shem tov* [Brooklyn: Kehot, 1987], 24 no. 88); and in the remarks of Nahman of Bratslav (*Sihot haRan* [Jerusalem: Hasidei Braslav, 1978], no. 77, 54). Hasidism's opponents claimed that, notwithstanding the antiquity of the concept, hasidic thought framed it as innovative, distorting it in the process. See Wilensky, *Hasidim and Mitnaggedim*, 2:163–64.

49. *Perush man*, 122.

50. Ibid., 132. For his critique of communism, see ibid., 269–70.

51. Ibid., 322.

52. A brief review of the book appeared in the *Bibliotek idishe visenshaft* (Iasi) 84 (1925): 144.

53. *Hahalom ufitrono*, 11–12, 29–30, 41–42. He also mentions dreams in other works. For instance, the conclusion of *Al ha'emet vehasheker* describes a dream in which he encountered a demonic serpent—the symbol of falsehood, according to Otto Weininger—in the heart of the forest, which showed him various visions, all the false fruits of deception and its destructive force in human society. Given its didactic character, this dream appears to be fictional. *Perush man* also concludes with a dream of this type.

54. See especially Friedman's chapter 6, 20–28. For responses by Orthodox and hasidic rabbis to the appearance of Freud's *Die Traumdeutung* (1900), see Assaf, *Ne'ehaz basevakh*, 296 note 55. Evidently, Freud's name and reputation had even penetrated the fortified walls of the hasidic community. The Viennese rabbi Chaim Bloch testified to meetings with Freud. Bloch even recounted how Wilhelm Stekel—one of Freud's first students, who split off from Freud to found an independent branch of psychoanalysis—showed him his notes on the erotic dream "of one of the leaders of Hasidism in Poland, who had a reputation for being a saint and free of the blemishes of eroticism and salaciousness." This rebbe, who dreamt nightly of having sexual relations with an unknown married woman, had sought Stekel's help. See Chaim Bloch, *Heikhal ledivrei haza"l upitgameyhem* (New York: Pardes, 1948), 35, 54–55. It has also recently been revealed that the Lubavitcher rebbe Shalom Ber Schneersohn visited Freud's clinic in 1902. See Stanley Schneider and Joseph H. Berke, "Sigmund

Freud and the Lubavitcher Rebbe," *Psychoanalytic Review* 87/1 (2000): 39–59; *Sefer hatoladot: Moharashab*, 53.

55. *Hahalom ufitrono*, 41–42.

56. Parts of this work were written much earlier. See, for example, 27, where he notes: "I wrote this chapter during the second year of the war [1915]."

57. *Al ha'emet vehasheker*, 3–6.

58. He explains Talmudic hyperbole as fanciful or allegorical, especially the stories concerning Rabbah bar bar Hannah, and gives an example from the events of his day: if someone wrote "that a Serb shot a rifle in the city of Sarajevo and killed five [fifteen] million people," this would be seen as an outrageous exaggeration, but "we, for whom this event took place in our day, will understand the fancy and recognize that it was the Serb who killed the Austrian crown prince in Sarajevo who sparked the World War in which five [fifteen] million died" (ibid., 20).

59. Ibid., 37.

60. Ibid., 12–13.

61. Ibid., 21.

62. Ibid., 23–24.

63. Ibid., 25. See also *Perush man*, 65.

64. *Al ha'emet vehasheker*, 29.

65. Ibid., 30–32.

66. On the notion of beauty in the early days of Hasidism, see Moshe Idel, "Female Beauty: A Chapter in the History of Jewish Mysticism," in *Within Hasidic Circles*, edited by Immanuel Etkes et al. (Jerusalem: Bialik Institute, 1999), 317–34 (Hebrew).

67. *Al hayofi*, 7.

68. *Ha'olam* (London) 17, 20 September 1929, 784.

69. *Al ha'adam*, 18–20.

70. Ibid., 20–23.

71. Ibid., 27.

72. *Al ha'emet vehasheker*, 26–27.

73. Avraham Isaac Hakohen Kook, "Ha-Milhamah," in *Orot*, translated with an introduction by Bezalel Naor (Northvale, N.J.: Aronson, 1993), 95 (emphasis in original). On the attitude of zaddikim in Poland to World War I and its results, see Piekarz, *Hasidism in Poland*, 232–45.

74. *Al ha'adam*, 45.

75. See, for example, *Perush man*, 43, where he objects to new strictures.

76. Ibid., 10.

77. See, for example, ibid., 21, 34–36, 160, and passim.

78. His critique of the neo-Romantic approach to Hasidism is an exception. He sharply denigrates those "modern maskilim who admire Hasidism," who have spoken the praises of Hasidism from the late nineteenth century, "praise of a type that leads to denigration." He accuses them of turning the Besht into a "reformer" because he opposed *pilpul* and, by interpreting Hasidism as a revolt against the Torah and the commandments, of turning Hasidism into a reflection of what they wish to see (ibid., 24–25).

79. On this type, see Immanuel Etkes, "Lishe'elat mevasrei hahaskalah beMizrah

Eyropa," in *East European Jewish Enlightenment* (Jerusalem: Shazar, 1993), 25–44 (Hebrew).

80. *Perush man*, 171.

81. Ibid., 183.

82. Ibid., 78. Darwin is also mentioned (212), as one of the "contemporary scholars."

83. Ibid., 338.

84. Ibid., 338–40. For details of other sharply worded, journalistic critiques of contemporary zaddikim and rabbis that he published pseudonymously, see Assaf, *Ne'ehaz basevakh*, 305 note 85.

85. The untitled article appeared in *Kvutsei Efrayim* (Seini) 5, nos. 7–8 (Tevet–Shevat 1926): 49–53.

86. He is apparently referring to Rabbi Hayyim Shmuel Schor, who appointed himself chief rabbi of Bucharest and enjoyed the support of the Romanian Ministry of Religion. Schor propagandized against a single representative body for Romanian Jewry and lobbied for the regime's recognition of the Orthodox community as an independent legal entity. See *Pinkas Hakehillot: Rumania*, 1:118–19; Jacob Geller, *The Rise and Decline of a Community: The Ashkenazim and Sephardim in Rumania (1919–1941)* (Tel Aviv: Moreshet, 1985), 233–38 (Hebrew).

87. Hophni and Pinhas, the sons of the priest Eli (1 Samuel 1–2), symbolize corrupt religious leadership.

88. See Jacob Katz, *A House Divided: Orthodoxy and Schism in Nineteenth-Century Central European Jewry* (Hanover. N.H.: Brandeis University Press, 1998).

89. Assaf, "The Clash over *Or Ha-Hayyim*," 201, 203.

90. For details, see Assaf, *Ne'ehaz basevakh*, 307 note 90.

91. *Aniyat amen*, 9, 18, 24, and passim. For another eulogy, by Rabbi Shmuel Schwemmer, see *Bibliotek idishe visenshaft* (Iasi), no. 187 (Tammuz 1933).

92. The following remarks are typical of Chortkov tradition regarding Menahem Nahum: "Although none questioned his prowess in revealed and hidden Torah, and his great knowledge of other fields and sciences . . . not all agreed with his particular doctrine . . . accordingly, despite their profundity and importance, the hasidim who followed the ways of their holy rabbis refrained from reading his various books" (*Madbarna de'umtei*, 2:460; note that this writer does not even name Friedman's works).

93. With one exception: the facsimile edition of *Sheloshah sefarim niftahim* (1987), the private initiative of the hasid Yitshak Hakham. The absence from this edition of the expected approbations by the zaddikim of the Ruzhin dynasty is apparently not fortuitous.

94. Zvi Aryeh of Zlatopol, a scion of the Chernobyl dynasty, married Yisrael of Chortkov's daughter in 1913 and moved with his father-in-law to Vienna. In 1939 he came to Palestine and settled in Tel Aviv. From 1958 until his death he served as the rebbe of the Chortkov hasidim. He also authored a booklet titled *Emunah veda'at* (Jerusalem: Beit Yetomim Diskin, 1940). On him, see *Madbarna de'umtei*, 2:431–55.

95. Zvi Aryeh Twersky does allude to Nietzsche, "one scholar among the nations" whose thought deals with the "superman" (*Hatov vehatakhlit*, 20–21).

96. Ibid., preface. The title may allude to Menahem Nahum's remarks in his *Al hayofi* (cited above) naming beauty the ultimate good (*takhlit hatov*).

97. *Madbarna de'umtei*, 2:447.

98. *Hatov vehatakhlit*, 17–19.

99. Ibid., 19.

100. Ibid., 21–22.

101. Shmuel Abba Horodezky, "Tsadik meyuhad bemino," *Hadoar* 3 (27 Tevet 1924): 9–10 (reprinted in *Hahasidut vehahasidim*, 4:179–81). See also Horodezky, "Mi-shulhan hasefarim," *Hayom* (Warsaw), 14 Iyyar 1925, 4.

102. But they did correspond, as mentioned above.

103. Although nowhere mentioned explicitly, Friedman's direct influence is clearly visible in his disciple Nahum Shmaryahu Schechter's *Perah shoshan* (Cluj: Weinstein and Friedman, 1925), a commentary on *Avot*. Like his friend and mentor, Schechter intended to explain Talmudic statements "according to the foundations of philosophy, research, and knowledge." Hayyim Yehuda Ehrenreich's comments are revealing: "I greatly doubt whether his work can achieve its desired end. For the readers of his book will not understand his investigations and philosophizing, and those who understand scholarship and philosophy will not read his book" (*Otsar hahayyim* 1 [1929]: 93). These remarks are also applicable to Menahem Nahum's writings. As noted, he and Schechter were closely acquainted, and Friedman even wrote an approbation to Schechter's book; however, it was never published. See Raphael, *Hasidut vehasidim*, 319 note 8.

104. Hakham, Introduction to *Sefarim niftahim*, 8. He published only *Divrei Menahem*, *Perush man*, and *Al ha'emet vehasheker* (which he characterizes as belonging to the genre of *musar* literature) and does not refer to Friedman's other treatises in his introduction.

105. Avraham Kahana, *Masot al sofrim veanshei shem vedivrei hasidut* (Pshemyshl: Yavneh, 1934), 21–22.

106. For additional examples of scions of rabbis and zaddikim who did not follow the ancestral path, see chapter 2, note 3. The following chapter contains an outstanding example of the misgivings of one such hasidic son.

107. His name was expunged from most genealogies of hasidic dynasties. For example, Efraim Elimelekh Dorf cites only Menahem Nahum of Itscan as a descendant of the rebbe of Adjud (*Ateret tiferet yisrael* [Tel Aviv: Mofet, 1969)], 15).

108. On Bernyu, see the end of the introduction.

109. On Matesl Friedman, see Reisen, *Lexicon*, 3:173–76; *Leksikon*, 7:471–72; *Pinkas Hakehillot: Rumania*, Introduction, 1:101–2; Wunder, *Meorei Galicia*, 4:147–48. For additional references, see Assaf, *Ne'ehaz basevakh*, 312 note 108.

110. For examples of his pseudonyms and the titles of his articles, see Assaf, *Ne'ehaz basevakh*, 312 note 109.

111. Reisen, *Lexicon*, 3:173–76.

112. See Shlomo Bikl, *Romanya* (Buenos Aires, 1961), 197–99. It is noteworthy that Menahem Nahum's close friend, Yaakov Botoshansky, also wrote a play about Bernyu. See Assaf, *Ne'ehaz basevakh*, 312 note 108, 313 note 111.

113. Like Menahem Nahum and his brother Matityahu, Yaakov Friedman was the great-grandson of Shalom Yosef, Yisrael of Ruzhin's oldest son. On the side of his mother, Margalit Twersky, Yaakov Friedman was also of distinguished lineage: a seventh-generation descendant of the Maggid Menahem Nahum of Chernobyl.

114. On his poetry, see Dan Miron, introduction, in Yaakov Friedman, *In the Beginning There Was Silence: Poems* (Tel Aviv: Hadekel, 1983), 5–38 (Hebrew); Dan Miron, "Koha shel hulshah," in *Man Is Nothing But . . . : Studies in Modern Hebrew Poetry* (Tel Aviv: Zmora-Bitan, 1999), 505–46 (Hebrew); Sela-Saldinger, *Torn Chord*; Joseph Bar-El, *Di shire fun Yankev Fridman* (Tel Aviv: Israel-Buch, 1996).

115. Sela-Saldinger, *Torn Chord*, 1:23–33.

116. *Leksikon*, 7:478–80. On how Yaakov Friedman passed muster and came to be included in Wunder's encyclopedia of Orthodox rabbis, see Wunder, *Meorei Galicia*, 4:229.

117. This scion of the Zhabno dynasty (Poland) remained observant but left the hasidic camp. For information on him and his brother Yisrael, who became a secular socialist, see Zvi Ankori, *Chestnuts of Yesteryear: A Jewish Odyssey* (Jerusalem: Carmel, 2001), 189–90 (Hebrew).

118. Bornstein (1895–1961), a well-known writer, journalist, and playwright, who wrote under the pseudonym M. B. Stein, was the son of the admor Shmuel Bornstein of Sochachev (the grandson of Menahem Mendel of Kotsk). For further details, see Assaf, *Ne'ehaz basevakh*, 313–14 note 117.

119. On Fischel Schneersohn, see chapter 2, note 149. For further information on him and on Stein, see also Menashe Unger, "Eduyot shel nekhadim," *Davar:* Sabbath and holiday supplement, 6 Kislev 1926.

120. Sadan, "Ro'eh vetson marito," 7–8.

121. Ibid., 12–13. See Dov Sadan, "Se'ifim bimegilat yuhasin," *Orhot ushevilim*, 28–29, 313–14; Sadan, "Firkha kefula," *Hadashim gam yeshanim*, 3:201.

122. Another intriguing figure is Rabbi Yaakov Friedman (1878–1956), the admor of Husyatin-Tel Aviv and the author of *Ohalei Yaakov*. Although fully Orthodox, he was ignored because of his surprising, original Zionist nationalist thought. See Yehuda Brandes, *In the Kingdom of Holiness* (Alon Shevut: Tevunot, 2006; Hebrew).

123. The reference is to Yitshak Hakham's facsimile edition of *Sheloshah sefarim niftahim*.

124. *Yated ne'eman*, Rosh Hashanah 2001, Shabbat supplement, 31.

Chapter 7. "Confession of My Tortured, Afflicted Soul": The World of Rabbi Yitshak Nahum Twersky of Shpikov

1. Glatstein, *Homecoming at Twilight*, translated by Norbert Guterman (New York: T. Yoseloff, 1968), 145–46 (slightly revised).

2. Dineson Collection, V.879/17, Department of Archives, NLIS. Dineson, seen as the father of the Yiddish sentimental novel, was then Y. L. Peretz's loyal assistant. See Shmuel Leib Zitron, *Dray literarishe doyres: Zikhroynes vegn yidishe shriftshteler* (Vilna: Shreberk, 1922), 1:56–104; *Leksikon*, 2:514–16. His date of birth is a matter of debate; his tombstone in the Warsaw cemetery puts it as 1858.

3. For comprehensive information on the founding of the Shpikov dynasty, see Twersky, *Hehatser hapnimit*, 26ff. It was written by Yitshak Nahum's nephew Yohanan Twersky (1900–67), who, like his uncle, grew up in this hasidic court. Despite its fic-

tional literary framework, this book is an important source of information about life in hasidic courts in the Ukraine on the eve of World War I. On Yohanan Twersky and his writings on Hasidism, see Lanuel, "The Maiden of Ludmir." Intriguing memoirs on the Shpikov hasidic court were also written by other townspeople. See Glubman, *Ketavim*; and *We Were as Dreamers* (Hebrew), by Pinchas Govrin, his son.

4. For the scant biographical information that is available on Yitshak Nahum, see Lewin, *"These Will I Remember!"* 4:132–36; Wunder, *Meorei Galicia*, 3:14–16; Shaul Gur-Arieh, *Beit tsadikim ya'amod* (Jerusalem: Makhon Or Hatsafon, 1984), 236–38; *Entsiklopediyah lehasidut*, 2:434. Written in the spirit of hasidic historiography, all of these books, especially the first, aim to glorify their heroes and obscure their anomalous characteristics. Well acquainted with Yohanan Twersky's memoirs, the editors of *"These Will I Remember!"* extracted from them only those things befitting a zaddik martyred during the Holocaust. Nonetheless, they too note that "in secret, in private [Rabbi Yitshak Nahum] would sometimes study kabbalah and mystical books. He was a silent person by nature, *who knew how to keep and conceal a secret*" (4:132).

5. Not in spring 1909, as according to Belz historiography (Shaul Gur-Arieh, *Beit tsadikim ya'amod*, 236). Written in 1910, the confession tells of his impending marriage.

6. See Bromberg, *Belz*, 127–53; Klapholtz, *Admorei Belz*, 3:3; Wunder, *Meorei Galicia*, 4:872–77.

7. Yisakhar Dov's daughter Hannah Rachel was married to Pinhas of Ustila (1880–1943), Yohanan of Rachmistrivke's grandson. Pinhas spent many years at the Belz court. See Wunder, *Meorei Galicia*, 3:23–28; *Kovets mishkenot Yaakov* 2 (1994): 9–10, 36–56; *Olam hahasidut* 32 (1997): 14–19. For an amusing Belz anecdote concerning how the Belz hasidim stole Reb Pinhas's Chernobyl-style clothing before his wedding, forcing him to wear Belz clothing, and how Yitshak Nahum earned a favorable reception because he came in Belz clothing, see *Rawa-Ruska*, 79; Assaf, *Ne'ehaz basevakh*, 319 note 8.

8. For a brief description of this wedding, see Twersky, *Hehatser hapnimit*, 220–21. Also, the wedding portrayed in the opening of I. J. Singer's famous novella *Yoshe Kalb* (1932) is probably this one (New York: Schocken, 1988). Although this book's historical kernel lies in a nineteenth-century episode, its atmosphere is grounded in the early-twentieth-century courts of Belz and Chernobyl. See Twersky, "Ha'otsar shebe-Shpikov."

9. Apart from the custom of *kest*, a prearranged agreement regarding the number of years the bridegroom would be supported by his in-laws so he could continue his studies, the economic straits of the Shpikov court also forced Yitshak Nahum to move to Belz, as he notes in the confession.

10. For a description of late-nineteenth-century Belz as a center of conservatism, where men and women dressed as nowhere else in Galicia, see Joseph Margoshes, *A World Apart: A Memoir of Jewish Life in Nineteenth Century Galicia*, translated by Rebecca Margolis and Ira Robinson (Boston: Academic Studies Press, 2008), 16–17.

11. Yohanan Twersky also wondered about his uncle's acclimation to Belz. He surmised: "How did he acclimate to Belz, with its internal and external fences? Perhaps because he placed Torah at the center of his life, or perhaps because of his fondness

for his wife, or because, he, the young one, was indulgent and not judgmental. All these together sweetened his difficult hours there" (*Hehatser hapnimit*, 243).

12. Wunder, *Meorei Galicia*, 3:15; Lewin, *"These Will I Remember!"* 4:133.

13. *Rawa-Ruska*, 79.

14. Twersky, *Hehatser hapnimit*, 243–54.

15. On the tribulations of the Belz hasidic court during World War I, see Klapholtz, *Admorei Belz*, 3:316–38.

16. Ibid., 3:44.

17. This dispute, started and fueled by the extremists Yisakhar Dov of Belz, on the one hand, and Hayyim Elazar Shapira of Munkatsh (1872–1937), on the other, brought Belzer cooperation with the Neologists and the Zionists. For sources on this little-researched controversy, see Assaf, *Ne'ehaz basevakh*, 320–21 note 17. Of special interest here is Shmuel Hakohen Weingarten's testimony that he personally sold Yitshak Nahum Twersky the Zionist shekel for two years (*Encyclopaedia of the Jewish Diaspora*, vol. 7: *Karpatorus* [Jerusalem: Encyclopaedia of the Jewish Diaspora Co., 1959], 229 [Hebrew]). The purchase of the shekel demonstrated Zionist sympathies; this is particularly outstanding against the background of the Belzer rebbe's ingrained opposition to Zionism.

18. On this period, see Klapholtz, *Admorei Belz*, 3:339–52.

19. Yitshak Nahum signed a letter sent from Belz in 1926 as the head of the Rawa rabbinical court. See *Be'oholei tsadikim: Tsmihatah vehithavutah shel shushilta dedehava beit Belze* (Jerusalem: Makhon Mehkar Ve'arkhiyon Keter Malkhut, 1993), 2:380–81. In an open letter to the press, the residents of Rawa requested of Rabbi Yitshak Nahum that he not accept the post of rabbi, not because they had anything against him personally, but because they had not been consulted. See *Di vokh fun'm togblat* (Lemberg), 21 Adar 1926, no. 10, 4.

20. On this community, see *Rawa-Ruska;* Danuta Dăbrowska, Abraham Wein, and Aharon Weiss, eds., *Pinkas Hakehillot: Encyclopaedia of Jewish Communities—Poland*, vol. 2: *Eastern Galicia* (Jerusalem: Yad Vashem, 1980), 500–501 (Hebrew).

21. Wunder, *Meorei Galicia*, 3:16. For some information about his tenure as rabbi in Rawa, see also Twersky, *Hehatser hapnimit*, 263; *Rawa-Ruska*, 89–90. For a description of his son's wedding in 1936 to the daughter of the Radomsk rebbe, see *Rawa-Ruska*, 187–88. Photocopies of the invitation to his son's wedding and of three letters in Yitshak Nahum's handwriting from his tenure in Rawa Ruska were published by Nathan Ortner, *Devar hen: Sefer zikaron . . .*, 2nd rev. ed. (Lod: privately printed, 2006).

22. For a description of the destruction of Rawa's Jews during the Holocaust, see Isaac Lewin, *Aliti miSpetsiyah: Reshimot ud mutsal migeto Lvov*, translated by Dov Shtok (Tel Aviv: Am Oved, 1947), 94–109. Perhaps his description of a beaten and battered elderly rabbi standing wrapped in his prayer shawl and phylacteries refers to Yitshak Nahum, then fifty-four years old (106). For some details on Yitshak Nahum's son, Yoel, who was also critical of the Belz court, see Twersky, *Hehatser hapnimit*, 263; *Rawa-Ruska*, 90.

23. Yitshak Nahum had a younger brother, Moshe David; little is known of him, but he apparently played almost no role in his brother's intellectual and spiritual world.

His sister, Yente Devorah, the third child in the family, died in childhood. On Yente, see Twersky, *Hehatser hapnimit*, 19, 34–35.

24. Efraim Elimelekh Dorf, *Ateret tiferet yisrael: Sefer hayahas leshoshalot Rizin-Tsernobil-Karlin* (Tel Aviv: privately printed, 1969), 15, 96; Wunder, *Meorei Galicia*, 4:227–28; *Tiferet yisrael lehasidei beit Ruzhin* 30 (1992): 28–29; *Be'er Yitshak: Me'asef letorah vehasidut* 3 (1993): 43–44.

25. In his brief autobiography, her son, the writer Yohanan Twersky, noted that in 1906, when he was six years old, his mother took him to Odessa and presented him to Hayyim Nahman Bialik, and asked him to read her son's poems (G. Kressel Collection, Twersky file, 4°1412, Department of Archives, NLIS [photocopy in Aliza Lanuel, "The Maiden of Ludmir," appendix 3]). For some information on "the noble woman" Haya, see also Aharon Pechenick, "Kisufei ge'ulah behasidut Tshernobl veRuzhin," *Shdemot* 79 (1981): 112–13, and her grandson David Twersky's response, ibid., p. 114.

26. Twersky, *Hehatser hapnimit*, 231, 235–36.

27. See a 1917 letter sent from Shpikov by Yohanan Twersky to Bialik in Odessa, published in M. Ungerfeld, "A Bundle of Letters to H. N. Bialik," *He'avar* 15 (1968): 303–4 (Hebrew).

28. As noted, Yohanan Twersky recorded some information on her personal world and history. He based his remarks on his own memories and on those of his mother, "written and oral," and on "the writings of Aunt Mirele and the writings of my uncle Yitshak-Nakhum'l." Indeed, in Haya's will, written on 16 December 1950 and kept in the Twersky Archive at the Tel Aviv Gnazim Institute, she requests that the letters of Yitshak Nahum in her possession be sent to her son. I was unable to locate either these memoirs or these letters in the Twersky Archive. If found, they would certainly shed additional light on this intriguing family.

29. On Menahem Nahum of Trisk-Warsaw, see Twersky, *Hehatser hapnimit*, 221–34; Menashe Unger, *Admorim shenispu bashoah* (Jerusalem: Mossad Harav Kook, 1969), 203–4. Some of his Torah teachings are cited in *Kerem hahasidut* 5 (1990): 42–43.

30. Yohanan Twersky's memoirs, where he notes Mirl's enthusiastic reception of his early literary efforts, also recall her exchange of letters with Yaakov Dineson (*Hehatser hapnimit*, 219–20). He recounts that Dineson chose her pseudonym (Bat Tovim) and that he printed her first poems, and describes Dineson's long letters, written "on thick blue paper, in round, fair letters" (231). To date, I have been unable to determine where Dineson published Mirl's poems.

31. The dates of Asher Perlow's birth and marriage are cited according to Aharon Hoyzman, *Yalkut divrei Aharon* (Jerusalem: Hatehiyah, 1962), 250. For a lively description of the wedding, see Baruch Chemerinsky, "Hatunat bat harabbi miShpikov (sipur zikhronot)," in *Sefer Chemerinsky: Derekh hayetsirah shel bamai ivri,* edited by Shlomo Shenhod (Tel Aviv: Hamenorah, 1947), 29–58.

32. Of his father, the admor Yisrael, it was said that he would play the violin, accompanied by four of his sons, at Saturday night *Melave Malka* repasts, including works by Bach and Beethoven. See *Stolin: A Memorial to the Jewish Communities of Stolin and Vicinity* (Tel Aviv: Former Residents of Stolin and Vicinity in Israel, 1952), 149, 171–73 (Hebrew).

33. For further information on Asher, see Assaf, *Ne'ehaz basevakh*, 324 note 33.

34. *Pinsk*, vol. 2, ed. N. Tamir (Mirski) (Tel Aviv: Irgun Yotsei Pinsk-Karlin, 1996), 270 (Hebrew).

35. Twersky, *Hehatser hapnimit*, 234. Although Twersky clearly rewrote this letter; he apparently preserved its spirit.

36. For a comprehensive treatment of this subject, see Iris Parush, *Reading Jewish Women: Marginality and Modernization in Nineteenth-Century Eastern European Jewish Society* (Waltham, Mass.: Brandeis University Press, 2004). For details on the daughters of specific hasidic dynasties and their conversance with modern Hebrew, Yiddish, and German literature, see Assaf, *Ne'ehaz basevakh*, 324–25 note 36.

37. For an illustrative description of how Chava combined old and new, see Glubman, *Ketavim*, 127–28.

38. Twersky, *Hehatser hapnimit*, 160. Yitshak Nahum's remarks make it clear that he was familiar with some of Dineson and Berdyczewski's works; however, his Hebrew style testifies to a broader acquaintance with the new Hebrew literature. On the marginality of belles-lettres among the Orthodox community in Poland between the world wars, see Nathan Cohen, *Books, Writers and Newspapers: The Jewish Cultural Center in Warsaw, 1918–1942* (Jerusalem: Magnes, 2003), 178–86 (Hebrew).

39. Twersky, *Hehatser hapnimit*, 212.

40. Glubman, *Ketavim*, 29. On Glubman and his memoirs, see chapter 5.

41. *Rawa-Ruska*, 89. This visit took place sometime between 1922 and 1926.

42. On the possible influence of wording by Peretz, Horodezky, and Berdyczewski, see below. It also appears that Yitshak Nahum was familiar with Moshe Leib Lilienblum's *Hatot ne'urim o vidui hagadol* (first published in 1876), and that he adopted from that source the secular use of the term *vidui* (confession). On this literary genre, see Hannah Naveh, *The Confession: A Study of Genre* (Tel Aviv: Papyrus, 1988; Hebrew).

43. Nor is Yitshak Nahum's image of the condition of Hasidism in Poland entirely accurate. His comment to Dineson that "your honor resides in Warsaw, the capital of Poland, where Hasidism still has all its power and its influence is still tremendous" is far from reflecting the reality.

44. This refers to three of Mordekhai of Chernobyl's sons who led important hasidic dynasties: Yitshak Nahum's great-grandfather Yitshak of Skvira; his grandmother's father, David of Talne; and his maternal grandfather, Yohanan of Rachmistrivke.

45. In 1902, similar wording was used to describe the decline of the Chernobyl leadership by Shmuel Abba Horodezky, a relative of Yitshak Nahum (*Rabbi Nahum miTshernobil vetse'etsa'av* [Berdichev, 1902], 46–47).

46. Professor Dov Samet called my attention to the fascinating analogy between the victimology presented by an individual named Yitshak (Isaac) and the biblical Akedah story. Not only does Yitshak Nahum see himself as "a sacrifice on his mother's altar," he also implicitly compares himself to Abraham: "I would . . . abandon my home, my family, my place of birth . . . and travel to a big city." The confessor is thus Abraham the sacrificer, and also Isaac the sacrifice.

47. In the following passage: "But my bitter, harsh fate forces me to spend most of my days among old men—whether old in years or in attitudes, what matter?—mummified, dismal, whose God is not my God, their views not my views, all their thoughts, goals, and desires foreign to me."

48. Y. L. Peretz, *Hasidut* (Tel Aviv: Dvir, 1960), 211. For further details on this play and other contemporary literary works that treat the question of tension between zaddikim and their rebellious sons who lost their faith, see Assaf, *Ne'ehaz basevakh*, 328–29 note 46.

49. The reference is to Berdyczewski's *Sefer hasidim* (Warsaw: Tushiya, 1900), because of which Berdyczewski was considered a leading figure in the neo-Romantic stream of modern Hebrew literature. For additional information on this work and treatments of Berdyczewski's ambivalent attitude toward Hasidism, see Assaf, *Ne'ehaz basevakh*, 329 note 47.

50. The preface of this book (*Nishmat hasidim*) indeed ends with the statement: "Only one short prayer is heard in the depths of my heart: Sovereign of the World! May I share their portion!" (*Sefer hasidim*, 20).

51. Berdyczewski in fact did not study at Heidelberg, but at the universities of Breslau and Berlin. He received his doctoral degree from Bern University, in Switzerland.

52. Quoted in Zvi Sharfstein, *Haya aviv ba'arets: Mekorot hayyai* (Tel Aviv: Masada, 1953), 291–92. For a similar attitude, see Simon Bernfeld, "Zikhronot," *Reshumot* 4 (1926): 165.

53. Yitshak Nahum was aware of these weaknesses, which he attributed to the lengthy process of writing that stretched over several weeks, broken up by his fear that the letter would be read by prying eyes.

54. For a description of the crisis of Jewish identity at the turn of the nineteenth century against the background of the contradiction between religion and life, see Luz, *Parallels Meet.*

55. These figures included not just Menahem Nahum Friedman of Itscan, the topic of the previous chapter, but also such famed individuals as Ahad ha-Am and Shmuel Abba Horodezky. Their attempt to mediate between the hasidic background they abandoned and their adopted path of secular Jewish nationalism is the product of the encounter between fossilized, degenerate Hasidism, still seen as possessing an aspect of a Judaism of emotions, and political Zionism, seen as Judaism of the intellect. For details and bibliography on these figures and their hasidic backgrounds, see Assaf, *Ne'ehaz basevakh*, 331 note 53.

56. For examples, see Assaf, *Ne'ehaz basevakh*, 331 note 54.

57. For detailed information on one such figure, Moshe Twersky, the grandson of Yohanan of Rachmistrivke through his son Menahem Nahum, see Assaf, *Ne'ehaz basevakh*, 331–32 note 55.

58. Aescoly, *Hasidism in Poland*, 128. For evidence of an atmosphere of secularization that penetrated hasidic courts prior to World War I, see the memoirs of Ita Kalish, the daughter of Mendele of Otwock, where she describes her circle of friends, all of whom had left the hasidic courts (*Etmoli* [Tel Aviv: Hakibbutz Hameuchad, 1970], 99–100).

59. For the full Hebrew text, see *Ne'ehaz basevakh*, 333–48. I thank David Louvish for his excellent translation of the Hebrew text of the confession into English. (Some minor revisions have been made.)

60. This is the date according to the Julian calendar; thus, this letter was written on 6 February 1910. The Hebrew date was 27 Shevat 5670.

61. Referring to his sister Mirl, who had corresponded earlier with Dineson.

62. The use of the Hebrew phrase "*tsar li hamakom*" (emphasis in original) reflects the influence of Micha Yosef Berdyczewski's autobiographical short story "Me'ever lanahar (Zikhronot ozev)" (Beyond the river [memoir of an abandoner]). First published in 1899, this story contains Berdyczewski's description of the agonies of a young husband who escaped from the suffocation of the old study house for the free, heretical world of the enlightenment, yet still feels committed to the world he abandoned. Berdyczewski's hero used this Hebrew phrase. See Berdyczewski, *Mibayit umihuts*, 50–52. I thank Professor Avner Holtzman for bringing this parallel to my attention; see also note 66 below.

63. Yitshak Nahum's image of nineteenth-century Jewish Lithuania as a place where modernity and enlightenment (as opposed to Hasidism) found greater expression than in the Ukraine is noteworthy.

64. This is almost an exact quote from Horodezky's remarks in *Rabbi Nahum mi-Tshernobil vetse'etsa'av* (Berdichev, 1902), 46–47.

65. This teacher was probably Mordekhai Glubman. In Glubman's memoirs, he relates his own attraction to Haskalah and philosophical works at that time (*Ketavim*, 141).

66. Here too the influence of Berdyczewski's "Me'ever lanahar" is apparent (*Mibayit umihuts*, 45–46).

67. All ellipsis points are in the original.

68. The *kapota* is a long black coat traditionally worn by observant Jewish men in Eastern Europe. The *shtrayml* is an expensive round hat made from sable or foxtails. Its origins are obscure. Over time it became a beloved symbol proudly worn by pious Jews. Usually given as a wedding present, the groom cherishes it throughout his lifetime.

69. He is probably referring to Haya and Mirl, who lived with their families in a special wing inside the court. The third sister, Feige, lived in the nearby hasidic court of Buhush (see above).

70. According to BT *Yoma* 66b.

71. On the Belz custom of shaving the groom's head with a razor and shaving off all the bride's hair, see Yisrael Klapholtz, *Minhagei raboteinu miBelz* (Bnei Brak: Hamesorah, 1982), 73–74.

72. See the description in the memoirs of the writer Yehoshua Twersky, a descendant of the Machnovka rebbes (Chernobyl), of the Belzer hasidim forcing women to give up their wigs and replace them with kerchiefs "because Belz despises wigs and the women's costume there is just to wear kerchiefs" (Yehoshua Twersky, *Behatsar hatsadik* [Tel Aviv: Zion, 1970], 120).

73. The rebbe, Yisakhar Dov Rokeah of Belz.

74. *Sha'atnez* is a pentateuchal prohibition against wearing clothing that combines wool and linen.

75. See Exodus 24:10.

76. This is the hasidic *gartl*, which divides the upper, spiritual part of the body, from the lower, physical part.

77. For additional testimony about objections to the use of electricity in Belz, see Joseph Rubin, ed., *Belz: Sefer zikaron* (Tel Aviv: Yotsei Belz, 1974), 65–76; for further

examples of Yisakhar Dov's fanaticism and conservatism, see Piekarz, *Hasidism in Poland*, 111–12.

78. Leviticus 11:20.

79. This phrase is noteworthy. It was indeed the title of the Spanish monk Tomás de Torquemada, but here it is probably a reference to Fyodor Dostoevsky's *The Brothers Karamazov* (1880), where one of the characters is given this title. As this book had not then been translated into Yiddish or Hebrew, Yitshak Nahum probably absorbed the term from a secondary source.

80. This is a reference to his sister Mirl, who was married to Asher Perlow of Stolin.

Works Cited

This section lists only those works cited at least twice in the book. For works cited only once, full publication information is provided in the notes. Where an English title was available for a Hebrew or Yiddish source, this is cited, with the original language noted using the key below. Where no English title was available, the title is provided in transliteration. Hasidic and rabbinic works are usually listed in this section by title; scholarly and academic works are listed by author's last name and title. Also, for books published before and in the early twentieth century, especially rabbinic works, the place of publication is provided, but not the publisher.

(H = Hebrew; Y = Yiddish)

Aescoly, *Hasidism in Poland*

Aescoly, Aaron Ze'ev. *Hasidism in Poland.* With an introduction by David Assaf. Jerusalem: Magnes, 1998 (H).

Alfasi, *Bisdeh hahasidut*

Alfasi, Yitshak. *Bisdeh hahasidut.* Jerusalem: Ariel, 1987.

Alfasi, *Hahozeh*

———. *Hahozeh miLublin: Rabbi Yaakov Yitshak Halevi Horvits.* Jerusalem: Mossad Harav Kook, 1969.

Alim litrufah

Alim litrufah mikhtavei Moharnat. New York: Y. D. Halevi, 1955.

Altshuler, "Braslaw *Ḥassidim*"

Altshuler, Mordecai. "The Braslaw *Ḥassidim* in the USSR in the Thirties." *Michael* 6 (1980): 129–34 (H).

Aniyat amen

Schechter, Nahum Shmaryahu. *Aniyat amen.* Cluj: Ipuron, 1936.

Arim veimahot beyisrael

Arim veimahot beyisrael. Vols. 1, 2, and 4: Edited by Y. L. Hakohen Fishman. Jerusalem: Mossad Harav Kook, 1946–50. Vol. 6: *Toldot yehudei Brody*, by Nathan M. Gelber. Jerusalem: Mossad Harav Kook, 1955.

Assaf, *Bibliography*

Assaf, David, comp. and ed. *Bratslav: An Annotated Bibliography.* Jerusalem: Shazar, 2000 (H).

Assaf, "The Clash over *Or Ha-Hayyim*"

———. "'A Heretic Who Has No Faith in the Great Ones of the Age': The Clash over the Honor of *Or Ha-Hayyim.*" *Modern Judaism* 29/2 (May 2009): 194–225.

Assaf, "Hasidut Polin bame'ah ha19"

———. "Hasidut Polin bame'ah ha19: Matsav hamehkar usekirah bibliografit." In *Hasidism in Poland*, edited by Israel Bartal, Rachel Elior, and Chone Shmeruk, 357–79. Jerusalem: Bialik Institute, 1994 (H).

Assaf, *Ne'ehaz basevakh*

———. *Ne'ehaz basevakh: Pirkei mashber umevukhah betoldot hahasidut.* Jerusalem: Shazar, 2006.

Assaf, *Regal Way*

———. *The Regal Way: The Life and Times of Rabbi Israel of Ruzhin.* Translated by David Louvish. Stanford, Calif.: Stanford University Press, 2002.

Hebrew edition: *Derekh hamalkhut: R. Yisrael miRuzhin umekomo betoldot hahasidut.* Jerusalem: Shazar, 1997.

Assaf, "*Yesod ha-Ma'ala*"

———. "*Yesod ha-Ma'ala:* A New Chapter in the Historiography of Hasidism in Eretz Israel." *Cathedra* 68 (1993): 57–63 (H).

Assaf, *Zaddik and Devotees*

———, ed. *Zaddik and Devotees: Historical and Social Aspects of Hasidism.* Jerusalem: Shazar, 2001 (H).

Assaf and Liebes, *The Latest Phase*

Assaf, David, and Esther Liebes, eds. *The Latest Phase: Essays on Hasidism by Gershom Scholem.* Jerusalem: Magnes, 2009 (H).

Avaneha barzel

Horowitz, Shmuel. *Avaneha barzel.* Jerusalem: Yeshivat Braslav, 1935.

Balaban, *Die Judenstadt von Lublin*

Balaban, Majer. *Die Judenstadt von Lublin.* Berlin: Jüdischer Verlag, 1919.

Bartal, "Shimon ha-Kofer"

Bartal, Israel. "'Shimon ha-Kofer': A Chapter in Orthodox Historiography." In *Studies in Jewish Culture in Honour of Chone Shmeruk*, edited by Israel Bartal, Ezra Mendelsohn, and Chava Turniansky, 243–68. Jerusalem: Shazar, 1993 (H).

Beit Rabbi

Heilman, Hayyim Meir. *Beit Rabbi.* 3 vols. Berdichev: Sheftl, 1902.

Beit tsadikim ya'amod

Beit tsadikim ya'amod. 3 vols. New York: Ma'arekhet Beit Tsadikim, 2004–5.

Be'oholei Habad

Deutsch, Shaul Shimon, ed. *Be'oholei Habad.* Vol. 1. New York: Mendelsohn, 1995.

Berdyczewski, "Dubova"

Berdyczewski, Micha Yosef. "Dubova." *Hatsefirah* 15, 23 February 1888, 3. Reprinted in Avner Holtzman and Yitzhak Kafkafi, eds., *Kitvei Micha Yosef Berdyczewski (Bin Gorion)*, vol. 1: *Early Writings, 1886–88* (Tel Aviv: Hakibbutz Hameuchad, 1996), 213–14 (H).

Berdyczewski, *Mibayit umihuts*

———. *Mibayit umihuts.* Piotrkov, 1899.

Berdyczewski, *Sipurim*

———. *Kitvei Micha Yosef Bin-Gorion.* Tel Aviv: Dvir, 1965.

Berdyczewski, "Tsiyun lenefesh"

———. "Tsiyun (lenefesh hagaon R. Akiva Chajes)." *Bet hamidrash* 1 (Krakow, 1888), 71–72. Reprinted in Avner Holtzman and Yitzhak Kafkafi, eds., *Kitvei Micha Yosef Berdyczewski (Bin Gorion)*, vol. 2: *Early Writings, 1888–1890* (Tel Aviv: Hakibbutz Hameuchad, 1996), 44–45 (H).

Bonar and M'Cheyne, *Mission of Inquiry to the Jews*

Bonar, Andrew A., and Robert M. M'Cheyne. *Narrative of a Mission of Inquiry to the Jews from the Church of Scotland in 1839.* Edinburgh, 1844.

Brayer, "Admorei Romaniyah"

Brayer, Menahem M. "Admorei Romaniyah veUngariyah veErets Yisrael." In *Hasidut veTsiyon,* edited by Shimon Federbush, 190–245. Jerusalem: Mossad Harav Kook, 1963.

Bromberg, *Belz*

Bromberg, Avraham Yitshak. *Ha'admorim leveit Belz.* Vol. 10 of *Migdolei hahasidut.* Jerusalem: Hamakhon Lehasidut, 1955.

Bromberg, *Hahozeh*

———. *Hahozeh miLublin.* Vol. 19 of *Migdolei hatorah vehahasidut.* Jerusalem: Hamakhon Lehasidut, 1962.

Buber, *For the Sake of Heaven*

Buber, Martin. *For the Sake of Heaven.* Translated by Ludwig Lewisohn. Philadelphia: Jewish Publication Society, 1945.

Darkhei hayyim veshalom

Gold, Yehiel Mikhl. *Darkhei hayyim veshalom . . . shenahag be'atsmo . . . Hayyim Elazar Shapira.* Munkatsh: Teichman, 1940.

Deinard, *Alata*

Deinard, Ephraim. *Alata.* St. Louis, Mo.: Moinester, 1927.

Deinard, *Zikhronot bat ami*

———. *Zikhronot bat ami: Memoirs of Jewish Life in Russia.* 2 vols. St. Louis, Mo.: Moinester, 1920 (H).

Deinard, *Zmir aritsim harishon*

———, ed. *Zmir aritsim harishon.* Kearny, N.J.: Deinard, 1904.

Deutsch, "Letters by Shmaryahu Schneersohn"

Deutsch, Shaul Shimon. "Letters by Shmaryahu Schneersohn." *Chasidic Historical Review* 1/2 (February 1996): 31–35; 1/3 (April–May 1996): 33–37.

Devarim arevim

Ehrmann, Dov. *Devarim arevim.* 2 vols. Munkatsh: Kahn and Fried, 1903–5.

Divrei hayamim hahem

Divrei hayamim hahem, al pi ha'atakot mireshimotav shel Admor haRayyats . . . Schneersohn miLubavitsh. Jerusalem [1964]. Limited edition [stencil].

Divrei yemei hahozrim

Kuntres divrei yemei hahozrim mikhvod kedushat Admor Yosef Yitshak . . . Schneersohn miLubavitsh. New York: Kehot, 2006.

Dubnow, *Jews in Russia and Poland*

Dubnow, Simon. *History of the Jews in Russia and Poland.* Translated by I. Friedlander. 3 vols. Philadelphia: Jewish Publication Society, 1916–20.

Dubnow, *Toldot hahasidut*

———. *Toldot hahasidut.* Tel Aviv: Dvir, 1930–31.

Edelbaum, “Letters”

Edelbaum, Meyer. “Letters from the S. Dubnow Archive.” *Tagim* 2 (1971): 47–55; *Tagim* 3–4 (1972): 78–81 (H).

Eliach, *HaGaon*

Eliach, Dov. *HaGaon: Hayyav umishnato shel haGra.* 3 vols. Jerusalem: Makhon Moreshet Hayeshivot, 2002.

Elior, “Between *Yesh* and *Ayin*“

Elior, Rachel. “Between *Yesh* and *Ayin:* The Doctrine of the Zaddik in the Works of Jacob Isaac, the Seer of Lublin.” In *Jewish History: Essays in Honour of Chimen Abramsky,* edited by Ada Rapoport-Albert and Steven J. Zipperstein, 393–455. London: P. Halban, 1988.

Elior, “Habad Movement”

———. “The Controversy over the Leadership of the Habad Movement.” *Tarbiz* 49 (1980): 166–86 (H).

Endelman, “Memories of Jewishness”

Endelman, Todd M. “Memories of Jewishness: Jewish Converts and Their Jewish Pasts.” In *Jewish History and Jewish Memory: Essays in Honor of Yosef Hayim Yerushalmi,* edited by Elisheva Carlebach, John M. Efron, and David N. Myers, 311–29. Hanover, N.H.: Brandeis University Press, 1998.

Entsiklopediyah lehasidut

Alfasi, Yitshak, ed. *Haentsiklopediyah lehasidut: Ishim.* 3 vols. Jerusalem: Mossad Harav Kook, 1986–2004.

“Erekh avot”

Rabinowitz, Yehoshua Heschel of Monastrich. “Erekh avot: Igeret hayahas.” Preface to his *Masekhet avot im be'ur torat avot.* New York: A. Rechtman, 1926.

Erter, *Hatsofeh leveit yisrael*

Erter, Isaak. *Hatsofeh leveit yisrael.* Edited by Yehuda Friedlander. Jerusalem: Bialik Institute, 1996.

Eser kedushot

Berger, Yisrael. *Sefer zekhut yisrael hanikra eser kedushot.* Piotrkov, 1906.

Eser orot

———, *Sefer zekhut yisrael hanikra eser orot.* Piotrkov, 1907.

Eser tsahtsahot

———, *Sefer zekhut yisrael hanikra eser tsahtsahot.* Piotrkov, 1910.

Etkes, *Gaon of Vilna*

Etkes, Immanuel. *The Gaon of Vilna: The Man and His Image.* Translated by Jeffrey M. Green. Berkeley: University of California Press, 2002.

Etkes, *Salanter*

———. *Rabbi Israel Salanter and the Mussar Movement: Seeking the Torah of Truth.* Translated by Jonathan Chipman. Philadelphia: Jewish Publication Society, 1993.

Fein, “Di londoner misyonern-geselshaft”

Fein, Y. “Di londoner misyonern-geselshaft far yidn: Ihr arbeit in Polyn un Rusland bemeshekh fun 19n yahrhundert.” *Yivo bleter* 24 (1944): 27–46.

Freid, *Yamim veshanim*

Freid, Meir Yaakov. *Yamim veshanim: Zikhronot vetsiyurim mitekufah shel hamishim shanah.* Vol. 2. Tel Aviv: Dvir, 1939.

Friedman, *Al ha'adam*

Friedman, Menahem Nahum. *Al ha'adam.* Kishinev, 1932.

Friedman, *Al ha'emet vehasheker*

———. *Al ha'emet vehasheker.* Kishinev, 1927.

Friedman, *Al hayofi*

———. *Al hayofi.* Kishinev, 1929.

Friedman, *Divrei Menahem*

———. *Divrei Menahem: 26 derashot.* Krakow, 1913.

Friedman, *Hahalom ufitrono*

———. *Hahalom ufitrono.* Chernovtsy, 1925.

Friedman, *Perush man*

———. *Masekhet avot im perush man.* Introduction, opening, chapter 1.Vienna, 1920. Chapter 2. Vienna, 1922. Chapter 3. Chernovtsy, 1925. Chapter 4. Kishinev, 1927. Chapters 5–6. Kishinev, 1928. Reprinted in Menahem Nahum Friedman, *Sheloshah sefarim niftahim*, edited by Yitshak Hakham. Holon: privately printed, 1987.

Fuenn, *Kiryah ne'emanah*

Fuenn, Shmuel Yosef. *Kiryah ne'emanah, vehu korot adat yisrael ba'ir Vilna . . .* Vilna, 1860.

Galant, *Zbirnik*

Galant, Ilya. "Do istrii borot'bi z tsadikizmom." In *Zbirnik prats evreis'koi istorichno-arkheografichnoi komissii*, 2:313–44. Kiev, 1929 (Ukrainian and Russian).

Gertner, "Kluger"

Gertner, Haim. "The Rabbinate and the Hasidic Movement in Nineteenth-Century Galicia: The Case of Rabbi Shlomo Kluger." In *Within Hasidic Circles: Studies in Hasidism in Memory of Mordecai Wilensky*, edited by Immanuel Etkes et al., 51–74. Jerusalem: Bialik Institute, 1999 (H).

Gidney, *At Home and Abroad*

Gidney, William T. *At Home and Abroad: A Description of the English and Continental Missions . . .* London, 1900.

Gidulei hanahal

Sternfeld, Noah Halevi. *Gidulei hanahal, vehu shem hagedolim kinus letsadikim letalmidav vetalmidei talmidav shel . . . morenu harav Nahman miBratslav . . .* Part 1 (to 1920). Jerusalem: Agudat Meshekh Hanahal, 1984.

Ginsburg, *Amolike Peterburg*

Ginsburg, Shaul M. *Amolike Peterburg* [*Historishe verk* (Naye serye) 1]. New York: Tsiko, 1944.

Ginsburg, *Historishe verk*

———. *Historishe verk.* 3 vols. New York, 1937–38.

Ginsburg, "Di legende"

———. "Di legende un di verklikhkeyt vegen dem 'alten rebn's zohn,' vos hot zikh getoyft." *Di tsukunft* 36/1 (January 1931): 61–64.

Ginsburg, *Meshumodim*

———. *Meshumodim in tsarishn rusland* [*Historishe verk* (Naye serye) 2]. New York: Tsiko, 1946.

Glubman, *Ketavim*

Glubman, Mordekhai. *Ketavim.* 2nd full ed. Jerusalem: privately printed, 2005 [stencil].

Gottlober, *Memoires and Travels*

Gottlober, Avraham Ber. *Memoires and Travels.* Edited and with an introduction by Reuven Goldberg. 2 vols. Jerusalem: Bialik Institute, 1976 (H).

Govrin, *We Were as Dreamers*

Govrin, Pinchas. *We Were as Dreamers: A Family Saga.* Jerusalem: Carmel, 2005 (H).

Granatstein, *Hashvil vehaderekh*

Granatstein, Yehiel. *Hashvil vehaderekh: Al hatsadik Rabbi Shmuel miKuriv . . . ve'al talmidav hakedoshim.* Tel Aviv: Pe'er, 1986.

Green, *Tormented Master*

Green, Arthur. *Tormented Master: A Life of Rabbi Nahman of Bratslav.* University: University of Alabama Press, 1979.

Hakham, Introduction to *Sefarim niftahim*

Hakham, Yitshak. "Kavim lidmuto shel . . . Rabbi Menahem Nahum Friedman . . . meItscani-Shtefanesht." Introduction to *Sheloshah sefarim niftahim*, by Menahem Nahum Friedman. Holon: privately printed, 1987.

"Hasidei Braslav ve'ir Uman"

Alef-Tav. "Hasidei Braslav ve'ir Uman." *Hamelits*, 25 February 1864, 106–7; 3 March, 126–28; 10 March, 140–41.

Hatov vehatakhlit

Twersky, Zvi Aryeh. *Hatov vehatakhlit.* Vienna, 1933.

Havlin, *Hamashpi'a*

Havlin, Shlomo Zalman. *Hamashpi'a . . . perakim betoldot Habad . . .* Jerusalem, 1982.

Hillman, *Igrot ba'al haTanya*

Hillman, David Z. *Igrot ba'al haTanya uvnei doro.* Jerusalem: Hamesorah, 1953.

Horodezky, *Hahasidut vehahasidim*

Horodezky, Shmuel Abba. *Hahasidut vehahasidim.* 4 vols. Berlin, 1923. Rev. ed. Tel Aviv: Dvir, 1951.

Horodezky, *Zikhronot*

———. *Zikhronot.* Tel Aviv: Dvir, 1957.

Igrot kodesh

Levin, Shalom Duber, ed. *Igrot kodesh me'et kevod kedushato Admor Hazaken . . .* 2 vols. New York: Kehot, 1987–93.

Igrot kodesh: Moharayyats

Igrot kodesh me'et . . . Admor Moharayyats . . . miLubavitsh. Vols. 1–7. New York: Kehot, 1983–84. Vol. 14. New York: Kehot, 1998.

Ikvei shalom

Siddur ikvei shalom im nehora me'alya shehiber harav hagaon R. Akiva Shalom Chajes za"l. Lublin, 1898.

Ish-Naomi, "Mitehom haneshiyah"

Ish-Naomi [Elimelekh Wexler]. "Mitehom haneshiyah." *Reshumot* 1 (1918): 166–77; 2 (1922): 174–86.

Kaftor vaferah

Dov, Yaakov Halevi. *Kaftor vaferah.* Vol. 2. Jerusalem: privately printed, 1972.

Kahana, *Sefer hahasidut*

Kahana, Avraham. *Sefer hahasidut.* Warsaw: Di Welt, 1922.

Karlinsky, *Counter History*

Karlinsky, Nahum. *Counter History: The Hasidic Epistles from Eretz-Israel, Text and Context.* Jerusalem: Yad Izhak Ben-Zvi, 1998 (H).

Kasdai, "Kit'ei zikhronot"

Kasdai, Zvi. "Kit'ei zikhronot." *Reshumot* 4 (1926): 216–19. Reprinted in Nurit Govrin, ed., *On Micha Josef Berdyczewski (Bin Gorion): Memoirs by His Contemporaries* (Holon: Dvora and Emmanuel House, 1998), 90–91 (H).

Katz, *Halakhah and Kabbalah*

Katz, Jacob. *Halakhah and Kabbalah: Studies in the History of Jewish Religion, Its Various Faces and Social Relevance.* Jerusalem: Magnes, 1984 (H).

Katz, "Igrot maskilim"

Katz, Simha. "Igrot maskilim bignutam shel hasidim." *Moznayim* 10 (1940): 266–76.

Katz, *Zikhronot*

Katz, Ben-Zion. *Zikhronot: Hamishim shanah bahistoriyah shel yehudei Rusiyah.* Tel Aviv: Twersky, 1963.

Kerem Chabad

Mondshine, Yehoshua, ed. *Kerem Chabad* 4/1–2 (1992).

Klapholtz, *Admorei Belz*

Klapholtz, Yisrael. *Admorei Belz: Te'ur demutam ufo'alam vetoldot hayyehem shel tsadikei Belz.* Vol. 3. Bnei Brak: Pe'er Hasefer, 1979.

Klausner, *Historiyah*

Klausner, Yosef. *Historiyah shel hasifrut haivrit hahadashah.* Vol. 2. Jerusalem: Ahiasaf, 1937. Vol. 3. Jerusalem: Ahiasaf, 1939. Vol. 5. Jerusalem: Ahiasaf, 1949.

Kotik, *Journey*

Kotik, Yehezkel. *Journey to a Nineteenth-Century Shtetl: The Memoirs of Yehezkel Kotik.* Edited by David Assaf. Detroit, Mich.: Wayne State University Press, 2002.

Kotik, *Wanderer*

———. *Wanderer: The Memoirs of Yechezkel Kotik.*Vol. 2. Edited and translated into Hebrew with an introduction by David Assaf. Tel Aviv: Tel Aviv University, 2005 (H).

Krauss, *Birkhot hahayyim*

Krauss, Hayyim. *Kuntres birkhot hahayyim.* Jerusalem: privately printed, 1979–80.

Krauss, "Chaikin"

Krauss, Shmuel. "Hehasid R. Zvi Hirsh Chaikin." *Beit mashiah* 60, 10 Heshvan 1995, 20–28.

Kressel, *Cyclopedia*

Kressel, Getzel. *Cyclopedia of Modern Hebrew Literature.* 2 vols. Merhavia: Sifriat Poalim, 1965–67 (H).

Lanuel, "The Maiden of Ludmir"

Lanuel, Aliza. "The Maiden of Ludmir." Master's thesis, Tel Aviv University, 2003 (H).

Lazarus, *Ebenezer*

Lazarus, Joshua George. *"Ebenezer" . . . A Narrative of the Lord's Dealings with One of His Ancient People . . .* London, 1841.

Leksikon

Leksikon fun der nayer yiddisher literatur: Biographical Dictionary of Modern Yiddish Literature. 8 vols. New York: Congress for Jewish Culture, 1956–81 (Y).

Levin, *Ma'asar*

Levin, Shalom Duber, ed. *Ma'asar: Ha'admor ha'emtsa'i.* New York: Kehot, 1997.

Levinsohn, *Divrei tsadikim*

See Levinsohn, *Emek refa'im*

Levinsohn, *Emek refa'im*

Levinsohn, Yitshak Ber. *Divrei tsadikim . . . im emek refa'im.* Odessa, 1867.

Lewin, *"These Will I Remember!"*

Lewin, Isaac, ed., *"These Will I Remember!" Biographies of Leaders of Religious Jewry in Europe . . . 1939–45.* Vol. 4. New York: Research Institute of Religious Jewry, 1961 (H).

Liberman, *Ohel Rahel*

Liberman, Haim. *Ohel Rahel.* 3 vols. New York: privately printed, 1980–84.

Likutei Moharan

Likutei Moharan. New York: Edison Lithographing, 1958.

Litvin, *Yudishe neshomes*

Litvin, A. [Shmuel Hurwitz]. *Yudishe neshomes.* 6 vols. New York, 1917.

Lublin

Blumenthal, N., and M. Korzen, eds. *Lublin.* Vol. 5, *Encyclopaedia of the Jewish Diaspora: A Memorial Library of Countries and Communities, Poland Series.* Jerusalem: Encyclopaedia of the Jewish Diaspora, 1957 (H).

Lurie and Zeltser, "Moses Berlin and the Lubavich Hasidim"

Lurie, Ilia, and Arkadii Zeltser. "Moses Berlin and the Lubavich Hasidim: A Landmark in the Conflict between Haskalah and Hasidism." *Shvut,* n.s. 5 (21) (1997): 32–64.

Luz, *Parallels Meet*

Luz, Ehud. *Parallels Meet: Religion and Nationalism in the Early Zionist Movement (1882–1904).* Translated by Lenn J. Schram. Philadelphia: Jewish Publication Society, 1988.

Madbarna de'umtei

Bekenrot, Aryeh. *Madbarna de'umtei.* 2 vols. Jerusalem: privately printed, 2001.

Mahler, "Hamisyonerim bePolin"

Mahler, Raphael. "Hamediniyut klapei hamisyonerim bePolin haKongresa'it bitekufat haberit hakedoshah." In *Sefer Shiloh: Kovets ma'amarim lezikhro,* edited by Michael Hendel, 169–81. Tel Aviv: Tel Aviv Municipality, 1960.

Mahler, *Hasidism and the Jewish Enlightenment*

———. *Hasidism and the Jewish Enlightenment: Their Confrontation in Galicia and Poland in the First Half of the Nineteenth Century.* Philadelphia: Jewish Publication Society, 1985.

Mahler, *Modern Times*

———. *History of the Jewish People in Modern Times.* Vol. 3. Merhavia: Hashomer Hatsair, 1955. Vol. 5. Tel Aviv: Sifriat Poalim, 1970. Vol. 6. Tel Aviv: Sifriat Poalim, 1976 (H).

Abridged English ed. *A History of Modern Jewry, 1780–1815.* London: Vallentine, Mitchell, 1971.

Marcus, *Hahasidut*

Marcus, Ahron. *Hahasidut.* Translated by Moshe Scheinfeld. Tel Aviv: Netsah, 1954. Rev. ed., Bnei Brak: Netsah, 1980. [For the German edition, see Verus, *Der Chassidismus.*]

Mark, *Mysticism and Madness*

Mark, Zvi. *Mysticism and Madness in the Work of R. Nahman of Bratslav.* Tel Aviv: Am Oved, 2003 (H).

Mayer, *Die Juden unserer Zeit*

Mayer, Bonaventura. *Die Juden unserer Zeit.* Regensburg, 1842.

Meir, *Words of the Righteous*

Meir, Jonatan, ed. *Words of the Righteous: An Anti-Hasidic Satire by Joseph Perl and Isaac Baer Levinsohn.* Los Angeles: Cherub, 2004 (H).

Mekler, *Fun rebns hoyf*

Mekler, David L. *Fun rebns hoyf (fun Tshernobil biz Talne).* 2 vols. New York: Jewish Book Publishing Company, 1931.

Mevorakh, *Napoleon utekufato*

Mevorakh, Barukh. *Napoleon utekufato: Reshumot ve'eduyot ivriyot shel bnei hador.* Jerusalem: Bialik Institute, 1968.

Mishpahat haRav miLiadi

Slonim, Menahem Shmuel. *Toldot mishpahat haRav miLiadi.* Tel Aviv: Zohar, 1947.

Mondshine, "Haskamot shtukot"

Mondshine, Yehoshua. "'Haskamot shtukot' miVolozhin umiVilna: Kabel et ha'emet mimi she'amarah?" *Ohr Yisroel: Torah Quarterly* 4/4 (Tammuz 1999): 151–59.

Mondshine, *Migdal oz*

———, ed. *Sefer migdal oz.* Kfar Habad: Makhon Lubavitch, 1980.

Nahalei emunah

Kenig, Nosson Zvi, and Shmuel Tuktsinski, comps. *Sefer nahalei emunah.* Bnei Brak, 1967.

Neharei esh

Neharei esh: Ma'amarim umikhtavim min Rabenu hagadol . . . Avraham Shimon Halevi Ish Horovits . . . 2nd ed. New York: C. Tescher, 1997.

Ner yisrael

Stern, Hayyim Dov. *Ner yisrael.* Vols. 3, 4, 6. Bnei Brak: privately printed, 1990–99.

Netiv tsadik

Kenig, Nosson Zvi, comp. *Netiv tsadik.* Bnei Brak: N. S. Kenig, 1971.

Netsah shebanetsah

Vinberg, Shlomo Zalmina. *Netsah shebanetsah: Toldot hayyav ufo'alo shel . . . David miTalne.* Jerusalem: privately printed, 1994.

Neveh tsadikim

Kenig, Nosson Zvi. *Neveh tsadikim.* Bnei Brak: N. S. Kenig, 1969.

Nifle'ot harabbi

Walden, Moshe Menahem. *Nifle'ot harabbi.* Warsaw: Wagmeister, 1911.

Ohel Naftali

Michelsohn, Avraham Hayyim. *Ohel Naftali.* Lemberg: Seidman, 1911.

Perl, *Al mahut kat hahasidim*

Perl, Yosef. *Über das Wesen der Sekte Chassidim.* Edited and annotated by Avraham Rubinstein (Hebrew introduction and notes; German text). Jerusalem: Israel Academy of Sciences and Humanities, 1977.

Perl, *Megaleh temirin*

———. *Megaleh temirin.* Vienna: A. Straus, 1819.

English ed.: *Joseph Perl's "Revealer of Secrets": The First Hebrew Novel,* translated by Dov Taylor (Boulder, Colo.: Westview, 1997).

Perls yidishe ksovim

Yosef Perls yidishe ksovim. Vilna: YIVO Institute for Jewish Research, 1937.

Piekarz, *Braslav Hasidism*

Piekarz, Mendel. *Studies in Braslav Hasidism.* Jerusalem: Bialik Institute, 1972 (H).

Piekarz, *Hasidism in Poland*

———. *Ideological Trends of Hasidism in Poland during the Interwar Period and the Holocaust.* Jerusalem: Bialik Institute, 1990 (H).

Pinkas Hakehillot: Lublin

Wein, Abraham, ed. *Districts Lublin-Kielce.* Vol. 7 of *Pinkas Hakehillot: Encyclopaedia of Jewish Communities—Poland.* Jerusalem: Yad Vashem, 1999 (H).

Pinkas Hakehillot: Rumania

Pinkas Hakehillot: Encyclopedia of Jewish Communities—Rumania. 2 vols. Edited by Theodor Lavi. Jerusalem: Yad Vashem, 1969–80 (H).

Radensky, "Biography of David Twersky"

Radensky, Paul Ira. "Hasidism in the Age of Reform: A Biography of David ben Mordkhe Twersky of Tal'noye." Ph.D. diss., Jewish Theological Seminary of America, 2001.

Raphael, *Hasidut vehasidim*

Raphael, Yitshak. *Al hasidut vehasidim.* Jerusalem: Mossad Harav Kook, 1991.

Rapoport-Albert, "Hagiography"

Rapoport-Albert, Ada. "Hagiography with Footnotes: Edifying Tales and the Writing of History in Hasidism." *History and Theory* 27 (1988): 119–59.

Rapoport-Albert, "Hasidism after 1772"

———. "Hasidism after 1772: Structural Continuity and Change." In *Hasidism Reappraised,* edited by Ada Rapoport-Albert, 76–140. London: Littman Library, 1996.

Rawa-Ruska

M. Ringel and J. H. Rubin, eds. *Rawa-Ruska Memorial Book.* Tel Aviv: Rawa Ruska Organization in Israel, 1973. (H and Y).

Rechtman, *Yidishe etnografye*

Rechtman, Avraham. *Yidishe etnografye un folklor.* Buenos Aires, 1958.

Reisen, *Lexicon*

Reisen, Zalman. *Lexicon of Yiddish Literature, Press and Philology.* Vol 3. Vilna: Kletskin, 1929 (Y).

Remba, *Banim akhlu boser*

Remba, Ayzik. *Banim akhlu boser.* Tel Aviv: Hava'ad Hatsiburi Lehotsa'at Kitvei Ayzik Remba, 1973.

Rodkinson, *Toldot amudei haHabad*

Rodkinskon, Michael Levi. *Toldot amudei haHabad.* Königsberg, 1876.

Rose, "Haharedim veha'internet"

Rose, Aharon. "Haharedim veha'internet." *Eretz Acheret* 41 (2007): 38–49.

Rosman, *Founder of Hasidism*

Rosman, Moshe. *Founder of Hasidism: A Quest for the Historical Ba'al Shem Tov.* Berkeley: University of California Press, 1996.

Sadan, *Betseitkha uveohalekha*

Sadan, Dov. *Betseitkha uveohalekha: Minyan hikrei sifrut.* Tel Aviv: Agudat Hasofrim, 1966.

Sadan, *Hadashim gam yeshanim.*

———. *Hadashim gam yeshanim.* 3 vols. Tel Aviv: Am Oved, 1987.

Sadan, *Ke'arat tsimukim*

———. *Ke'arat tsimukim.* Tel Aviv: Neumann, 1950.

Sadan, *Orhot ushvilim*

———. *Orhot ushvilim: Kerekh ha'ishim.* Tel Aviv: Am Oved, 1977.

Sadan, "Ro'eh vetson marito"

———. "Ro'eh vetson marito." Introduction to Yaakov Friedman, *Sheleg bamidbar.* Tel Aviv: Y. L. Peretz, 1970.

Sagiv, "Chernobyl Dynasty"

Sagiv, Gad. "The Chernobyl Hasidic Dynasty: Its Historical Thought from Its Beginning till the Eve of the First World War." Ph.D. diss., Tel Aviv University, 2009 (H).

Sefer hasihot

Yosef Yitshak Schneersohn. *Sefer hasihot . . . 5701 [1941] . . . 5704 [1944] . . . 5705 [1945] . . .* New York: Kehot, 1986.

Sefer hatoladot: Admor Hazaken

Glizenstein, Avraham Hanokh. *Sefer hatoladot: Rabbi Shneur Zalman miLiadi, Admor Hazaken.* New York: Kehot, 1967.

Sefer hatoladot: Admor Hazaken (1986)

———. *Sefer hatoladot: Rabbi Shneur Zalman miLiadi, Admor Hazaken.* 4 vols. Rev. and expanded ed. Kfar Habad: Kehot, 1986.

Sefer hatoladot: Moharash

———. *Sefer hatoladot: Rabbi Shmuel Schneersohn miLubavitsh, Admor Moharash.* Kfar Habad: Kehot, 1970.

Sefer hatoladot: Moharashab

———. *Sefer hatoladot: Rabbi Shalom Duber Schneersohn miLubavitsh, Admor Moharshab.* Kfar Habad: Kehot, 1972.

Sefer hatoladot: Moharayyats

———. *Sefer hatoladot: Rabbi Yosef Yitshak Schneersohn miLubavitsh, Admor Moharayyats.* Vol. 2. Kfar Habad: Kehot, 1972.

Sefer hatse'etsa'im

Heilprin, Shmuel Eleazar, comp. *Sefer hatse'etsa'im: Ilan yohasin letse'etsa'ei . . . Rabbi Shneur Zalman miLiadi* . . . Jerusalem: privately printed, 1980.

Sela-Saldinger, *Torn Chord*

Sela-Saldinger, Eliahu. *A Torn Chord Trembling in the Dark: A Study of Yaakov Friedman's Literary Works.* 2 vols. Jerusalem: Leivik, 1996 (Y and H).

She'erit yisrael

Kenig, Nosson Zvi. *She'erit yisrael.* Bnei Brak: privately printed, 1963.

Shivḥei haBesht

In Praise of the Baal Shem Tov [*Shivḥei ha-Besht*]: *The Earliest Collection of Legends about the Founder of Hasidism.* Translated and edited by Dan Ben-Amos and Jerome R. Mintz. Bloomington: Indiana University Press, 1970.

Shivḥei haBesht (Rubinstein)

Shivḥei haBesht. Introduction and annotations by Avraham Rubinstein. Jerusalem: Rubin Mass, 1991.

Shmeruk, "Hashehitah hahasidit"

Shmeruk, Chone. "Mashma'utah hahevratit shel hashehitah hahasidit." In *Zaddik and Devotees: Historical and Social Aspects of Hasidism*, edited by David Assaf, 160–80. Jerusalem: Shazar, 2001 (H).

Shmeruk, *Yiddish Literature*

———. *Yiddish Literature: Aspects of Its History.* Tel Aviv: Porter Institute for Poetics and Semiotics, 1978 (H).

Shmu'ot vesipurim

Hakohen, Raphael Nahman. *Shmu'ot vesipurim mirabotenu hakedoshim.* 3 vols. New York: [Yitzchok Gansburg], 1990.

Shochat, "Leadership of the Jewish Communities"

Shochat, Azriel. "Leadership of the Jewish Communities in Russia after the Abolition of the 'Kahal.'" *Zion* 42 (1977): 143–233 (H).

Siah sarfei kodesh

———. *Siah sarfei kodesh.* 6 vols. Jerusalem: Agudat Meshekh Hanahal, 1988–2000. Index. Jerusalem, 2003.

Siah sarfei kodesh (Rakats)

Rakats, Yoets Kim Kadish. *Siah sarfei kodesh.* 5 vols. Lodz, 1928–31. *Sefer milu'im.* Frishtik, 1932.

Sihot vesipurim

Hazan, Avraham. *Sihot vesipurim.* Bnei Brak: Hasidei Bratslav, 1961.

Spektor, *Mayn lebn*

Spektor, Mordekhai. *Mayn lebn.* 3 vols. Warsaw: Ahisefer, 1927.

Stanislawski, "Jewish Apostasy in Russia"

Stanislawski, Michael. "Jewish Apostasy in Russia: A Tentative Typology." In *Jewish Apostasy in the Modern World,* edited by Todd M. Endelman, 189–205. New York: Holmes and Meier, 1987.

Studies in Hasidism

Assaf, David, Joseph Dan, and Immanuel Etkes, eds. *Studies in Hasidism. Jerusalem Studies in Jewish Thought* 15 (1999) (H).

Teitelbaum, *HaRav miLiadi*

Teitelbaum, Mordekhai. *HaRav miLiadi umifleget Habad.* 2 vols. Warsaw: Tushiya, 1910–13.

Tishby, *Studies in Kabbalah*

Tishby, Isaiah. *Studies in Kabbalah and Its Branches: Researches and Sources.* 3 vols. Jerusalem: Magnes, 1982–83 (H).

Tovot zikhronot

Kokhav Lev, Avraham. *Tovot zikhronot.* Jerusalem: n.p., 1951.

Twersky, "Ha'otsar shebeShpikov"

Twersky, David. "Ha'otsar shebeShpikov." *Shdemot* 77 (1981): 78.

Twersky, *Hehatser hapnimit*

Twersky, Yohanan. *He"hatser" hapnimit: Korot mishpahah.* Tel Aviv: Twersky, 1954. [An earlier version of the first part appeared in *Reshumot*, n.s., 5 (1953): 226–83.]

Verus, *Der Chassidismus*

Verus [Ahron Marcus]. *Der Chassidismus.* Pleschen, 1901. [For the Hebrew edition, see Marcus, *Hahasidut.*]

Weiss, *Braslav*

Weiss, Joseph G. *Studies in Braslav Hassidism.* Jerusalem: Bialik Institute, 1974 (H).

Werses, *From Language to Language*

Werses, Shmuel. *From Language to Language: Literary Works and Their Transformation in Hebrew Literature.* Jerusalem: Magnes, 1996 (H).

Wigdermann, "Kevurat hamor"

Wigdermann, S. "Kevurat hamor." *Reshumot* 2 (1922): 448–53.

Wilensky, *Hasidim and Mitnaggedim*

Wilensky, Mordecai. *Hasidim and Mitnaggedim: A Study of the Controversy between Them in the Years 1772–1815.* 2 vols. Jerusalem: Bialik Institute, 1970 (H).

Wunder, *Meorei Galicia*

Wunder, Meir. *Meorei Galicia: Encyclopedia of Galician Rabbis and Scholars.* 6 vols. Jerusalem: Institute for Commemoration of Galician Jewry, 1978–2005 (H).

Yemei hatela'ot

Hazan, Avraham. *Yemei hatela'ot.* Jerusalem: Hasidei Bratslav, 1966.

Zederbaum, *Keter kehunah*

Zederbaum, Alexander. *Keter kehunah, o divrei hayamim lekohanei haemunah hayisraelit uvnoteha.* Odessa, 1867.

Zitron, *Avek fun folk*

See Zitron, *Meshumodim*

Zitron, *Meshumodim*

Zitron, Shmuel Leib. *Meshumodim: Tipn un siluetn funem nontn over.* Vols. 1–2. Vilna, 1921. [Partial Hebrew translation: *Me'ahorei hapargod: Mumarim, bogdim, mitkahashim,* vols. 1–2 (Vilna, 1923–25)]. Vols. 3–4: *Avek fun folk.* Warsaw [1923?].

Index